Lecture Notes in Artificial Intelligence   6069

Edited by R. Goebel, J. Siekmann, and W. Wahlster

Subseries of Lecture Notes in Computer Science

W0246065

Julian Padget   Alexander Artikis
Wamberto Vasconcelos   Kostas Stathis
Viviane Torres da Silva   Eric Matson
Axel Polleres (Eds.)

Coordination, Organizations, Institutions, and Norms in Agent Systems V

COIN 2009 International Workshops
COIN@AAMAS 2009, Budapest,Hungary, May 2009
COIN@IJCAI 2009, Pasadena, USA, July 2009
COIN@MALLOW 2009, Turin, Italy, September 2009
Revised Selected Papers

 Springer

Series Editors

Randy Goebel, University of Alberta, Edmonton, Canada
Jörg Siekmann, University of Saarland, Saarbrücken, Germany
Wolfgang Wahlster, DFKI and University of Saarland, Saarbrücken, Germany

Volume Editors

Julian Padget, E-mail: jap@cs.bath.ac.uk
Alexander Artikis, E-mail: a.artikis@iit.demokritos.gr
Wamberto Vasconcelos, E-mail: w.w.vasconcelos@abdn.ac.uk
Kostas Stathis, E-mail: kostas.stathis@cs.rhul.ac.uk
Viviane Torres da Silva, E-mail: viviane.silva@ic.uff.br
Eric Matson, E-mail: ematson@purdue.edu
Axel Polleres, E-mail: axel.polleres@deri.org

Library of Congress Control Number: 2010931699

CR Subject Classification (1998): I.2, H.4, D.2, C.2, H.5, H.3

LNCS Sublibrary: SL 7 – Artificial Intelligence

ISSN   0302-9743

ISBN-10   3-642-14961-8 Springer Berlin Heidelberg New York
ISBN-13   978-3-642-14961-0 Springer Berlin Heidelberg New York

springer.com

© Springer-Verlag Berlin Heidelberg 2010
Printed in Germany

Typesetting: Camera-ready by author, data conversion by Scientific Publishing Services, Chennai, India
Printed on acid-free paper   06/3180

Preface

This volume is the fifth in a series that started in 2005, collecting papers from the Coordination, Organizations, Institutions and Norms (COIN) Workshops. The papers in this volume are drawn from the three meetings that took place in 2009.

AAMAS

COIN@AAMAS 2009 took place on May 12, 2009, as a satellite event of the 8th International Conference on Autonomous Agents and Multiagent Systems (AAMAS 2009), in Budapest, Hungary. With 35 registered participants, the workshop was an exciting and fruitful gathering where discussions followed the papers presented by an international group of speakers. We had participants from Australia, Italy, The Netherlands, New Zealand, Portugal, Spain, UK and USA, to name a few. Of the 19 submissions, 12 were selected for presentation and, subsequently, 10 were invited to be revised and included in the proceedings.

IJCAI

COIN@IJCAI 2009 took place on July 11, 2009, as a satellite event of the 21st International Joint Conference on Artificial Intelligence (IJCAI 2009), in Pasadena, California, USA. We had 15 submissions, 10 of which were selected for presentation at the workshop. The workshop sessions gave rise to a stimulating and productive gathering with an invited talk from Maarten Sierhuis of NASA entitled "Towards Organization-Aware Multi-Agent Systems," followed by presentations of accepted papers. An international audience from countries such as Australia, Brazil, India, Canada, Spain, France, UK and USA participated in the workshop. From the 10 presented papers, 6 were invited to be revised and included in the proceedings.

MALLOW

COIN@MALLOW 2009 took place September 7-11, 2009, as one of the federated Multi-Agent Logics, Languages, and Organizations Workshops, in Turin, Italy. The particular theme of this edition of COIN was to explore how the COIN topics are manifested in on-line communities. To this end, Axel Polleres was invited as co-organizer and there was an invited talk by Alexandre Passant entitled "Using Semantics to Improve Corporate Online Communities." In addition there were nine presentations, comprising five regular papers and four project reports. Of these, four regular papers and one project report were invited to submit revised, extended versions for inclusion in this volume.

The papers in this volume are extended, revised versions of the best papers presented at the three workshops. The result is a balanced collection of high-quality papers that really can be called representative of the field at this moment. For this volume, the papers from the three workshops were re-grouped around three themes: *Building and Managing Organizations*, *Social Norms and Semantics* and *Norms and Reasoning*. We now summarize each of these themes and present a synopsis of the papers in each.

Building and Managing Organizations

The papers in this section address issues covering requirements capture, policy realization and both virtual and mixed human-agent organizations.

1. Boella et al. in "Conditional Dependence Networks in Requirements Engineering," present a way to extend dependence networks, a graphical notation used in requirements analysis, to represent norms. Moreover, they show how coalitions may be defined with the use of the extended dependence networks.
2. Criado et al. in "A Norm-Based Organization Management System," describe a platform for virtual organizations that supports norm specification and management, while accommodating (norm) change.
3. van Diggelen et al. in "Implementing Collective Obligations in Human-Agent Teams using KAoS Policies," explore the relationship between teamwork models and collective obligations and use the scenario of a Mars mission to show how team performance is affected by different teamwork models.
4. Lam et al. in "Building Multi-Agent Systems for Workflow Enactment and Exception Handling," propose a method for building norm-governed multi-agent systems to enact workflows. The novelty here lies in having the agents use organizational and domain knowledge, combined with task and capability information, to identify appropriate remedial actions when exceptions arise.
5. Hormazabal et al., in "An Approach for Virtual Organizations' Dissolution," tackle the problem of examining the conditions under which a virtual organization might be dissolved, by drawing parallels with circumstances that apply in commercial law for real-world organizations. An agent-based simulation is used to explore the particular circumstance of the organizational goals being unachievable and quantifies the benefits of timely dissolution.
6. Urovi and Stathis, in "Playing with Agent Coordination Patterns in MAGE," introduce the Multi-Agent Game Environment (MAGE), a logic-based framework that uses games as a metaphor for agent activities within an artificial society. They use their approach to specify the coordination patterns required to form a virtual organization in the context a scenario for oil-spill detection.
7. Coutinho et al. in "A Model-Based Architecture for Organizational Interoperability in Open Multiagent Systems," apply ideas from model-driven software engineering to multi-agent systems by specifying organizational meta-models and model transformations in order to address the problem of how agents can access a particular organizational infrastructure and interpret its underlying model without prior knowledge of the organization.

8. Hübner et al. in "Normative Programming for Organization Management Infrastructures," propose the Organization Modelling Language to define the organizational function of a system and the capture of organizational properties. This specification is then translated to a simpler normative language, thus avoiding the potential awkwardness — for the human designer — of a purely normative approach.

Social Norms and Semantics

The second part of this volume highlights the theme that was a key topic for the MALLOW workshop, although this thread was also apparent at other meetings earlier in the year. Thus the topics in this section explore the modelling of social attributes and of social structures, both in artificial environments and in virtual worlds that reflect the physical world.

1. Cranefield and Li, in "Monitoring Social Expectations in Second Life," discuss the formal definition of social expectations in temporal logic and their subsequent on-line monitoring by means of model-checking. The idea is demonstrated through Second Life, where a user can be notified whether their expectations of others have been fulfilled or violated, subject to the limitations of the Linden Scripting Language's capacity to detect events of (social) significance.

2. Lorini and Verdicchio, in "Towards a Logical Model of Social Agreement for Agent Societies," formalize the notion of agreement, as a bottom-up counter to the more conventional top-down approach that organizational modelling normally encourages. The key here is to focus on the agreement as the basic building block and to define a modal logic that has agreement as its primitive object and establishes relationships through the concept of preference, hence leading to notions of norms and commitments.

3. Sadedin and Guttmann, in "Promotion of Selfish Agents in Hierarchical Organizations," investigate the hypothesis that agents that misrepresent their achievements for the purpose of promotion will achieve a more influential status in an organization, in contrast to agents that report truthfully. An agent-based simulation is used to explore the consequences for multi-layered organizations over a range of employee populations, the main result being that judgement of individual performance rather than team performance appears to have the effect of promoting selfish behavior.

4. Passant et al. in "SIOC Project: Semantically Interlinked Online Communities," describe how Semantic Web technologies can be used to express information about the nature, structure and content of on-line communities. The information thus created—and maintained via human-centric social interactions—becomes processable by software agents and can, for example, enable interoperability between applications from the Social Web.

5. Stankovic et al. in "Directing Status Messages to their Audience in Online Communities," seek ways to govern the delivery of so-called status messages (short text messages usually broadcast to a large audience). The user survey that begins the paper suggests adding the concept of audience to such

messages and follows this with a discussion of the requirements for such a mechanism and how it might be realized by Semantic Web technologies.

6. Sen and Sen, in "Effects of Social Network Topology and Options on Norm Emergence," study how and when norms emerge in social networks, depending on parameters such as the topology of the network, population size, neighborhood size, and a number of behavior alternatives. The approach outlined can be used to model and to analyze social networks such as those generated by Facebook, Flickr and Digg and, it is posited, to predict how norms emerge and spread in human societies.

Norms and Reasoning

Here we focus on a core topic of the COIN community, namely, norms, exploring the formalization of obligations, how agents make sense of normative environments, handle incomplete information and might regulate themselves.

1. Cardoso and Oliveira, in "Directed Deadline Obligations in Agent-Based Business Contracts," use temporal logic to formalize directed contractual obligations, as well as a mechanism for flexible deadlines of the obligations. This latter is presented as a lifecycle for directed obligations with temporal restrictions, based on authorizations and implemented by means of a rule-based system.

2. Savarimuthu et al. in "Internal Agent Architecture for Norm Identification," propose an agent architecture that identifies the norms of a society using a bottom-up approach, in that agents infer norms rather than being told them explicitly. The paper demonstrates how a norm can be inferred by an agent using the proposed architecture, via an illustrative case scenario, in which an agent observes the actions of another and when sanctions occur.

3. Kemmerich, in "Influence of Communication Graph Structures on Pheromone-Based Approaches in the Context of a Partitioning Task Problem," has the goal of finding a cost-optimal, distance minimizing, and uniform partitioning of an agent set to a set of targets in a two-dimensional world using an ant colony optimization algorithm. In particular it is shown that new pheromone traces are unable to develop in the presence of establish structures. Although the approach is proven non-optimal, it is also shown that the solution quality is high.

4. Salazar et al. in "An Infection-Based Mechanism in Large Convention Spaces," describe a distributed regulation mechanism to handle emergent social conventions. Intuitively, the size of the convention space should affect emergence and in this paper, it is shown empirically how the problem of finding a common vocabulary enables perfect communication and hence the capacity to handle large convention spaces.

5. Swarup, in "The Classification Game: Complexity Regularization Through Interaction," shows that if a population of neural network agents is allowed to interact during learning, so as to arrive at a consensus solution to the learning problem, then they can implicitly achieve complexity regularization. This

learning paradigm is called the classification game. Through experimentation, it is shown how low complexity equilibria are selected, leading to better generalization.

6. Serrano and Saugar, in "Dealing with Incomplete Normative States," put forward a normative framework that enables the specification of incomplete theories and their management through incomplete normative states—identified as 'pending.' The framework lets designated agents resolve this category through the speech acts allow and forbid. The proposal is formalized by using the action language K, taking advantage of its support for incompleteness, and subsequently illustrated with some scenarios drawn from the management of university courses.

7. Burgemeestre et al. in "Towards an Architecture for Self-Regulating Agents: A Case Study in International Trade," use an example of norm-enforcement from the physical world as inspiration for the virtual world, from which they construct an architecture for self-regulating agents derived from BDI. Validation of the approach is demonstrated through a study of the self-certification EU customs regulations.

We are grateful to all the conference organizers who accepted our proposals for COIN workshops and the workshop organizers who together created the fora in which our discussions flourish. We are equally pleased to acknowledge the continuing support of Springer, and Alfred Hofmann in particular, for the annual publication of the COIN workshop series, providing both a research record and a dissemination channel to reach those researchers not able to attend the meetings in person.

March 2010

Julian Padget
Alexander Artikis
Wamberto Vasconcelos
Kostas Stathis
Viviane Torres da Silva
Eric Matson
Axel Polleres

Organization

Program Committee Members

COIN@AAMAS

Alexander Artikis	NCSR "Demokritos", Greece
Guido Boella	University of Turin, Italy
Olivier Boissier	ENS Mines Saint-Etienne, France
Stephen Cranefield	Otago, New Zealand
Cristiano Castelfranchi	ISTC, Rome, Italy
Virginia Dignum	University of Utrecht, The Netherlands
Marc Esteva	IIIA-CSIC, Spain
Nicoletta Fornara	University of Lugano, Switzerland
Jomi Fred Hübner	University of Blumenau, Brazil
Lloyd Kamara	Imperial College, UK
Victor Lesser	University of Massachusetts Amherst, USA
Christian Lemaitre	Universidad Autonoma Metropolitana, Mexico
Eric Matson	Purdue University, USA
John-Jules Meyer	University of Utrecht, The Netherlands
Daniel Moldt	University of Hamburg, Germany
Pablo Noriega	IIIA-CSIC, Spain
Tim Norman	University of Aberdeen, UK
Eugenio Oliveira	Universidade do Porto, Portugal
Sascha Ossowski	URJC, Spain
Julian Padget	University of Bath, UK
Alessandro Ricci	Università di Bologna, Italy
Antonio Carlos da Rocha Costa	UCPEL, Brazil
Juan Antonio Rodriguez-Aguilar	IIIA-CSIC, Spain
Jaime Sichman	University of São Paulo, Brazil
Carles Sierra	IIIA-CSIC, Spain
Kostas Stathis	Royal Holloway, University of London, UK
Catherine Tessier	ONERA, France
Wamberto Vasconcelos	University of Aberdeen, UK
Leon Van Der Torre	University of Luxembourg, Luxembourg
Harko Verhagen	Stockholm University, Sweden
George Vouros	University of the Aegean, Greece

COIN@IJCAI

Alexander Artikis	NCSR "Demokritos", Greece
Guido Boella	University of Turin, Italy

COIN@MALLOW

Frances Brazier	Vrije Universiteit Amsterdam, The Netherlands
Dan Brickley	FOAF Project
John Breslin	DERI, National University of Ireland
Antonio Carlos da Rocha Costa	UCPEL, Brazil
Stephen Cranefield	University of Otago, New Zealand
Harry Halpin	W3C
Jomi Fred Hübner	University of Blumenau, Brazil
Joris Hulstijn	Vrije Universiteit Amsterdam, The Netherlands
Lloyd Kamara	Imperial College, University of London, UK
Eric Matson	Purdue University, USA
Pablo Noriega	IIIA-CSIC, Spain
Eamonn O'Neill	University of Bath, UK
Alexandre Passant	DERI, National University of Ireland
Jeremy Pitt	Imperial College, University of London, UK
Juan Antonio Rodriguez Aguilar	IIIA-CSIC, Spain
Sascha Ossowski	Universidad Rey Juan Carlos, Madrid, Spain
Sebastian Schaffert	Salzberg Research, Austria
Jaime Simão Sichman	University of São Paulo, Brazil
Maarten Sierhuis	NASA, USA
Kostas Stathis	Royal Holloway, University of London, UK
Harko Verhagen	Stockholm University, Sweden
Niek Wijngaards	THALES, Delft, The Netherlands

Additional Reviewers

Roberto Centeno	University Rey Juan Carlos, Madrid, Spain
Luciano Coutinho	University of Sao Paulo, Brazil
Sindhu Joseph	IIIA, Spain
Rosine Kitio	Ecole Nationale Superieure des Mines de Saint-Etienne, France
Thomas Kurz	Salzburg Research, Austria
Pieter De Leenheer	Vrije Universiteit Amsterdam, The Netherlands
Henrique Lopes Cardoso	Universidade do Porto, Portugal
Jan Ortmann	University of Hamburg, Germany
Marco Remondino	University of Turin, Italy
Birna van Riemsdijk	Technical University of Delft, The Netherlands
Olga Streibel	Free University of Berlin, Germany
Matthias Wester-Ebbinghaus	University of Hamburg, Germany

Workshop Organizers

COIN@AAMAS   Alex Artikis   Software & Knowledge Engineering Laboratory, Institute of Informatics & Telecommunications National Centre for Scientific Research "Demokritos", Athens, Greece. `a.artikis@iit.demokritos.gr`

Wamberto Vasconcelos   Department of Computing Science, University of Aberdeen, Scotland, UK. `w.w.vasconcelos@abdn.ac.uk`

COIN@IJCAI   Kostas Stathis   Department of Computer Science, Royal Holloway, University of London, Egham, Surrey, UK. `kostas.stathis@cs.rhul.ac.uk`

Viviane Torres da Silva   Computer Science Department, Universidade Federal Fluminente, Rio de Janeiro, Brazil. `viviane.silva@ic.uff.br`

Eric Matson   M2M Laboratory, Department of Computer and Information Technology, Purdue University, Indiana, USA. `ematson@purdue.edu`

COIN@MALLOW   Julian Padget   Department. of Computer Science, University of Bath, UK. `jap@cs.bath.ac.uk`

Axel Polleres   Digital Enterprise Research Institute, National University of Ireland, Galway, Ireland. `axel.polleres@deri.org`

COIN Steering Committee

Guido Boella   University of Turin, Italy
Olivier Boissier   ENS Mines Saint-Etienne, France
Nicoletta Fornara   University of Lugano, Italy
Christian Lemaître   Universidad Autonoma Metropolitana, Mexico

Eric Matson   Purdue University, USA
Pablo Noriega   IIIA-CSIC, Spain
Sascha Ossowski   Universidad Rey Juan Carlos, Spain
Julian Padget   University of Bath, UK
Jeremy Pitt   Imperial College London, UK
Jaime Sichman   University of São Paulo, Brazil
Wamberto Vasconcelos   University of Aberdeen, UK
Javier Vázquez Salceda Universitat Politècnica de Catalunya, Spain
George Vouros   University of the Aegean, Greece

Table of Contents

Part III: Norms and Reasoning

Part I

Building and Managing Organizations

Conditional Dependence Networks
in Requirements Engineering

Guido Boella[1], Leendert van der Torre[2], and Serena Villata[1]

[1] Dipartimento di Informatica, University of Turin
{boella,villata}@di.unito.it
[2] Computer Science and Communication, University of Luxembourg
leendert@vandertorre.com

Abstract. In this paper we present a new model for the requirements analysis of
a system. We offer a conceptual model defined following a visual modeling language, called dependence networks. TROPOS uses a visual modeling language
called dependence networks in the requirements analysis of a system, and in this
paper we propose a new conceptual model extending dependence networks with
norms. This improvement allows to define a new type of dependence networks,
called conditional dependence networks, representing a new modeling technique
for the requirements analysis of a system. Our model, moreover, allows the definition of coalition depending on different kinds of networks. We illustrate our
model using the scenario of virtual organizations based on a Grid network.

1 Introduction

The diffusion of software applications in the fields of e-Science and e-Research under-
lines the problem to develop open architectures, able to evolve and include new software
components. In the late years, the process of design of these software systems became
more complex. The definition of appropriate mechanisms of communication and coordination between software components and human users motivates the development of
methods with the aim to support the designer for the whole development process of the
software, from the requirements analysis to the implementation.

The answer to this problem comes from software engineering that provided numerous methods and methodologies allowing to treat more complex software systems. One
of these methodologies is the TROPOS methodology [7], developed for agent-oriented
design of software systems. The intuition of the TROPOS methodology [7] is to couple,
together with the instruments offered by software engineering, the multiagent paradigm.
In this paradigm, the entities composing the system are agents, autonomous by definition [2], characterized by their own sets of goals, capabilities and beliefs. TROPOS
covers five phases of the software development process: early requirements allowing the
analysis and modeling of the requirements of the context in which the software system
will be inserted, late requirements describing the requirements of the software system,
architectural and detailed design of the system and, finally, the code implementation.

The TROPOS methodology [7] is based on the multiagent paradigm but it does not
consider the addition of a normative perspective to this paradigm. Since twenty years,
the design of artificial social systems is using mechanisms like social laws and norms

J. Padget et al. (Eds.): COIN 2009, LNAI 6069, pp. 3–18, 2010.
© Springer-Verlag Berlin Heidelberg 2010

to control the behavior of multiagent systems [3]. These social concepts are used in the conceptual modeling of multiagent systems, for example in requirements analysis, as well as in formal analysis and agent based social simulation. For example, in the game theoretic approach of Shoham and Tennenholtz [17], social laws are constraints on sets of strategies. In this paper, we propose to add norms, presented thanks to the normative multiagent paradigm, both to the requirements analysis phases and to the conceptual meta-model. This paper addresses the following research question:

- How to apply a normative multiagent approach to the early and late requirements analysis?

The research question beaks down in the following sub-questions: which ontology have to be defined for the normative multiagent requirements engineering model? and how to model sanctions, contrary-to-duty and coalition's stability in dependence networks?.

Our approach is based, following the approach of TROPOS [7], on the semiformal language of visual modeling called dependence networks and it is composed by the following components. First, we present our ontology that defines the set of concepts composing our conceptual metamodel. The elements composing the ontology are agents, goals, facts, skills, dependencies, coalitions with the addition of the normative notions of roles, institutional goals, institutional facts, institutional skills, dynamic dependencies and obligations, sanctions, secondary obligations and conditional dependencies. Second, our model is defined as a directed labeled graph whose nodes are instances of the metaclasses of the metamodel, e.g., agents, goals, facts, and whose arcs are instances of the metaclasses representing relationships between them such as dependency, dynamic dependency, conditional dependency. Finally, we have a set of rules and constraints to guide the building of the main concepts of the metamodel, e.g. the formation of coalitions and their stability is constrained to the kind of dependencies linking its members. In TROPOS [7], the requirements analysis phase is split in two main phases, the early requirements and the late requirements. In our methodology, these two phases share the same conceptual and methodological approach, thus we refer to them just as requirements analysis. Dynamic dependence networks have been firstly introduced by Caire *et al.* [9] and then treated in Boella *et al.* [5] in which the existence of a dependency depends on the actions of the agents which can delete it.

We introduce the normative issue of obligations, representing them directly in dependence networks. This introduction allows the definition of a third kind of modeling called conditional dependency modeling based on the structure of conditional dependence networks. This new kind of networks represent obligations as particular kinds of dependencies and these obligations are related to notions by means of sanctions if the obligation is not fulfilled and contrary to duty when the primary obligation, not fulfilled, actives a secondary obligation. Moreover, we introduce the notion of coalition and we propose to use methods of social order such as obligations and sanctions to efficiently achieve the maintenance of the stability and the cohesion of these groups. Our model is intended to support the requirements specification for high level open interaction system where heterogeneous and autonomous agents may interact.

Our aim is not to present an new theorem that, using norms semantics, checks whether a given interaction protocol complies with norms. We are more interested in considering, in the context of requirements analysis, how agents' behaviour is effected by norms and in analyzing how to constrain the modeling of coalitions' evolution thanks to a normative system. There are two main assumptions in our approach. First of all we assume that norms can sometimes be violated by agents in order to keep their autonomy. The violation of norms is handled by means of sanctions and contrary to duty mechanisms. Second, we assume that, from the institutional perspective, the internal state of the external agents is neither observable nor controllable but the institutional state or public state of these agents is note since connected to a role and it can be changed by the other agents. Our model is not intended to support all analysis and design activities in software development process, from application domain analysis down to the system implementation as in the TROPOS methodology [7], but only the requirements analysis phases which involve dependence networks. Of course, our model is not intended for any type of software. For system software, e.g., a compiler, or embedded software, the operating environment of the system-to-be is an engineering artifact, with no identifiable stakeholders. In such cases, traditional software development techniques may be most appropriate. However, a large and growing percentage of software operates within open, dynamic organizational environments. This paper is organized as follows. Section 2 describes a Grid computing scenario. In Section 3, we present the dependency and the dynamic dependency modeling while in Section 4 we present a new kind of dependence network, called conditional dependence network. Related work and conclusions end the paper.

2   The Grid Scenario

The Grid Computing paradigm provides the technological infrastructure to facilitate e-Science and e-Research. Grid technologies can support a wide range of research including amongst others: seamless access to a range of computational resources and linkage of a wide range of data resources. It is often the case that research domains and resource providers require more information than simply the identity of the individual in order to grant access to use their resources. The same individual can be in multiple collaborative projects, each of which is based upon a common shared infrastructure. This information is typically established through the concept of a virtual organization (VO) [12]. A virtual organization allows the users, their roles and the resources they can access in a collaborative project to be defined. In the context of virtual organizations, there are numerous technologies and standards that have been put forward for defining and enforcing authorization policies for access to and usage of virtual organizations resources. Role based access control (RBAC) is one of the more well established models for describing such policies. In the RBAC model, virtual organization specific roles are assigned to individuals as part of their membership of a particular virtual organization.

As presented by Zhao *et al.* [22], obligations are requirements and tasks to be fulfilled, which can be augmented into conventional systems to allow extras information to be specified when responding to authorization requests. For example in [22], administrators can associate obligations with permissions, and require the fulfillment of the obligations when the permissions are exercised. The general idea of the RBAC model is that, permissions are associated with functional roles in organizations, and members of the roles acquire all permissions associated with the roles. Allocation of permission to users is achieved by assigning roles to users. Failure of the fulfilling an obligation will incur a sanction.

Some of the main features of a node in a Grid are reliability, degree of accepted requests, computational capabilities, degree of faults and degree of trust for confidential data. These different features set up important differences among the nodes and the possible kinds of coalitions that can be formed and maintained. Reciprocity-based coalitions can be viewed as a sort of virtual organizations in which there is the constraint that each node has to contribute something, and has to get something out of it. The scenario of virtual organizations based on Grid networks represents a case study able to underline the benefits of a normative multiagent paradigm for requirements analysis. First of all, in the normative multiagent paradigm as well as in the common multiagent one, the autonomy of agents is the fixed point of all representations, i.e., the Grid philosophy imposes the autonomy of the nodes composing it. Second, the normative multiagent paradigm allows a clear definition of the notion of role and its associated permissions, i.e. the role based access control policy needs a design able to assign roles and represents to all the consequent constraints based on them. Third, the normative multiagent paradigm allows the introduction at requirements analysis level of obligations able to model the system. Fourth, the concept of coalition and the constraints introduced by this concept can model the concept of "local network" in virtual organizations. Finally, the presented modeling activities depict the system using structures similar to the Grid network itself.

3 Dependency and Dynamic Dependency Modeling

Figure 1 shows the ontology on which is based our model containing a number of concepts related to each other. We divide our ontology in three submodels: the agent model, the institutional model, and the role assignment model, as shown in Figure 1. Roughly, an institution is a structure of social order and cooperation governing the behavior of a set of individuals. Institutions are identified with a social purpose and permanence, with the enforcing of rules governing cooperative human behavior. The Figure depicts, following the legend of Figure 2, the three submodels which group the concepts of our ontology.

Such a decomposition is common in organizational theory, because an organization can be designed without having to take into account the agents that will play a role in it. For example if a node with the role of simple user becomes a VO administrator, then this remains transparent for the organizational model. Likewise, agents can be developed without knowing in advance in which institution they will play a role.

As shown in Figure 1, the agent view is composed by concepts like agent, goal and skill or ability and they are represented by means of a social dependence networks in which nodes are the agents and the edges are the representation of goal-based dependencies. The institutional view, instead, is composed by the notion of role and its institutional goals, skills and facts. As for the agent view, also the institutional one is represented by means of a social institutional dependence network representing the norm-based dependency relations between roles. The role assignment view associates to each agent the roles it plays, depending on the organization in which the agent is playing. All these notions are unified in the combined view where the dependence network

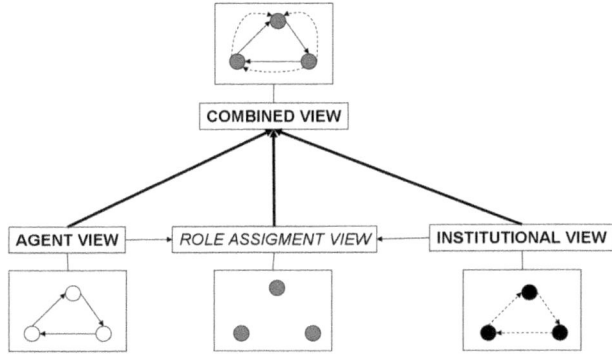

Fig. 1. The conceptual metamodel

represents at the same time both goal-based dependencies and norm-based ones connecting the agents playing roles. In this way, early and late requirements can be based both on agents and on roles. Models are acquired as instances of a conceptual metamodel resting on the concepts presented in the following sections. For more details on the three conceptual submodels, see Boella *et al.* [5] and Boella *et al.* [4].

3.1 Dependence Networks

Figure 2 shows the components of our model. Our model is a directed labeled graph whose nodes are instances of the metaclasses of the metamodel, e.g., agents, goals, facts, and whose arcs are instances of the metaclasses representing relationships between them such as dependency, dynamic dependency, conditional dependency.

Dependence networks [18] represent our first modeling activity consisting in the identification of the dependencies among agents and among roles. In the early requirements phase, we represent the domain stakeholders using these networks while in the late requirements phase, the same kind of approach is followed representing the agents of the future system involved in the dependence network. Figure 2-(a) shows the graphical representation of the model obtained following this modeling activity, the *dependency modeling*. The legend describes the agents (depicted as white circles), the roles (depicted as black circles), the agents assigned to roles (depicted as grey circles), the agents'/roles' goals (depicted as white rectangles) and the dependency among agents (one arrowed line connecting two agents with the addition of a label which represents the goal on which there is the dependency). The legend considers dependencies among agents but they can be also among roles or agents assigned to roles.

3.2 Dynamic Dependence Networks

Concerning dynamic dependence networks [5], as shown in Figure 2-(a), here we distinguish "negative" dynamic dependencies where a dependency exists unless it is removed by a set of agents due to removal of a goal or ability of an agent, and "positive"

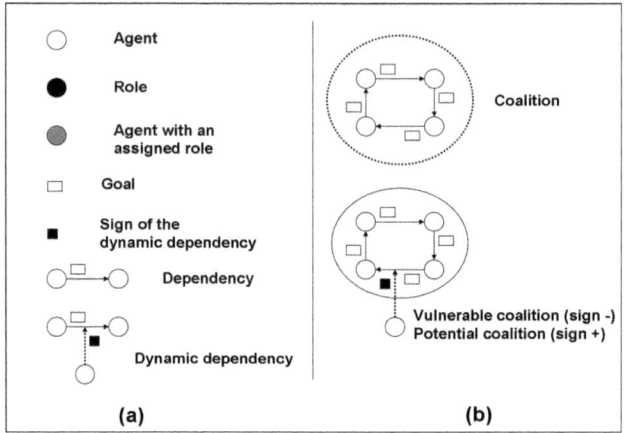

Fig. 2. Legend of the graphical representation of our model

dynamic dependencies where a dependency may be added due to the power of a third set of agents. *Dynamic dependency modeling* represents our second modeling activity for requirements analysis. A formal definition of dynamic dependence networks is given in Boella *et al.* [4].

The legend of Figure 2-(a) describes the sign of the dynamic dependency (depicted as a black square) and the dynamic dependency among agents (depicted as one arrowed line connecting two agents with the addition of a label which represents the goal on which there is the dependency and another arrowed dotted line with the sign's label connecting an agent to the arrowed plain line that can be deleted or added by this agent). Figure 3 presents an example of dynamic dependence network on the Grid. In this figure, each node plays a role inside a virtual organization and a number of goal-based dependencies link the nodes to each other, making explicit the fact that a major number of goals can be achieved thanks to cooperation. The dynamic dependency depicted in the figure is related to the institutional goal of obtaining an authorization and it can be removed or added due to the institutional power of the role played by agent n_6. Thanks to our model, we can represent portions or complete virtual organizations, explicating what are the played roles, what are the goals of each node and what are its capabilities, both from the agent point of view and from the institutional one.

A coalition can be defined in dependence networks, based on the idea that to be part of a coalition, every agent has to contribute something and has to get something out of it. The graphical representation of coalitions is depicted in Figure 2-(b) which describes coalitions (depicted as sets of agents and dependencies included in a dotted circle) and vulnerable and potential coalitions (depicted as sets of agents and dependencies in a circle in which one or more of these dependencies can be added or deleted by another agent with a labeled dynamic dependency). Definition 1 makes a distinction between *coalitions* which are actually formed, *vulnerable coalitions* which can be destroyed by the deletion of dynamic dependencies and, *potential coalitions*, which can be formed depending on additions and deletions of dynamic dependencies.

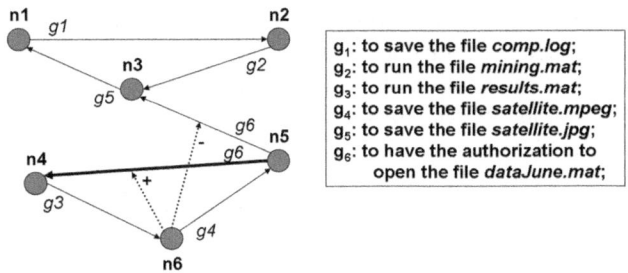

Fig. 3. An example of dynamic dependence network

Definition 1 (Coalition). *Let A be a set of agents and G be a set of goals. A coalition function is a partial function $C : A \rightarrow 2^A \times 2^G$ such that $\{a \mid C(a, B, G)\} = \{b \mid b \in B, C(a, B, G)\}$, the set of agents profiting from the coalition is the set of agents contributing to it. Let $\langle A, G, dyndep^-, dyndep^+, \geq \rangle$ be a dynamic dependence network, and dep the associated static dependencies.*

1. *A coalition function C is a coalition if $\exists a \in A, B \subseteq A, G' \subseteq G$ such that $C(a, B, G')$ implies $G' \in dep(a, B)$. Coalitions which cannot be destroyed by addition or deletion of dependencies by agents in other coalitions.*
2. *A coalition function C is a vulnerable coalition if it is not a coalition and $\exists a \in A, D, B \subseteq A, G' \subseteq G$ such that $C(a, B, G')$ implies $G' \in \cup_D dyndep^-(a, B, D)$. Coalitions which do not need new goals or abilities, but whose existence can be destroyed by removing dependencies.*
3. *A coalition function C is a potential coalition if it is not a coalition or a vulnerable coalition and $\exists a \in A, D, B \subseteq A, G' \subseteq G$ such that $C(a, B, G')$ implies $G' \in \cup_D (dyndep^-(a, B, D) \cup G' \in dyndep^+(a, B, D))$ Coalitions which could be created or which could evolve if new abilities or goals would be created by agents of other coalitions on which they dynamically depend.*

Figure 3 presents two different coalitions. On the one hand, we have an *actual* coalition composed by agents n_1, n_2 and n_3. On the other hand, we have a potential coalition, such as a coalition which could be formed if agent n_6 really performs the dynamic addition, making agent n_5 dependent on agent n_4.

4 Conditional Dependency Modeling

In this section, we answer to the question *how to model sanctions, contrary-to-duty and coalition's stability in dependence networks* by defining the conditional dependency modeling. Normative multiagent systems are "sets of agents (human or artificial) whose interactions can fruitfully be regarded as norm-governed; the norms prescribe how the agents ideally should and should not behave. [...] Importantly, the norms allow for the possibility that actual behavior may at times deviate from the ideal, i.e., that violations of obligations, or of agents' rights, may occur" [6]. In this paper, we represent general regulative norms. The notion of conditional obligation with an associated sanction is the base of the so called regulative norms. Obligations are defined in terms of goals of the agent and both the recognition of the violation and the application of the sanctions are the result of autonomous decisions of the agent.

A well-known problem in the study of deontic logic is the representation of contrary-to-duty structures, situations in which there is a primary obligation and what we might call a secondary obligation, coming into effect when the primary one is violated [16]. A natural effect coming from contrary-to-duty obligations is that obligations pertaining to a particular point in time cease to hold after they have been violated since this violation makes every possible evolution in which the obligation is fulfilled inaccessible. A classical example of contrary-to-duty obligations is given by the so called "gentle murder" by Forrester [11] which says "do not kill, but if you kill, kill gently". A contrary-to-duty obligation is not a type of norm. A regulative norm represented by a rule *"if a then obliged x"* is a contrary-to-duty if there is another norm of the kind *"forbidden a"*. Note that this is not a property of the norm *"if a then obliged x"* and thus not a type of norm.

4.1 Conditional Dependence Networks

The introduction of norms in dependence networks is based on the necessity to adapt the requirements analysis phases to model norm-based systems. An example of application of this kind consists in the introduction of obligations in virtual Grid-based organizations [22] where obligations, as shown in Section 2, are used to enforce the authorization decisions. On the one hand, in approaches like [22], obligations are considered simply as tasks that have to be fulfilled when an authorization is accepted/denied while, on the other hand, in approaches like [15], the failure in fulfilling the obligation incurs a sanction but there is no secondary obligation.

The introduction of obligations brings us to introduce a new kind of goal, the normative one. These goals originate from norms and they represent the obligation itself. We define a new set of normative concepts, based on Boella *et al.* [2] model of obligations, and we group them in a new view, called the normative view. The normative view is composed by a set of norms N and three main functions, *oblig*, *sanct* and *ctd* representing obligation, sanctions and contrary-to-duty obligations. The UML diagram of Figure 4 provides a unified vision of the presented concepts of the ontology representing our conceptual metamodel.

Definition 2 (Normative View). *Let the institutional view* $\langle RL, IF, RG, X, igoals : RL \rightarrow 2^{RG}, iskills: RL \rightarrow 2^X, irules^1 : 2^X \rightarrow 2^{IF}\rangle$, *the normative view is a tuple* $\langle RL, RG, N, oblig, sanct, ctd \rangle$ *where:*

- *RL is a set of roles, RG is a set of institutional goals, N is a set of norms;*
- *the function $oblig : N \times RL \rightarrow 2^{RG}$ is a function that associates with each norm and role, the institutional goals the agent must achieve to fulfill the norm. Assumption:* $\forall n \in N$ *and* $rl \in RL$, $oblig(n, rl) \in power(\{rl\})^2$.

---

[1] *irules* associate sets of institutional actions with the sets of institutional facts to which they lead.

[2] Power relates each role with the goals it can achieve.

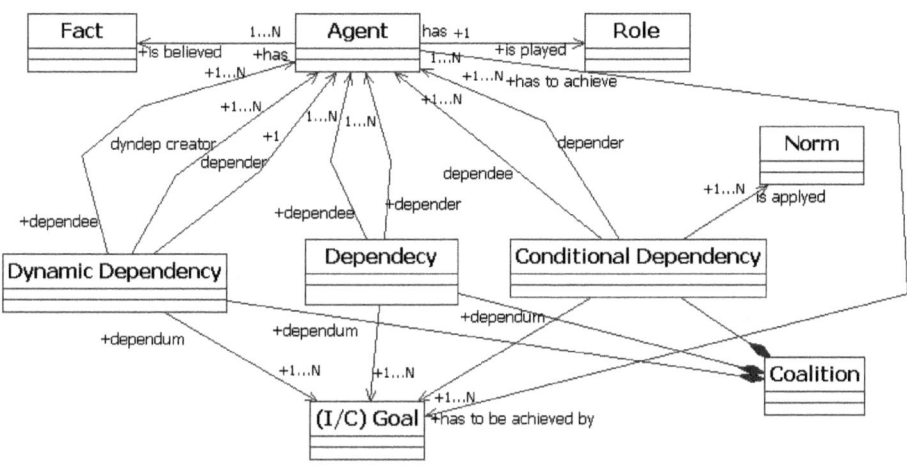

Fig. 4. The UML class diagram specifying the main concepts of the metamodel

- the function $sanct : N \times RL \rightarrow 2^{RG}$ is a function that associates with each norm and role, the institutional goals that will not be achieved if the norm is violated by role rl. Assumption: for each $B \subseteq RL$ and $H \in power(B)$ that $(\cup_{rl \in RL} sanct(n, rl)) \cap H = \emptyset$.
- the function $ctd : N \times RL \rightarrow 2^{RG}$ is a function that associates with each norm and role, the institutional goals that will become the new institutional goals the role rl has to achieve if the norm is violated by rl. Assumption:$\forall n \in N$ and $rl \in RL$, $ctd(n, rl) \in power(\{rl\})$.

We relate norms to goals following a twofold direction. First, we associate with each norm n a set of institutional goals $oblig(n) \subseteq RG$. Achieving these normative goals means that the norm n has been fulfilled; not achieving these goals means that the norm is violated. We assume that every normative goal can be achieved by the group, i.e., the group has the power to achieve it. Second, we associate with each norm a set of institutional goals $sanct(n) \subseteq RG$ which will not be achieved if the norm is violated and it represents the sanction associated with the norm. We assume that the group of agents does not have the power to achieve these goals. Third, we associate with each norm (primary obligation) another norm (secondary obligation) represented by a set of institutional goals $ctd(n) \subseteq RG$ that have to be fulfilled if the primary obligation is violated.

We define a new modeling activity, called *conditional dependency modeling*, to support in the early and late requirements analysis the representation of obligations, sanctions and contrary-to-duty obligations. Conditional dependence networks are defined as follows:

Definition 3 (Conditional Dependence Networks (CDN))
A conditional dependence network is a tuple $\langle A, G, cdep, odep, sandep, ctddep \rangle$ *where:*

- *A is a set of agents and G is a set of goals;*
- $cdep : 2^A \times 2^A \to 2^{2^G}$ *is a function that relates with each pair of sets of agents all the sets of goals on which the first depends on the second.*
- $odep : 2^A \times 2^A \to 2^{2^G}$ *is a function representing a obligation-based dependency that relates with each pair of sets of agents all the sets of goals on which the first depends on the second.*
- $sandep \subseteq (OBL \subseteq (2^A \times 2^A \times 2^{2^G})) \times (SANCT \subseteq (2^A \times 2^A \times 2^{2^G}))$ *is a function relating obligations to the dependencies which represent their sanctions. Assumption:* $SANCT \in cdep$ *and* $OBL \in odep$.
- $ctddep \subseteq (OBL_1 \subseteq (2^A \times 2^A \times 2^{2^G})) \times (OBL_2 \subseteq (2^A \times 2^A \times 2^{2^G}))$ *is a function relating obligations to the dependencies which represent their secondary obligations. Assumption:* $OBL_1, OBL_2 \in odep$ *and* $OBL_1 \cap OBL_2 = \emptyset$.

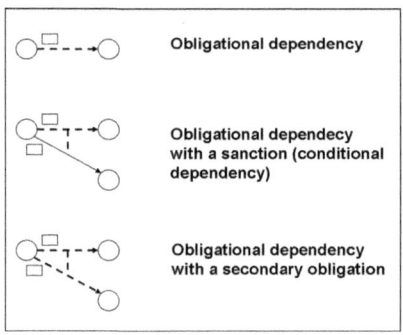

Fig. 5. Legend of the graphical representation of the *conditional dependency modeling*

Figure 5 gives a graphical representation of the *conditional dependency modeling*. It describes the obligation-based dependency (depicted as a dashed arrowed line), the obligation-based dependency with the associated sanction expressed as conditional dependency (depicted as a dashed arrowed line representing the obligation connected to a common arrowed line representing the sanction by a dashed line) and the obligation-based dependency with the associated secondary obligation (depicted as a dashed arrowed line representing the primary obligation connected to another dashed arrowed line representing the secondary obligation by a dashed line). The two functions *ctddep* and *sandep* are graphically represented as the dashed line connecting the obligation to the sanction or to the secondary obligation.

Example 1. Considering Grid's nodes of Figure 3, we can think to add two constraints under the form of obligations and we build the following conditional dependence network $CDN = \langle A, G, cdep, odep, sandep, ctddep \rangle$ depicted in Figure 6:

1. Agents $A = \{n_1, n_2, n_3, n_4, n_5, n_6\}$;
2. Goals $G = \{g_1, g_2, g_3, g_4, g_5, g_6, g_7, g_8\}$;
3. $cdep(\{n_1\}, \{n_2\}) = \{\{g_1\}\}$: agent n_1 depends on agent n_2 to achieve the goal $\{g_1\}$: to save the file *comp.log*;
   $dep(\{n_2\}, \{n_3\}) = \{\{g_2\}\}$: agent n_2 depends on agent n_3 to achieve the goal $\{g_2\}$: to run the file *mining.mat*;
   $dep(\{n_3\}, \{n_1\}) = \{\{g_5\}\}$: agent n_3 depends on agent n_1 to achieve the goal $\{g_5\}$: to save the file *satellite.jpg*;
   $dep(\{n_4\}, \{n_6\}) = \{\{g_3\}\}$: agent n_4 depends on agent n_6 to achieve the goal $\{g_3\}$: to run the file *results.mat*;
   $dep(\{n_6\}, \{n_5\}) = \{\{g_4\}\}$: agent n_6 depends on agent n_5 to achieve the goal $\{g_4\}$: to save the file *satellite.mpeg*;
   $dep(\{n_5\}, \{n_4\}) = \{\{g_6\}\}$: agent n_5 depends on agent n_4 to achieve the goal $\{g_6\}$: to have the authorization to open the file *dataJune.mat*;
   $odep(\{n_2\}, \{n_1\}) = \{\{g_7\}\}$: agent n_2 is obliged to perform goal $\{g_7\}$ concerning agent n_1 : to run the file *mining.mat* with the highest priority;
   $odep(\{n_4\}, \{n_5\}) = \{\{g_8\}\}$: agent n_4 is obliged to perform goal $\{g_8\}$ concerning agent n_5 : to share results of the running of file *dataJune.mat* with agent n_5;
   $odep(\{n_4\}, \{n_6\}) = \{\{g_8\}\}$: agent n_4 is obliged to perform goal $\{g_8\}$ concerning agent n_6 : to share results of the running of file *dataJune.mat* with agent n_6;
   $sandep\{((\{n_2\}, \{n_1\}) = \{\{g_7\}\}, (\{n_1\}, \{n_2\}) = \{\{g_1\}\})\}$;
   $ctddep\{((\{n_4\}, \{n_5\}) = \{\{g_8\}\}, (\{n_4\}, \{n_6\}) = \{\{g_8\}\})\}$;

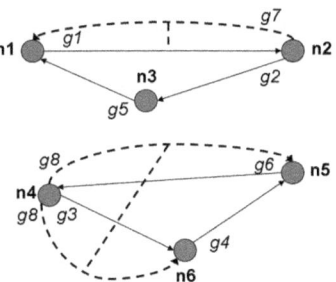

Fig. 6. Conditional Dependence Network of Example 1

Example 1 is depicted in Figure 6 which shows the network in the step after the deletion and the insertion of the two dynamic dependencies of Figure 3. In Figure 6, following the definition of coalition, we have two coalitions composing, e.g., two local groups of a virtual organization. The first one is composed by nodes n_1, n_2, n_3 and the other one is composed by nodes n_4, n_5 and n_6. Since these two subsets of the virtual organization have to work with a good cohesion then it is possible to insert some constraints, made clear by obligations. The first obligation consists in giving the highest priority to, for example, a computation for an agent composing the same local coalition as you. This first obligation is related to a sanction if it is violated. This link is made clear by the function *sandep* and it means the deletion of a dependency concerning a goal of the agent that has to fulfill the obligation. We represent sanctions as avoiding the achievability of a goal by the punished agent but a sanction would be represented also by imposing something unpleasant, for example an additional goal, on an agent. In this paper, we concentrate the discussion only on the first point and the second one is left for future research. The second obligation, instead, is related to a secondary obligation and it means that the agent has to share the results of a computation with a member of its coalition but, if it does not fulfill this obligation then it has to share these results with another member of its coalition.

Figure 7 shows the graphical representation of how an obligation in a conditional dependence network can evolve toward the application of a sanction or of a secondary obligation. In the first case, if the obligation is fulfilled and it is linked to a sanction then the obligation can be removed and also the connection among the obligation and the sanction can be removed. The only dependency that remains in the network is the one related to the sanction that passes from being a conditional dependency to a common dependency. If the obligation is not fulfilled then it is deleted and the deletion involves also the conditional dependency representing the sanction. The sanction consists exactly the deletion of this conditional dependency associated to a goal that the agent would achieve. In the second case, if the obligation is fulfilled and it is linked to a secondary obligation then the obligation is deleted and also the secondary obligation is deleted since there is no reason to already exists. If the obligation, instead, is not fulfilled then the primary obligation is deleted but the secondary obligation not. Note that in Figure 7 are depicted only the conditional dependencies and the obligational dependencies and not all the other kinds of possible dependencies present in the network.

Summarizing, we represent obligations, sanctions and contrary-to-duty obligations as tuples of dependencies related to each other. An obligation is viewed as a particular kind of dependency and it is related to dependencies due to sanctions and dependencies

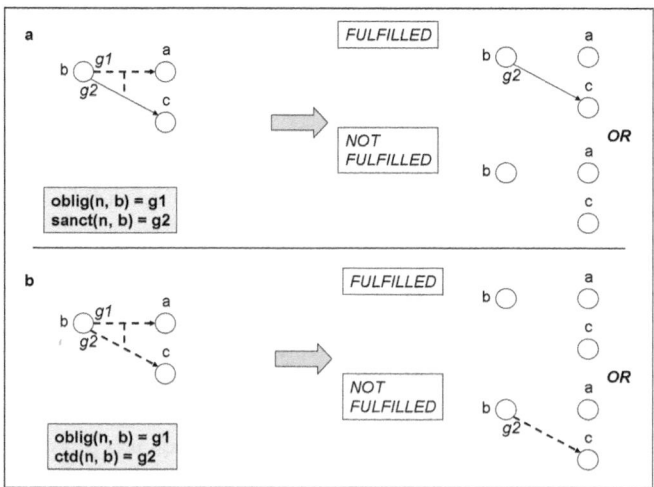

Fig. 7. The evolution of conditional dependence networks

due to secondary obligations. In the first case, we have that sanctions are common dependencies, already existing inside the system that, because of their connection with the obligation, can be deleted. These obligations can be of different kinds depending on the involved agents. For example, we can have a primary obligation linked to two secondary obligations: a first case con involve the same agents, e.g., agent a has to pay agent b for a service but he does not do the payment thus the secondary obligation is to pay to agent b an additional cost, and second case can involve a third agent, e.g., agent a continues to not pay you thus a third agent c is obliged to punish it for example with the deletion of all the services he has to perform for this agent.

4.2   Coalitions in Conditional Dependence Networks

In Section 3, we presented a definition of coalition based on the structure of dynamic dependence networks. In these dynamic coalitions we deal with conditional goals but there is not the presence of obligations intended as sets of dependencies linked together by a relation of the kind obligation-sanction or primary obligation-secondary obligation. Conditional dependence networks have to be taken into account when a system is described in terms of coalitions, vulnerable coalitions and potential coalitions since they can change depending on the conditional dependencies set by obligations. A coalition has to consider sanctions and secondary obligations, according to these constraints:

Definition 4 (Constraints for Coalitions in Conditional Dependence Networks).
Let A be a set of agents and G be a set of goals. A coalition function is a partial function $C \subseteq A \times 2^A \times 2^G$ such that $\{a \mid C(a, B, G)\} = \{b \mid b \in B, C(a, B, G)\}$, the set of agents profiting from the coalition is the set of agents contributing to it.

Introducing conditional dependence networks, the following constraints arise:

- *$\forall (dep_1, dep_2) \in sandep$, $dep_2 \notin C$ if and only if $dep_1 \notin C$. If the obligation, associated to the dependency dep_1 is not part of the coalition C then also the sanction dep_2 associated to the obligation is not part of the coalition C. If the obligation, associated to the dependency dep_1 is part of the coalition C then also the sanction dep_2 associated to the obligation is part of the coalition C.*
- *$\forall (dep_1, dep_2) \in ctddep$, $dep_2 \in C$ if and only if $dep_1 \notin C$. If the primary obligation, associated to the dependency dep_1 is not part of the coalition C then the secondary obligation dep_2 is part of the coalition C. If the primary obligation, associated to the dependency dep_1 is part of the coalition C then the secondary obligation dep_2 is not part of the coalition C.*

Example 2. Let us consider conditional dependence network of Example 1, depicted in Figure 6. Applying these constraints, we have that if the obligation on goal g_7 is fulfilled then the coalition composed by agents n_1, n_2 and n_3 already exists since the dependency associated to the sanction is not deleted. If the obligation on goal g_7 is not fulfilled then the obligation is deleted but also the sanction is deleted and the coalition does not exist any more. Concerning the second coalition, if the obligation on goal g_8 is fulfilled then both the primary and the secondary obligation are removed but if the primary obligation is not fulfilled then the secondary obligation is part of the coalition composed by agents n_4, n_5 and n_6.

5   Related Work

The idea of focusing the activities that precede the specification of software requirements, in order to understand how the intended system will meet organizational goals,
is not new. It has been first proposed in requirements engineering, specifically in Eric
Yu's work with his i* model [21]. The i* model offers actors, goals and actor dependencies as primitive concepts. The rationale of the i* model is that by doing an earlier
analysis, one can capture not only the what or the how, but also the why a piece of
software is developed. This supports a more refined analysis of system dependencies
and encourages a uniform treatment of system's requirements. As stated throughout the
paper, the most important inspiration source for our model is the TROPOS methodology [7] that spans the overall software development process, from early requirements
to implementation. Other approaches to software engineering are those of KAOS [10],
GAIA [20], AAII [14] and MaSE [13] and AUML [1]. The comparison of these works
is summarized in Figure 8.

	Early requirements	Late requirements	Architectural design	Detailed design
i*	X	X		
Kaos		X		
GAIA		X	X	
AAII and MaSE			X	X
AUML				X
TROPOS	X	X	X	X

Fig. 8. Comparison among different software engineering methodologies

The main difference between these approaches and our one consists in the introduction of the notion of obligation with its related concepts of contrary-to-duty and
sanction to the requirements analysis and in the graphical modeling language based on
dependencies among agents. Moreover, these approaches do not consider the notion of
coalition, as group of actors with a common set of goals and the possible constraints on
their structure.

6   Conclusions

This paper provides a detailed account of a new requirements analysis model based
on the normative multiagent paradigm, following the TROPOS methodology [7]. The
paper presents and discusses the early and late requirements phases of systems design [19]. We present the key concepts of the ontology of our methodology, agents,
roles, skills, goals, as shown by the UML diagram of Figure 4. We divide our ontology in three submodels: the agent model, the institutional model, and the role assignment model. The modeling activities based on this ontology, the dependency and

the dynamic dependency modeling, use a visual language in order to model the stakeholders and their relationships. Moreover, we introduce in the ontology the notion of coalition for dependence networks. The modeling of normative concepts is an improvement to requirements analysis since it allows, first, to constrain the construction of the requirements modeling and, second, to represent systems, as for example Grid-based systems, in which there are explicit obligations regulating the behaviour of the components composing it. We define a new modeling activity, called conditional dependency modeling, to support in the early and late requirements analysis the representation of obligations and contrary-to-duty obligations. This representation is realized as tuples of dependencies related to each other where an obligation is viewed as a particular kind of dependency, related to the dependencies due to sanctions and secondary obligations. Moreover, we model the requirements analysis phases also in a context in which there is the possible presence of coalitions in conditional dependence networks.

Concerning future work, we are interested in representing the coalitions' evolution process by means of our modeling techniques and in defining more powerful constraints on coalitions with the aim to maintain, thanks to the application of norms, coalitions' stability during this evolution process. In our opinion, this would be a relevant improvement to the studies concerning coalitions' stability because of the application, at the same time, of a social network approach, providing measures and graph-based methods, and a normative multiagent approach, providing mechanisms like social laws and norms. Finally, we are improving our conditional dependency modeling by adding also the representation of prohibitions.

References

1. Bauer, B., Müller, J.P., Odell, J.: Agent UML: A formalism for specifying multiagent software systems. Software Engineering and Knowledge Engineering 11(3), 207–230 (2001)
2. Boella, G., Caire, P., van der Torre, L.: Autonomy implies creating one's own norms norm negotiation in online multi-player games. Knowl. Inf. Syst. 18(2), 137–156 (2009)
3. Boella, G., van der Torre, L., Verhagen, H.: Introduction to normative multiagent systems. Computational and Mathematical Organization Theory 12, 71–79 (2006)
4. Boella, G., van der Torre, L., Villata, S.: Changing institutional goals and beliefs of autonomous agents. In: Bui, et al. (eds.) [8], pp. 78–85
5. Boella, G., van der Torre, L., Villata, S.: Social viewpoints for arguing about coalitions. In: Bui, et al. (eds.) [8], pp. 66–77
6. Boella, G., van der Torre, L.W.N.: Regulative and constitutive norms in normative multiagent systems. In: Dubois, D., Welty, C.A., Williams, M.-A. (eds.) Principles of Knowledge Representation and Reasoning (KR), pp. 255–266. AAAI Press, Menlo Park (2004)
7. Bresciani, P., Perini, A., Giorgini, P., Giunchiglia, F., Mylopoulos, J.: Tropos: An agent-oriented software development methodology. Autonomous Agents and Multi-Agent Systems 8(3), 203–236 (2004)
8. Bui, T.D., Ho, T.V., Ha, Q.T. (eds.): 11th Pacific Rim International Conference on Multi-Agents (PRIMA 2008). LNCS (LNAI), vol. 5357. Springer, Heidelberg (2008)
9. Caire, P., Villata, S., Boella, G., van der Torre, L.: Conviviality masks in multiagent systems. In: Padgham, L., Parkes, D.C., Müller, J., Parsons, S. (eds.) 7th International Joint Conference on Autonomous Agents and Multiagent Systems (AAMAS), pp. 1265–1268. IFAAMAS (2008)

10. Dardenne, A., van Lamsweerde, A., Fickas, S.: Goal-directed requirements acquisition. Sci. Comput. Program. 20(1-2), 3–50 (1993)
11. Forrester, J.W.: Gentle murder, or the adverbial samaritan. Journal of Philosophy 81, 193–197 (1984)
12. Foster, I.T.: The anatomy of the grid: Enabling scalable virtual organizations. In: First IEEE International Symposium on Cluster Computing and the Grid (CCGRID), pp. 6–7. IEEE Computer Society, Los Alamitos (2001)
13. García-Ojeda, J.C., DeLoach, S.A., Robby, W.H.O., Valenzuela, J.: O-maSE: A customizable approach to developing multiagent development processes. In: Luck, M., Padgham, L. (eds.) Agent-Oriented Software Engineering VIII. LNCS, vol. 4951, pp. 1–15. Springer, Heidelberg (2008)
14. Kinny, D., Georgeff, M.P., Rao, A.S.: A methodology and modelling technique for systems of bdi agents. In: Perram, J., Van de Velde, W. (eds.) Modelling Autonomous Agents in a Multi-Agent World, MAAMAW 1996. LNCS, vol. 1038, pp. 56–71. Springer, Heidelberg (1996)
15. Minsky, N.H., Lockman, A.: Ensuring integrity by adding obligations to privileges. In: International Conference on Software Engineering (ICSE), pp. 92–102 (1985)
16. Prakken, H., Sergot, M.J.: Contrary-to-duty obligations. Studia Logica 57(1), 91–115 (1996)
17. Shoham, Y., Tennenholtz, M.: On social laws for artificial agent societies: Off-line design. Artif. Intell. 73(1-2), 231–252 (1995)
18. Sichman, J.S., Conte, R.: Multi-agent dependence by dependence graphs. In: The First International Joint Conference on Autonomous Agents & Multiagent Systems (AAMAS), pp. 483–490. ACM, New York (2002)
19. van Lamsweerde, A.: Requirements Engineering: From System Goals to UML Models to Software Specifications. Wiley, Chichester (2009)
20. Wooldridge, M., Jennings, N.R., Kinny, D.: The GAIA methodology for agent-oriented analysis and design. Autonomous Agents and Multi-Agent Systems 3(3), 285–312 (2000)
21. Yu, E.: Modeling organizations for information systems requirements engineering. In: First IEEE International Symposium on Requirements Engineering, pp. 34–41 (1993)
22. Zhao, G., Chadwick, D.W., Otenko, S.: Obligations for role based access control. In: AINA Workshops (1), pp. 424–431. IEEE Computer Society, Los Alamitos (2007)

A Norm-Based Organization Management System

Natalia Criado, Vicente Julián, Vicente Botti, and Estefania Argente*

Grupo de Tecnología Informática - Inteligencia Artificial
Departamento de sistemas informáticos y computación
Camino de Vera S/N 46022 Valencia (Spain)
{ncriado,vingalda,vbotti,eargente}@dsic.upv.es

Abstract. Virtual organizations are conceived as an effective mechanism for ensuring coordination and global goal fulfilment of an open system, in which heterogeneous entities (agents or services) interact and might also present self-interested behaviours. However, available tools rarely give support for organizational abstractions. The THOMAS multi-agent architecture allows the development of open multi-agent applications. It provides a useful framework for the development of virtual organizations, on the basis of a service-based approach. In this paper, the Organization Management System component of the THOMAS architecture is presented. It is in charge of the organization life-cycle process, including the normative management. It provides a set of structural, informative and dynamic services, which allow describing both specification and administration features of the structural elements of the organization and their dynamics. Moreover, it makes use of a normative language for controlling the service request, provision and register.

Keywords: Multi-Agent Systems, Normative Language, Virtual Organizations, Web Services.

1 Introduction

A promising approach in the multi-agent systems (MAS) area is the development of open systems. The main features of open systems are: (i) they are populated by heterogeneous agents which can enter or leave the system dynamically; and (ii) they are situated in dynamic environments. Therefore, organizations are conceived as an effective mechanism for coordinating the behaviour of heterogeneous agents, imposing not only structural restrictions on their relationships, but also normative restrictions on their behaviour [1,2]. Thus, organizations describe the system functionality (i.e. roles, tasks, services), the norms that control agent behaviours, the formation of groups of agents, the global goals pursued by these

---

* This work is supported by TIN2005-03395 and TIN2006-14630-C03-01 projects of the Spanish government, GVPRE/2008/070 project, FEDER funds and CONSOLIDER-INGENIO 2010 under grant CSD2007-00022, FPU grant AP-2007-01256 awarded to N.Criado.

J. Padget et al. (Eds.): COIN 2009, LNAI 6069, pp. 19–35, 2010.

groups and the relationships between entities and their environment. Moreover, the potential changes on the dynamic environment might require the adaptation of the organizational structure and functionality.

The "computing as interaction" paradigm [3] defines computation as an inherent social activity that takes place by means of communication between computing entities. More specifically, large distributed systems are conceived in terms of service provider or consumer entities [4]. Therefore, the relevant technological approaches of this paradigm are service oriented architectures (SOA) and MAS. On the one hand, services provide a standard infrastructure for the interaction among heterogeneous software entities. On the other hand, MAS offer a more general and complex notion of SOA; agents, due to their intelligent and social capabilities, allow the redefinition of traditional services adding new features such as dynamic service composition, negotiation about quality of service, etc. In the last years, several works have focused on the problem of integrating these two approaches, in order to model autonomous and heterogeneous computational entities in dynamic and open environments. Their main effort is directed at masking services for redirection, integration or administration purposes [5].

Taking this integrating view into account, THOMAS has been defined as an open architecture for large-scale open multi-agent systems, based on a service-oriented approach [6]. This architecture provides agents with a set of services for offering and discovering entities' functionality and for managing the organization life-cycle. With this purpose of achieving a better integration among MAS and Web Services, all the functionalities (i.e. agent and also THOMAS functionalities) are provided, required and published in THOMAS employing Web Services standards (such as OWL-S), and they can also make use of traditional Web Services.

One of the main components of the THOMAS architecture is the Organization Management System (OMS), which is responsible for the management of the organizations and their constituent entities. In order to allow this management, the OMS must provide a set of structural, informative and dynamic services for describing both specification and administration features of the structural elements of the organization and their dynamics. In this sense, the OMS provides adaptive mechanisms for creating organizational structures that allow optimizing the coordination in Virtual Organizations (VOs), taking into account the heterogeneity of agents and services.

With the aim of allowing the organization management, the OMS requires a normative language for controlling how services can be employed, i.e., when and how agents can request, provide or publish not only their services, but also these ones provided by the open architecture. In this sense, a normative language that imposes a deontic control over agents for requesting, providing or publishing services has been defined. Then the OMS provides regulatory mechanisms that guarantee a globally efficient coordination in open systems taking into account the impossibility of controlling (the majority of) the agents and services directly.

Following, a description of the proposed OMS component, in charge of the organization management by means of organizational services is detailed. Its norm management process, both with a description of its norm representation language is detailed in section 3. The implementation of this OMS component is explained in section 4. A case study is contained in section 5. Finally, discussion and conclusions are detailed in sections 6 and 7, respectively.

2 Organization Management System

As previously mentioned, the THOMAS architecture has the aim of integrating both multi-agent systems and service-oriented computing technologies as the foundation of virtual organizations. This open architecture for large-scale open multi-agent systems is composed of a range of services included on different modules or components[1]. In this sense, agents have access to the architecture infrastructure through the following components:

- **Service Facilitator** (SF). This component provides a mechanism and support by which organizations and agents can offer and discover services.
- **Platform Kernel** (PK). It maintains the basic management services for an agent platform. It integrates the FIPA AMS and the FIPA communication network layer.
- **Organization Management System** (OMS). This component is mainly responsible of the management of the organizations and their entities. Thus, it gives support to the organization life-cycle management.

The present paper is focused on this last component. It is in charge of controlling the organizational life-cycle process. In THOMAS, organizations are structured by means of *Organizational Units* (OU) [7] which represent a set of agents that carry out some specific and differentiated activities or tasks, following a predefined pattern of cooperation and communication. An OU is formed by different entities along its life-cycle which can be either single agents or other OUs. They represent a virtual meeting point because agents can dynamically enter and leave organizational units, by means of adopting (or leaving) roles inside. An OU has also an internal topology (i.e. hierarchical, team, plain), which imposes restrictions on agent relationships (for example, supervision, monitoring or information relationships). A more detailed explanation of the OU concept and a description of different topologies can be found in [7].

The OMS is in charge of controlling how the Organizational Units are created, which entities are participating inside them, how these entities are related and which roles they are playing through time. For this reason, the OMS offers agents a set of services for organization life-cycle management, classified in:

- **Structural services**, which enable agents to request the OMS to modify the structural and normative organization specification. They comprise services for adding/deleting norms (*RegisterNorm, DeregisterNorm*), adding/deleting roles (*RegisterRole, DeregisterRole*) and creating new organizational units or deleting them (*RegisterUnit, DeregisterUnit*). Publishing these services enables agents to modify the organization structure through its life-time.

---

[1] http://www.fipa.org/docs/THOMASarchitecture.pdf

- **Informative services**, that provide information of the current state of the organization, detailing which are the roles defined in an OU (*InformUnitRoles*), the roles played by an agent (*InformAgentRoles*), the specific members of an OU (*InformMembers*), its member quantity (*InformQuantity*), its internal structure (*InformUnit*), and the services and norms related with a specific role (*InformRoleProfiles*, *InformRoleNorms*).
- **Dynamic services**, which allow defining how agents can adopt roles inside OUs (*AcquireRole*, *LeaveRole*) or how agents can be forced to leave a specific role (*Expulse*), normally due to sanctions. Publishing these services enables external agents to participate inside the system.

This set of services for organization life-cycle management allows defining specification and administration features of the structural components of the organization (roles, units and norms) and their dynamics (entry/exit of entities). However, a specific control on who can make use of these services and in which conditions is needed. This type of control is defined by means of norms.

3   Norm Management

Normative systems have been defined as a mechanism for enabling cooperation inside Open MAS. In this sense, norms are persuasive methods for obtaining the desired behaviour from agents. In addition, norms can be viewed as a coordination skill for organizing MAS, since they specify the desired behaviour of the society members [8]. Regarding this second conception of norms, our proposal consists on employing norms for regulating agent organizations. More specifically, this work has the purpose of applying the normative theory for defining the way in which agents may modify the structure of their organization (norms, organizational units and roles) and its execution components, in order to adapt it dynamically to environmental changes.

Recently, works on norms have focused on overcoming the gap between theoretical works on normative systems and practical MAS. They give a computational interpretation of norms that allows norm execution. However, none of them raises the normative management problem or gives an infrastructure that enables including the normative theory inside the implementation of real MAS applications. With this aim, we have developed both a normative language for controlling agent organizational dynamics and a normative management engine, which are explained in the following sections.

3.1   Norm Representation Language

Before addressing the norm controlling problem, the definition of a formal language for the representation of the normative concepts is needed. Our normative language is mainly based on previous works for defining norms inside Electronic Institutions (EI) [9,10]. These works define a normative language for controlling the communicative acts (illocutions) of agents inside an EI. In addition, they propose an extension of this language for allowing the definition of norms concerning non-dialogical actions. Our language takes these approaches as a starting point and increases them in order to give support to functional and organizational management. More concretely, it makes possible the definition of constraints on agent behaviours in terms of actions related to service controlling and organizational processes. The main contributions of the proposed language are: (i) it allows the definition of consequences of norms by means of sanctions and rewards; (ii) it gives support to organizational concepts such as roles or organizational units and; (iii) the definition of agents' functionality by means of the OWL-S standard increases norm expressiveness, as will be argued lately.

Following, some issues about the developed normative language are commented. For a more detailed description of this language see [11].

The proposed language is a coordination mechanism that attempts to: (i) promote behaviours satisfactory to the organization, i.e. actions that contribute to the achievement of global goals; and (ii) avoid harmful actions, i.e. actions that prompt the system to be unsatisfactory or unstable. Norm semantics is based on deontic logic since it defines obligations, permissions and prohibitions. Our approach conceives norms as expectations that may not be fulfilled. Thus, norms are not impositions (i.e. they are not automatically regimented on agents by their designer), but they are methods for persuading agents to behave correctly by means of the application of sanctions and rewards. For example, an agent would be expelled from the organization as sanction if it violates norms systematically. An analysis on the effectiveness of both sanctions and rewards as mechanisms for enforcing norms is over the scope of this article. However, this work assumes that agents are aware of norms, punishments and rewards. In this sense, a normative reasoning process for norm-aware agents has been proposed in [12].

Norms define agent rights and duties in terms of actions that agents are allowed or not to perform. Actions have been divided in two categories: actions related to the organizational aspects of MAS; and actions concerning service accessing. Hence, two main types of norms have been defined:

- **Organizational Norms:** related to services offered by the OMS to members of the organization. They establish organizational dynamics, e.g. role management (role cardinalities, incompatibility between roles) and the protocol by which agents are enabled to acquire roles.
- **Functional Norms:** related to services offered by the members of the organization or the SF. They define role functionality in terms of services that can be requested/provided, service requesting order, service conditions, protocols that should be followed, etc. They establish service management according to previous service results, environmental states, etc.

Table 1 details the reduced BNF syntax of this language. A norm is defined by means of a deontic operator (<*deontic_concept*>), an addressed entity and an action, that concerns organizational (<*organizational_action*>) or functional (<*functional_action*>) management. The <*temporal_situation*> field establishes a temporal condition for the activation of the norm. It can be expressed as a deadline, an action or a service result. A norm may also contain a state condition

Table 1. On the left side, BNF syntax of norms is detailed. On the right side, its semantics expressed by means of dynamic logic is given. α is an action description. β is an state description. V, $DO(\alpha)$ and $DONE(\alpha)$ are the well-known predicates for representing violation states, an action α that will be done next and an action α that has been performed. Finally, ϕ represents a norm.

<norm>::=<deontic> <entity> <action> [<temporal>] [*IF* <if_condition>] | *norm_id*	
<ext_norm>::=<norm> [*SANCTION*(<norm>)] [*REWARD*(<norm>)]	$\phi : FORBIDDEN\ \alpha \equiv [\alpha]V$ $\phi : OBLIGED\ \alpha \equiv [\neg\alpha]V$ $\phi : PERMITTED\ \alpha \equiv [\alpha]\neg V$
<deontic>::=*OBLIGED* | *FORBIDDEN* | *PERMITTED*	
	$\phi : \phi'SANCTION\ \alpha \equiv \phi' \wedge [V]DO(\alpha)$ $\phi : \phi'REWARD\ \alpha \equiv \phi' \wedge [\neg V]DO(\alpha)$
<entity>::=<agent>: <role> [− <unit>] | <role> [− <unit>] | <entity_id> <agent>::=?*variable* | *agent_id* <role>::=?*variable* | *role_id* <unit>::=?*variable* | *unit_id* <entity_id>::=*agent_id* | *role_id* | *unit_id*	$\phi : \phi'BEFORE\ \alpha \equiv \phi' \vee DONE(\alpha)$ $\phi : \phi'AFTER\ \alpha \equiv [\alpha]\phi'$ $\phi : \phi'BETWEEN(\alpha_1,\alpha_2) \equiv [\alpha_1]\phi' \vee$ $DONE(\alpha_2)$
<action>::=<functional_action> | <organizational_action>	$\phi : \phi'IF\beta \equiv \beta \to \phi'$
<temporal>::=*BEFORE* <sit> | *AFTER* <sit> | *BETWEEN*(<sit> , <sit>)	

for its activation (<*if_condition*>). It is a boolean condition expressed over variables, identifiers, failed or satisfactory states of norms or service results.

Usually, obligations and prohibitions have sanctions and rewards as persuasive methods. Sanctions and rewards are represented through norms addressed to entities that will act as norm defenders or promoters. The definition of sanctions and rewards recursively as norms can create an infinite chain of norms. Thus, not only addressed agents might be controlled by norms, but also their controllers (defenders or promoters). Following M. Luck et al. proposal [13], our normative model does not impose any restriction on this fact, so it is the norm designer who is in charge of specifying when to stop this recursive process, i.e. when a controller is trustworthy enough. For example, norm 1 obliges a *Supervisor* agent to request *AddUnit* service; if the *Supervisor* agent does not respect the norm, then it will be expelled from the organization by the OMS as sanction. Norm 1 contains a state condition and a temporal condition also. In this case, these conditions indicate that the agent is obliged to request *AddUnit* service before 10 seconds if it is the only *Supervisor* inside the organization.

$$?agent : Supervisor\ OBLIGED\ REQUEST\ AddUnit$$
$$IF\ InformQuantity(``Supervisor") = 1$$
$$BEFORE(10'') \tag{1}$$
$$SANCTION\ oms\ OBLIGED\ PROVIDE\ Expulse$$
$$MESSAGE(CONTENT(?agent, ``Supervisor"))$$

Organizational norms are related to actions that allow agents to request organizational services (<*org_service*>) for adopting roles, registering new norms, etc. These services are provided by the OMS. Functional norms are defined in terms of actions related to the publication (REGISTER), provision (SERVE) or usage (REQUEST) of services. The BNF syntax of both organizational and functional actions is detailed in Table 2. Norm 2 contains an example of a functional norm. It obliges a service *Provider* agent to register its own *SearchService* service.

$$?agent : Provider\ OBLIGED$$
$$REGISTER\ SearchService$$
$$PROFILE \qquad (2)$$
$$INPUT(ServiceDescription : String)$$
$$OUTPUT(ServiceID : Identifier)$$

Table 2. BNF syntax of organizational and functional actions

<organizational_action>::=REQUEST <org_service> MESSAGE(<msg_cont>)

    <org_service>::=<structural_service> | <dynamic_service> | <informative_service>

  <structural_service>::=RegisterNorm | RegisterRole | DeregisterNorm |
DeregisterRole | DeregisterUnit | RegisterUnit

<informative_service>::=InformUnitRoles | InformAgentRoles | InformUnit | InformMembers |
InformRoleProfiles | InformRoleNorms | InformQuantity

  <dynamic_service>::=AcquireRole | LeaveRole | Expulse

  <functional_action>::=<serv_publication> | <serv_provision> | <serv_usage>

  <serv_publication>::=REGISTER *service_name* PROFILE <profile_desc>
[PROCESS<process_desc>]

  <service_provision>::=SERVE *service_name* PROCESS <process_desc>
[MESSAGE(<msg_cont>)]

    <service_usage>::=REQUEST *service_name* MESSAGE(<msg_cont>)

As previously mentioned, the specification of functionalities by means of OWL-s standard allows defining functionality more expressively: representing service preconditions and effects; global functionalities are described as complex services that are composed of atomic services, so a complex service specification describes how agent behaviours are orchestrated; and functionality is detailed in two ways: services that entities perform and services that entities need. Thus, Service Oriented Computing (SOC) concepts such as ontologies, process models, choreography, facilitators, service level agreements and quality of service measures can be applied to MAS. Our proposal of normative language offers support for specifying knowledge about a service following OWL-s ontology. The profile (*<profile_desc>*) for advertising and discovering services contains input and output parameters of the service and its preconditions and postconditions. The process model (*<process_desc>*) gives a detailed description of a service's operation. It details the sequence of actions carried out by the service. These actions are linked through each other by means of different control constructs: CONNECTS indicates a sequential ordering between two actions; JOIN indicates a concurrence between actions and a final synchronization of them; IF-THEN-ELSE and

Table 3. BNF syntax of service profile and process

<profile_desc>::=[INPUT(<param_list>)] [OUTPUT (<param_list>)]
        [PRE(<cond_exp>)][POST(<cond_exp>)] | *profile_id*

<process_desc>::=*process_id* | *?variable* | <action> CONNECTS <process_desc> |
        <action> JOIN <process_desc> |
        IF <cond_exp> THEN(<process_desc>) [ELSE (<process_desc>)] |
        WHILE <cond_exp> DO(<process_desc>)

<msg_cont>::=[SENDER(<entity>)] [RECEIVER (<entity>)]
        [PERFORMATIVE (*performative_id*)] CONTENT (<args>)

<action>::=*task_id*(<param_list>) | <service_usage>

<param_list>::=*variable* : *type* [,<param_list>]

WHILE-DO define the classical control structures. Finally, the grounding provides details on how to interoperate with a service, via messages <*msg_cont*>).
Table 3 contains syntax of service processes, profiles and requesting messages.

In this section, a general language for controlling agent service access has been
briefly described. For further details and examples see [11].

3.2   Norm Management Process

This section describes aspects related to the management of organizational
norms. As previously mentioned, our formalism allows representing constraints
over organizational dynamics. Thus, the controlled norms define access to the
organizational services provided by our architecture.

Recently, the line of research on computational implementation of norms is
based on the Electronic Institution (EI) proposal [9,10]. The EIs provide a framework for heterogeneous agent cooperation. However, they are not an open environment in its broadest sense, because agents interact inside the institution
through the infrastructure provided by the EI. Therefore, the behaviour of external agents is completely controlled by the institution, which allows or not
agents to pronounce certain illocutions. Thus, norms are pre-imposed on agents.
The institutional mediation prevents agent behaviour from deviating from desired behaviour. Moreover, the fact that all communications are made through
the institution allows an easy regimentation and enforcement of norms. In this
sense, the existence of a middle-ware for mediating the agent communication
avoids the need to take into consideration the limitations that exist in open environments. Such limitations are related to the detection of fact occurrence and
the extra capabilities needed in order to impose norms upon other agents.

Our proposed virtual organization architecture is completely different since it
does not have any mediator layer. On the contrary, agents are allowed to interact
freely. In this sense, our architecture is more related to the notion of *Partially
Controlled MAS* [14], in which agents may deviate from ideal behaviour. As a
consequence, there has to be a control mechanism for motivating agents to obey
the norms. However, our architecture offers a set of services for the management
of the organizations life-cycle. In this sense, the OMS is not a centralised entity
that controls all the interactions performed by agents. On the contrary, it is
a *controllable* entity (which is directly controlled by the system designer [14])

which offers a set of organizational services in order to give support to agent cooperation. One of these coordination mechanisms is the definition of norms that regulate agent behaviour. The OMS does not control the agent communications, it is only in charge of implementing the norms that regulate access to OMS services. The verifiability issue of a norm is a crucial aspect in the normative management process since there is not any mediator middle-ware that controls all the communications.

Norm Verifiability. Works on norm implementation conceive norms as a mechanism for enabling coordination and cooperation inside open MAS. Nevertheless, none of them faces with one of the main problems inside open systems, which is the existence of limitations. The term *limitation* refers to the fact that an entity needs extra information and capabilities in order to act as a norm supervisor or controller. Therefore, an analysis of normative verifiability is needed, before dealing with norm implementation.

The OMS can control norms which are related to the provision of organizational services. Therefore, the set of OMS verifiable norms is a subset of the organizational norms. Verifiable norms are *regulative* norms that define ideal behaviour by means of obligations, prohibitions and permissions. More specifically, permissive and prohibition norms concerning the access to OMS services are controllable, since the OMS checks whether the client agent is allowed to perform such request before providing it. On the other hand, obligation norms can not be imposed by the OMS as it has not capabilities to force agents to carry out an action. However, the OMS can detect the violation of an obligation norm related to an OMS service and perform the associated sanction. On the contrary, if the norm has been fulfilled then the OMS will carry out the actions specified by the reward. Logically, obligation norms should be active for a certain period of time, i.e. normative activation and deactivation events must be defined in order to allow the OMS to determine the norm fulfilment.

Verifiable conditions are related to informative services provided by the OMS such as role cardinalities, information about roles played by agents, etc. Regarding detectable events, they are the request and provision of services offered by the OMS. Both verifiable condition and detectable events syntax are a refinement of the general condition syntax proposed in [11]. Finally, sanctions and rewards can be defined by means of norms that oblige the OMS to request or provide a specific service, as shown in norm 2.

In this section, issues concerning the formal language for representing norms and syntax of verifiable organizational norms have been detailed. Not only an abstract component in charge of the management of organizations has been proposed, but also an implementation of the OMS component has been made. Next, this implementation is described.

4   Organization Management System Implementation

As previously argued, the OMS is a *controllable* entity which offers a set of organizational services. This system maintains a fact base representing the

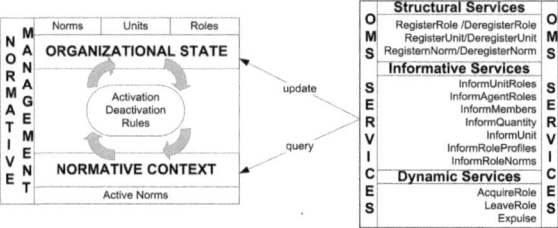

Fig. 1. OMS Implementation

organizational state, and it is also in charge of controlling verifiable norms. The implementation has been included in a prototype of the THOMAS architecture[2]. As Figure 1 illustrates, the OMS implementation is composed by two main elements: the implementation of the organizational services and the implementation of the normative management process, which are described next.

4.1 OMS Services Implementation

As previously stated, the set of services provided by the OMS are those ones related to the organizations life-cycle management, i.e. the management of their structural components (unit, roles and norms) and the organizational dynamics.

The service request management process consists of:

- (i) Firstly, the normative context must be analysed in order to determine whether the client agent is allowed to request this service according to the organizational state.
- (ii) If so, then the OMS provides the requested service.
- (iii) If the organizational state changes as a result of the service provision, then this state is updated.

Mainly, the service provision process consists of an input verification phase and the updating of the organizational state according to the produced changes. As an example, the process of registering of a new norm involves:

- (i) Verification of input data, i.e. checking the adequacy of norm syntax as well as the uniqueness of the provided norm identifier.
- (ii) Norm verifiability detection, i.e. determine if the norm control should be carried out by the OMS. Verifiability checking is done by means of an interpreter, which has been automatically built from the BNF syntax of our organizational normative language employing the JavaCC[3] tool.
- (iii) Inconsistency checking. Taking [15,16] as a starting point, an inconsistent situation is that one in which an action is forbidden and permitted or forbidden and obliged simultaneously. The off-line detection of all norm inconsistencies is not possible, since the norm activation conditions are based

---

[2] http://www.dsic.upv.es/users/ia/sma/tools/Thomas/
[3] https://javacc.dev.java.net/

on the detection of events and facts that may occur during execution. For the moment, the inconsistency detection mechanism is restricted to the determination of *static inconsistencies*, which are situations in which the same action is defined unconditionally as permitted and forbidden to the same entity. As future work, we will employ results of theoretical works on norm change[4] as well as conflict resolution techniques for solving *dynamic inconsistencies* among norms.

- (iv) The fact corresponding to the new norm is registered in the normative system.

Due to lack of space, only the organizational service for registering a new norm has been explained in detail. However, all services needed for the management of units, roles, norms and organizational dynamics, have been implemented in a similar way.

4.2   Norm Management Implementation

This process covers the maintenance of the organizational state and the determination of the allowed actions according to the normative context and the organizational state. These two functionalities have been implemented as internal services of the OMS, by means of a rule-based system in Jess[5] that maintains a fact base representing the organizational state and it also detects norm activation. Thus, the *update* service is in charge of adding and deleting facts into the rule system in order to register the organizational current state.

The determination of the allowed actions is made by means of the analysis of the normative context. It has been performed as an internal *query* service offered by the normative manager to the OMS services. This checking is performed by the OMS each time it receives a new service request. Then the OMS checks whether it exists a norm addressed to the client agent that forbids such service request. Thus, an action is considered as allowed when there is not any norm that forbids it explicitly. Norms can be addressed to any agent that plays a specific role or they can affect a specific agent also. Consequently, a criterion for norm precedence is needed. In this case, a rule known as *lex specialis* has been employed [17]. Therefore, the normative analysis begins with checking agent addressed norms. If there is not any norm, norms related to the roles played by the agent are considered.

Regarding detection of norm activation and deactivation, this functionality has been implemented through a set of rules that detect the occurrence of the activation and deactivation events. This implementation of norms by means of rules is based on a previous work aimed at implementing norms for Electronic Institutions [9]. Next, some details about the implementation of each type of norm are commented:

---

[4] http://icr.uni.lu/normchange07/
[5] http://herzberg.ca.sandia.gov/

- *Service access norms.* As previously mentioned, these norms allow the definition of prohibitions and permissions concerning the use of organizational services. More formally, the semantics of permission norms, expressed as Event-Condition-Action rules (ECA-rules), is:

$$
\begin{aligned}
&\textbf{on } event_{start} \textbf{ if } if_{condition} \textbf{ do } \oplus permitted(a)\\
&\quad\textbf{on } a \textbf{ if } permitted(a) \textbf{ do } \oplus provided(a)\\
&\quad\quad\textbf{on } event_{end} \textbf{ do } \ominus permitted(a)\\
&\textbf{if } not(if_{condition}) \textbf{ do } \ominus permitted(a)
\end{aligned}
\tag{3}
$$

According to this, a general service access norm is controlled by means of the definition of four new rules in the expert system. The first rule detects norm activation and asserts the permission ($\oplus permitted(a)$). If the action (a) occurs and it is allowed, then the service is provided ($\oplus provided(a)$). The last two rules retract the norm from the expert system when the norm is deactivated, i.e. when the condition ($if_{condition}$) is not true or the completion event is detected ($event_{end}$). In case of prohibition norms, a prohibition ($\oplus forbidden(a)$) is asserted. Thus, if an action a is forbidden, then a *notAllowed* fact is asserted.
- *Obligation norms.* They cannot be directly imposed by the OMS, since it is not able to force another agent to carry out a specific action. However, it might persuade agents to behave correctly by performing sanctions and rewards; i.e. the OMS acts as norm enforcer. Following, a formal description of obligation semantics is shown:

$$
\begin{aligned}
&\textbf{on } event_{start} \textbf{ if } if_{condition} \textbf{ do } \oplus expected(a)\\
&\textbf{on } a \textbf{ if } expected(a) \textbf{ do } \ominus expected(a) \bullet reward\\
&\textbf{on } event_{end} \textbf{ if } expected(a) \textbf{ do } \ominus expected(a) \bullet sanction
\end{aligned}
\tag{4}
$$

Thus, the implementation of obligation norms consists on controlling the activation of the obligation. Then the OMS waits for the fulfilment of the expected action (a), i.e. the OMS asserts a new expectation ($\oplus expected(a)$). If the action is performed before the deadline ($event_{end}$) then the reward is carried out. Otherwise the OMS will perform the sanction.

This section has illustrated some details of the implementation of the OMS entity. The next section illustrates a case study which describes how an untrusted external agent is prevented from participating in the agent society.

5 Case Study

In order to illustrate the performance of the OMS services and the normative management process carried out by the OMS, a case-study example of a customised information system has been employed in this section. This example, named *InformationSystem*, aims at distributing relevant information of different topics in an efficient way, trying to guarantee the maximum quality of this information. Thus, users might ask the system for information about some specific topic punctually or they might request to be a member of the system. As a member, a user can supply its own information for a specific topic, he can also create new topics and even classify or evaluate the quality of the information given by others.

In this section, this system is modelled as an Open MAS in which external agents can participate as information requesters, providers or even information evaluators. Following, a description of the organizational structure of the *InformationSystem* organization is explained, and also a dynamical usage of the organization is detailed, providing an execution scenario.

5.1   Organization Structure

Three roles have been identified in the *InformationSystem* example: (i) *Consultant*, that requests information to the system; (ii) *Provider*, that is allowed to provide new information (documents); and (iii) *Evaluator*, who is in charge of evaluating the documents and controlling member behaviours. Two domain services have been identified: *ProvideInfo* service, that allows *Providers* to add new documents; and *EvaluateInfo* service, which is offered by *Evaluators* in order to assess the quality of a given document.

5.2   Dynamic Usage

This scenario shows how a *provider* agent, which is not providing good documents, is expulsed permanently from the *InformationSystem* (Figure 2). P1, E1, C1 have been previously registered as a *provider*, an *evaluator* and a *consultant* inside the *InformationSystem*, respectively. Then C1 requests P1 to give information related to hotels (Figure 2 message 1). P1 returns a *Document* as a result of the *ProvideInfo* service (message 2). Then C1 requests agent E1 to provide the *EvaluateInfo* service so as to known quality of this information (message 3). After evaluating the provided document, E1 answers by informing C1 about the low quality of this information (message 4). Then, E1 decides to expel P1 from the *InformationSystem*, since its provided documents are of low quality, by requesting the OMS to execute the expulsion service (messages 5 and 6). Then the OMS informs P1 about its expulsion as an information *provider* (message 7). Next E1 creates a new norm in order to prevent P1 acting as a *provider* in the future (messages 7 and 8). Therefore, when P1 tries to become an information *provider* inside the *InformationSystem* (message 9) the OMS will not allow P1 to acquire the *provider* role (message 10), since there is a norm which forbids it explicitly.

Due to lack of space, a detailed application example illustrating all the new features of the proposal has not been included here. However, this example illustrates how the OMS services are employed in order to change the normative context dynamically. The normative context defines the way in which agents behave inside THOMAS. For further details a simple demo example can be found together with an available prototype of the THOMAS architecture[6]. Following, conclusions and a discussion on related works are presented.

---

[6] http://www.dsic.upv.es/users/ia/sma/tools/Thomas/index.html

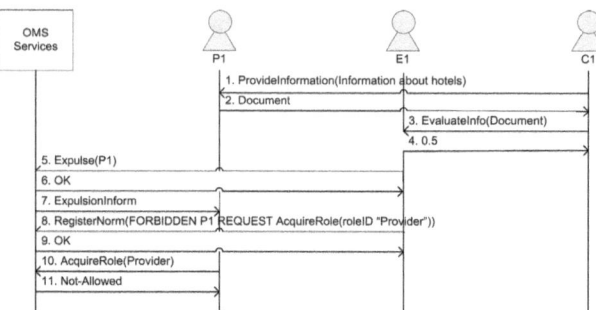

Fig. 2. Case Study Dynamics

6   Discussion

Organizations represent an effective mechanism for activity coordination, not only for humans but also for agents. They have recently been used in agent theory to model coordination in open systems and ensure social orders [18].

Virtual Organizations include the integration of organizational and individual perspectives, and the dynamic adaptation of models to organizational and environmental changes [1]. The necessity of managing the organizational life-cycle has been taken into account in several approaches such as the S-Moise+ middleware [19] (based on Moise+ [20] organizational model), the Brain system [21], the ORA4MAS proposal [22] and the Rade system [23]. In our architecture the OMS entity acts in a similar way; it offers dynamical services for allowing agents to take roles at runtime, accordingly to the established organizational norms. However, the main contributions of our proposal are: (i) all this functionality has been designed following a Service Oriented approach. The OMS services have been implemented as Web Services independently of the agent platform. Thus, the OMS gives support for the coordination among agents which belong to different platforms. In addition, the OMS services are registered and published by the architecture in order to allow agents to discover them and to know how to make use of them. (ii) The OMS also offers structural services for allowing the organizational structure (i.e the roles, units and norms) to be modified at runtime. As argued previously, the characteristics of open environments make mandatory supporting the organizational structure evolution and facilitating its growth and update through execution time.

Open systems need the existence of normative mechanisms that coordinate agent behaviours. Regarding works on norms, they traditionally have a theoretical point of view. Recently, norms have received a more practical conception in order to allow the regulation of open distributed systems. More specifically, traditional approaches based on deontic logic have evolved to a more operational conception of norms that allows their employment inside the design and execution of real MAS applications as a coordination mechanism. These approaches must allow reasoning about the global system performance as well as the agent individual reasoning. The *normative learning* term has been defined as the process by which agents take norms into consideration inside their decision making process [24]. Works concerning the normative reasoning are related to the norm emergence [25,26] and the norm acceptance [27,28]. Taking these later works as a starting point, the OMS component described in this paper is aware of the existence of norms that regulate access to its services. On the other hand, proposals for computational operationalization of norms are based on the e-institution metaphor [9,10]. They assume the existence of an "special" entity, which is the institution itself, that acts as a middle-ware for agent communications. Therefore, the institution has an unlimited knowledge about occurrence of facts as well as extra capabilities for controlling norms.

In order to allow the definition of MAS as Open Systems a new normative framework that gives support to agent normative reasoning is needed. With this aim, we have proposed a general normative language for expressing norms and a normative implementation that allows agents to take into consideration the existence of norms and their limitations as norm controllers. This proposal of normative language is a more general and expressive formalism mainly focused on controlling service registering and usage, making it possible a better integration of both MAS and Web Service Technologies. The main and new aspects of the proposed language are: (i) it allows the definition of norms that cover organizational dynamics; and (ii) norms define agent functionality in terms of services requested and provided by each role. Both the organizational performance and functionality of the system are established by means of norms.

7   Conclusions

This work belongs to a higher project whose goal is to develop models, frameworks, methods and algorithms for constructing large-scale open distributed computer systems. Our aim is to employ this architecture for building demonstrators on e-procurement, e-healthcare and water conflict resolution. Thus, the Organizational Management System implementation has been included in a prototype of the THOMAS architecture. This component is mainly responsible for the management of organizations and their entities. The OMS allows the creation and management of both norms and organizations. Therefore, our normative implementation has been employed for controlling access to the organizational services. In this sense, norms can be conceived as a method for regulating the dynamical organizational adaptation to the environmental changes.

References

1. Dignum, V., Dignum, F.: A landscape of agent systems for the real world. Tech. report 44-cs-2006-061, Inst. Information and Computing Sciences, Utrecht University (2006)
2. Boissier, O., Gâteau, B.: Normative multi-agent organizations: Modeling, support and control. In: Normative Multi-agent Systems, Dagstuhl Seminar (2007)

3. Luck, M., McBurney, P., Shehory, O., Willmott, S.: Agent Technology: Computing as Interaction (A Roadmap for Agent Based Computing). AgentLink (2005)
4. Luck, M., McBurney, P.: Computing as interaction: Agent and agreement technologies. In: IEEE SMC Conference on Distributed Human-Machine Systems, pp. 1–6 (2008)
5. Greenwood, D., Calisti, M.: Engineering web service - agent integration. In: IEEE Int. Conf. on Systems, Man and Cybernetics, vol. 2, pp. 1918–1925 (2004)
6. Carrascosa, C., Giret, A., Julian, V., Rebollo, M., Argente, E., Botti, V.: Service Oriented MAS: An open architecture. In: AAMAS, vol. 2, pp. 1291–1292 (2009)
7. Argente, E., Palanca, J., Aranda, G., Julian, V., Botti, V., García, A., Espinosa, A.: Supporting agent organizations. In: Burkhard, H.-D., Lindemann, G., Verbrugge, R., Varga, L.Z. (eds.) CEEMAS 2007. LNCS (LNAI), vol. 4696, pp. 236–245. Springer, Heidelberg (2007)
8. Boella, G., van der Torre, L., Verhagen, H.: Introduction to the special issue on normative multiagent systems. Journal of. Auton. Agents Multi-Agent Syst. 17, 1–10 (2008)
9. García-Camino, A., Noriega, P., Rodríguez-Aguilar, J.A.: Implementing norms in electronic institutions. In: EUMAS, pp. 482–483 (2005)
10. Torres, V.: Implementing norms that govern non-dialogical actions. In: Sichman, J.S., Padget, J., Ossowski, S., Noriega, P. (eds.) COIN 2007. LNCS (LNAI), vol. 4870, pp. 232–244. Springer, Heidelberg (2008)
11. Argente, E., Criado, N., Julian, V., Botti, V.: Designing Norms in Virtual Organizations. In: CCIA, vol. 184, pp. 16–23. IOS Press, Amsterdam (2008)
12. Criado, N., Julian, V., Argente, E.: Towards the Implementation of a Normative Reasoning Process. In: 7th International Conference on Practical Applications of Agents and Multi-Agent Systems (PAAMS 2009), pp. 319–328. Springer, Heidelberg (2009)
13. López, F., Luck, M.: Modelling norms for autonomous agents. In: ENC, pp. 238–245. IEEE Computer Society, Los Alamitos (2003)
14. Brafman, R.I., Tennenholtz, M.: On Partially Controlled Multi-Agent Systems. Journal of Artificial Intelligence Research 4, 477–507 (1996)
15. Kollingbaum, M.J., Vasconcelos, W.W., García-Camino, A., Norman, T.J.: Conflict resolution in norm-regulated environments via unification and constraints. In: Baldoni, M., Son, T.C., van Riemsdijk, M.B., Winikoff, M. (eds.) DALT 2007. LNCS (LNAI), vol. 4897, pp. 158–174. Springer, Heidelberg (2008)
16. Vasconcelos, W., Kollingbaum, M.J., Norman, T.J.: Resolving conflict and inconsistency in norm-regulated virtual organizations. In: AAMAS, pp. 632–639 (2007)
17. Boella, G., van der Torre, L.: Permissions and obligations in hierarchical normative systems. In: ICAIL (2003)
18. Dignum, V., Meyer, J., Weigand, H., Dignum, F.: An organization-oriented model for agent societies. In: RASTA: 31–50 (2002)
19. Hubner, J., Sichman, J., Boissier, O.: S-moise+: A middleware for developing organised multi-agent systems. In: EUMAS, pp. 64–78 (2006)
20. Hubner, J., Sichman, J., Boissier, O.: MOISE+: towards a structural, functional, and deontic model for MAS organization. In: AAMAS, pp. 501–502 (2002)
21. Cabri, G., Leonardi, L., Zambonelli, F.: BRAIN: A Framework for Flexible Role-Based Interactions in MAS. In: CoopIS/DOA/ODBASE, pp. 145–161 (2003)
22. Kitio, R., Boissier, O., Hbner, J.F., Ricci, A.: Organisational artifacts and agents for open multi-agent organisations: "Giving the power back to the agents". In: Sichman, J.S., Padget, J., Ossowski, S., Noriega, P. (eds.) COIN 2007. LNCS (LNAI), vol. 4870, pp. 171–186. Springer, Heidelberg (2008)

23. Xu, H., Zhang, X.: A Methodology for Role-Based Modeling of Open Multi-Agent Software Systems. In: ICEIS, pp. 246–253 (2005)
24. Verhagen, H.J.E.: Norm Autonomous Agents. PhD thesis, The Royal Institute of Technology and Stockholm University (2000)
25. Walker, A., Wooldridge, M.: Understanding the emergence of conventions in multi-agent systems. In: ICMAS, pp. 384–390 (June 1995)
26. Savarimuthu, B.T.R., Cranefield, S., Purvis, M., Purvis, M.: Role model based mechanism for norm emergence in artificial agent societies. In: Sichman, J.S., Padget, J., Ossowski, S., Noriega, P. (eds.) COIN 2007. LNCS (LNAI), vol. 4870, pp. 203–217. Springer, Heidelberg (2008)
27. Castelfranchi, C., Dignum, F., Jonker, C.M., Treur, J.: Deliberative normative agents: Principles and architecture. In: Jennings, N.R. (ed.) ATAL 1999. LNCS, vol. 1757, pp. 364–378. Springer, Heidelberg (2000)
28. Dignum, F., Morley, D., Sonenberg, L., Cavedon, L.: Towards socially sophisticated BDI agents. In: ICMAS, pp. 111–118. IEEE Computer Society, Los Alamitos (2000)

Implementing Collective Obligations in Human-Agent Teams Using KAoS Policies

Jurriaan van Diggelen[1], Jeffrey M. Bradshaw[2], Matthew Johnson[2],
Andrzej Uszok[2], and Paul J. Feltovich[2]

[1] TNO Defense, Security and Safety,
Soesterberg, The Netherlands
[2] Florida Institute for Human and Machine Cognition (IHMC),
40 S. Alcaniz, Pensacola, FL 32502, USA
`jurriaan.vandiggelen@tno.nl,`
`{jbradshaw,mjohnson,auszok,pfeltovich}@ihmc.us`

Abstract. Obligations can apply to individuals, either severally or collectively. When applied severally, each individual or member of a team is independently responsible to fulfill the obligation. When applied collectively, it is the group as a whole that becomes responsible, with individual members sharing the obligation. In this paper, we present several variations of common teamwork models involving the performance of collective obligations. Some of these rely heavily on a leader to ensure effective teamwork, whereas others leave much room for member autonomy. We strongly focus on the implementation of such models. We demonstrate how KAoS policies can be used to establish desired forms of cooperation through regulation of agent behavior. Some of these policies concern invariant aspects of teamwork, such as how to behave when a leader is present, how to ensure that actions are properly coordinated, and how to delegate actions. Other policies can be enabled or disabled to regulate the degree of autonomy of the team members. We have implemented a prototype of a Mars-mission scenario that demonstrates varying team behavior when applied across these different teamwork models.

Keywords: Human-agent teams, Policies, Collective Obligations.

1 Introduction

Autonomy is a core property of an agent. Generally speaking, we might say that the more control an agent has over its own actions and internal state, the greater its autonomy. By this definition, collaboration almost always entails a reduction in autonomy. In collaboration, we are willing to give up some degree of autonomy in the service of achieving joint objectives [18].

Our research interest has been to understand how this can be realized through the use of *policies* in KAoS [2]. A KAoS policy is defined as "an enforceable, well-specified constraint on the performance of a machine-executable action by a subject in a given situation". There are two main types of polices; authorizations and obligations. Authorization policies specify which actions are permitted (*positive*

J. Padget et al. (Eds.): COIN 2009, LNAI 6069, pp. 36–52, 2010.

authorizations) or forbidden (*negative authorizations*) in a given situation. Obligation policies specify which actions are required (*positive obligations*) or waived (*negative obligations*) in a given situation. KAoS uses OWL (Web Ontology Language: http://www.w3.org/2004/OWL) to represent policies. These policies can be used for regulation of a variety of systems including agent-based systems, web services, and grid services.

KAoS policies have already been successfully applied to some important aspects of joint activity in the context of human-robot teamwork [17] In this paper, we extend this research by adding the notion of a *collective obligation* [7]. The difference between an individual obligation (IO) and a collective obligation (CO) is that in IO's each individual or member of a team is independently responsible to fulfill the obligation. On the other hand, in CO's, it is the group as a whole that becomes responsible, with individual members sharing the obligation. CO's are especially useful in governing complex abstract behavior—in our case, for example, the obligation that agents have to ensure safety. The difficulty of writing individual obligations for *ensure-safety* is that it is probably not an action that can be directly executed by any one agent. Most likely, a plan must be created to decompose *ensure-safety* into more concrete actions. It is also difficult to decide, beforehand, who is the best candidate to carry out the plan, as a different plan might be adopted in different circumstances. Moreover, agents may have different capabilities, enabling them to contribute individually or jointly in particular roles. For such reasons, constraints requiring the performance of abstract team actions like *ensure-safety* are usually better implemented as collective, as opposed to individual, obligations.

Because a CO often does not direct activity at the level of the single agent's behavior, we must find a way to translate the CO to the individual level. Our research aim in this paper can thus be described: to develop general policies to fulfill collective obligations, and to map these obligations to individuals dynamically, based on the current context.

Inspired by previous theoretical groundwork on these issues [7][14], we follow a very practical approach. First, we demonstrate how to represent and reason about collective obligations in OWL. Second, we describe three sets of KAoS policies that we defined to govern agent behavior in the execution of collective obligations. Third, we provide a configuration policy set that is used to adjust specific aspects of the teamwork model for use in a given situation. Finally, we present a prototype we have implemented to demonstrate the use of these policies in the context of a Mars mission scenario [19].

We claim several benefits for developers of agent teams. The first concerns *reusability*. Because the policies describe near-universal teamwork aspects, they are domain independent and can apply to many kinds of applications, thus saving development time. The second benefit concerns *sharedness*. Because teamwork requires maintaining common ground among the participants [18], agents benefit when the code that generates team behavior can be shared by all agents. By introducing a shared collection of teamwork policies for the whole system, in conjunction with KAoS monitoring and enforcement capabilities, newly added agents fit easily into the team, no matter who developed them or which language they are programmed in. The policies accommodate even the most primitive agents by eliminating the requirement that each agent be capable of sophisticated deliberation in order to collaborate. Next, there is the benefit of *separation of concerns*. By using KAoS policies, the code that implements teamwork is cleanly segregated from the rest of the agent code. This avoids the typical clutter experienced when teamwork code is scattered in arbitrary locations among all agents. Finally, we believe that KAoS policies are very *straightforward to read* and understand, making them more suitable to implement this kind of behavior than more low-level programming languages.

In addition to the benefits for agent developers, we also believe that this approach is more conducive to scientific progress towards the much more ambitious goal of human and machine joint activity [23][10]. Although the policies described in this paper are relatively simple, they are fundamental in normal human teamwork. Hence, when agents adopt important aspects of human teamwork, people may find them more predictable and understandable.

The remainder of the paper is outlined as follows. Section 2 explains the basic teamwork model. Section 3 provides an overview of the KAoS policy services framework. In Sections 4, 5 and 6, we describe how we used KAoS to implement the teamwork model: ontological aspects in Section 4; policies in Section 5; an implemented prototype with agents in a Mars-mission scenario in Section 6. Related work is discussed in Section 7, followed by conclusions in Section 8.

2   Team Design

Teamwork is a topic of great complexity and breadth. Here, our focus is only on one aspect of teamwork, i.e., collective obligations. Collective obligations require teams to perform some action whenever some event or state triggers the obligation. Performing such actions typically involves planning, delegation and coordination. The aim of team design is to ensure that this process is adequately supported.

Not every team member is necessarily equally involved in each phase. For example, special responsibilities are often attributed to the *leader* of the team. What it means to be a leader may vary in different domains [17]. In this paper, we adopt a very light definition of leadership, i.e. being authorized to delegate actions, and being authorized to create plans. Whether the presence of a leader is a strict necessity in our approach is further discussed in Section 7.

Three primary aspects of team design are pertinent to the issues discussed in this paper: leadership assumption, task allocation, and plan coordination. Each of these aspects can vary, resulting in different team behavior. Figure 1 depicts these aspects in three dimensions, where each combination of aspects represents a different kind of team.

Along the x-axis, two possibilities for leadership assumption are shown. We can appoint someone as a leader beforehand (i.e. pre-established leadership), or we can defer the choice and allow leaders to volunteer on demand (i.e. *ad hoc* leadership assumption). Whereas "pre-established" and "*ad hoc*" qualify as two extremes on the leadership assumption dimension, there are, of course, intermediate options possible that we do not consider here. One example is that of a predefined line of succession which is used to determine leadership if all higher-ranking leaders are unavailable.

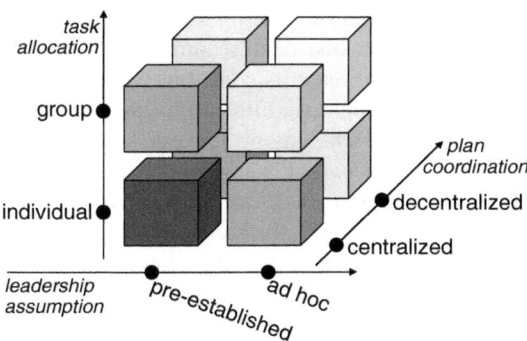

Fig. 1. Three dimensions in team design

The task allocation dimension is shown along the z-axis. Individual task allocation means that requests are directed at individual agents. In group task allocation, the request is directed to the group as a whole, without specifying which individual must perform the task.

Plan coordination is depicted on the y-axis, with the two alternatives being centralized and decentralized. Figure 2 depicts the communication pattern for these two ways of coordinating plans. The left side of the figure depicts centralized coordination, i.e. the requester (the grey agent) is responsible for making sure that the actions are executed in the right order. The right side of the figure shows decentralized coordination, i.e. the agents executing the plan take care of the coordination themselves. In the latter case, the requester delegates plan coordination. It may do so by sending a request for action *a,* together with information about who will perform the subsequent action *b.* In the figure, this is written as "creq a,b."

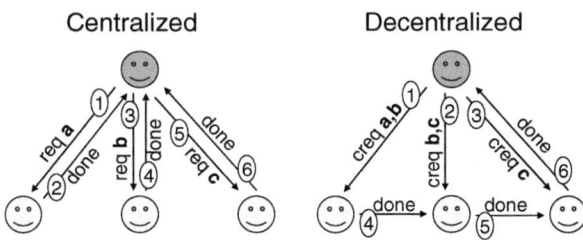

Fig. 2. Centralized and decentralized coordination patterns

With centralized coordination, the requested agents may not be aware that their actions are part of a larger plan. With decentralized coordination, the requested agents require more knowledge about the action's context, i.e. they must know which agent is responsible for performing the next action in the plan.

The three dimensions outlined above can be regarded as different aspects of the dichotomy between *central authority* and *member autonomy* [3]. Pre-established leadership means that one central authority remains in charge of the team, whereas *ad hoc* leadership allows for more member autonomy because each team member may become a leader under certain circumstances. Centralized plan coordination allocates the task of coordinating plans to one central authority, whereas decentralized plan coordination allows each agent to make its contribution to coordination, i.e. reflecting more member autonomy. Individual task allocation implies that one central authority decides who performs the tasks; whereas group task allocation yields more member autonomy as the team members decide this among themselves.

In Figure 1, the team with most central authority is represented as the black cube. For the other teams, we can say that the further away the cube is from the black cube, the more member autonomy exists in the team. The white cube represents the team with most member autonomy. Which of these eight team configurations is the best one depends on the circumstances and cannot be decided in general. Below, we outline some general considerations when choosing between central authority and member autonomy; the discussion is not intended to be exhaustive. An advantage of using a central authority might be that it allows the team designer to select the best agent for the most important tasks. In this way, the team can be better adapted to the different qualities of agents. Another advantage of a central authority approach might be accountability: that is, that it would be easier to identify the responsible agent when things go wrong.

A disadvantage of a central authority might be that it would be less robust in certain circumstances, e.g., when the leader becomes unavailable, the entire team becomes dysfunctional. Another disadvantage of central authority might arise when not every team member has the same access to the situation. For example, it may be better to have a crisis operation led by someone on site than by a predefined leader who is far away. As a last disadvantage, we mention the potentially increased response time of strongly hierarchical teams. For example, when an incident happens, this must communicated all the way up to a leader, after which the leader makes a decision and communicates it all the way down to those carrying out the work. A faster response may be obtained by allowing the observer of the incident to take immediate action.

Because the models are implemented on the KAoS infrastructure, we will first give some more background on the KAoS policy framework.

3 Implementing Team Behavior

KAoS provides the basic services for distributed computing, including message transport and directory services, as well as more advanced features like domain and policy services. The two main components of the KAoS Framework are the Directory Service and the Guard. Agents register with the Directory Service, which provides normal white and yellow page services as well as acting as the policy repository. The policies themselves are distributed to local guards deployed on each platform to allow for fast policy checking that is robust to network problems.

An important part of building systems in this way is deciding where to implement a given behavior. In general, there are three possible places; in the agent, in the policies, or in the ontology (cf. Figure 3). For example, in our implementation, system development in KAoS takes place at different locations, in different languages, using different tools. The agent or application is typically were most systems keep their knowledge, so we will address ontologies and policies in more detail and explain the advantages and disadvantages each brings.

	Language	**Development Tool**
Agents or other Applications	E.g., Java	E.g., Eclipse
Policies	KAoS Policies (OWL)	KPAT
Ontologies	OWL	E.g., Protégé, COE

Fig. 3. KAoS system development components

OWL ontologies provide the vocabulary used in specifying policies. They define all actions, action properties, and actor types and can be developed directly in OWL or using an ontology editor, such as Protégé (http://protege.stanford.edu/) or COE (Cmap Ontology Editor).

Policies are also represented in OWL. They can be created using the KAoS Policy Administration Tool (KPAT). KPAT hides the complexity of OWL from the human users and allows the user to create, modify and manage policies in a very natural hypertext interface. Policies can be ranked in terms of their *priorities*. In case two conflicting policies are applicable at the same moment, the policy with the highest priority takes precedence.

The policies are used to govern the actions of agents (or other applications) within the system being developed. We use Java and Eclipse (http://www.eclipse.org/) to implement the agents for our prototype, although any other combination of a programming language and IDE could be used. KAoS includes a number of features that can be exploited in the development of agent-based systems.

As an example of system development in KAoS, suppose that we have a set of robots and we want to obligate them to beep before they move, in order to alert any nearby people of the pending movement. First, we would specify the terms Robot, Beep and Move in an ontology. Then, we would create a policy using KPAT, which would look like the following:

```
1 Robot is obligated to start performing Beep
2         which has any attributes
3 before Robot starts performing Move
4         which has any attributes
```

Fig. 4. KAoS policy example

Once the policy has been created, it is sent by KPAT to the Directory Service for analysis and deconflication, before it is distributed for run-time enforcement. Since this policy applies only to robots, it is automatically distributed only to the *guards* responsible for governing robots. Local enforcement mechanisms on each platform intercept movements as appropriate and check with the guard resident on that platform for policy constraints. With the new policy in place, an obligation to beep would be applied prior to each movement.

Each approach has advantages and disadvantages in different situations. Without policy, we would be forced to represent everything in the agent itself, so, for our beep example, the beep action might simply be coded in Java within the move method. This is not very flexible and is hidden from those unfamiliar with the code. In situations where the source code is unavailable, it simply cannot be implemented at all. A second option is to implement the behavior by adapting the ontology, i.e. by defining a move as a beep that is followed by a physical move, and having the agents query the ontology for the definition of the action. This would amount to redefining the commonly accepted meaning of *move* into something else entirely – not a good idea either. The third option is to add the policy of Figure 4. This seems to us the cleanest method. The policy is defined external to the robot's program and thus is viewable and editable by anyone using the system. To give an example that pushes some knowledge back into the robots, suppose that we modify our policy to state "robots must warn before they move." The main idea is still modeled in policy, though less specific. The ontology could be used to model the knowledge that beeping and flashing lights are both appropriate methods to warn. Finally, the robot could chose the appropriate warning method based on its own capabilities and preferences.

In the following three sections we will explain how the teamwork model described in Section 3 can be implemented by developing ontologies, policies, and agents.

4 Ontology

Extending KAoS so it can handle collective obligations posed some additional requirements to the core ontology. The first issue concerns the representation of teams. The property `teamMemberOf` was used to assert that an agent (represented by an individual in class `agent`) is a member of some team (represented by an individual in class `team`). To represent the collective obligation of a team, the property `HasCollectiveObligation` was used to refer to the instance representation[1] of the action that constitutes the CO.

The second issue concerning collective obligation is the representation of plans. Because a plan typically consists of multiple actions (that may be partialed out to different team members), we can represent that an action contains subactions by using the properties `subAction1` and `subAction2`. The property `subActionRelation` specifies whether the two subactions are composed in parallel or sequence. In this way, composite actions can be represented as an AND-OR graph, or planning tree [22].

The last ontological issue concerns the relationship between the plan and the action the plan seeks to achieve. Because different circumstances require different plans and adjustments of players, roles, and tools, we specify this as a context-dependent relation, using a rule of the form "X *counts-as* Y in context C." These so-called *counts-as* rules can be used in an ontology to translate between actions of different levels of abstraction [13]. For example, the sequence of actions *bring-to-habitat* and *nurse* (the plan) counts as *ensure-safety* (what the plan is designed to achieve) in the context of *spacesuit-failure-of-Benny-at-11:00am* (the context). An action and its associated context are related by the property `hasContext`. To represent the fact that an action has been performed, the property `hasStatus` is set to `performed`. Because we represent *counts-as* rules as subclass relations (e.g. "X subClassOf Y" represents the fact

---

[1] Because OWL-DL does not allow the use of classes as property values, we created a prototypical instance for every action class (e.g. `ensureSafety`). This prototypical instance represents the same (e.g. `ensureSafetyPrototypicalInstance`). In this way, we can refer to actions both at the class level, and at the instance level.

```
1 Leader is obligated to start performing Action which has attributes:
2  all prototypicalInstance values equal the Trigger action's
3    triggerOfCollectiveObligation of the prototypicalInstance values
4  the performedBy value equals the Trigger action's performedBy values
5 after Leader finishes performing Action which has attributes:
6  any prototypicalInstance values are in the set of this action's
7    HasCollectiveObligationTrigger of the teamMemberOf of the
8    performedBy values
```

Fig. 5. KAoS hypertext statement representing the policy of Definition 1.1

that X counts as Y), the OWL reasoner automatically derives that if X hasStatus performed, then also Y hasStatus performed.

The issues discussed above are important when monitoring policy compliance regarding collective obligation. An agent complies with an obligation to do action X, if X has the status performed before the deadline set by the obligation. This definition has two important consequences. First, the agent to which the obligation applies is not required to perform the action itself, but may also delegate the action to another agent. Second, the agent can choose to perform a plan which counts as action X (in the current context), because performance of the plan entails performance of X. Both of these two issues play a fundamental role in our approach to teamwork and are therefore implemented at the ontology level.

5 Policies for Agent Teams

The general pattern of the teamwork described in this paper consists of three steps. First, the collective obligation is triggered. Second, a plan is created. Third, this plan is carried out. The policies described in this section serve to support this process by governing issues such as: how is the CO-trigger communicated to the agent creating the plan? Who creates the plan? Who carries out the plan? How is the plan coordinated to ensure the right order of actions?

5.1 Leader Policy Set

If there is a team leader, it has a special responsibility and must be treated by the other agents in a special way. The purpose of the Leader Policy Set is to lay down these responsibilities, managing both task allocation and plan coordination.

Definition 1. Leader Policy Set

1. *The leader of a team should adopt the collective obligations of its team as its own individual obligations*
2. *Team members should notify their leader when the collective obligation of their team is triggered*
3. *The leader of a team may request members of its team to perform actions*
4. *The leader of a team may create plans*

The first policy captures the intuition that leaders must take responsibility for their team. Definition 1.1 states more precisely what this means for collective obligations. The policy as implemented in KAoS is shown in Figure 5. The trigger of the policy is implemented at line 5,6,7 and 8 using a role-value map [1] which compares the values of two properties of the Action which the agent has just finished performing. It states that the property prototypicalInstance must have a value in common with the concatenation of the properties performedBy, teamMemberOf and HasCollectiveObligationTrigger. As an example of an action that would trigger the obligation, consider agent Herman performing the action observeSpaceSuitFailure (i.e. observeSpaceSuitFailure performedBy Herman) and that Herman is teamMemberOf MecaTeam and that MecaTeam HasCol-lectiveObligationTrigger observeSpaceSuitFailurePrototypicalInstance. The obligation is described in lines 1, 2, 3 and 4 of Figure 5. Lines 2-3 is a role-value map which describes that the actor must do the action which is given by the property triggerOfCollectiveObligation of the action that triggered the obligation. In our example, observeSpaceSuitFailure is triggerOfCollectiveObligation of ensureSafety. Hence, the actor is obliged to perform ensureSafety. Line 4 describes that the agent that must fulfill the obligation is the same agent that has triggered the obligation.

The second policy of Definition 1 ensures that, in case nobody else in the team triggers the collective obligation (for example by observing a spacesuit failure), this agent will notify the leader about the event. This captures the intuition that team members must help their leader. This policy is implemented in a similar fashion to policy 1.1 (Figure 5).

The third policy in the leader policy set states that leaders do not have to do the work all by themselves, but they are authorized to request actions from their team members.

The fourth policy states that the leader is authorized to create a plan. Plan creation is done by adding a *counts-as* rule to the ontology (see Section 4). The effect of this is that all agents may perform a different action than the action they were initially obliged to do. Therefore, the right to create new plans is not self-evident. It is, however, a right that belongs to a leader.

5.2 Coordination Policy Set

The coordination policy set describes how actions in a plan should be coordinated. We consider two coordination patterns (as depicted in Figure 2), which are both governed by this policy set.

Definition 2. Coordination Policy Set

1. *An agent should notify the requester after it has performed a requested action*
2. *If the agent knows who will perform the subsequent action, it should notify that agent after it finishes performing its own action*
3. *If the agent knows who will conduct the subsequent action, it is not required to notify the requester after it finishes performing its action*

The first policy ensures that, in case of centralized coordination, the requester knows when the subsequent action may begin. This is due to the "done" messages 2, 4 and 6 on the left side of Figure 2. In case of decentralized coordination, the requester is notified after the plan is finished, i.e. by "done" message 6 on the right side of the figure.

The second policy of Definition 2 concerns the case of decentralized coordination. When an agent has received a request for a coordinated action, it knows who will perform the subsequent action, and must notify that agent after it has finished its action.

The third policy is enforced with high priority, and can be regarded as an exception to the first policy of Definition 2. This policy prevents requested agents from notifying their requester when the plan is only partially completed. As can be seen on the right hand side of Figure 2, the two agents that are requested to perform action a and action b of the plan do not send a "done" message to their requester. The rationale behind this is that, in the decentralized case, partially-finished notifications are not needed for *plan coordination*, which is the purpose of this policy set. There may be other reasons why this may be desirable, e.g., to monitor plan progress to respond to unexpected events in a timely way [10]. This can always be implemented in an additional higher priority policy set, which is specially designed for that purpose. However, issues such as dealing with plan failure or replanning are beyond the scope of this paper.

5.3 Leader Absence Policy Set

What if the agents find themselves in a leaderless team? This may happen either because nobody has been appointed as a leader or else the leader is (temporarily) unavailable. In this case, the other agents in the team must take care of the collective obligation themselves. This issue is handled by ensuring that one agent assumes the leader role, and thereby becomes subject to the leadership policies of Definition 1.

Definition 3. Leader Absence Policy Set

1. *When no leader is present, the CO is triggered, and the agent knows it can fulfill the CO, it should assume the leader role*
2. *When no leader is present, the CO is triggered, but the agent cannot fulfill the CO, it should notify the whole team of the CO trigger*
3. *An agent should not notify its team about a CO trigger, when it has been notified itself by another team member about that CO trigger*

The first policy ensures that a capable leader will volunteer in case the collective obligation is triggered in a leaderless team. An agent may assume leadership by registering with the KAoS directory-service, which only accepts such a registration when there are no other leaders already currently available. In this way, we prevent multiple agents from taking leadership at the same time, on a first come, first served basis.

The second policy is a variation on the policy of Definition 1.2, adapted to the leaderless scenario. For example, when an agent observes a safety critical event (the CO is triggered), but the agent is not capable of ensuring safety, the agent should notify all of its team members about it, so someone else in the team can fulfill the CO.

The third policy is an exception to the second rule, and prevents agents from re-peatedly notifying one another about the same collective obligation trigger.

5.4 Configuration Policy Set

The policies discussed so far are the same for all eight different kinds of teams de-picted in Figure 1. In this section, we will discuss the configuration policy set which states which of the eight team strategies the agents must follow.

Definition 4. Configuration Policy Set

1. *Do not request distributed coordinated actions*
2. *Do not request actions to a team*

In contrast to the policy sets we discussed earlier, these policies are optional, and can be switched on and off depending on the way the team designer wishes to configure the team. If the first policy is switched on, the team will apply centralized plan coor-dination. If it is switched off, the team will apply decentralized plan coordination.

If the second policy is switched on, the team will apply individual task allocation. If it is switched off, the team applies group task allocation. Group task allocation can be implemented using collective obligations that are dealt with using the policies described in the previous sections. For example, to request action a to a group, the action a is added as a collective obligation to that group. The leader absence policy set (Definition 3) ensures that a leader which is capable of performing action a stands up, after which the leader policy set (Definition 1) ensures that this agent performs action a.

To implement pre-established leadership assumption, a leader must be appointed beforehand, using KPAT. To implement *ad hoc* leadership assumption, no leader should be defined beforehand, such that the policy in Definition 3.1 ensures that a leader will volunteer at runtime if needed.

6 Meca Scenario

We tested the policies using a Mars mission scenario developed in the Mission Execu-tion Crew Assistant (MECA) project [19]. This long-term project aims at enhancing the cognitive capacities of human-machine teams during planetary exploration mis-sions by means of an electronic partner. The e-partner helps the crew to assess a situa-tion and determine a suitable course of actions when problems arise. A large part of the project is devoted to developing a requirements baseline, taking into account hu-man factors knowledge, operational demands, and envisioned technology. Developing new prototypes using emerging technologies, such as this one, is a continuous activity in the project.

One of the major themes is dealing with the long communication delays between Earth and Mars. This has led researchers to consider new forms of mission control that are less centralized on Earth, allowing greater autonomy to the astronauts on Mars [12]. We believe that our work on policies and team strategies is a useful contri-bution to this problem.

One of the use-cases that has driven the development of MECA's requirements baseline concerns an astronaut suffering from hypothermia. The initial situation is depicted in Figure 6.

Herman is in the Habitat; Anne, Albert and two rovers are in team A; Benny and Brenda are in team B. Benny and Brenda are on a rock-collecting procedure. Suddenly, Benny's space suit fails. Brenda and the MECA system diagnose the problem together and predict hypothermia. Immediate action is required. A rover from team B comes to pick Benny up and brings him to the habitat. Someone with surgery skills and someone with nursing skills await him there and take care of Benny, after which he safely recovers.

One of the requirements of MECA is that safety of the crew must be ensured at all times. We implemented this requirement using a collective obligation of the MECA team to *EnsureSafety*. The trigger of this collective obligation is *ObserveSafetyCriticalEvent*. Within the scenario, both of these actions are added in a specific MECA-action ontology which extends the KAoS core action ontology. The ontology also specifies several subconcepts of *ObserveSafetyCriticalEvent*, such as *ObserveSpaceSuitFails*. This causes *ObserveSpaceSuitFails* to trigger the collective obligation.

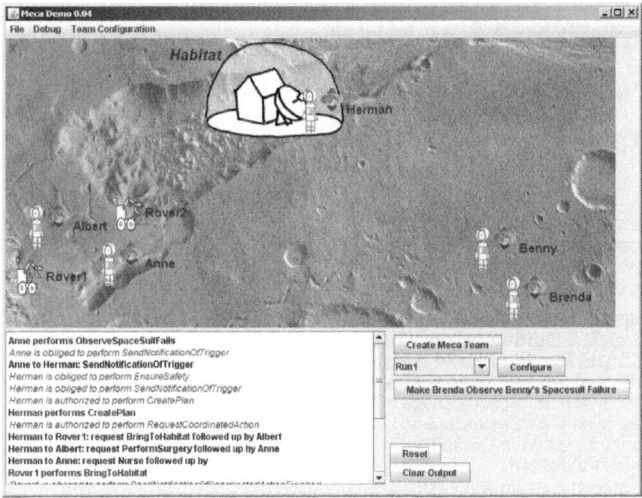

Fig. 6. MECA prototype

The seven agents in the example (five astronauts and two rovers) are implemented in Java. Because most of the agent behavior in this demonstration is implemented by the policies, the Java implementation could remain very simple. We used Java to implement how the actions, such as *BringToHabitat*, are performed. For the purposes of this demonstration, a simple screen animation was sufficient. We also implemented in Java how the agents remain policy-compliant. This means that they consult the KAoS guard to check which obligations and authorization policies apply. They fulfill an obligation by simply executing the code that implements the action concerned. It fulfills a negative authorization by refraining from executing the corresponding piece of code.

The most important aspect of this demonstration is the implementation of collective obligations after the action *ObserveSpaceSuitFails* is performed. This is driven exclusively by KAoS policies. By applying the different team configurations described in Section 2, we obtain different event traces which demonstrate the functioning of the team. The event trace for the most centrally organized team (represented by the black cube in Figure 1) is shown below.

Brenda performs ObserveSpaceSuitFails
Brenda is obliged to perform SendNotificationOfTrigger
Brenda to Herman: SendNotificationOfTrigger
Herman is obliged to perform EnsureSafety
Herman is authorized to perform CreatePlan
Herman performs CreatePlan
Herman is not authorized to perform RequestCoordinatedAction
Herman is authorized to perform RequestAction
Herman to Rover1: request BringToHabitat
Rover1 performs BringToHabitat
Rover1 is obliged to perform SendNotificationOfRequestedActionFinished
Rover1 to Herman: SendNotificationOfRequestedActionFinished
Herman to Albert: request PerformSurgery
Albert performs PerformSurgery
Albert is obliged to perform SendNotificationOfRequestedActionFinished
Albert to Herman: SendNotificationOfRequestedActionFinished
Herman to Anne: request Nurse
Anne performs Nurse
Anne is obliged to perform SendNotificationOfRequestedActionFinished
Anne to Herman: SendNotificationOfRequestedActionFinished

Fig. 7. Event trace of MECA team with maximal central authority

Brenda performs ObserveSpaceSuitFails
Brenda is obliged to perform SendNotificationOfTrigger
Brenda to Rover1: SendNotificationOfTrigger
Brenda to Anne: SendNotificationOfTrigger

Brenda to Albert: SendNotificationOfTrigger
Brenda to Rover2: SendNotificationOfTrigger
Brenda to Herman: SendNotificationOfTrigger
Brenda to Benny: SendNotificationOfTrigger
Anne is obliged to perform AssumeLeaderRole
Anne is obliged to perform EnsureSafety
Anne is authorized to perform CreatePlan
Anne performs CreatePlan
Anne is authorized to perform RequestCoordinatedAction
Anne is authorized to perform TeamRequestAction
Anne to MecaTeam: request BringToHabitat
Anne to MecaTeam: request PerformSurgery after BringToHabitat
Anne to MecaTeam: request Nurse after PerformSurgery
Rover1 is obliged to perform AssumeLeaderRole
Rover1 performs BringToHabitat
Rover1 is obliged to perform SendNotificationOfTrigger
Rover1 to MecaTeam: SendNotificationOfTrigger
Albert is obliged to perform AssumeLeaderRole
Albert performs PerformSurgery
Albert is obliged to perform SendNotificationOfTrigger
Albert to MecaTeam: SendNotificationOfTrigger
Herman is obliged to perform AssumeLeaderRole
Herman performs Nurse

Fig. 8. Event trace of MECA team with maximal member autonomy

The events printed in bold are actions; the underlined events are communication actions; the italicized events represent policies that were triggered. Typical to this event trace is that Brenda immediately knows that she must contact Herman after she observed the spacesuit failure. This is due to the pre-established leadership of Herman. Furthermore, Herman delegates the parts of the plan to individual agents (i.e. individual task allocation), and he waits until the requested agent is finished before he requests the next action in the plan (i.e. centralized plan coordination).

The event trace for the team with most member autonomy (represented by the white cube in Figure 1) is shown in Figure 8.

Typical to this event trace is that Brenda notifies the whole team about the CO trigger, after which Anne becomes a leader (i.e. *ad hoc* leadership assumption). Furthermore, Anne delegates her actions to the MECA team (i.e., group task allocation). Also, she delegates all actions at once and instructs the agents how to coordinate the actions (i.e., decentralized plan coordination). More information about applying computational policies in space mission design can be found in [6].

7 Related Work

In this paper, we have investigated how collective obligations can be projected on individuals using KAoS policies. More generally, the problem addressed can be regarded as a coordination problem. In this section, we will discuss similarities and differences with related approaches for multi-agent coordination.

Policies are constraints that are imposed and enforced prescriptively on agents. Related to policy systems, are *normative* systems, such as electronic institutions, and agent organizations, e.g. [8],[15]. Researchers who study *norms* generally focus on the ways in which agents learn, recognize, and adopt such obligations through their own deliberation, including the consideration of incentives and sanctions [5]. Several approaches exist in which norm-based electronic institutions have been applied to coordination problems, e.g. [9][11],[21]. Whereas these approaches also solve coordination problems by explicitly constraining the behavior of agents, their underlying motivation is to effectively model an organization. Our starting point in this paper has been the idea of a collective obligation, and what this means in terms of policies for individual agents.

Another approach to solving coordination problems is to use coordination artifacts [20], which are part of the platform, and provide coordination services for the agents using them. Because these artifacts are much simpler than agents, they can solve (simple) coordination problems in a more straightforward way. We have chosen to solve also the simple coordination problems with agents (or humans), which are guided by policies. A benefit of this approach could be that, in human-agent teams, coordination requests might be easier accepted when performed by humans than when performed by electronic artifacts.

Yet another approach to teamwork and collaboration is based on common goals. For example, the pioneering research of Cohen and Levesque [4] introduced the notion of a *joint persistent goal* as the ultimate driving force behind teamwork. In our framework, a collective obligation serves a similar purpose. A difference is that Cohen and Levesque based their approach on mentalistic notions, such as goals, beliefs and intentions, whereas our approach is based on institutional notions, such as obligations and authorizations. This allows the approach to be used by both simple and sophisticated agents, of heterogeneous varieties. Another approach to teamwork, based on mentalistic notions is STEAM [24]. STEAM is based on Soar, a general cognitive architecture for intelligent systems, whereas our approach is based on KAoS, which is a policy framework. A correspondence between our implementation and STEAM is that both approaches heavily rely on plans in the teamwork process. A crucial requirement for effective teamwork is maintaining a sufficient level of common ground [18]. By adopting the KAoS framework, some important aspects of common ground were naturally ensured. The common ontology, which is maintained by the directory service and distributed to the guards, ensures that every agent shares understanding of the domain terms. Also the collective obligations of the team, which are represented in the ontology, are mutually known.

8 Conclusion

In this paper, we have proposed a policy-based approach for addressing collective obligations in human-agent teams. We have implemented a variety of common teamwork models using KAoS policies. These models have demonstrated their value in a simulation of a Mars-mission scenario, where a delicate decision must be made between central authority and member autonomy.

We believe that our approach to teamwork has considerable benefits in terms of reusability, clarity, and generality. Although the types of teamwork we support are still relatively simple, we believe that more complex teamwork can be implemented by utilizing additional policies on top of the policies we have proposed here.

In the future, we plan to extend the teamwork model to deal with unexpected events. This requires a leader to monitor his or her plan, and to perform re-planning if the plan does not go as expected. In another envisioned augmentation, the team members can be of help by notifying their leaders when their requested actions fail or are encountering trouble (cf. [10]). Such policies can be implemented in KAoS, in a similar fashion as we have described in this paper.

Another topic of future research is to investigate teams which are less dependent on a leader. Whereas we have solved the problem of leaderless teams by obliging one agent to become an ad-hoc leader, it is perhaps possible to fulfill a collective obligation without a leader at any stage of the process. In this way, a more peer to peer organization is obtained, where agents collectively reach agreement about the plan to be followed. As this organization form is much more complex, it can be regarded as an extension of the work we presented in this paper.

References

[1] Baader, F., Calvanese, D., McGuinness, D.L., Nardi, D., Patel-Schneider, P.F. (eds.): The Description Logic Handbook: Theory, Implementation, and Applications. Cambridge University Press, Cambridge (2003)

[2] Bradshaw, J.M., et al.: Representation and reasoning for DAML-based policy and domain services in KAoS and Nomads. In: Proceedings of the Autonomous Agents and Multi-Agent Systems Conference (AAMAS). ACM, New York (2003)

[3] Burton, R.M., DeSanctis, G., Obel, B.: Organizational Design. Cambridge University Press, Cambridge (2006)

[4] Cohen, P.R., Levesque, H.J.: Teamwork. SRI International, Menlo Park (1991)

[5] Davidsson, P.: Emergent Societies of Information Agents. In: Klusch, M., Kerschberg, L. (eds.) CIA 2000. LNCS (LNAI), vol. 1860, pp. 143–153. Springer, Heidelberg (2000)

[6] van Diggelen, J., Bradshaw, J.M., Grant, T., Johnson, M., Neerincx, M.: Policy-Based Design of Human-Machine Collaboration in Manned Space Missions. In: Proceedings of the Third IEEE International Conference on Space Mission Challenges for Information Technology, SMC-IT09 (2009)

[7] Dignum, F., Royakkers, L.: Collective Obligation and Commitment. In: Proceedings of 5th Int. conference on Law in the Information Society, Florence (1998)

[8] Dignum, V.: A Model for Organizational Interaction. SIKS Dissertation Series (2003)

[9] Esteva, M., Rodriguez-Aguilar, J., Rosell, B., Arcos, J.: Ameli: An agent-based middleware for electronic institutions. In: Proceedings of the 3rd International Joint Conference on Autonomous Agents and Multi-Agent Systems (AAMAS), pp. 236–243 (2004)

[10] Feltovich, P.J., Bradshaw, J.M., Clancey, W.J., Johnson, M., Bunch, L.: Progress appraisal as a challenging element of coordination in human and machine joint activity. In: Artikis, A., O'Hare, G.M.P., Stathis, K., Vouros, G.A. (eds.) ESAW 2007. LNCS (LNAI), vol. 4995, pp. 124–141. Springer, Heidelberg (2008)

[11] Gómez, M., Plaza, E.: Dynamic Composition of Electronic Institutions for Teamwork. In: Sichman, J.S., Padget, J., Ossowski, S., Noriega, P. (eds.) COIN 2007. LNCS (LNAI), vol. 4870, pp. 155–170. Springer, Heidelberg (2008)

[12] Grant, T., Soler, A.O., Bos, A., Brauer, U., Neerincx, M., Wolff, M.: Space Autonomy as Migration of Functionality: The Mars Case. In: Proceedings of the 2nd IEEE international Conference on Space Mission Challenges For information Technology(SMC-IT), pp. 195–201. IEEE, Los Alamitos (2006)

[13] Grossi, D.: Designing Invisible Handcuffs. Formal Investigations in Institutions and Organizations for Multi-agent Systems. SIKS Dissertation Series 2007-16, Utrecht University (2007)

[14] Grossi, D., Dignum, F., Royakkers, L., Meyer, J.-J.C.: Collective Obligations and Agents: Who Gets the Blame? In: Lomuscio, A., Nute, D. (eds.) DEON 2004. LNCS (LNAI), vol. 3065, pp. 129–145. Springer, Heidelberg (2004)

[15] Hübner, J.F., Sichman, J.S., Boissier, O.: A Model for the Structural, Functional, and Deontic Specification of Organizations in Multiagent Systems. In: Bittencourt, G., Ramalho, G.L. (eds.) SBIA 2002. LNCS (LNAI), vol. 2507, pp. 118–128. Springer, Heidelberg (2002)

[16] Hubner, J.F., Sichman, J.S., Boissier, O.: Developing organised multiagent systems using the MOISE+ model: programming issues at the system and agent levels. Int. J. Agent-Oriented Softw. Eng. 1(3/4), 370–395 (2007)

[17] Johnson, M., Feltovich, P.J., Bradshaw, J.M., Bunch, L.: Demonstrating Human-Robot Coordination through Dynamic Regulation, policy. In: IEEE Workshop on Policies for Distributed Systems and Networks, pp. 231–232 (2008)

[18] Klein, G., Woods, D., Bradshaw, J.M., Hoffman, R.R., Feltovich, P.J.: Ten Challenges for Making Automation a Team Player. IEEE Intelligent Systems in Joint Human-Agent Activity 19(6) (2004)

[19] Neerincx, M.A., Bos, A., Olmedo-Soler, A., Brauer, U., Breebaart, L., Smets, N., Lindenberg, J., Grant, T., Wolff, M.: The Mission Execution Crew Assistant: Improving Human-Machine Team Resilience for Long Duration Missions. In: Proc. of the 59th International Astronautical Congress, IAC 2008 (2008)

[20] Omicini, A., Ricci, A., Viroli, M., Castelfranchi, C., Tummolini, L.: Coordination Artifacts: Environment-Based Coordination for Intelligent Agents. In: Proceedings of the Third international Joint Conference on Autonomous Agents and Multiagent Systems (2004)

[21] Rubino, R., Omicini, A., Denti, E.: Computational institutions for modelling Norm-regulated MAS: an approach based on coordination artifacts. In: Boissier, O., Padget, J., Dignum, V., Lindemann, G., Matson, E., Ossowski, S., Sichman, J.S., Vázquez-Salceda, J. (eds.) ANIREM 2005 and OOOP 2005. LNCS (LNAI), vol. 3913, pp. 127–141. Springer, Heidelberg (2006)

[22] Steffik, M.: Introduction to Knowledge Systems. Morgan Kaufmann, San Francisco (1995)

[23] Sycara, K., Lewis, M.: Integrating intelligent agents into human teams. In: Team Cognition: Understanding the Factors that Drive Process and Performance, pp. 203–232. American Psychological Association, Washington (2004)

[24] Tambe, M.: Towards Flexible Teamwork. Journal of Artificial Intelligence Research, 83–124 (1997)

Building Multi-Agent Systems for Workflow Enactment and Exception Handling*

Joey Lam, Frank Guerin, Wamberto Vasconcelos, and Timothy J. Norman

Department of Computing Science
University of Aberdeen, Aberdeen, U.K. AB24 3UE
{j.lam,f.guerin,w.w.vasconcelos,t.j.norman}@abdn.ac.uk

Abstract. Workflows represent the coordination requirements of various distributed operations in an organisation. Typical workflow management systems are centralised and rigid; they cannot cope with the unexpected flexibly. Multi-agent systems offer the possibility of enacting workflows in a distributed manner, via software agents which are intelligent and autonomous, and respect the constraints in a norm-governed organisation. Agents should bring flexibility and robustness to the workflow enactment process. In this paper, we describe a method for building a norm-governed multi-agent system which can enact a set of workflows and cope with exceptions. We do this by providing agents with knowledge of the organisation, the domain, and the tasks and capabilities of agents. This knowledge is represented with SemanticWeb languages, and agents can reason with it to handle exceptions autonomously.

1 Introduction

Workflows represent the coordination requirements of various distributed operations in an organisation, and can automate business processes, for example. Workflows can be formalised and expressed in a machine readable format, and this makes it possible for them to be employed in service-oriented computing scenarios. In such scenarios we may be dealing with open heterogeneous computing systems, where errors and exceptions are likely to occur. We would like the computing systems to cope with these exceptions. Ideally we would like to be able to deal with the unexpected; while we could write specific exception handling routines to deal with some common exceptions which we expect to arise, it will be difficult to anticipate all possible exceptions. We can use Artificial Intelligence techniques to deal with a set of possible exceptions, where the response to each situation is not hand-coded at design-time, but rather worked out at run-time by reasoning with hand-coded knowledge. Typical workflow management systems (e.g., [12,13]) are centralised and rigid; they have not been designed for dynamic environments requiring adaptive responses. To overcome this we argue that it is necessary to use agents to control the enactment of a workflow in a distributed manner; agents can be endowed with sufficient intelligence to allow them to

---

* This work is funded by the European Community (FP7 project ALIVE IST-215890).

J. Padget et al. (Eds.): COIN 2009, LNAI 6069, pp. 53–69, 2010.

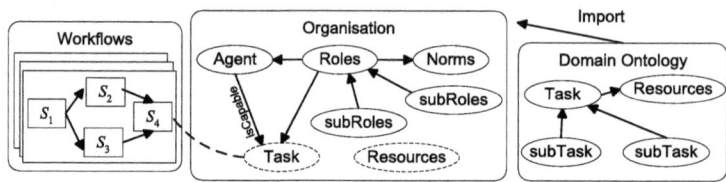

Fig. 1. Overview of the Proposed Approach

manage exceptions autonomously. This should bring flexibility and robustness to the process of enacting workflows.

We are interested in building multi-agent systems (MASs) which simulate the operations in large organisations, and so must adhere to constraints defined by the organisation[1]. We propose a method for building such agent systems, given the appropriate knowledge as an input. The knowledge input to the system is divided into three main components, as illustrated in Figure 1. Firstly there is the *organisational knowledge*, consisting of such things as roles, norms, role classification, and resources available. Secondly there are the *workflows*, describing the tasks to be executed, and appropriate flow of control, and also including variable definitions which are used to control flow. Thirdly there is the *domain ontology*, describing concepts of the world including tasks and resources. Some tasks are atomic and can be directly executed by agents, but some tasks require a workflow to be executed. In this case the name of the task matches the name of a workflow. As indicated by the dashed line there are links between the workflow tasks and the organisation and imported domain ontology. Tasks and resources are not described in the organisation directly; the domain ontology is imported to the organisation ontology. This knowledge allows us to firstly allocate tasks in an agent system where workflow tasks are distributed among the agents in a way which is consistent with the organisational constraints. Secondly, it allows the agents to enact the workflows, updating the organisation as appropriate. Thirdly it allows agents to cope with exceptions as they arise, because the agents can query the ontology to find alternative agents or tasks when problems arise.

In our system the workflow specifications and the ontologies are available to be queried by any of the agents in the system, and the ontologies can also be updated as events add or modify instances in the ontology. This requires a centralised service which maintains the knowledge, and updates it, when instructed to by an agent. This centralised approach is somewhat undesirable in a distributed agent system (lack of robustness, and scalability), however additional robustness could be introduced by having multiple copies of the knowledge, and some synchronisation processes to ensure that all copies are identical. Both of these possibilities entail challenges which go beyond the scope of the current paper; we will merely assume the knowledge is available.

---

[1] Our focus for the moment is simulation, but eventually we envisage that our agents will support real human users in executing tasks as part of human-agent teams.

This paper is structured as follows. In Section 2 we briefly introduce Semantic Web languages. In Section 3 we describe norm-governed organisations represented in Semantic Web languages. We describe the representation of workflows and explain allocation of tasks in Sections 4 and 5 respectively. The details of agents enacting workflows and dealing with exceptions are given in Sections 6 and 7 respectively. Section 8 looks at related work and Section 9 concludes and proposes future work.

2   Semantic Web Languages

The OWL-DL [6] ontology language is a variant of the $\mathcal{SHOIN}(\mathbf{D})$ Description Logic [7], which provides constructs for full negation, disjunction, a restricted form of existential quantification, cardinality restrictions, and reasoning with concrete datatypes. We make use of the open world assumption, which requires that something is false if and only if it can be proved to contradict other information in the ontology. Since we assume a MAS as an open system, its knowledge of the world is incomplete, and the knowledge is extendable. If a formula cannot be proved true or false, we draw no conclusion[2].

Formally, an ontology $\mathcal{O}$ consists of a set of *terminology* axioms $\mathcal{T}$ (TBox), *role* axioms (RBox) and assertional axioms $\mathcal{A}$ (ABox), that is, $\mathcal{O} = \langle \mathcal{T}, \mathcal{R}, \mathcal{A} \rangle$. An axiom in $\mathcal{T}$ is either of the form $C \sqsubseteq D$ or $C \doteq D$, where C and D are arbitrary concepts (aka. classes in OWL); the RBox contains assertions about roles (such as functional, transitive roles) and role hierarchies; an axiom in $\mathcal{A}$ is either of the form $C(a)$ (where C is a concept and a is an individual name; a belongs to C), or of the form $R(a,b)$ (where a,b are individual names (aka. instances in OWL) and R is a role name (aka. a datatype or object property in OWL); b is a filler of the property R for a). The meaning of concepts, roles and individuals is given by an interpretation. An *interpretation* $\mathcal{I} = (\Delta^{\mathcal{I}}, \cdot^{\mathcal{I}})$ consists of a non-empty set of individuals (the *domain* of the interpretation) and an *interpretation function* $(\cdot^{\mathcal{I}})$, which maps each atomic concept $\mathsf{CN} \in \mathbf{C}$ ($\mathbf{C}$ is a set of concept names) to a set $\mathsf{CN}^{\mathcal{I}} \subseteq \Delta^{\mathcal{I}}$ and each atomic role $R \in \mathbf{R}$ ($\mathbf{R}$ is a set of role names) to a binary relation $R^{\mathcal{I}} \subseteq \Delta^{\mathcal{I}} \times \Delta^{\mathcal{I}}$. The interpretation function can be extended to give semantics to concept descriptions. An interpretation $\mathcal{I}$ is said to be a model of a concept C, or $\mathcal{I}$ models C, if the interpretation of C in $\mathcal{I}$ is not empty. A concept A is *unsatisfiable* w.r.t. a terminology $\mathcal{T}$ if, and only if, $A^{\mathcal{I}} = \emptyset$ for all models of $\mathcal{I}$ of $\mathcal{T}$. An ontology $\mathcal{O}$ is *inconsistent* if it has no models. Note that from this point onwards we will refer to OWL-DL roles as properties, to avoid confusion with agents' roles in an organisation.

OWL DL benefits from many years of DL research, leading to well defined semantics, well-studied reasoning algorithms, highly optimised systems, and well understood formal properties (such as complexity and decidability) [3].

---

[2] We can reason in an inconsistent ontology by tolerating a limited number of contradictions. A formula is *undefined* (or *undetermined*) if it entails neither true nor false; a formula is *overdefined* (or *over-determined*) if it entails both true and false.

The Semantic Web Rule Language (SWRL)[3] extends the set of OWL axioms to include Horn-Clause-like rules that can be expressed in terms of OWL classes and that can reason about OWL instances. SWRL provides deductive reasoning capabilities that can infer new knowledge from an existing OWL knowledge base. However, OWL DL extended with SWRL is no longer decidable. To make the extension decidable, Motik et al. [15] propose DL-safe rules where the applicability of a rule is restricted to individuals explicitly named in a knowledge base.

For example:

parent(x,y) $\wedge$ brother(y,z) $\wedge \mathcal{O}(x) \wedge \mathcal{O}(y) \wedge \mathcal{O}(z) \rightarrow$ uncle(x,z)

where $\mathcal{O}(x)$ must hold for each explicitly named individual x in the ontology. Hence, DL-safe rules are SWRL rules that are restricted to known individuals.

The language SPARQL-DL [18] supports mixed TBox/RBox/ABox queries for OWL-DL ontologies. Throughout the paper we will use qnames to shorten URIs with rdf, rdfs, and owl prefixes to refer to standard RDF (Resource Description Framework), RDF-S (RDF Schema) and OWL namespaces, respectively. We also use the prefix dom and org to refer to the namespace of the Domain and Organisation ontologies. Our agents will be able to query the ontology to access the knowledge. For example, agents can search for all roles working in the finance department which are obliged to perform task "WriteReport" by using this query[4]:

Type(_:x, ?role), PropertyValue(_:x, org:worksIn, _:y), Type(_:y, org:FinanceDept), PropertyValue(_:x, org:isObliged, _:z), Type(_:z, dom:WriteReport)

3   Norm-Governed Organisations

In this section, we describe how to represent roles, role classification, and norms using OWL and SWRL. Our specification in this section is adequate to allow agents to query an organisation at a certain point in time and ask questions such as "is agent x prohibited from doing task t", or "is agent y empowered to do task b". However, we do not provide a specification for how the organisation is changed as a result of agents performing speech acts, or as a result of other events. We assume that the system provides other specifications for this purpose, and we focus only on the specifications necessary for workflow enactments.

We represent the agent organisation using Semantic Web languages. The agent literature has many examples of different approaches to the specification of norm-governed organisations, using languages such as the event calculus or C+, for example [2]. Semantic Web languages are not as expressive as these, but they have the advantage of having very efficient DL reasoners, and being standardised. To specify the organisational knowledge relevant to our workflows we can get by without the expressiveness of more sophisticated languages; for example we only need to do static queries on current knowledge, and we do not require the

---

[3] http://www.w3.org/Submission/SWRL/
[4] Type(?a,?C) gives the most specific classes an instance belongs to.

ability to reason over different time intervals. We do allow modalities to change over time, but we only represent the new (changed) ontology; agents can only query the current version, not any prior states.

3.1   Roles and Their Constraints

The ontology we propose in this paper models the concepts of a role, its role classification(s), restrictions on roles (such as mutually exclusive roles, cardinality, prerequisite roles) [16], and other aspects of the organisation. Roles are modelled in a classification to reflect the subsumption of role descriptions. Sub-roles inherit the properties from the super-roles; the properties of a sub-role override those of its super-roles if the sub-role has more restrictive properties (the sub-role cannot be less restrictive or the ontology would be inconsistent). Cardinality restrictions can be used for example to restrict the number of agents a task can be assigned to. Disjointness axioms can represent separation of duty restrictions.

We now give an example specification to illustrate these ideas. In Figure 2, a role classification is shown. Sub-roles inherit the properties from super-roles. For example, Staff are obliged to work from 9am to 5pm during weekdays; its sub-roles inherit this obligation. The properties of a sub-role override those of its super-role. Manager is permitted to employ staff; its sub-roles inherits this property. However, this property of the AccountingManager is more restrictive; it is only permitted to employ AccountingStaff (see axioms 4 and 5 below). For the cardinality restrictions, we can model that only one agent can fill the role of the general manager (see axioms 11 and 12 below); a member of staff works in exactly one department (see axiom 6 below). An example of mutually exclusive roles is that a department manager cannot be a general manager simultaneously (see axiom 8 below). An example of separation of duty is that a staff submitting a project proposal is prohibited from approving the proposal (see axiom 9 below). Prerequisite roles means that a person can be assigned to role $r1$ only if the person already is assigned to role $r2$ (see axiom 10).

(1) Programmer ⊔ Manager ⊔ Secretary ⊑ Staff

(2) DeptManager ⊔ GeneralManager ⊑ Manager

(3) AccountingManager ⊔ ITManager ⊑ DeptManager

(4) Manager ⊑ ∃ isPermitted.(∃ employs.Staff) ⊓ ∀ isPermitted.(∃ employs.Staff)

(5) AccountingManager ⊑ ∃ isPermitted.(∃employs.AccountingStaff)⊓ ∀isPermitted.(∃employs.AccountingStaff)

(6) Staff ⊑ =1 worksIn

(7) range(worksIn) = Department

(8) DeptManager ⊑ ¬ GeneralManager

(9) Staff(x) ∧ ProjectProposal(p) ∧ ApproveProjectProposal(act) ∧ submits(x,p) ∧ approves(act,p) ∧$\mathcal{O}$(x) ∧$\mathcal{O}$(p) ∧$\mathcal{O}$(act) → isProhibited(x,act)

(10) AccountingManager ⊑ ∃ prerequisites.Accountant

(11) GeneralManager ⊑ =1 takenBy

(12) range(takenBy) = Agent

(13) canDelegate ⊑ hasPower

(14) Staff ⊑ ∃ isObliged.(∃ works.(Weekdays ⊓ OfficeHour)) ⊓ ∀ isObliged.(∃ works.(Weekdays ⊓ OfficeHour))

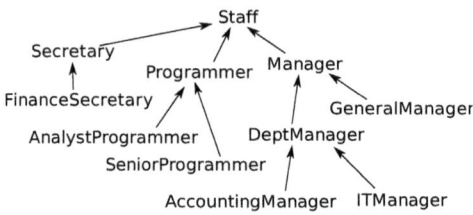

Fig. 2. Roles and a Role Classification

3.2 Normative Notions

We firstly describe norms concerning agents performing some task Task. We model permission[5], obligation, prohibition and power as isPermitted, isObliged, isProhibited and hasPower OWL object properties to relate roles in the organisation and tasks. Their domain and range is Role and Task respectively. Permissions allow the agent to achieve a state of affairs or perform an action (see for example axioms 4 and 5 above). Permission and prohibition are distinct from power because a member may be empowered to do something even though he is prohibited from doing it. Prohibitions forbid the agent from achieving a state of affairs or performing an action (see for example axiom 9 above). An obligation indicates that some act has to be done (see for example axiom 14 above). It is common to specify a time-limit or a condition for obligations. The axiom 14 above states a conditional obligation, such that staff have to work during office hours and weekday. Due to limited space, we will not describe time-limit constraints in the paper. We now model the relations between the basic notions; the relations can be equivalence, compatibility or incompatibility (or conflict) [20]. The following rules list some of these relations.

(1) If an act is permitted and prohibited then there is a conflict.

$\quad$ isPermitted(x,act) $\wedge$ isProhibited(x,act) $\wedge \mathcal{O}(x) \wedge \mathcal{O}(act) \rightarrow$ owl:Nothing(x)

(2) If an act is obligatory, then it is permitted.

$\quad$ isObliged(x,act) $\wedge \mathcal{O}(x) \wedge \mathcal{O}(act) \rightarrow$ isPermitted(x,act)

(3) If an act is obligatory and prohibited then there is a conflict.

$\quad$ isObliged(x,act) $\wedge$ isProhibited(x,act) $\wedge \mathcal{O}(x) \wedge \mathcal{O}(act) \rightarrow$ owl:Nothing(x)

(4) If a prohibited act is performed then there is a violation.

$\quad$ performed(x,act) $\wedge$ isProhibited(x,act) $\wedge \mathcal{O}(x) \wedge \mathcal{O}(act) \rightarrow$ violated(x,act)

Compared to standard deontic logic, here these deontic notions are being given quite a different interpretation by the Semantic Web languages. For example in deontic logic we could say that "obliged" is equivalent to "not permitted not to", however in Semantic Web languages we cannot express this. SWRL does not allow us to negate the atoms within the scope of isPermitted(...). Nevertheless,

---

[5] Explicitly defined permission means *strong* permission in our system. Undefined permission axioms represent *weak permission*.

the Semantic Web version of these norms seems to be adequate for representing simple agent scenarios, as illustrated in our examples below. One thorny issue is contraposition; a DL axiom such as $A \sqsubseteq B$ entails $\neg B \sqsubseteq \neg A$. This entailment is not desirable in exceptional situations where there is a special condition such that some type of A is not a B. The only way we can deal with this is to explicitly state all exceptions in the axioms, for example Bird $\sqcap \neg$ Penguin $\sqcap \neg$ Ostrich $\sqsubseteq$ CanFly.

In this paper we distinguish between institutional tasks (such as authorising a purchase), and physical tasks (such as printing a document). An institutional task can only be performed by an agent which has power to do that task. For example we say that action 'manager x employs staff y' is valid if x is empowered to employ a staff at that time, therefore y is now a member of staff. Otherwise, it is an invalid action due to its lacking of institutional power. The following axioms mean that a manager has the power to employ staff; when the manager performs EmployStaff, the person will become a staff:

EmployStaff $\doteq$ $\exists$ employ.Staff $\sqcap$ $\forall$ employ.Staff

Manager $\sqsubseteq$ $\exists$ hasPower.EmployStaff

Manager(m) $\land$ Person(p) $\land$ EmployStaff(act) $\land$ hasPower(m,act) $\land$ employ(act,p) $\land$ performed(m,act) $\land \mathcal{O}$(m) $\land \mathcal{O}$(p) $\land \mathcal{O}$(act) $\rightarrow$ Staff(p)

4 Workflows

We now introduce a representation for workflows. A common way to represent a workflow is using Petri Nets [19] or BPEL (Business Process Execution Language) [1]. In this paper we represent a workflow as a digraph, which is a simplified and minimalistic way to capture the basic concepts of workflows.

Definition 1. *A workflow is a tuple $\langle N, \mathbf{S}, \mathbf{E}, s_0, \mathbf{S}_f \rangle$, where*

1. *N is the name of the workflow,*
2. *$\mathbf{S}$ is a finite set of states of the form $\langle id, T \rangle$, where id is the number identifying this state, and T is the task;*
3. *$\mathbf{E}$ is a set of edges linking states. Edges take the form $\langle id_1, l, v, id_2 \rangle$, where id_1 is the state this edge leaves from, id_2 is the state this edge arrives at, v is the variable associated with the edge, and l is a label indicating the type of edge. There are four types of edge, $l \in \{AND, OR, JOIN\text{-}AND, JOIN\text{-}OR\}$ where AND-edges and OR-edges describe exclusive-or branches, and JOIN-AND-edges and JOIN-OR-edges describe joins. For any pair of states with multiple edges linking them, the edges must be of the same type;*
4. *s_0 is the initial state of the workflow, and $\mathbf{S}_f \subseteq \mathbf{S}$ is the set of final states.*

We consider a travel request workflow example in a company. Figure 3 graphically depicts the example. Figure 4 shows the representation of the workflow. The figure annotates edges with the name of the variable associated with the edge. We refer to *input* and *output* variables of the workflow; for example the state $\langle 2, \text{checkRequestForm} \rangle$ has input variable "TravelRequestForm" and output

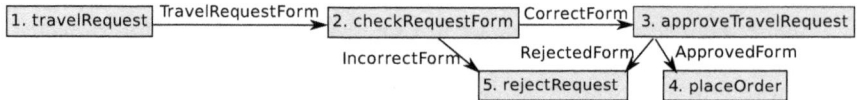

Fig. 3. Travel Request Workflow Example

$W = \langle \text{travelRequest\_WF}, \mathbf{S}, \mathbf{E}, 1, \{4, 5\}\rangle$
$\mathbf{S} = \{\langle 1,\text{travelRequest}\rangle, \langle 2,\text{checkRequestForm}\rangle, \langle 3,\text{approveTravelRequest}\rangle, \langle 4,\text{placeOrder}\rangle, \langle 5,\text{rejectRequest}\rangle\}$
$\mathbf{E} = \{\langle 1,\text{AND},\text{TravelRequestForm}, 2\rangle, \langle 2,\text{OR},\text{CorrectTravelRequesForm}, 3\rangle,$
$\quad \langle 2,\text{OR},\text{IncorrectTravelRequesForm}, 5\rangle \langle 3,\text{OR},\text{ApprovedForm}, 4\rangle, \langle 3,\text{OR},\text{RejectedForm}, 5\rangle\}$

Fig. 4. Travel Request Workflow as a Digraph

variable "CorrectTravelRequestForm". In this example, we assume the workflow
is triggered by an agent who issues a travel request. Firstly a travel request
form is issued; the request form should be checked to have correct information.
The checked form is then passed to be approved. The output of "approveTrav-
elRequest" is either "ApprovedForm" or "RejectedForm". If the output variable
is "ApprovedForm", the order for the travelling can be placed; otherwise, the
request is rejected.

5   Allocating Tasks to Agents

In this section we describe how we allocate tasks to software agents which,
together, will enact a set of workflows. Agents are parameterised by the roles
they take up – these roles dictate the tasks agents become responsible for.

The input to the ontological creation of agents is a set of workflows $\mathcal{W}$ and an
ontology $\mathcal{O}$, and the output is an updated ontology with a set of software agents
introduced as subclasses of the Agent concept, with roles and tasks associated
with them. In Figure 5 we show how we create agents in our ontology. The
algorithm collects in $\mathcal{T}$ all tasks of the workflows and distributes them among
the roles of the organisation. The distribution gives priority to *i)* obligations,
then *ii)* institutionalised power and permissions, and finally *iii)* permissions,
captured in the algorithm by the order of the nested **if** constructs. All tasks
should be distributed among roles, otherwise the algorithm fails, that is, the
organisation represented in the ontology cannot enact one of the workflows. If
all tasks have been assigned to roles, then for each role R_i we create in $\mathcal{O}$ a
subclass Ag_i of Agent, with tasks $\mathcal{T}_i = \{T_0^i, \ldots, T_m^i\}$ associated to the agent via
isCapable.

For each Ag_i in $\mathcal{O}$ we start up an independent computational process – a
software agent – which will support the enactment of workflows. Each software
agent, upon its bootstrapping, will use the definition of the subclass as the
parameterisation of its mechanisms: the role and tasks associated to the agent
will guide its behaviour, explained in Section 6. For simplicity, in our algorithm
above, we assume that each agent will enact exactly one role; however this could
easily be changed if required.

algorithm $agent\_creation(\mathcal{W} = \{W_1, \ldots, W_n\}, \mathcal{O})$
$\mathcal{T} = \bigcup_{i=1}^{n} \mathbf{S}_i, \langle N_i, \mathbf{S}_i, \mathbf{E}_i, s_{0_i}, \mathbf{S}_{f_i} \rangle \in \mathcal{W}$
  for each role R_i in $\mathcal{O}$ **do**
    for each $\langle id, T \rangle \in \mathcal{T}$ **do**
      if $R_i \sqsubseteq \exists$ isObliged.T **then**
        $\mathcal{T} := \mathcal{T} \setminus \{\langle id, T \rangle\}$; $\mathcal{T}_i := \mathcal{T}_i \cup \{T\}$
      else if $R_i \sqsubseteq \exists$ hasPower.$T \sqcap \exists$ isPermitted.T **then**
        $\mathcal{T} := \mathcal{T} \setminus \{\langle id, T \rangle\}$; $\mathcal{T}_i := \mathcal{T}_i \cup \{T\}$
      else if $R_i \sqsubseteq \exists$ isPermitted.T **then**
        $\mathcal{T} := \mathcal{T} \setminus \{\langle id, T \rangle\}$; $\mathcal{T}_i := \mathcal{T}_i \cup \{T\}$
  if $\mathcal{T} \neq \emptyset$ **then fail** // org. cannot enact a workflow
  else
    for each role R_i in $\mathcal{O}$ with $\mathcal{T}_i = \{T_0^i, \ldots, T_m^i\}$ **do**
      $\mathcal{O} := \mathcal{O} \cup \{Ag_i \sqsubseteq \mathsf{Agent}\}$
      $\mathcal{O} := \mathcal{O} \cup \{Ag_i \doteq \exists$ hasRole.$(R_i) \sqcap \exists$ isCapable.$(T_0^i \sqcup \cdots \sqcup T_m^i)\}$
return $\mathcal{O}$;

Fig. 5. Creation of Agents in $\mathcal{O}$

6 Enactment of Workflows

After allocation, the next step is that agents take up roles in the organisation and enact workflows. Agents plan their actions in real-time. The workflow provides an outline plan, but many of the details need to be decided by agents. During the enactment, an ontology is used by the agents to check what actions they can perform. There is a relationship between the tasks and variables in the workflows, and the concepts and instances in the ontology. Each time the agents perform workflow tasks or assign values to variables, they update the instances in the ontology. Some agent actions will involve the consumption of organisational resources, in which case the agent will update the instances in the ontology. Thus the ontology maintains a record of the current status of the workflow enactment, as well as relevant aspects of the organisation. In this paper we avoid details of how the implementation could work, but the update of the ontology can be done by the agents whenever they are about to do a task; the agent sends an update instruction to the service which maintains the ontology.

We will detail the relationship between the ontology and the workflow enactment; this is easiest to illustrate by referring to an example. We continue with the travel request example from Section 4, and we add to it an ontology (see the axioms below) which describes roles, norms, and descriptions of tasks. The following axioms state the norms governing agents and the tasks to be executed.

(1) Secretary $\sqsubseteq \exists$ isObliged.checkRequestForm
(2) Manager $\sqsubseteq \exists$ hasPower.approveRequest
(3) DeptManager $\sqsubseteq \exists$ hasPower.approveTravelRequest
(4) Manager(m) $\wedge$ TravelRequestForm(f) $\wedge$ approveTravelRequest(act) $\wedge$ requestedFrom(f,m) $\wedge$
    approves(act,f) $\wedge \mathcal{O}$(m) $\wedge \mathcal{O}$(m) $\wedge \mathcal{O}$(f) $\rightarrow$ isProhibited(m,act)
(5) checkRequestForm $\doteq \exists$ checks.(TravelRequestForm $\sqcap \exists$ isCorrect.xsd:boolean)
(6) Staff(s) $\wedge$ requestedFrom(f,s) $\wedge$ hasName(s,n) $\wedge$ filledName(f,n) $\wedge$ hasStaffID(s,id) $\wedge$
    filledStaffID(f,id) $\wedge \mathcal{O}$(s) $\wedge \mathcal{O}$(f) $\wedge \mathcal{O}$(n) $\wedge \mathcal{O}$(id) $\wedge \cdots \rightarrow$ isCorrect(f, { "true" ^^$\langle$ xsd:boolean$\rangle$})
(7) CorrectTravelRequestForm $\doteq$ TravelRequestFrom $\sqcap \exists$ isCorrect.{ "true" ^^$\langle$ xsd:boolean$\rangle$}
(8) InCorrectTravelRequestForm $\doteq$ TravelRequestForm $\sqcap \exists$ isCorrect.{ "false" ^^$\langle$ xsd:boolean$\rangle$}
(9) checkRequestForm $\sqsubseteq \exists$ hasInput.TravelRequestForm $\sqcap$
    $\exists$hasOutput.(CorrectTravelRequestForm $\sqcup$ InCorrectTravelRequestForm)
(10) functional(isCorrect)
(11) ApprovedForm $\doteq$ TravelRequestForm $\sqcap \exists$ isApproved.{ "true" ^^$\langle$ xsd:boolean$\rangle$}

Each state in a workflow is mapped to a task in the domain ontology by matching the same name (i.e. each task is a concept in the ontology). For example, state 2 in the workflow (Figure 4) is mapped to checkRequestForm in the domain ontology. When a task in a workflow is about to be executed by an agent, an instance of the corresponding task in the ontology is created by the agent (in real-time).

Similarly, each input (or output) variable from a workflow task maps to a concept in the ontology. For example, the variable "ApprovedForm" in the workflow (Figure 4) is mapped to the concept ApprovedForm (see axiom 11 above) in the domain ontology. Every time an agent assigns a value to an input (or output) from a workflow task, then a new instance is also created in the ontology, corresponding to the value of the variable.

The creation of instances in the ontology allows an agent to check if its next action complies with the constraints of the organisation. The agent who is about to execute a workflow task first tentatively creates an instance in the ontology, and then calls the DL reasoner to check the ontology's consistency and also to check if violations have been introduced. If the ontology is inconsistent, then the agent knows that the task it was about to execute is an error; on the other hand, if the ontology entails violated(x,task) for some agent "x", then the agent knows that the task it was about to execute would cause it to violate norms. Thus the agent should not carry out the task, and should revert to the ontology before the instance was added. This type of check can pick up on such things as an agent performing a prohibited action (see axiom 4 in subsection 3.2) or axiom (4) above which forbids a manager from approving his own travel request. Of course an autonomous agent may choose to execute the task regardless, in which case the instance is added, and the ontology may now have recorded violations (in the case of broken prohibitions) or may be inconsistent (in the case of an agent updating wrong information). In the second case, the inconsistent ontology can still be used thereafter for agents to check proposed actions. Ontology reasoners can reason with inconsistent ontologies by selecting consistent subsets [8]. In our case, the reasoner can identify the set of "Minimal Unsatisfied Preserving Sub-Ontologies" (MUPSs) in an inconsistent ontology [17]; each MUPS is a minimal set of problematic axioms. Thus, given an inconsistent ontology, an agent can add an instance and check if the number of MUPSs has increased; if so, then this instance has caused further inconsistencies, otherwise the instance (and hence the proposed workflow task) is acceptable.

We now describe how the agent's behaviour is related to the ontology and the workflow using the "travel request" workflow in Figure 4. Let us look at the second state of the workflow in Figure 4, i.e., the "checkRequestForm" task. When control passes to this state there already exists an instance of a TravelRequestForm in the ontology, say this is TF124. Now the above axioms (1) states that the Secretary is obliged to perform the "checkRequestForm" workflow task. The secretary is going to perform this action, so the secretary agent creates an instance of checkRequestForm, say this is CRF54. Axiom (5) states that checkRequestForm is defined as having at least one checks relationship, and therefore the secretary agent must also add an ABox axiom for the relationship checks(CRF54, TF124); the agent can also deduce that the form TF124 should be correct or incorrect (i.e. boolean). Now due to axiom (6), assuming the form has been filled correctly, then its isCorrect property should have a true value; this corresponds to ABox axiom isCorrect(TF124, { "true" ^^⟨ xsd:boolean⟩}), which can now be inferred from the ontology. Now from axiom (7) it can be inferred that the travel request form TF124 is an instance of the concept CorrectTravelRequestForm. Finally axiom (9) tells us that this instance TF124 is the value to be assigned to the output variable "CorrectTravelRequesForm" of this workflow task. However, the secretary might erroneously decide to assign the output TF124 as the output value "CorrectTravelRequesForm" or "IncorrectTravelRequesForm" in the workflow. As mentioned above, whenever an agent assigns a value to a workflow input (or output) variable, the agent must add an instance of the corresponding concept to the ontology. Thus the secretary's choice is between adding the ABox axiom CorrectTravelRequestForm(TF124) or InCorrectTravelRequestForm(TF124). Of course if the latter choice is made, then the ontology becomes inconsistent, because the form passed all the tests of axiom (6), hence CorrectTravelRequestForm(TF124) can already be inferred. Thus the secretary knows that declaring the form incorrect breaks the organisation's constraints. Likewise, if the form was incorrectly filled, the secretary would break the organisation's constraints by declaring it to be correct. Axiom (10) states that the isCorrect property can only have one value (i.e. the form's correctness cannot be both true and false).

7   Dealing with Exceptions

During the enactment of workflows, exceptions may occur easily, for example due to unavailable resources, or agent failures. One way to deal with exceptions is to classify exceptions into classes and pre-define rules or policies to handle each case; specialised agents then perform defined remedial actions [9]. However, exceptions are difficult to predict during design, especially in open and dynamic environments. It is preferable to program agents with intelligence and adaptivity so they can accommodate unexpected changes in their environment. To satisfy this requirement we have associated the workflow tasks with semantic information in the OWL ontology, and we have also represented the background knowledge for the organisation. This allows agents to reason about the description of tasks and agents in the organisation and find alternative ways to deal with workflow tasks when exceptions arise.

Exceptions often involve the inability to execute some particular task in the workflow. This can be repaired by breaking off from the execution of the workflow at that point, and executing some sequence of actions which can act as a substitute for the problematic task. The appropriate sequence of actions may itself involve another workflow which is nested inside the original workflow. A simple example of this could be when a member of an organisation is absent and unable to execute a task in a workflow; then another member of the organisation may repair this problem by invoking a delegation workflow to delegate the absent member's duties to another suitable member of staff.

We provide exception handlers for the following two types of exception: (1) an agent exception, where an agent may have crashed, or is not performing for some reason; and (2) a task exception, where a task is unachievable.

The "Agent_Exception_handler" in Figure 6 handles Exceptions regarding unavailable agents. The input to this routine consists of the problematic workflow state and the agent who is handling the exception (Ag_H); this is the agent who completed the preceding workflow state, and was unable to pass control to the next agent. This routine first tries to find an alternative agent which has the appropriate capability (and institutional power if necessary), and to delegate the task to that agent. If no suitable agent can be found, then a substitute task is sought; the subroutine "Find_Alternative_Task" (Figure 8) tries to find a task with the same inputs and outputs. If no suitable task can be found, then the Agent_Exception_handler tries to procure additional staff, and this is done via a nested workflow for staff procurement. The agent uses its own internal procedure "callWorkflow" to initiate a workflow to procure a new member of staff who can do task T_p; this procedure returns true if the workflow successfully procures new staff. We do not detail the procurement workflow, but it will make a selection between either hiring contract staff or recruiting new staff, depending on the organisational rules governing that class of staff.

The "Task_Exception_handler" in Figure 6 deals with unachievable tasks. Its inputs are the problematic workflow state and the agent who is handling the exception (Ag_H); in this case this is the agent who attempted to execute the problematic task, and was unable to. The routine begins by checking if the task has failed due to the unavailability of a required resource. If so, an alternative resource is sought. This is done by finding siblings of the original resource in the ontology. This could for example replace a black and white laser printer with a colour laser printer for a simple print job; the colour printer is less desirable as it is more costly, but it can do the job. If no suitable substitute resource can be found, then a substitute task is sought; the subroutine "Find_Alternative_Task" (Figure 8) tries to find a task with the same inputs and outputs. If no suitable task can be found, then the Task_Exception_handler tries to procure the resource, and this invokes a nested workflow for resource procurement. This workflow is shown in Figure 9, it will make a selection between either hiring the equipment or purchasing it, depending on the organisational rules governing that type of equipment (we do not give the details of these rules).

We now describe dealing with exceptions with examples. We consider the workflow example shown in Figure 9 which deals with printing a finance report. When a finance report is written, its format is then checked. Next, the report is to be approved, and printed locally, finally the report is posted. Below we list some of the ontology axioms which are relevant to this workflow.

(1) ApproveReport ⊑ Institutional_Task
(2) Manager ⊑ ∃ hasPower.ApproveReport ⊓ ∀ hasPower.ApproveReport ⊓ ∃ isCapbale.ApproveReport ⊓
     ∃ isPermitted.ApproveReport
(3) ITManager ⊑ ∃ hasPower.ApproveITReport ⊓ ∀ hasPower.ApproveITReport
(4) FinanceManager ⊑ ∃ hasPower.ApproveFinanceReport ⊓ ∀ hasPower.ApproveFinanceReport
(5) FinanceManager ⊔ ITManager ⊔ GeneralManager ⊑ Manager
(6) ApproveFinanceReport ⊔ ApproveITReport ⊑ ApproveReport
(7) ApproveFinanceReport ⊑ ¬ ApproveITReport
(8) Secretary ⊑ ∃ isObliged.checkReportFormat

The FinanceManager has the power to do ApproveFinanceReport. If the FinanceManager is not available, then control returns to state 2 of the workflow, where the

algorithm Agent_Exception_handler($\langle id, T_p \rangle, Ag_H$)
    // Try to find an alternative agent who has the capability to do T_p
    if Find_Alternative_Agent($\langle id, T_p \rangle, Ag_H, \mathcal{O}$) **return** true;
    // Try to find an alternative task (or workflow) with the same input/output as T_p
    else if Find_Alternative_Task($\langle id, T_p \rangle, Ag_H, \mathcal{O}$) **return** true;
    else if callWorkflow(procureStaff_WF,T_p) **return** true; // initiate the staff procurement workflow
    else return false;

algorithm Task_Exception_handler($\langle id, T_p \rangle, Ag_H$)
    // if something is missing try alternative resources
    if there exists some resource R such that
        $T_p \sqsubseteq \exists$uses.R and ! available (R)
      then for each R_i, where sibling(R, R_i)
        let r be an instance of R
        let r_i be an instance of R_i
        let t be an instance of T_p
        $\mathcal{O}' := \{$uses$(t, r_i)\} \cup \mathcal{O} \setminus \{$uses$(t, r)\}$
        if consistent($\mathcal{O}'$) **then** $\mathcal{O} := \mathcal{O}'$; **return** true;
    end for
    // Try to find an alternative task (or workflow) with the same input/output as T_p
    if Find_Alternative_Task($\langle id, T_p \rangle, Ag_H, \mathcal{O}$) **then return** true;
    // If resources are missing
    if there exists some resource R such that $T_p \sqsubseteq \exists$ uses.R and ! available (R)
      then if callWorkflow(procureResource_WF,R) **return** true
      // initiate the resource procurement workflow
    return false;

Fig. 6. Dealing with Exceptions

algorithm Find_Alternative_Agent($\langle id, T_p \rangle, Ag_H, \mathcal{O}$)
    $Ag_H = \langle \mathcal{R}_H, \mathcal{T}_H \rangle$
    // if T_p is a type of institutional task, then it needs institutional power
    if $T_p \sqsubseteq$ Institutional_Task $\in \mathcal{O}$
    // then find agents having the capability and power to do T_p
    then Agent_list := RunQuery("Type(_:y, ?agent), PropertyValue(_:x, org:isPermitted, _:z),
        PropertyValue(_:x, org:hasPower, _:z), PropertyValue(_:y, org:isCapable, _:z),
        PropertyValue(_:y, org:hasRole, _:x), Type(_:z,dom:T_p)")
    // else find agents having the capability to do T_p
    else Agent_list := RunQuery("Type(_:y, ?agent), PropertyValue(_:y, org:isCapable, _:z), Type(_:z,dom:T_p)")
    for each Ag_i in Agent_list do
      // if Ag_H has power to delegate to Ag_i, then Ag_H gives him the order to do it
      if $\exists Role \in \mathcal{R}_H$ such that canDelegate($Role, Ag_i$)
        then SpeechAct(Ag_H, Ag_i,order,T_p)   **return** true;
      else   // Ag_H requests Ag_i to take the obligation
        if callWorkflow(request_WF, Ag_H, Ag_i, T_p)   **then return** true;
    end for
    return false;

Fig. 7. Finding Alternative Agents

secretary must handle the exception using the routine in Figure 6. This leads to
the routine "Find_Alternative_Agent" (in Figure 7) being run. After running the
query within "Find_Alternative_Agent", the agent whose role is GeneralManager
is returned as an appropriate candidate to carry out the approval task. This is
because GeneralManager inherits power from its superclass Manager, while IT-
Manager is restricted to approve IT reports only. The final stage of the exception
handling is for the secretary to initiate a "request" workflow, to request that the
general manager take on the obligation to approve the finance report. If this is
successful, then the workflow can resume with the new substitute agent.

    The next step is to print the report. To show an example of an unachievable
task, let us assume no printer or toner is available; therefore printReportLocally
cannot be implemented. As the secretary is responsible for this unachievable task,

algorithm Find_Alternative_Task($\langle id, T_p \rangle, Ag_H, \mathcal{O}$)
$\quad Ag_H = \langle \mathcal{R}_H, \mathcal{T}_H \rangle$
$\quad$ // find any task T with same input/output
$\quad$ Task_list := RunQuery("Type(_:t, ?task),Type(_:z, dom:T_p), PropertyValue(_:z, dom:hasInput, _:xi),
$\qquad$ PropertyValue(_:z, dom:hasOutput, _:xo), PropertyValue(_:t, dom:hasInput, _:xi),
$\qquad$ PropertyValue(_:t, dom:hasOutput, _:xo)")
$\quad$ **for** each $T \in$ Task_list $\quad$ // check the consistency for each alternative task
$\qquad$ let t be an instance of T_p
$\qquad$ $\mathcal{O}' := \{T(t)\} \cup \mathcal{O} \setminus \{T_p(t)\}$
$\qquad$ **if** consistent($\mathcal{O}'$) **then** $\mathcal{O} := \mathcal{O}'$
$\qquad\quad$ **if** T is a workflow, **then** Ag_H initiates T
$\qquad\quad$ **else if** T is a task $\quad$ // then check if the Ag_H can do T
$\qquad\qquad$ **if** $T_p \sqsubseteq$ Institutional_Task $\in \mathcal{O}$ $\quad$ // then find agents having the capability and power to do T_p
$\qquad\qquad\quad$ **if** $\exists Role \in \mathcal{R}_H$ such that isCapable(Ag_H, T)∧ hasPower($Role, T$)∧ isPermitted($Role, T$)
$\qquad\qquad\qquad$ **then** $Ag_H := \langle \mathcal{R}_H, \mathcal{T}_H \cup \{T\} \rangle$; **return** true;
$\qquad\qquad$ **else if** $\exists Role \in \mathcal{R}_H$ such that isCapable(Ag_H, T)
$\qquad\qquad\qquad$ **then** $Ag_H := \langle \mathcal{R}_H, \mathcal{T}_H \cup \{T\} \rangle$; **return** true;
$\qquad\qquad$ // otherwise call routine for finding alternative agent
$\qquad\qquad$ **if** Find_Alternative_Agent($\langle id, T \rangle, Ag_H, \mathcal{O}$) **then return** true;
$\quad$ **end for**
$\quad$ **return** false;

Fig. 8. Finding Alternative Task

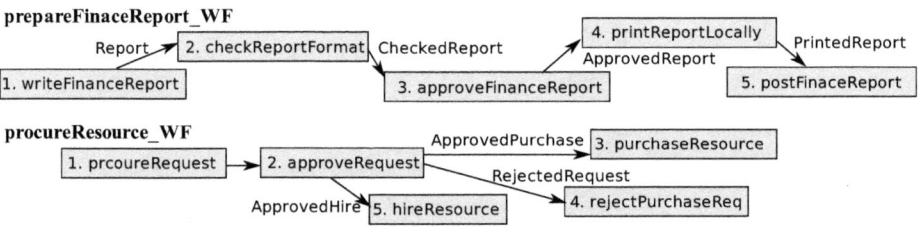

Fig. 9. Finance Report and Purchase Workflows

the secretary must execute of the routine "Task_Exception_handler" (in Figure 6), which reveals that a resource is missing, and no suitable alternative resource exists in the organisation. The routine then searches for alternative tasks and finds that the task printReportCommercially is a sibling task of printReportLocally, has the same input ApprovedReport and output PrintedReport. However, if the report is sensitive, it is not allowed to print it commercially (see axiom 6 below). Assume that printRpt322 is the instance of printReportLocally, which is to be replaced by printReportCommercially; according to "Find_Alternative_Task" (in Figure 8) we move the instance printRpt322 from printReportLocally to printReportCommercially. If the report is sensitive, i.e., printRpt322 is also an instance of SensitiveReport, then from axiom 6 below we could infer that the agent performing the commercial print act is violating norms. Hence, printReportCommercially should not be executed. If the agent chooses not to violate the norms, then "Find_Alternative_Task" fails and control returns to "Task_Exception_handler" (in Figure 6). Having failed to find an alternative resource or task, this routine now tries to procure the resource required for the task. This means that the secretary must initiate the "procureResource_WF" workflow (in Figure 9), and if successful, the printing resource is available, and the workflow can progress.

(1) printReportLocally $\doteq$ $\exists$ print.(Report $\sqcap$ $\exists$ printedBy.(Printer $\sqcap$ $\exists$ hasToner.(Toner $\sqcap$
    $\exists$ hasAmt.GreaterThanZero)))
(2) Printer $\sqcup$ Toner $\sqsubseteq$ Resource
(3) procureRequest $\doteq$ $\exists$ requests.(Resource $\sqcap$ $\exists$ hasAmt.LessThanOne $\sqcap$ $= 1$ hasPrice)
(4) printReport $\sqsubseteq$ $\exists$ hasInput.ApprovedReport $\sqcap$ $\exists$ hasOutput.PrintedReport
(5) printReportLocally $\sqcup$ printReportCommercially $\sqsubseteq$ printReport
(6) Staff(s) $\wedge$ SensitiveReport(r) $\wedge$ printReportCommercially(act) $\wedge$ print(act,r) $\wedge$ performed(s,act) $\wedge\mathcal{O}$(s)
    $\wedge\mathcal{O}$(r) $\wedge\mathcal{O}(act)$ $\rightarrow$ violated(s,act)
(7) Secretary $\sqsubseteq$ $\exists$ isObliged.printReportLocally

8   Related Work

Various works use agents to enact workflows. Buhler and Vidal [4] proposed to
integrate agent services into BPEL4WS-defined workflows. The strategy is to
use the Web Service Agent Gateway to slide agents between a workflow engine
and the Web services it calls. Thus the workflow execution is managed centrally
rather than by the agents. On the other hand Guo et al. [5] describe the development of a distributed multi-agent workflow enactment mechanism from a
BPEL4WS specification. They proposed a syntax-based mapping between some
of main BPEL4WS constructs to the Lightweight Coordination Calculus (LCC).
This work however does not address organisational or normative aspects of an
agent system; we believe that these high level aspects are important for agent
systems that are to model real processes in human organisations; such simulations can be useful to reveal potential problems in organisational and normative
specifications for a system, for example in a crisis management scenario. Furthermore we have shown how the use of ontologies to describe aspects of the
organisation and domain can be valuable in exception handling, as agents are
part of an organisation and will be unable to deal with exceptions entirely on
their own.

Klein and Dellarocas [9] explicitly deal with the issue of exceptions; they
propose the use of specialised agents that handle exceptions. The exception handling service is a centralised approach, in which a coordination doctor diagnoses
agents' illnesses and prescribes specific treatment procedures. Klein and Dellarocas [10] identified an exception taxonomy which is a hierarchy of exception types,
and then described which handlers should be used for what exceptions. Klein et
al. [11] describe a domain-independent but protocol-specific exception handling
services approach to increasing robustness in open agent systems. They focus on
"agent death" in the Contract Net protocol. We would argue that our approach
is more generic in that it is neither domain-specific, nor protocol-specific. When
seeking alternative ways to achieve workflow tasks, our agents can use the same
handling routine regardless of the workflow in progress. A further distinction between our work and the above related works use some device which is added into
the system to deal with exceptions, for example: specialised agents, an exception repository, or a directory to keep track of agents. In contrast, our approach
aims to endow the agents of the system themselves with the ability to deal with
exceptions by querying ontologies to find alternative ways.

Perhaps the closest approach to our work in the literature is from Mallya and
Singh [14]. Building on the commitment approach, they have proposed novel

methods to deal with exceptions in a protocol. They distinguish between expected and unexpected exceptions. Unexpected exceptions are closest to the types of exceptions we tackle here. Mallya and Singh's solution makes use of a library of sets of runs (sequences of states of an interaction) which could be spliced into the workflow at the point where the exception happens. This is similar to the way our exception handling can sometimes include a nested workflow in place of a failed task, to repair the workflow. However, they do not describe how these sets of runs can be created, but it is likely that one would need access to observed sequences from previous enactments of similar workflows. The aim of the commitment approach is in line with our work, as it endows the agents with some understanding of the meaning of the workflow they are executing, by giving them knowledge of the commitments at each stage. This would make it possible for agents to find intelligent solutions when exceptions arise. Similarly, in our approach, agents are endowed with semantic knowledge (represented in an ontology) about the capabilities and norms of the other roles so that they can find suitable candidates to execute tasks in the case of exceptions.

9   Conclusions and Future Work

In this paper we have described a method by which an agent system could be constructed to enact a set of given workflows, while respecting the constraints of a given organisation. We have shown how Semantic Web languages can be used to describe the organisational knowledge, as well as domain knowledge which can be used by the agents if exceptions arise during the enactment of a workflow; the agents can then use this knowledge to make intelligent decisions about how to find alternative ways to complete the workflow.

Some issues which have not been addressed include the updating of the organisational knowledge by agent activities outwith the workflows, for example speech acts that may change norms in the system. Also, we have not included any mechanism to detect when an obligation is violated. This could be addressed by associating time limits with obligations and including timer events which are triggered when obligations time out, and then checking if they have been fulfilled; this remains for future work.

Our aim has been to allow agents to deal with unexpected exceptions, rather than coding specific exception handlers for a predefined set of expected exceptions. Nevertheless we have had to define exception handling routines for some predefined situations, such as agent exceptions, or task exceptions. However, our predefined situations cover a broad class of exceptions, and there can be many possible solutions if the ontological knowledge is suitably rich.

References

1. IBM, BEA Systems, Microsoft, SAP AG and Siebel Systems, business Process Execution Language for Web Services version 1.1. Technical report (July 2003)
2. Artikis, A.: Executable Specification of Open Norm-Governed Computational Systems. PhD thesis, Imperial College London (2003)

3. Baader, F., Calvanese, D., McGuinness, D.L., Nardi, D., Patel-Schneider, P.: The Description Logic Handbook: Theory, Implementation and Applications. Cambridge University Press, Cambridge (2003)
4. Buhler, P., Vidal, J.M.: Integrating agent services into BPEL4WS defined workflows. In: Proceedings of the Fourth International Workshop on Web-Oriented Software Technologies (2004)
5. Guo, L., Robertson, D., Chen-Burger, Y.-H.: Using multi-agent platform for pure decentralised business workflows. Web Int. and Agent Systems 6(3) (2008)
6. Horrocks, I., Patel-Schneider, P.F.: Reducing OWL entailment to description logic satisfiability. In: Fensel, D., Sycara, K., Mylopoulos, J. (eds.) ISWC 2003. LNCS, vol. 2870, pp. 17–29. Springer, Heidelberg (2003)
7. Horrocks, I., Sattler, U.: A tableaux decision procedure for $\mathcal{SHOIQ}$. In: Proc. of the 19th Int. Joint Conf. on Artificial Intelligence, pp. 448–453 (2005)
8. Huang, Z., van Harmelen, F., ten Teije, A.: Reasoning with inconsistent ontologies. In: Kaelbling, Saffiotti (eds.) IJCAI'05 (2005)
9. Klein, M., Dellarocas, C.: Exception handling in agent systems. In: AGENTS '99: 3rd Annual Conference on Autonomous Agents, pp. 62–68 (1999)
10. Klein, M., Dellarocas, C.: Towards a systematic repository of knowledge about managing multi-agent system exceptions. Technical Report ASES Working Report ASES-WP-2000-01, Massachusetts Institute of Technology (2000)
11. Klein, M., Rodriguez-Aguilar, J., Dellarocas, C.: Using domain-independent exception handling services to enable robust open multi-agent systems: The case of agent death. Auton. Agents and Multi-Agent Systems 7(1-2), 179–189 (2003)
12. Lanzén, A., Oinn, T.: The taverna interaction service: enabling manual interaction in workflows. Bioinformatics 24(8), 1118–1120 (2008)
13. Ludäscher, B., Altintas, I., Berkley, C., Higgins, D., Jaeger, E., Jones, M., Lee, E.A., Tao, J., Zhao, Y.: Scientific workflow management and the Kepler system: Research articles. Concurr. Comput.: Pract. Exper. 18(10), 1039–1065 (2006)
14. Mallya, A.U., Singh, M.P.: Modeling exceptions via commitment protocols. In: AAMAS '05: Proceedings of the fourth international joint conference on Autonomous agents and multiagent systems, pp. 122–129. ACM, New York (2005)
15. Motik, B., Sattler, U., Studer, R.: Query Answering for OWL-DL with Rules. In: McIlraith, S.A., Plexousakis, D., van Harmelen, F. (eds.) ISWC 2004. LNCS, vol. 3298, pp. 549–563. Springer, Heidelberg (2004)
16. Sandhu, R.S., Coyne, E.J., Feinstein, H.L., Youman, C.E.: Role-based access control models. Computer 29(2), 38–47 (1996)
17. Schlobach, S., Cornet, R.: Non-standard reasoning services for the debugging of description logic terminologies. In: Proceedings of the 8th International Joint Conference on Artificial Intelligence (IJCAI'03), pp. 355–362 (2003)
18. Sirin, E., Parsia, B.: SPARQL-DL: SPARQL query for OWL-DL. In: 3rd OWL Experiences and Directions Workshop, OWLED-2007 (2007)
19. van der Aalst, W.: The Application of Petri Nets to Workflow Management. The Journal of Circuits, Systems and Computers 8(1), 21–66 (1998)
20. von Wright, G.H.: Deontic logic. Mind, New Series 60(237), 1–15 (1951)

An Approach for Virtual Organisations' Dissolution

Nicolás Hormazábal[1], Henrique Lopes Cardoso[2],
Josep Lluis de la Rosa[1], and Eugénio Oliveira[2]

[1] Universitat de Girona, Agents Research Lab,
Av. Lluis Santaló S/N, Campus Montilivi, Edifici PIV, 17071 Girona, Spain
{nicolash,peplluis}@eia.udg.edu
[2] Universidade do Porto, LIACC, DEI / Faculdade de Engenharia,
R. Dr. Roberto Frias, 4200-465 Porto, Portugal
{hlc,eco}@fe.up.pt

Abstract. Current research on virtual organisations focuses mainly on their formation and operation phases, devoting only little attention to the dissolution phase. These passages typically suggest that dissolution should occur when the organisation has fulfilled all its objectives or when it is no longer needed. This last definition is quite vague and hard to define, as the need for an organisation is not always easy to measure.

We believe that, besides fulfilment of objectives, more causes should be considered for the dissolution of a virtual organisation, since an organisation is not always capable of achieving its goals or continuing operations. Organisations can change during their operation, as might the environment in which they operate, and these changes may affect their performance to the point that they should not continue operating. In addition, the causes that could lead to dissolution could affect the formation of future organisations. Considering the correspondence between virtual organisations and real-life organisations, some portions of real-world commercial law related to dissolution can be applied to the virtual world.

In this paper we introduce the different causes that should be considered for virtual organisation dissolution, and a case study focused on one of these causes is presented as a way to emphasise the significance of the dissolution process.

1   Introduction

Generally speaking, virtual organisations (VOs) are composed of a number of autonomous agents with their own capabilities and resources for problem-solving, task execution and performance. Being autonomous, agents usually pursue individual goals, but in some cases, these goals can be achieved with better performance or higher benefits inside a cooperative environment with other agents, where the resulting organisation can even offer new services through the combination of complementary abilities. For example, in an economic environment,

J. Padget et al. (Eds.): COIN 2009, LNAI 6069, pp. 70–85, 2010.

agents may represent different units or enterprises that come together in response to new market opportunities that require a combination of resources that no partner alone can fulfil [1]. These cooperative organisations have been researched mainly from the point of view of their formation and operation. However, their lifecycle has been outlined as having an additional phase and therefore is comprised of *formation*, *operation* and *dissolution*.

Although the automation of the dissolution process has been mentioned as a research and development challenge in the study of VOs [2], there is not much work addressing dissolution. This phase is often overlooked by deeper research, yet, in economic terms, if an organisation's dissolution is not properly managed, it can generate tremendous costs [3]. The timeliness of dissolution is dictated by the existing agents and resource availability. If a VO is underperforming without a chance for reconfiguring itself (or if the possible reconfiguration is not sufficient to improve performance), then it should dissolve in order to free assigned resources and members.

Under normal circumstances, the dissolution should happen after the VO has fulfilled its objectives [4]. Some researchers also mention that such partnerships should dissolve when they are no longer sustainable [5] or the VO is no longer needed. The main topic of this paper is the clarification of these terms, through an identification of the causes that should be considered for the dissolution of a VO.

The paper is organised as follows: Section 2 briefly describes some real-life organisations and the normative environment that provides the context for the dissolution process of virtual organisations. Section 3 describes the normative framework used for supporting the dissolution process. Section 4 explains the dissolution process, describing the steps needed for dissolution and the causes that should lead to a VOs dissolution. Section 5 presents a case study focused on one of the causes for dissolution presented. Finally, in section 6, the conclusions of the current work are presented.

2   Real-World Organisations

In virtual environments, agent societies enable interactions between agents and are therefore the virtual counterpart of real-life societies and organisations [6]. As such, when seeking to support VO dissolution, issues related to the dissolution of real-life organisations should be considered.

The most common type of regulated social organisation is the commercial organisation, such as a limited or public limited company. These organisations are regulated by law, and therefore they exist inside a normative environment enforced by its respective legal institution. Every country has its own laws, but there are several common key features among Western countries that can be used for reference. We shall use Spanish Commercial Law ([7], [8]) as a starting point, specifically those laws concerning the dissolution of this type of commercial organisation.

The dissolution of a commercial organisation is divided into two phases. First, there is the identification of a *dissolution cause*. In some cases, the agreement of the organisation's members is also needed to move forward to the next phase. The second phase is *liquidation*, wherein, once a dissolution cause is identified, the organisation moves forward to perform the tasks needed to enact its end, producing a dissolution report that summarises the organisation's activity.

From the text above, the dissolution causes can be classified into two different groups:

- Causes that, when identified, dissolve the organisation automatically without needing of the members' (or the boards) agreement.
- Causes that, when identified, need an agreement from the members (or the board) before going on to the next step, the *liquidation*.

These causes depend on, besides the law itself, the contents of the organisations articles of association, their statutes (where, for example, the duration of the organisation is specified, in case the partners decide to have a fixed duration) or the organisation's assets. The law may also include slightly different legislation on some aspects depending on the organisation's scope.

Institutions regulate interactions between the members of a society, defining the "rules of the game", what is permitted and what is forbidden and in what conditions [9]. Similarly, a VO needs to operate within a normative environment, enforced in this case by an electronic institution (EI), which is the electronic counterpart of real-life institutions.

3   Normative Framework

Commercial organisations are restricted externally by the legal context in which they operate and internally by the statutes or articles of association created during the organisation's formation. There are, then, different normative layers related to the organisations' activities. First, a common set of norms for every organisation exists in the form of the law; specific norms for each one of them consist of the statutes or articles of association. An institutional normative framework should therefore include a hierarchical organisation of norms. Borrowing from [11], we consider norms to be organised into three levels (see Figure 1).

The EI aims to support agent interaction as a framework of coordination and provides a level of trust by offering an enforceable normative environment. This means that the EI will facilitate both the creation and the enforcement of contracts among agents [12]:

- Institutional norms, at the higher level, influence the formation of VO constitutional and operational contracts; they set up the normative background upon which cooperative commitments can be established. Regulations on general contracting activities and the behaviour of every agent in the EI are included on this level.
- Constitutional norms represent the core of the cooperative agreement between the agents. The agreement is represented by norms that regulate the created coalition, which usually exists for a specified period of time. Norms at this level only affect the agents that participate in the VO.

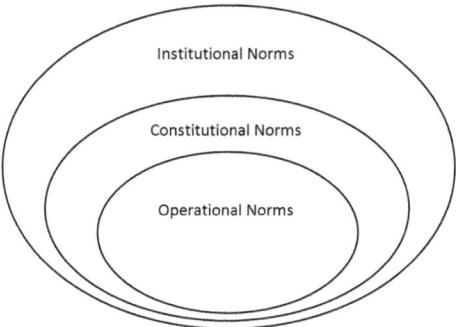

Fig. 1. Normative Framework

- Operational norms indicate the actions to be performed by contractual agents by specifying operational contracts, which may be established among a subset of the VO's agents.

Drawing a parallel between the real-life organisations (like commercial organisations) and the EI framework, institutional norms map commercial law, constitutional norms correspond to the organisation's articles of association or statutes, and the operational norms represent the individual task commitments inside the organisation (table 1).

Table 1. Parallel between societies and EI

Real-Life Societies	Electronic Institution Framework
The Law	Institutional Norms
Statutes	Constitutional Norms
Task Commitments	Operational Norms

The VOs activity is therefore governed by norms established for different layers in the institutional normative framework. When we focus on the dissolution phase of a VO lifecycle, we posit that there should be some norms related to the identification of when a VO has to be dissolved, thus helping to identify the causes of dissolution.

4   Dissolution Process

Inspired by commercial law, in this work we suggest a two-step dissolution process. First is the dissolution activation (which will be called *activation*), consisting of the identification of a cause of dissolution for the VO, and then the execution of the dissolution process follows, where the needed tasks for the dissolution will be run (this step will be called *liquidation*).

4.1   Activation

In the current literature, the causes for VO dissolution are mainly the successful achievement of all its goals or a decision by the involved partners to stop the operation [10]. But if the partners decide to stop the operation of the VO, they should somehow specify the cause of the decision; if the organisation is ending its activities before fulfilling its goals, this could be considered an unsuccessful venture. This information should be used for future organisation formation and partner selection.

Before dissolving, VOs can attempt to adapt themselves to environmental changes or perform a reorganisation in order to maintain or improve performance, depending on different causes. This means that it is not always the right choice to move forward to the dissolution, yet in some cases, it may be better to dissolve instead of trying to reorganise a VO.

We suggest then distinguishing two type of causes of dissolution: first, the causes that need the decision of the involved members for moving on to the dissolution, which will be called *Necessary Causes*, as they are necessary for the dissolution but not sufficient, as they need the members agreement.

Additionally, there are some causes that should automatically dissolve the organisation without needing the partners' decision. These causes are the *Sufficient Causes*.

During the VO operation, *necessary* or *sufficient* causes could be identified, which could lead the VO to different dissolution sub-states (figure 2). If a *sufficient cause* is identified, the VO goes directly to *liquidation*, the mandatory step before the complete dissolution, where the organisation enters into an *on-liquidation* sub-state until it finishes related tasks. But if a *necessary cause* is identified, the VO goes to a *pending dissolution* sub-state, where the VO waits for the partners' confirmation for the dissolution, or for the VO modifications (the adaptation or evolution of the VO) that will avoid the dissolution and make the VO return to the operation phase. If no measures are taken for returning to the operation phase after a period of time defined by the EI, the VO dissolves, going to the *on-liquidation* sub-state.

In short, during the dissolution, if a *sufficient cause* is detected, the organisation goes into *liquidation*. If a *necessary cause* is detected and no actions on the VO are taken to solve the issues related to the dissolution cause, the VO goes into *liquidation*.

Sufficient Causes. *Sufficient causes*, once identified, are sufficient for the automatic dissolution of the VO. The causes of this type that we have identified are as follows:

- *Deadline:* In the VO cooperation agreement, created during its formation, the duration of the organisation can be specified. During the operation of a VO, partners can modify their own normstheir cooperation agreementso they can extend the lifespan of the organisation, but once it is reached, the organisation should dissolve, as it was created to exist only for this duration.

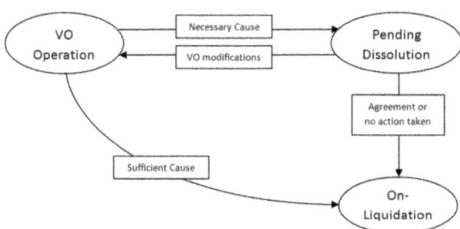

Fig. 2. Dissolution Sub-States

- *Reduction:* During the formation of a VO, the agents specify in the cooperation agreement the resources that they are willing to devote to the organisation. This is what defines the organisation's assets: the total amount of resources that the organisation has. The EI should establish the minimum required resources for a VO to be considered as such. If for some reason the VO suffers a reduction of its resources below the minimum, the VO dissolves. For example, on a football (soccer) team, the minimum amount of resources for a team is 7 players; below that number, one no longer has a team.
- *Agreement:* As we cannot disregard the case where VO partners arbitrarily decide to dissolve the organisation, the agreement for the dissolution should be considered too. For that, a minimum percentage (typically over 50%) of partners must decide to dissolve the organisation.

Necessary Causes. *Necessary causes* are necessary, but not sufficient. To be made sufficient, they need the agreement of the VO partners. Putting it another way, the partners have to take action to prevent the dissolution.

- *Fulfilment:* As mentioned before, the dissolution can be reached by the successful achievement of all the VO goals. During the formation of the VO, agents must define the organisation's goals in the cooperation agreement. Once they are fulfilled, the Institution can be dissolved. The reason that this is a *necessary cause* and not a *sufficient* one is that once the goals have been achieved, the agents can evaluate whether they want to set new ones based on the performance and continue operating.
- *Unfeasibility:* There are some cases when a VO cannot fulfil its goals. This could happen due to internal issues, such as the loss of key resources for achieving all the goals, or it could be brought about by external causes, such as changes in the environment that affect the organisation, such as the arrival of a new organisation that competes for the same goals. The VO can make changes to improve its performance, change its goals or add new resources, among other measures, to prevent the dissolution.
- *Inactivity:* For any reason, it could happen that the VO could show no activity during a period of time; after a specified period, the organisation could be considered as idle or dead, and after that, it could go on to the dissolution phase.

- *Loss:* This dissolution cause makes sense only when the benefits of the VO are measurable and in the same unit as the assets specified in the VO formation (see the *Reduction sufficient cause* above). In the cooperation agreement, the organisational assets are specified based on the resources that each member is willing to spend. If, during the operation of the VO, instead of benefits there are losses and these losses are over the half of the organisational assets, the VO can be dissolved as it can be considered unviable.

Some examples of possible action for the VO to take to avoid dissolution after a *necessary cause* are identified below:

- New goal definition or reallocation of resource and agent assignments for given tasks.
- Addition of new agents to the VO or replacing partners.
- Force the resumption of VO activities after a period of inactivity.
- Modify the VO assets by adding new resources or removing them.

In short, there are seven different dissolution causes, grouped by *sufficient causes* and *necessary causes* (table 2).

Table 2. Dissolution Causes

Sufficient Causes	Deadline
	Reduction
	Agreement
Necessary Causes	Fulfilment
	Unfeasibility
	Inactivity
	Loss

Activation within an Electronic Institution Framework. In the different layers of the EI normative framework (from section 3), we should have norms that support the VO dissolution at both the institutional and constitutional levels. Institutional norms should contain at least four values for dissolution support, which we will call *dissolution support elements*:

- Minimum Resources (R): The minimum resource requirements that a VO needs to have to be considered as such. The VO assets have to be greater than this value.
- Time of inactivity (Ti): The time that a VO has to be inactive before considering its dissolution.
- Maximum loss over assets (Ml): The maximum percentage of loss over the VO's initial assets before considering its dissolution.
- Minimum votes for the majority (V): The default value for the minimum percentage of the total number of participants needed to agree on the dissolution.

These values in the top level of the norms hierarchy (Institutional Norms) can be context-dependent. The grouping of predefined norms by appropriate contexts mimics the real-world enactment of legislation applicable to specific activities [13]. So, depending on the type of organisation, it could have some different *dissolution support elements*.

The following is an abstraction of the concepts that should be included in a VO contract. Regarding the constitutional norms, the VO contract should include at least the VO duration D (or the starting and ending dates for the VO operation). The contract structure should contain the cooperation effort to which each agent has committed as a result of the negotiation process prior to the VO formation. For each agent A_i, with the assigned resources R_k, based on the cooperation effort structure specified in [11]:

$$CoopEff = \{\langle A_i, R_k, W \rangle\}$$
$$W = \langle MinQt, MaxQt, Freq, UnitPr \rangle$$

W represents the workload for each participant agent A_i specified between a minimum ($MinQt$) and a maximum value ($MaxQt$), with a frequency ($Freq$) during the lifetime of the organisation and the unit price ($UnitPr$) that the agent has assigned for performing the assigned workload.

The frequency depends on the unit used for measuring the VOs duration (i.e., days, weeks, computer cycles), which in turn depends on the VO's scope. For example, when the duration unit is *days*, if the workload is specified for each week then the frequency $Freq$ is 7 (every seven days).

The significance of the cooperation effort for the dissolution is that with it, the organisational asset Oa of the organisation can be calculated, given the total duration of the organisation D for each agent A_i in the VO:

$$Oa = \sum_{A_i} MaxQt * UnitPr * \frac{D}{Freq}$$

This organisational asset will be used to evaluate the *Reduction* and *Loss* dissolution causes.

Each one of the causes of dissolution depends on one normative level (table 3) except for *Reduction* and *Loss*, which depend on both institutional and constitutional norms, as they depend on the initial VO assets (and thus on the constitutional norms) and on a minimum value specified in the institutional norms in the case that the VO has not redefined this for itself.

Unfeasibility is a different case. Although it can be considered as a constitutional norms-dependent cause, the truth is that it is more complicated to identify than by observing the assigned resources for each VO goal. A VO could find itself in a situation where it cannot fulfil its objectives for causes beyond the control of the organisation itself. Sometimes for external causes, VO performance could decrease, and the organisation should adapt to the environment, making modifications by reconfiguring itself (some authors introduce a separate phase for adaptation, and others mention the adaptation as a part of the operation phase), or dissolve. Tools for monitoring the VO are needed for identifying cases such as *Unfeasibility*, which, once identified, can enable the VO to avoid a useless extension of operation time if the expected results are to be negative.

Table 3. Dependence between dissolution causes and normative framework levels

Normative Level	Dissolution Cause
Institutional Norms	Agreement Inactivity Reduction Loss
Constitutional Norms	Deadline Fulfilment Reduction Loss

4.2   Liquidation

Liquidation is the last step before the complete dissolution of the VO. Every running task must be stopped and the VO activity frozen for realising the *liquidation* step. The organisation goes into an *on-liquidation* sub-state inside the dissolution phase (see Figure 2).

During the organisation's operation, a profit and expenses log must be maintained, which will allow the VO to create the final balance during this step. Some of the other main aspects that should be supported [10] are:

- Definition of general liabilities upon the dissolution of the VO.
- Keeping track of the individual contributions to a product/service that is jointly delivered (in terms of the quality and product life cycle maintenance).
- Redefinition/discontinuing information access rights after ceasing the cooperation.
- Assessing the performance of partners and generating information to be used by partner selection tools in future VO creation.

This last item is especially relevant, as it not only supports the formation of future VOs but can also support the identification of dissolution causes based (such as *unfeasibility*) on past experiences. An organisation can use this information to identify whether it is possible to fulfil its objectives given its status at a specific time.

For evaluating the partners' performance, it is better not to make a single evaluation at dissolution time, but at several times during the organisation's lifespan in order to have a complete picture of the performance evolution. In the best case the evaluation should be made at every moment during the organisation's operation time, but as this is not always possible, at least three fixed times are recommended for evaluating the organisation: at the moment of its formation, at half of its expected lifespan and at the end, before dissolving [14]. Additionally, new evaluations should be made if key elements are changed within the VO, such as the cooperation agreement.

The evaluation of performance depends upon the VO's scope. A suggestion for the evaluation elements is:

$$Ev = \langle Time, CA, Ben, Exp, Wf, Wr \rangle$$

Where:

- $Time$: The time when the evaluation has been made.
- CA: The VO cooperation agreements.
- Ben, Exp: A balance of the VO's benefits and expenses.
- Wf: The workload (in time or price unit) used for the fulfilled tasks.
- Wr: The expected workload needed for fulfilling the remaining tasks.

The output of the *liquidation* process should be a dissolution report (DR), which will contain all the evaluations made during the organisation's lifespan Evs, together with the dissolution cause DC. Additionally, it can contain an assessment Sc (a score between 0 and 1) from each agent A_i evaluating the VO's performance based on the fulfilment of the agents individual goals. We suggest the following for the content of the dissolution report DR:

$$DR = \langle Evs, DC, Vals \rangle$$
$$Evs = \{Ev_1, Ev_2, ..., Ev_n\}$$
$$Vals = \{Val_1, Val_2, ..., Val_n\}$$
$$Val_i = \langle A_i, Sc \rangle$$
$$DC \in \{Deadline, Reduction, Agreement,$$
$$Fulfilment, Unfeasibility, Inactivity, Loss\}$$

This dissolution report, stored in a knowledge base, will facilitate future VO formation and partner selection, giving information about the performance (from the benefits and expenses) and evaluation of each agent, and it also provides information for the reasons why the VO has not fulfilled its objectives, when that is the case.

5   Unfeasibility Case Study

We developed a simple digital environment for simulating the creation of agent organisations and for testing a way to identify the *unfeasibility* dissolution cause. In this environment, agents form organisations (as the idea is to focus only on the dissolution, the organisation formation process is done automatically) with a fixed duration (in time steps), after which the organisation dissolves.

The mechanism is simple: agents move and interact asynchronously through a grid space (which represents the environment), and when they find another agent in their neighbourhood (nearer than two cells), they send a message proposing the creation of an organisation. In the next time step, agents reply with whether they accept or not. Every agent in the system offers a single (not unique) service, where the advantage of forming an organisation lies in that two agents together can offer their own service plus their service combination, expanding their own markets.

The idea is to demonstrate the utility of supportive tools to automate the identification of dissolution causes, as well as to demonstrate how the dissolution can affect the overall system performance, comparing the results with cases without the *unfeasibility* cause. Additionally, agents have a transitional step between *dissolution activation* and *liquidation* for deciding whether to proceed or not, based on the evaluation results of the organisation's performance.

At the moment of their dissolution, each organisation will generate a *dissolution report* containing evaluations of the organisation at different time periods. Each evaluation will contain only the benefits since the last evaluation (or the benefits so far if it is the first evaluation), the diversity of the offered services and the time steps passed from the last evaluation. These evaluations will be generated at three time periods of the VO's lifespan: at the first third of its expected lifespan, at the second third, and at the moment of its dissolution, when the *dissolution report* containing the evaluations is created (thus, if a VO has a fixed lifespan of 30 steps, the report will contain evaluations of the VO's benefits at steps 10, 20 and 30). If an organisation decides to extend its lifespan, new evaluations will be added to the report.

A knowledge base with previous cases will be used to identify cases in which the agents' expectations will probably not be fulfilled. At first, this knowledge base will be empty, and it will be filled with the *dissolution reports* that each dissolved organisation generates.

For the simulation, the following assumptions related to the agents have been made:

1. Each agent offers a single service.
2. Agents who coalesce are more likely to reap benefits, to the extreme that, in this case, single agents receive no benefits.
3. When agents coalesce, there are three options related to the organisation's lifespan: a) set a fixed lifespan, b) do not fix a lifespan and c) set an initial lifespan that can be changed.
4. In the specific negotiation scenario, at least two agents coalesce; one agent who makes an offer for creating an organisation and one or more who receive the offer. Each offer has a 50% chance of being accepted. This is to simplify the negotiation process while still having the chance to offer refusals.

As for the calculated benefits and organisation services, it is assumed that:

1. Two or more agents offering the same service can't be part of the same organisation.
2. Benefits are calculated based on the services an organisation offers and the demand for these services.
3. The organisations will offer the individual services of each member agent, as well the combination of these services. For example, if an organisation is composed of two agents, which respectively offer the services A and B, the organisation will offer the services A, B and A+B (figure 3)
4. Every service has the same base demand, as do the combined services.
5. The demand of a service depends on the competition within this service (how many organisations offer the same service). For example, if an organisation offers the services A, B and A+B, and another active organisation offers the services A, C and A+C, there will be two competitors for the service A.

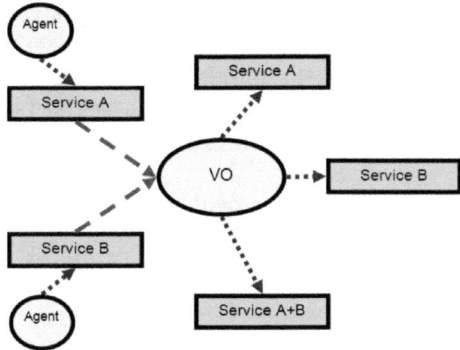

Fig. 3. Services of an organisation

Benefits for each time step are calculated by the following equation:

$$E = \sum_i \left(\frac{B}{C_i} + N \right)$$

Where:

- E are the total earnings or benefits of the organisation at each step.
- B is the base earnings for each service i.
- C_i is the number of organisations that offer the same service i (including the organisation whose earnings are being calculated).
- N is a random number from a normal distribution with average 0 and variance (B/2).

This implies that the greater the diversity in the services that an organisation offers, the lower competition and the higher benefits it will likely experience.

The organisation's goal is to receive at each time step a minimum "acceptable" benefit E above B/5; if it identifies that the goal is not achievable, an *unfeasibility* cause is detected. On the other hand, if the organisation estimates that its expected benefits can be over B/2, it considers whether to extend its lifetime, as the expected benefits are good.

To support the identification of the dissolution cause, a knowledge base with previous cases will be used. In this experiment, we will use a case-based algorithm (which from now on will be referred as *the algorithm*) to identify those cases in which it is better to dissolve the organisation if the goal cannot be fulfilled, which means that it finds itself in an *unfeasibility* case. The same algorithm will be used when the organisation's lifespan is about to reach its end, identifying whether it is better to extend it rather than to proceed to *liquidation*, as the benefit expectancies are good.

As said before, during the organisation's *dissolution*, a *dissolution report* will be created and stored in the knowledge base with different evaluation cases containing the VO's benefits, service diversity and the time step when the evaluation was made.

The algorithm, in its retrieving step, will identify pairs of consecutive evaluations similar to the current and last evaluations. Once a similar case is found, the algorithm will try to predict the following state based on the past case and to evaluate, reusing the past similar case, which is the best action for the organisation to take: whether it is better to continue operating by extending its lifespan or to dissolve.

The similarity for the algorithm is calculated by:

$$Sim = (Div_k * w_1 + Ben_k * W_2) + (Div_{k-1} * w_1 + Ben_{k-1} * W_2)$$

Where:

- Div is the diversity similarity at a time k and a time $k - 1$. This value is calculated by the percentage difference of the amount of different agent types (identified by the service they offer) that are members of organisations. For example, having in one case 4 different agents in an organisation, and in another 5, the diversity similarity will be $4/5 = 0, 8$.
- Ben are the benefits similarity per time step at a time k and a time $k - 1$. This is calculated by the same method as above, but using the benefits per step instead of the number of different agents.
- w_n are the respective weights for the similarity values. For this case, the weight will be equal for every similarity value.

In the knowledge base, there must be an evaluation at a time $k + 1$ in order to estimate the future benefits given the current state.

To distinguish positive cases (when it seems the that goal can be fulfilled for the next time step) from negative ones (when the goal cannot be fulfilled), the algorithm will compare earning expectations with the benefits found in similar past cases from the knowledge base, reusing values from past cases.

5.1   Setup

The simulation environment has been developed in RePast[1]. RePast is an open source agent modelling toolkit developed in Java that provides different tools for tracking and displaying agent and environment values. The tests were done in a grid of 50x50 cells, with 500 different agents who can each offer one of the ten different services. The base earning for each service was fixed at 1, and the default duration time of an organisation was 15 time steps. It was tested over 10,000 time steps through three different experiments:

Experiment 1: Organisations start with a defined lifespan, which can be extended or reduced, with support from the algorithm.

Experiment 2: Organisations have an unlimited lifespan, so new organisations can never be dissolved. Since agents only get benefits when they are part of an organisation (from hypothesis 2), this could be a reasonable strategy to guarantee benefits for each agent at each time step once the agents have formed an

---

[1] http://repast.sourceforge.net

organisation, as opposed to the other experiments where, due the organisations dissolution, there will more often be agents without organisations wandering in the grid without getting benefits.

Experiment 3: Organisations have a fixed lifespan that cannot be modified, so they always dissolve when the expected deadline is reached.

5.2   Results

After ten runs of 10,000 steps for each experiment, the results for the average benefits at each step can be seen on Figure 4. After step 8,600 the benefits per step seem to stabilise and reach the 98% of the steady value, so for the conclusions and the results calculation, we will consider the average benefits from step 8,600 onward. The average benefits per step are in Table 4.

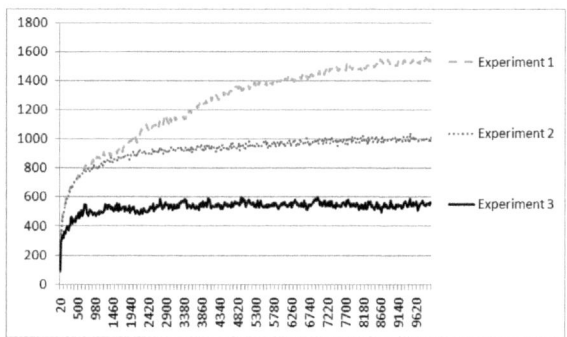

Fig. 4. Average organisation's benefits per step, 3 experiments, 10 runs, 10,000 steps each

Table 4. Average benefits per time step from the step 8600 onward

	Average Benefits	Std. Deviation
Experiment 1	1,530.04	12.69
Experiment 2	997.21	13.35
Experiment 3	543.77	16.26

There is a significant improvement when the algorithm enables identification of the unfeasibility dissolution cause for an organisation and when the organisation is allowed to modify its own lifespan (experiment 1). In Experiment 2, there are not many agents outside of an organisation, so most of them are getting benefits, but this does not guarantee that they are in the best possible organisation. They may do better to leave their organisationand not reap benefitsto search for new ones, instead of remaining part of a badly performing organisation. In this case, the unfeasibility dissolution cause not only helps to prevent organisations from operating when goals cannot be achieved, but it also helps to improve overall performance if goals are related to benefits.

6   Conclusions

VOs have been approached from different perspectives, but most of these approaches are focused mainly on the first phases of their lifecycle, (*formation* and *operation*), leaving the *dissolution* phase as an unresolved issue pending future work. The current paper makes an approach to this phase, presenting it as a two-step phase of (*activation* and *liquidation*), with two sub-states, (*pending dissolution* and *liquidation*).

One of the main contributions of this work is in the description of the causes of dissolution, besides VO goal fulfilment or the partners decision to dissolve. We also use elements from the dissolution process for supporting future VO formation, recording the resulting dissolution report from the *liquidation* step. This could be significant for future partner selection and for future identification of dissolution causes such as the unfeasibility cause, which can be identified by experience from past similar cases (see section 5).

Dissolution prevents the operation of badly performing or unnecessary organisations, and it can improve overall performance by correctly identifying those cases when an organisation should no longer operate.

Not all the dissolution causes are mandatory for dissolving the VO; some of them need the partners' approval for going on to the dissolution, as they could be also a cause for VO reconfiguration. The VO formation phase should consider new issues during the negotiation process, related to the norms for the *dissolution* phase.

Finally, the basis for the dissolution process was inspired by real-world organisations' dissolution; because of this, a normative framework is needed for supporting the dissolution process with a structure similar to that of real-life norms (the law at a higher level, and the organisations' statutes below). Although commercial law is used as an inspiration, this approach is not restricted to economically based organisations; assets, costs and benefits are not restricted to economical approaches, as they can be identified within the amount of workload inside a VO.

The *dissolution* phase is not trivial, so we offer an approach to it. Hopefully this work will fulfil the goal of emphasising its significance and provide a good reference for contributing to the formalisation of VO process. Future work will be focused on completing the formalisation of the dissolution phase and extend the work to other types of organisations.

References

1. Dignum, F., Dignum, V.: Towards an Agent-based Infrastructure to Support Virtual Organisations. In: PRO-VE '02: Proceedings of the IFIP TC5/WG5.5 Third Working Conference on Infrastructures for Virtual Enterprises, vol. 213, pp. 363–370 (2002)
2. Luck, M., McBurney, P., Shehory, O., Willmott, S.: Agent Technology: Enabling Next Generation Computing (A Roadmap for Agent Based Computing), AgentLink (2005)

3. Van Dyke, P.H.: Technologies for Virtual Enterprises. Agility Journal (1997)
4. Katzy, B., Zhang, C., Löh, H.: Reference Models for Virtual Organisations Virtual Organizations Systems and Practices, pp. 45–58. Springer, US (2005)
5. De Roure, D., Jennings, N.R., Shadbolt, N.R.: The Semantic Grid: Past, Present, and Future. Proceedings of the IEEE 93(3), 669–681 (2005)
6. Dignum, V., Dignum, F.: Modelling Agent Societies: Co-ordination Frameworks and Institutions. In: Brazdil, P.B., Jorge, A.M. (eds.) EPIA 2001. LNCS (LNAI), vol. 2258, pp. 7–21. Springer, Heidelberg (2001)
7. Ley de Sociedades Anónimas, Texto Refundido de la Ley de Sociedades Anónimas, Aprobado por el RDLeg 1564/1989, de 22 de diciembre, BOE del 27/12/1989 (1989)
8. Ley de Responsabilidad Limitada, Ley 2/1995, de 23 de marzo, BOE del 24/03/1995 (1995)
9. Esteva, M., Rodríguez-Aguilar, J.A., Sierra, C., Garcia, P., Arcos, J.L.: On the formal specification of electronic institutions. In: Sierra, C., Dignum, F.P.M. (eds.) AgentLink 2000. LNCS (LNAI), vol. 1991, pp. 126–147. Springer, Heidelberg (2001)
10. Camarinha-Matos, L.M., Afsarmanesh, H.: Virtual Enterprise Modeling and Support Infrastructures: Applying Multi-agent System Approaches. In: Luck, M., Mařík, V., Štěpánková, O., Trappl, R. (eds.) ACAI 2001 and EASSS 2001. LNCS (LNAI), vol. 2086, pp. 335–364. Springer, Heidelberg (2001)
11. Lopes Cardoso, H., Oliveira, E.: Virtual Enterprise Normative Framework Within Electronic Institutions. Engineering Societies in the Agents World V, 14–32 (2005)
12. Lopes Cardoso, H., Oliveira, E.: Electronic institutions for B2B: dynamic normative environments. Artificial Intelligence and Law 16(1), 107–128 (2007)
13. Lopes Cardoso, H., Oliveira, E.: A Contract Model for Electronic Institutions. In: Sichman, J.S., Padget, J., Ossowski, S., Noriega, P. (eds.) COIN 2007. LNCS (LNAI), vol. 4870, pp. 73–84. Springer, Heidelberg (2008)
14. Collier, B., DeMarco, T., Fearey, P.: A Defined Process For Project Postmortem Review. IEEE Software 13(4) (1996)

Playing with Agent Coordination Patterns in MAGE

Visara Urovi and Kostas Stathis

Department of Computer Science,
Royal Holloway, University of London, UK
{visara,kostas}@cs.rhul.ac.uk

Abstract. MAGE (Multi-Agent Game Environment) is a logic-based framework that uses games as a metaphor for representing complex agent activities within an artificial society. More specifically, MAGE seeks to (a) reuse existing computational techniques for norm-based interactions and (b) complement these techniques with a coordination component to support complex interactions. The reuse part of MAGE relates physical actions that happen in an agent environment to count as valid moves of a game representing the social environment of an application. The coordination part of MAGE supports the construction of composite games built from component sub-games and corresponds to coordination patterns that support complex activities built from sub-activities. To illustrate the MAGE approach, we discuss how to use the framework to specify the coordination patterns required to form a virtual organisation in the context of a service-oriented scenario.

1 Introduction

Early work in multi-agent system has focused on the representation of agent interaction construed in terms of communication protocols that agents can use to interact with each other. As these protocols standartise the way in which agents partake in social activities, more recent work has put the emphasis on normative concepts such as obligation, permission, and prohibition, amongst other, to specify the social rules that represent agent protocols (see [3,17]). However, despite the plethora of frameworks that support agent interactions about social concepts, there is relatively less work on how to represent systematically more complex activities that require agents to coordinate their actions when playing many protocols at the same time. There is, in other words, the need for computational frameworks that compose complex interactions and allow for their coordination.

Our specific motivation results from our participation in ARGUGRID [1], a research project that aims at providing a new model for programming a service Grid at a semantic, knowledge-based level of abstraction through the use of argumentative agent technology. Agents act on behalf of (a) users who specify abstract service requests and (b) providers who offer electronic services on the Grid. Agents interact with other agents by forming dynamic Virtual Organisations (VOs) in

J. Padget et al. (Eds.): COIN 2009, LNAI 6069, pp. 86–101, 2010.

order to enable the transformation of abstract user requests to concrete services that can be supported by the Grid. To guarantee that interactions in VOs are of a certain standard, agent-oriented provision of services must conform to service level agreements, while agent interaction more generally must be governed by electronic contracts. One of the requirements of ARGUGRID is that agreements and contracts need to be negotiated on the fly by agents, so there is the need to support protocols and workflows that enable the activities of VO creation, operation, and dissolution. One of the issues then becomes how to represent these complex activities at a knowledge-based level, suitable for argumentation-based agents to use as a framework to coordinate their interactions.

To manage agent coordination for VOs we present a logic-based framework that we call MAGE (Multi-Agent Game Environment). MAGE is based on the games metaphor for interactive systems [19,18] where the rules of a communication protocol between agents are viewed as the rules of an atomic game played amongst players, the speech acts uttered by agents represent the legal moves in the game, and the roles of agents in the interaction represent the roles of the players in the game. The game here is more like a dialogue game [16] to represent agent interactions from an observer's point of view and not from the strategy agents play, as in game theory [13].

The contribution of MAGE is that given the representation of atomic games it provides a computational framework in which atomic games can be composed into composite ones and provides a systematic framework for their coordination. To illustrate how the resulting framework can be applied to a practical application, we show how to apply it in an ARGUGRID scenario that specifies workflows in terms of agent protocols to support the creation of a VO and its relevant electronic contracts.

The rest of the paper is organised as follows. Section 2 presents the context of the problem and relates it to two kinds of games: atomic and compound. Atomic games and their specification are discussed in Section 3, while compound games and their specification are discussed in Section 4. Section 5 places our research in the context of existing literature and compares it to related work. We conclude with Section 6 where we also discuss our plans for future work.

2   ARGUGRID Games

We present a scenario that has motivated our work together with negotiation protocol used to negotiate services. We also discuss the link between the envisaged agent interactions and their representation as games. Once we have established this relation, we use it as the base of the MAGE computational framework developed in the next section.

2.1   The Earth Observation Scenario

This ARGUGRID scenario considers a government ministry official requiring data about the detection of an offshore *oil spill* [20]. The oil spill is an abstract and high-level goal that cannot be immediately satisfied by data within the ministry itself and requires the help of satellite companies that observe parts of the earth at different days. These companies publicise their services on a service Grid that is managed by agents. In this scenario a software agent takes the abstract request of the official and tries to instantiate it in a detailed set of services that can be invoked in sequence to provide the requested information. The scenario further assumes that satellite companies provide different services, each with different capabilities and costs, and one satellite may be more appropriate than another given certain conditions that the ministry sets. The official's software agent based on a set of preferences over the services requested, selects the suitable satellite companies and engages in a contract negotiation process with provider agents to create a VO that will instantiate the lower level services required to meet the official's request.

2.2   The Minimal Concession Protocol

Negotiation of contract terms in ARGUGRID uses a minimal concession protocol, with or without rewards, described in Dung et al [7], see Fig.1.

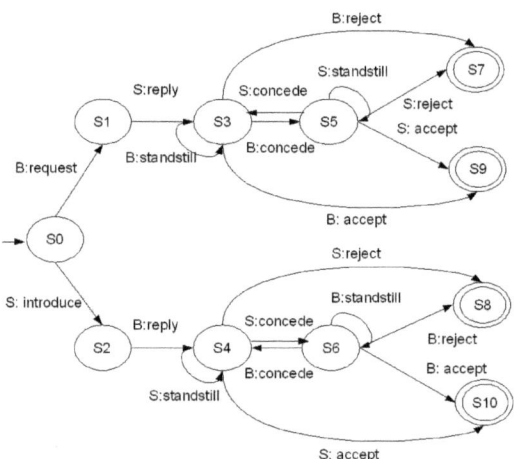

Fig. 1. The *Minimal Concession* protocol with Rewards [7]

The protocol provides the following set of locutions available to agents: *request, introduce, reply, concede, standstill, accept, reject*. The protocol assumes two agent roles, a *buyer* (B) and a *seller* (S). The protocol can start with an *introduce* move made by the seller or with a *request* move made by the buyer. These moves are used to respectively request or introduce an offer e.g. an oil spill detection service with some properties. Afterwards, a *reply* move can be made from the buyer to reply to an *introduce* move, or from a seller to reply to a *request* move. After this move, *standstill, reject* or *concede* an offer are all moves that can be made by any role. The *accept* move terminates successfully the protocol and the accepted offer is considered the value of the result of the game. Three consecutive *standstill* moves are considered as a *reject* move, which terminates the protocol with no agreement.

An important property of this protocol is that if two agents use the protocol in conjunction with a minimal concession strategy, then every negotiation terminates successfully and the minimal concession strategy is in symmetric Nash equilibrium [7]. A minimal concession strategy is used if the offered service/product does not match what is requested. An agent can concede on a property of the service/product when it is possible to do so. Afterwards the agent will expect the other agent to concede as well allowing the offer to get closer to match the request and vice versa. If the agent decides not to concede, it can standstill. The other agent will reply to a standstill with a concede locution if standstill is not a consecutive locution, otherwise it will standstill as well.

2.3   The VO Life-Cycle in ARGUGRID

The minimal concession protocol is only a component of the more complex activities that in ARGUGRID allow agents to form and participate in VOs, as shown in Fig. 2.

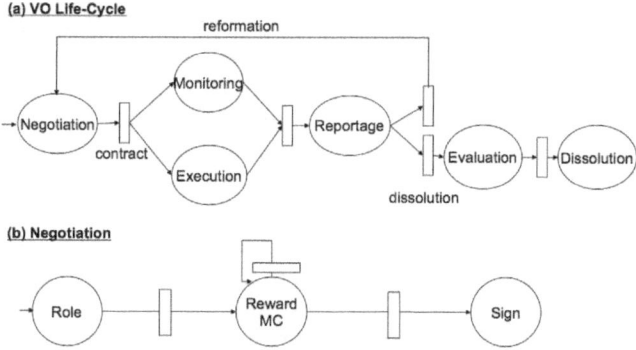

Fig. 2. Negotiation in the *VO Life-cycle* of ARGUGRID

Fig. 2(a) shows how by negotiating a successful contract starts the execution and monitoring activities of a VO. Issues raised by the monitoring or execution activities are reported and the VO must in this case be reformed via re-negotiation. If, however, reformation does not apply to these issues or if the execution has fulfilled the goals of the VO creation, the VO is dissolved by having its result being evaluated first. Activities in VOs may require further control-flows for sub-activities as shown in Fig. 2(b); this illustrates how the activity of negotiation is in fact a more complex activity that requires first to determine the roles of the agents in the VO, then negotiate the terms of the VO contract using the minimal concession protocol, and finally the complete contract must be signed by all relevant parties. The details for the remaining activities of monitoring, execution, reportage, evaluation, and dissolution, are beyond the scope of this work. In the remainder of this paper we focus on how to model the control flows of activities as a complex game exemplified by the negotiation activity.

2.4   VO Activities as Complex Games

The games metaphor was originally proposed to model human-computer interaction by Stathis and Sergot in [19] and was subsequently applied to formulate agent interaction protocols in [18]. We extend this model to support agent coordination patterns in ARGUGRID as games.

The basic unit of the games metaphor is the notion of an atomic game, which describes a set of rules about an initial state, a set of player roles, a set of game moves, the effects the moves have on the state, a specification of when a move is legal, a set of terminating states, and a set of results [18]. The minimal concession protocol described earlier seen as a game implies that the initial state of the protocol is the initial state of the game, the roles of the participating agents are the roles of the players, the protocol locutions are the game moves, the effects of locutions on the protocol state are the effects of moves on the state of the game, the preconditions of locutions are the valid moves, the final protocol states are the terminating states of the game, the set of protocol outcomes are the possible game results. The result of a game does not necessarily need to be zero-sum [13], by requiring a winner and a loser, but it can also give rise to a win/win or loose/loose situations.

To obtain complex interactions we combine atomic games to build more complex, composite games. An example of a complex interaction is the control flow of the Fig. 2(b), where we need to combine three different games: first the agents can play a *role negotiation* game to determine their roles, after establishing their roles, they play a *minimal concession with reward* game to agree on the terms of the contract, they can reiterate this game for as long they find an agreement and, finally, the *sign* game becomes active for the agents to sign the contract.

In a composite game we want to be able to parallelise, choose and synchronise atomic games. To capture these control-flow aspects of complex games we produce a coordination framework that allows us to coordinate complex interactions build from simpler ones. The resulting framework is then applied to support workflow coordination patterns. In general, the term *workflow* refers to the specification of a work procedure or a business process in a set of *atomic activities* and relations between them in order to coordinate the *participants* and the activities they need to perform [2]. The link with the definition of the workflow here is that the *participants* are the agents and the *atomic activities* are the atomic games. By relating atomic games as atomic activities we then use basic coordination patterns to enable agents to play more complex activities as complex games. We will see later how our example of the negotiation composite game (illustrated in Fig. 2(b)) will be defined as an aggregation of three patterns: a sequence, a conditional, and an iteration pattern.

3   Atomic Games in MAGE

Following earlier work on the games metaphor [19], we view communicative interactions within an agent society abstractly as game interactions [18]. As the rules of a game represent all valid evolutions of the game's state, we use the following logic program to describe the rules of a game:

```
game(State, Result)←
    terminating(State, Result).
game(State, Result)←
    not terminating(State, Result),
    valid(State, Move),
    effects(State, Move, NewState),
    game(NewState, Result).
```

To formulate a particular game we need to decide how to represent a game state, its initiating and terminating states, how players make valid moves, and how the effects of these moves change the current state to the next one until the terminating state is reached.

3.1   The State of Atomic Games

To represent the State of a game we use a term of the form Id@T, where Id is a unique identifier of a complex term describing the attributes of the state's configuration, and T is the system's time that uniquely identifies the actual evolutions of the complex term as a result of the interaction. The rationale behind this kind of representation is that in MAGE we acknowledge the fact that the interaction within a multi-agent system application can become quite complex. To cater for the complexities of practical applications we assume that complex terms have an underlying object-based data-model. To represent complex terms we use the syntax of C-Logic [5]. A term of the form:

```
min_concession:mc1 [
    parties⇒ {agent:a1 [role ⇒ seller], agent:a2 [role⇒buyer]},
    buyer_position ⇒ offer:o1 [price ⇒80, resolution⇒20, delivery ⇒2],
    seller_position ⇒ offer:o2 [price ⇒100, resolution⇒20, delivery ⇒2],
    standstill_count ⇒ 1,
    result ⇒ nil
]
```

is identified by mc1 denoting an instance of an object whose class is the minimal concession protocol with two participating agents a1 and a2, complex terms whose role attribute is seller and buyer respectively, where the buyer in the previous round has made an offer o1 (a complex term), while the seller has made another offer o2 (another complex term), there is one standstill move that has been encountered, and the result of the interaction is still incomplete as the value is still nil. Such a complex term has a first-order logic translation, see [5] for details.

3.2   State Evolution

The moves of the game are represented by complex terms too. The complex term below

speech_act:m1[actor ⇒ a1, act⇒introduce, offer ⇒ o1, role⇒ seller],

describes that the seller agent a1 utters introduce about an offer o1. Such moves are used as the contents of events that happen at a specific time. An assertion of the form happens(m1, 12), states that move m1 has happened at time 12. Such an event changes the state of a game.

holds_at(Id, Class, Attr, Val, T)←
  happens(E, Ti), Ti ≤ T,
  initiates(E, Id, Class, Attr, Val),
  not broken(Id, Class, Attr, Val, Ti, T).

broken(Id, Class, Attr, Val, Ti, Tn)←
  happens(E, Tj), Ti < Tj ≤Tn,
  terminates(E, Id, Class, Attr, Val).

holds_at(Id, Class, Attr, Val, T)←
  method(Class, Id, Attr, Val, Body),
  solve_at(Body, T).

attribute_of(Class, X, Type)←
  attribute(Class, X, Type).
attribute_of(Sub, X, Type)←
  is_a(Sub, Class),
  attribute_of(Class, X, Type).

instance_of(Id, Class, T)←
  happens(E, Ti), Ti ≤ T,
  assigns(E, Id, Class),
  not removed(Id, Class, Ti, T).
removed(Id, Class, Ti, Tn)←
  happens(E, Tj), Ti < Tj ≤ Tn,
  destroys(E, Id).

assigns(E, Id, Class)←
  is_a(Sub, Class),
  assigns(E, Id, Sub).

terminates(E, Id, Class, Attr, _)←
  attribute_of(Class, Attr, single),
  initiates(E, Id, Class, Attr, _).

terminates(E, Id, _, Attr, _)←
  destroys(E, Id).
terminates(E, Id, _, Attr, IdVal)←
  destroys(E, IdVal).

Fig. 3. A subset of the *Object-based Event Calculus* from [10]

We use the object-based event calculus (OEC) of Kesim and Sergot [10] to capture state changes of complex terms. A subset of the OEC is given in Fig. 3. The first two clauses derive the value of an attribute for a complex term holds at a specific time. The third clause describes how to represent derived attributes of object as method calls computed by means of a solve_at/2 meta-interpreter as specified in [11]. The fourth and fifth clauses support a monotonic inheritance of attributes for a class limited to the subset relation. The sixth and seventh clauses determine how to derive the instance of a class at a specific time. The effects of an event on a class is given by assignment assertions; the eighth clause states how any new instance of a class becomes a new instance of the super-classes. Finally, the ninth clause deletes single valued attributes that have been updated, while the tenth and eleventh clauses delete objects and dangling references.

3.3   Valid Moves and Their Effects

Before the event of a move being made in the state of the game, we must have a way to check that the move is valid. One simple definition is to make valid moves equivalent to the legal moves of the game:

valid(State, Move) ↔ legal(State, Move).

To specify valid moves, we specify when moves are legal. We specify when a request move is legal in the minimal concession protocol as:

legal(Id@T, Move) ←
    instance_of(Id, min_concession, T),
    speech_act:Move[actor ⇒ A, act⇒request, offer ⇒ Product, role⇒ buyer],
    holds_at(S, agent_of, A, T),
    holds_at(A, role, buyer, T).

Other definitions of valid moves are possible, for instance, Artikis et al [3] provide a more detailed account of valid moves in terms of social concepts such as obligations, permission and power. The important point here is that our framework can accommodate these for an application by providing a different definition of valid/2.

Once a set of moves is determined as valid, a new game state is brought about due to their effects. If we assume that the happening of such moves take only one unit of time, we can specify their effects as:

effects(Id@T, Moves, Id@NewT) ←
      forall(member(Move, Moves), add(happens(Move T))),
      NewT is T + 1.

In our representation of state, once an event has happened, its effects are added to the state implicitly, via inititiates/4 definitions that initiate new values for attributes of a state term, terminates/4 clauses that remove attribute values from a state term, and assigns/3 definitions for assigning new instances of terms. An example, of how new values are initiated for attributes for the minimal concession protocol is given below:

initiates(Ev, Id, seller_position, Offer)←
    happens(Ev, T),
    instance_of(Id, min_concession, T),
    Ev[act ⇒ Act, actor ⇒ Aid, role ⇒ seller, offer ⇒ Offer],
    changes_seller_position(Act).

changes_seller_position(introduce).
changes_seller_position(concede).
changes_seller_position(reply).

The above definition initiates the current position made by a seller to be stored
in the state of the game as a result of a request, reply or concede move. The
old offer is terminated and substituted by a new request because of the way the
object event calculus is specified (see the ninth clause in Fig. 3).

It is important to note that other specifications of effects/3 are possible depending on what assumptions we make about the duration of moves captured in
events. In addition, the state could be represented explicitly as a set of assertions
as in [18] rather that implicitly, with rules that define what holds in it, as in
MAGE. Both of these issues, however, are beyond the scope of this paper. It
suffices to say here that once a choice of state representation has been made, the
framework can accommodate it by suitably adjusting the effects/3 definition.

3.4   Initial and Final States of a Game

For the state of an atomic game to be created, the framework discussed so far
requires the assertion of an event that will first create the term via an assigns/3
assertion. The assertion:

assigns(Ev, Id, min_concession)←
    Ev[act ⇒ construct, protocol ⇒ min_concession, id ⇒ Id].

will allow the creation of an instance for the minimal concession protocol, which
can then be queried using the sixth clause of Fig. 3. To complete the instantiation
process we also need to specify the initial values for the attributes of the complex
term representing the minimal concession protocol. For this we need to define
separately the initiates/4 rules as the one below:

initiates(Ev, Id, party_of, Val)←
    Ev[act ⇒ construct, protocol ⇒ min_concession, parties ⇒ agent: Val].

Additional initiates/4 clauses are needed to define the whole of the initial state,
one for each attribute value.

The initial state of the game will evolve as a result of moves been made in
the state of a game. This state will eventually reach the final state from which
we can extract the game's result. We specify this via terminating/2 predicates.
For example, the definition:

```
terminating(Id@T, Result)←
    instance_of(Id, min_concession, T),
    holds_at(Id, result, Result, T),
    not Result==nil.
```

specifies the conditions under which the minimal concession protocol terminates
and at the same time returns the result.

4   Compound Games in MAGE

Compound games are complex games composed from simpler, possibly atomic,
sub-games. Based on our previous work in applying compound games to develop
multi-agent systems [18], in this section we show how to develop compound
games in the MAGE framework, with aim to support the coordination of complex
agent activities such as ARGUGRID workflows.

4.1   A Compound Game

To give an example of how sub-games will appear in the main game, consider
as an example the state of the VO negotiation in ARGUGRID, as specified in
Fig. 2.

```
vo_negotiation: Id [
  parties ⇒ {agent:a1, agent:a2, agent:a3},
  process ⇒ seq([
                roles:r1,
                if(r1[result⇒success], repeat(mcwr:r1, m1[result⇒exit])),
                if(m1[agreement⇒achieved], sign:s1)
  ])).
```

The above term states that the process of the negotiation is a sequence (seq)
of sub-games involving first a sub-game of roles game with identifier r1. This
game must be played, and if the result of the roles game is success, it means
that the roles of the agents in the VO have been agreed, and the workflow
must continue with repeatedly creating a minimal concession protocol mcwr
with identifier m1 and playing it until the result of this game is exit (meaning
that either an agreement has been achieved during the negotiation or the game
has been played more than a certain maximum and no agreement was achieved).
Only if the agreement attribute of m1 is set to achieved, the sign game with
identifier s1 is started and played to complete the negotiation process.

4.2   Coordination of Active Sub-games

The main issue to be considered in compound games is the coordination of moves
in active sub-games. We define coordination specifying the predicate active_at/3.
Using active sub-games, we can define valid moves in a complex game to include
all the valid moves in the active sub-games:

valid(Id@T, Move) ←active_at(Id, SubId, T), valid(SubId@T, Move).

For VO negotiation we define active subgames as follows:

active_at(Id, SubId, T)←
    instance_of(Id, neg, T),
    Id [process⇒Workflow],
    pattern(Workflow),
    runs(Id, Workflow, SubId, T).

Patterns in our framework are interpreted by a runs/4 predicate that parses the coordination structure and checks which sub-games are running. For the VO negotiation process three patterns are required: a sequence, an if-conditional, and a repeat loop, as specified below.

runs(G, seq([A|_]), A, T)←
    not pattern(A),
    not terminating(A@T,_).
runs(G, seq([A|B]), C, T)←
    not pattern(A),
    terminating(A@T,_),
    runs(G, seq(B), C, T).

runs(G, seq([A|B]), C, T)←
    pattern(A),
    (runs(G, A, C, T);
    runs(G, seq(B), C, T)).

runs(G, if(Id[Prop⇒Val], P), C, T)←
    holds_at(Id, Prop, Val, T),
    (pattern(P) →
    runs(G, P, C, T); C=P).
runs(G, repeat(P, Id[Prop⇒Val]), A, T)←
    not holds_at(Id, Prop, Val, T),
    runs(G, P, A, T).

pattern(P)← sequence(P).
pattern(P)← if_conditional(P).
pattern(P)← repeat_loop(P).

sequence(seq(_)).
if_conditional(if(_,_)).
repeat_loop(repeat(_,_)).

Note that the top-level game G is required as a parameter in the definition of runs/4 as a reference to the global variables of the interaction. Note also that the definition of the above patterns can be combined to form arbitrary complex structures, which is indicative of the expressive power of the framework.

More workflow primitives [21] can be specified in a similar manner. We show next an and_split pattern to illustrate how to support parallel composition. This pattern is specified as

and_split(A, Condition, Activities)

and states that after activity A is completed, if the Condition is true, then the set of Activities must be carried out in parallel. To support the parallel composition required for this coordination pattern, we define runs/3 as follows:

runs(G, and_split(A,_,_), A, T) ←
    not pattern(A),
    not terminating(A@T, _).
runs(G, and_split(A, Id[Prop ⇒Val], Activities), C, T)←
    terminating(A@T,_),
    holds_at(Id,Prop,Val,T),
    member(Activity,Activities),
    not terminating(Activity@T,_),
    (pattern(Activity) → runs(G,Activity,C,T); C=Activity).

We have formulated similarly the patterns for and_join, xor_split, and xor_join, but we cannot discuss them here due to lack of space. We plan to present these in future work.

4.3   Status of the Work

Implementation. We have built a prototype of MAGE that allows the deployment of a set of distributed objects in the GOLEM platform [4]. We call these objects *Game Calculators*. They are used by GOLEM agents to interact with each other and to coordinate their interactions, see Fig. 4. More specifically, GOLEM agents can call methods of a calculator object by means of actions performed in the environment. The content of such actions represents a move in the compound game. We believe this to be advantageous in two ways: (a) space and time decoupling, i.e. because game calculators are a mediation service, agents do not need to be in the same place at the same time in order to interact; and (b) we do not have to treat everything as an agent to develop an application.

To implement games, we link the internal part of the Game Calculator object with a TuCSoN tuple centre [14], a Linda-like extension of the concept of tuple space as a reactive logic based blackboard. The reason why we chose TuCSoN to implement Game Calculators is that it allows us to use a main tuple centre and distribute the state of a compound game in other tuple centres, each tuple centre

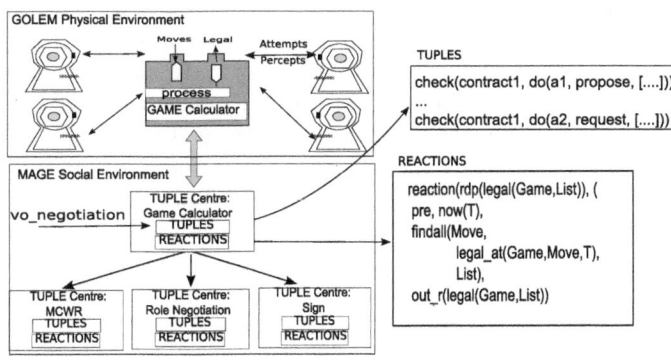

Fig. 4. Implementing MAGE using TuCSoN and GOLEM

could in principle map to atomic or compound sub-games. To support this we use a combination of the ReSPeCT language [14] and the OEC discussed here. A Game Calculator can be configured from an agent (either a coordinator agent or the agent who is interested to start the negotiation) to work as a specific compound game (such as VO negotiation). Further details of the implementation are beyond the scope of this work; we plan to present the implementation separately in future work.

Evaluation. MAGE is a mediation framework acting as a social environment that supports interactions between heterogeneous self-interested agents. We have developed MAGE so that it can work as a component-based social infrastructure for the GOLEM agent environment [4] to support practical applications. To do this we have tried to be flexible with the way norms are incorporated in the system using the notion of valid moves and we have focused on coordination. One of our contributions is that we have extended the games metaphor, presented in previous work, with the treatment of coordination patterns that this framework did not support before. From our experimentation with the minimal concession protocol in ARGUGRID VOs, a feature that we have found interesting is that we can specify the interaction with workflows at run-time, by keeping the same Game Calculator but changing the protocol and the workflow activities in a plug-and-play style. Moreover, using object-based indexing of events already available in the Event Calculus, we have experimented with interactions that give rise to approximately 1,000 events within a protocol, with acceptable performance. Again, we plan to discuss these details separately, as future work.

5 Related Work

The Electronic Institution (EI) approach [8] and the AMELI framework [9] uses organisational concepts to model the interaction of agents. Our framework is similar to EIs in the sense that their *scenes* are our atomic games and their *norms* as the rules that capture the valid moves for the agent as the game progresses. EIs also support a *performative structure* that enables a developer to define dependencies such as choice points, synchronization and parallelism mechanisms between scenes based on role flow policies among scenes specifying which paths can be followed by which agent's role. In our framework the EI performative structures are defined as compound games that structure atomic games, which can be coordinated by activity patterns. One of the differences of MAGE with AMELI is that we expect agents to interact via Game Calculators and we do not use mediating agents such as AMELI governors. An explicit feature of our approach is that the state of the interaction in a Game Calculator is easily inspectable, while in EIs agent playing specific roles need to communicate to build a coherent state. In addition we naturally support complex games that consist of complex sub-games, while EIs would require hierarchical performative structures and thus increase the complexity of the overall EI approach.

Artikis et al [3] propose a model for norm-governed multi-agent systems as executable specification of open agent societies. This work represents social constraints by making a clear distinction between physical capabilities, institutional power, permissions and sanctions to enforce policies. Social constrains are a sophisticated version for defining our valid moves of a game that captures the social state of the interaction. We too distinguish between possible actions happening in the environment supported by GOLEM, from social actions happening in MAGE, and we link them via physical objects that support agent coordination. As our focus is on coordination and as their emphasis is on normative concepts, the two approaches can be seen as complementary to each other, especially as they both use the Event Calculus as the underlying computational mechanism, even if we assume an object-based data-model. However, in our model we do not prove properties of interactions, which can be an extension of our work.

McBurney and Parson [12] present an abstract framework to represent complex dialogues as sequences of moves in a combination of dialogue games. Agents agree the game they need to play at a control layer, in our terms a compound game, and then play the protocol at an execution layer, in a our case a subgame. The framework admits combinations of different dialogue types that in our framework corresponds to the coordination of compound games. However, McBurney and Parson's dialogical games abstract away from the game state and they do not define the valid moves as a way of analysing the different kinds of pre-conditions and post-conditions on the state of the interactions. Instead their formalism is based on agents selecting and agreeing to play these dialogues. On the contrary our framework seeks to provide a computational mechanism for coordination in complex interactions that are construed as compound games.

Kesim et al [6] propose a framework to specify and execute workflows based on Event Calculus. In Kesim et al the Event Calculus is used to describe the specification and execution of activities in a workflow. The activities are assigned to agents using a coordinator agent that knows which agents can perform which activities. Like Kesim's work we use the EC to define workflows but we use games to dynamically define compositions of workflows. Similarly, Omicini et al [15] propose a model to distribute a workflow among different tuple centres (conceived as the entities that coordinate agent's activities) by linking tuple centres with linkability operators. In our approach we use the linkability of tuple centres as the coordination mechanism that the Game Calculator uses to start and terminate new games. We also provide a representational framework that can be used systematically to represent patterns of interactions, like workflows.

6 Conclusions and Future Works

We have presented MAGE, a logic-based framework that uses games as a metaphor for representing complex agent activities within an artificial society. We have illustrated how MAGE can reuse existing computational techniques for norm-based interactions and support their coordination. Using examples from the ARGUGRID project, we have illustrated how the reuse part of MAGE relates physical actions that happen in an agent environment to count as valid moves of a game representing the social environment of an application. Coordination in MAGE supports the construction of complex games built from component sub-games and corresponds to coordination patterns that support complex activities built from sub-activities. We have discussed how to use the framework to specify the coordination patterns required to form a virtual organisation in ARGUGRID.

Future work involves formulating the VO lifecycle of ARGUGRID in MAGE to build a library of reusable coordination patterns for similar applications.

References

1. ARGUmentantion as a foundation for the semantic GRID, ARGUGRID (2009), http://www.argugrid.eu/
2. Workflow Management Coalition (2009), http://www.wfmc.org/
3. Artikis, A., Sergot, M.J., Pitt, J.V.: Specifying Norm-Governed Computational Societies. ACM Trans. Comput. Log. 10(1) (2009)
4. Bromuri, S., Stathis, K.: Situating Cognitive Agents in GOLEM. In: Weyns, D., Brueckner, S.A., Demazeau, Y. (eds.) EEMMAS 2007. LNCS (LNAI), vol. 5049, pp. 115–134. Springer, Heidelberg (2008)
5. Chen, W., Warren, D.S.: C-logic of Complex Objects. In: PODS '89: Proceedings of the eighth ACM SIGACT-SIGMOD-SIGART symposium on Principles of database systems, pp. 369–378. ACM Press, New York (1989)
6. Cicekli, N.K., Yildirim, Y.: Formalizing Workflows Using the Event Calculus. In: Ibrahim, M., Küng, J., Revell, N. (eds.) DEXA 2000. LNCS, vol. 1873, pp. 222–231. Springer, Heidelberg (2000)
7. Dung, P.M., Thang, P.M., Toni, F.: Argument-based Decision Making and Negotiation in E-business: Contracting a Land Lease for a Computer Assembly Plant. In: Fisher, M., Sadri, F., Thielscher, M. (eds.) CLIMA IX. LNCS, vol. 5405, pp. 154–172. Springer, Heidelberg (2009)
8. Esteva, M., Rodríguez-Aguilar, J.A., Sierra, C., Garcia, P., Arcos, J.L.: On the formal specifications of electronic institutions. In: Sierra, C., Dignum, F.P.M. (eds.) AgentLink 2000. LNCS (LNAI), vol. 1991, pp. 126–147. Springer, Heidelberg (2001)
9. Esteva, M., Rosell, B., Rodriguez-Aguilar, J.A., Arcos, J.L.: Ameli: An agent-based middleware for electronic institutions. In: AAMAS '04: Proceedings of the Third International Joint Conference on Autonomous Agents and Multiagent Systems, Washington, DC, USA, pp. 236–243. IEEE Computer Society, Los Alamitos (2004)
10. Nihan Kesim, F., Sergot, M.: A Logic Programming Framework for Modeling Temporal Objects. IEEE Transactions on Knowledge and Data Engineering 8(5), 724–741 (1996)
11. Kesim, N.: Temporal Objects in Deductive Databases. PhD thesis, Imperial College (1993)
12. McBurney, P., Parsons, S.: Games that agents play: A formal framework for dialogues between autonomous agents. Journal of Logic, Language and Information 11(3), 315–334 (2002)
13. Myerson, R.B.: Game Theory: Analysis of Conflict. Harvard University Press, Cambridge (September 1997)
14. Omicini, A., Denti, E.: From Tuple Spaces to Tuple Centres. Science of Computer Programming 41(3), 277–294 (2001)
15. Omicini, A., Ricci, A., Zaghini, N.: Distributed workflow upon linkable coordination artifacts. In: Ciancarini, P., Wiklicky, H. (eds.) COORDINATION 2006. LNCS, vol. 4038, pp. 228–246. Springer, Heidelberg (2006)

16. Parsons, S., McBurney, P., Sklar, E., Wooldridge, M.: On the relevance of utter-ances in formal inter-agent dialogues. In: Durfee, E.H., Yokoo, M., Huhns, M.N., Shehory, O. (eds.) 6th International Joint Conference on Autonomous Agents and Multiagent Systems (AAMAS 2007), p. 240. IFAAMAS (2007)
17. Paschke, A., Bichler, M.: SLA Representation, Management and Enforcement. In: EEE '05: Proceedings of the 2005 IEEE International Conference on e-Technology, e-Commerce and e-Service (EEE'05) on e-Technology, e-Commerce and e-Service, Washington, DC, USA, pp. 158–163. IEEE Computer Society, Los Alamitos (2005)
18. Stathis, K.: A Game-based Architecture for Developing Interactive Components in Computational Logic. Journal of Functional and Logic Programming (5) (2000)
19. Stathis, K., Sergot, M.J.: Games as a Metaphor for Interactive Systems. In: HCI'96, People and Computers XI, pp. 19–33. Springer, Heidelberg (1996)
20. Toni, F.: E-business in ArguGRID. In: Veit, D.J., Altmann, J. (eds.) GECON 2007. LNCS, vol. 4685, pp. 164–169. Springer, Heidelberg (2007)
21. van der Aalst, W.M.P., Hofstede, A.t., Kiepuszewski, B., Barros, A.: Workflow patterns home page (2009), http://www.workflowpatterns.com/

A Model-Based Architecture for Organizational Interoperability in Open Multiagent Systems

Luciano R. Coutinho[1,*], Anarosa A. F. Brandão[2,**], Jaime S. Sichman[2,***],
Jomi F. Hübner[3,†], and Olivier Boissier[4,‡]

[1] DEINF/ CCET / UFMA - Avenida dos Portugueses, s/n
65085-580 São Luís, MA, Brazil
lrc@deinf.ufma.br
[2] LTI / EP / USP - Av. Prof. Luciano Gualberto, 158, trav. 3
05508-900 São Paulo, SP, Brazil
{anarosa.brandao,jaime.sichman}@poli.usp.br
[3] DAS / CTC / UFSC - PO Box 476
88040-900 Florianópolis, SC, Brazil
jomi@das.ufsc.br
[4] SMA / G2I / ENSM.SE - 158 Cours Fauriel
42023 Saint-Etienne Cedex, France
Olivier.Boissier@emse.fr

Abstract. In this paper, we report on MAORI, a Model-based Architecture for ORganizational Interoperability between agents and open MASs that were designed and implemented with heterogeneous organizational models/infrastructures. MAORI is structured along three layers: the Organizational Metamodels (OMM), the Model Transformations (M2M) and the Organizational Interoperability (ORI) layers. Building upon previous work, we focus on the rationale, design and implementation of the ORI layer.

1 Introduction

In the last few years, several organizational models [1,2,3,4] and infrastructures [5,6,7] were put forward for the engineering of organization-centered open multiagent systems (MASs) [8] . On the one hand, the availability of a wide range of diverse models and infrastructures has made the design and implementation of ordered open MASs feasible. On the other hand, such a diversity introduced an important new interoperability challenge for agent designers: how to deal with heterogeneous organizational models and infrastructures? Whenever an autonomous agent comes to enter some MAS it has to be able to interact with the other participants using a particular agent communication language as well as to understand received messages against a given domain ontology. Besides this, if the MAS was designed by following an organization-centered approach,

* Supported by FAPEMA, Brazil, grant 127/04 and CAPES, Brazil, grant 1511/06-8.
** Supported by CNPq, Brazil, grant 310087/2006-6.
*** Partially supported by CNPq, Brazil, grants 304605/2004-2, 482019/2004-2, 506881/2004-0.
† Supportedby ANR Project ForTrust (ANR-06-SETI-006).
‡ Partially supported by USP-COFECUB, grant 98/-4.

J. Padget et al. (Eds.): COIN 2009, LNAI 6069, pp. 102–113, 2010.
© Springer-Verlag Berlin Heidelberg 2010

the entering agent has also to be able to access a particular organizational infrastructure and to interpret its underlying organizational model. In this way, the agent design becomes tailored to a particular organizational approach and cannot be reused.

For instance, suppose that several e-business applications designed as open agent organizations are available on the Internet. Therefore, it is realistic to assume that these applications will be heterogeneous w.r.t. the organizational technology applied to build them. To put it in more concrete terms, suppose two agents organizations: one built upon the S-MOISE+ [6] organizational middleware and the other by using MADKIT [5] organizational platform. In this setup (and assuming a shared common agent communication language and domain ontology), the agent designers face the following problem: the native S-MOISE+ agents (based on the MOISE+ model [2]) do not interoperate with the MADKIT organizational infrastructure (based on the AGR model [1]), and vice-versa. Thus, it is not possible, for instance, to write an agent code that enter both e-business agent organizations in the search of products and/or services on behalf of its users. Such fact limits the S-MOISE+ and MADKIT agents actions' range which, in other turn, limits the idea of open MASs.

Given this problem, four approaches (at least) can be envisioned as candidate solutions [9]. The first one is to avoid the problem altogether by creating standards for organizational models and infrastructures (in a way similar to the FIPA standards for agent communication languages and platforms, or the W3C standards for writing ontologies). This approach solves the problem at the cost of imposing homogeneity and this sometimes is a high or even prohibitive cost (homogeneity can not be assumed in the case of legacy MASs). The second approach consists in conceiving an universal agent architecture able to function in all organizational infrastructures. This is an ambitious and technically challenging approach. Beyond an integrated view of organizational models, it requires the definition of a general organizational reasoning for the agent that could be specialized to each organizational infrastructure. The third approach comprises the delegation of the organizational reasoning needed to participate in an agent organization to middle-agents that "understand" the underlying organizational model and are able to function in the corresponding organizational infrastructure. This approach is technically feasible and it seems as an extension of the idea proposed by some organizational infrastructures (e.g., in AMELI [7] there is an internal active component called *governor* that helps external agents to reason about the structure and functioning of an e-institution). However, the basic drawback of this organizational middle-agent approach is that it turns the MAS in a semi-closed society [10] where the external agents have lost their organizational autonomy. The external agents do not "understand" the structure and functioning of the MAS and pass to react to the organizational requests coming from the middle-agent. Finally, the forth envisioned approach is to bridge the interfaces between the external agents and the organizational models/infrastructures of the MASs by means of some run-time interoperator middleware [11]. The basic function of such a middleware is to provide adapted copies of the state of some MAS (running on a source organizational model/infrastructure) on top of the target organizational models/infrastructures in which the external agents run. In this manner, the organizational interoperability problem is solved by translating a given agent organization (its running state) to the "language" (expected interface) of the external agents. Com-

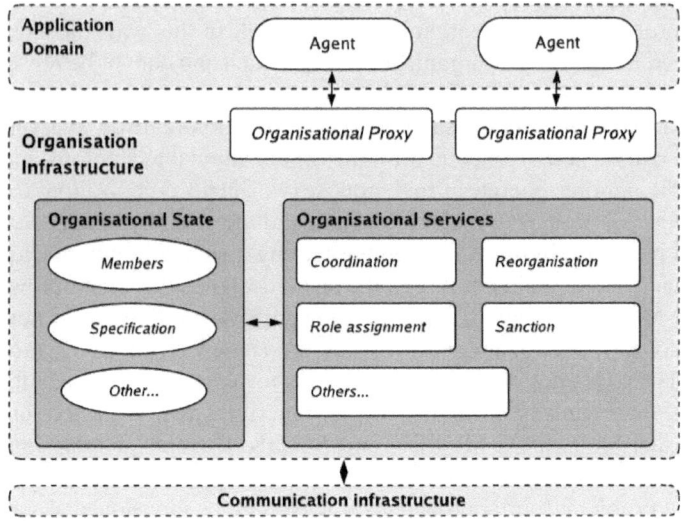

Fig. 1. Organization-centered open MAS

pared to the previous approaches, this last approach works with legacy MASs, does not requires a general organizational reasoning, and preserves the external agents' organizational autonomy. Nonetheless, its downside is that not all existing organizational models/infrastructure are full compatible (i.e., some present concepts/features that are not found in the other; or are found, but with some variations of meaning) and this can hinder the translations of the agent organization state.

In this paper, we present MAORI, a Model-based Architecture for ORganizational Interoperability between external agents and open MASs that were designed and implemented with heterogeneous organizational models/infrastructures. MAORI mainly follows the forth approach described in the previous paragraph. In order to tackle the issue of organizational models/infrastructures incompatibility, we also propose the use of organizational middle-agents (the third approach) to guide the external agents when its underlying organizational model/infrastructure cannot represent concepts or features found in the organizational model/infrastructure of the MAS.

The rest of the paper is structured as follows. Section 2 discuss some basic assumptions regarding the engineering of organization-centered open MASs. In section 3, an overview of MAORI is presented. The section 4 is dedicated to detail the top level organizational interoperability layer of MAORI. In section 5, some aspects of the implementation and validation of MAORI are described. In section 6, related work is discussed. In section 7, the main contributions and future directions are summarized.

2   Organization-Centered Open MASs

Following an organization-centered perspective [8], the engineering of an open MAS can be described as a process that starts with the creation of an *organizational specification*.

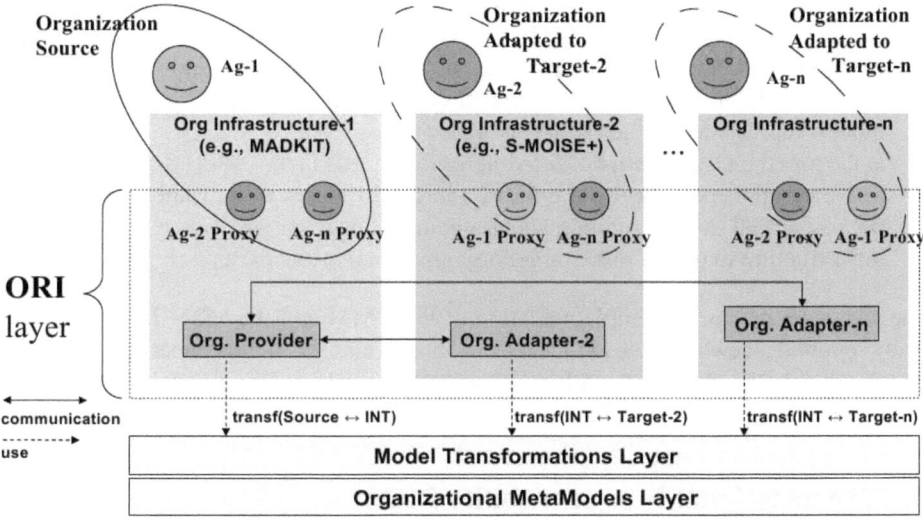

Fig. 2. MAORI overview

The organizational specification is written in conformance to an organizational model; it consists in an explicit computational representation of the desired patterns of joint activity that should occur inside the MAS in order to drive the agents interactions towards some desired purpose.

Once the organizational specification is done, it is used as the input to an organizational infrastructure. In general, the organizational infrastructure is supposed to interpret the specification and reify the organization of the MAS. In this respect, it maintains an internal organizational state of the MAS and offers to the agents an interface of organizational services. The list of the agents acting as members of the organization, what roles the agents are playing, what groups are active in the organization, among others, are some of the informations maintained in the organizational state. Some organizational services offered are: the global coordination of joint activity, role assignment requests/queries, sanctions, etc. These services are available to the participating agents by means of components called *organizational proxies*.

Finally, with the organizational infrastructure materializing the organization of the MAS, application domain agents (developed independently of the organization) can enter and interact inside it by accessing the available organizational services. This brief account is depicted in Figure 1.

3 MAORI

This section presents an overview of MAORI, our proposal for addressing the problem of organizational interoperability described in the Introduction. MAORI is structured along three main layers (Figure 2):

- at the bottom, the *Organizational Metamodels* (OMM) layer – in this layer, the existing organizational models are represented by means of explicit *metamodels*;
- in the middle, the *Model Transformations* (M2M) layer – the purpose of this layer is to provide an integrated view and transformations between the organizational models represented in the OMM layer;
- at the top, the *Organizational Interoperability* (ORI) layer – this layer is formed by active components that use the M2M and OMM layers to translate and adapt the organizational state of running agent organizations from one source organizational infrastructure to one or more target organizational infrastructures.

The rationale, design and implementation of the OMM and the M2M layers were already reported elsewhere (see [12] and [13]). In this manner, in this paper, we will bring into focus only the structure and functioning of the ORI layer and how it relates to the OMM and M2M layers.

4   Organizational Interoperability Layer

The Organizational Interoperability (ORI) layer function as an extension of the organizational infrastructures of MASs. It adds to each organizational infrastructure three basic components: *organization providers*, *organization adapters* and *agent proxies* (see Figure 2).

4.1   Providers and Adapters

Organizational providers are responsible for exporting the organizational state of running MASs. The exported state is called *source organization*. Organizational adapters are responsible for importing the organizational state of running MASs. An imported state is named *target* or *adapted organization*.

Imagine a scenario where an agent functions on a given organizational infrastructure and consider a MAS running on a different organizational infrastructure. If the agent wants to enter the MAS, an organizational adapter has to be instantiated in the organizational infrastructure of the entering agent. Initially, the responsibility of the adapter is to locate the appropriate organizational provider, establish a connection with it, ask for the organizational state and finally translate this organizational state to a target organization on top of the organizational infrastructure of the entering agent. In this way, for each MAS there will be one organizational provider. Connected to this provider, there will be several organizational adapters; one for each organizational infrastructure in which there are external heterogeneous agents.

In order to establish connections, the organizational providers and adapters must share a communication medium and protocol. The shared communication infrastructure is presented in the following. Some aspects of the communication protocol are discussed in section 4.3.

Organizational Interoperability Society. To describe the communication infrastructure, it helps to conceive of the organizational providers and adapters as internal agents

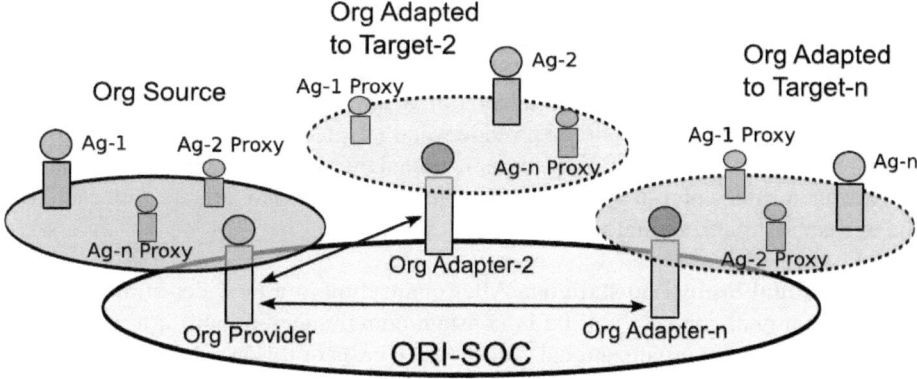

Fig. 3. Organizational Interoperability Society

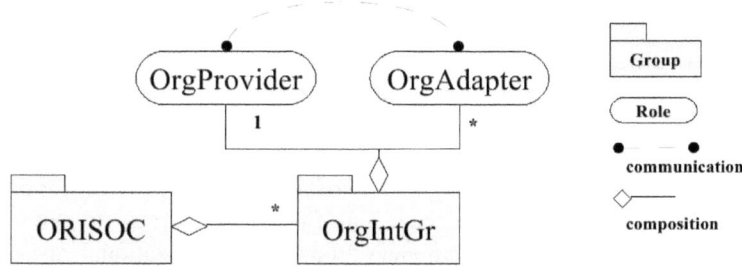

Fig. 4. MOISE+ structural specification for the ORISOC

that participate as members of an *Organizational Interoperability Society* (ORISOC, Figure 3). Thus, the ORI layer itself is conceived of as a MAS.

By following an organization-centered approach (sec. 2), the organization of the ORISOC can be represented by means of an organizational specification. The (structural part of the) organizational specification for the ORISOC is depicted in the diagram of Figure 4. The diagram is a MOISE+ structural specification. In it, ORISOC is represented as a super group formed by several sub groups (*OrgIntGr*). In each OrgIntGr, there is only one organizational provider and several organizational adapters; provider can communicate with adapters, and vice-versa; and, adapter cannot communicate with adapter. In this way, each OrgIntGr represents the inter-connection between one organizational provider with several organizational adapters (or one source organization being exported to several different target organizational infrastructures).

Once having represented the ORISOC in the form of an organizational specification, the major benefit is that available organizational infrastructures can be reused to implement it[1]. Following this way, the communication link between organizational providers and adapters will be provided by the (underlying communication infrastructure of the)

---

[1] In our prototype implementation (discussed in section 5) we have used the S-MOISE+ organizational infrastructure.

organizational infrastructure used. The localization of a given source organization will be reduced to a query for some OrgIntGr (issued by an adapter in the organizational infrastructure used to implement ORISOC). And, the act of connecting to a provider will simply mean the entering of an adapter in an appropriate OrgIntGr.

Summing up, the organizational providers and adapters are components that by one side interact with the internals of the organizational infrastructures, and that by the other side are agents that enter in an agent organization (ORISOC) to interact with each other and exchange organizational states.

Organizational State Translations. After connecting to a provider in the ORISOC, the organizational adapters will be in constant communication with it to synchronize the source and target organizational states. At the basis of this synchronization process are the M2M and OMM layers.

In the M2M layer, there is an integrated organizational metamodel [13]. This metamodel merges the concepts and structures present in all organizational models that compose the OMM layer [12]. The rationale of having an integrated metamodel is to minimize the number of transformations between n organizational metamodels. Therefore, when an organizational adapter asks the source organizational state to an organizational provider, the following occurs: (*i*) the organizational provider inspects the current organizational state and translate it (via the M2M layer) to an integrated format conforming to the integrated metamodel; (*ii*) the organizational adapter receives the result of the transformation and; (*iii*) the organizational adapter applies a transformation from the M2M layer that converts the received state from the integrated format to a format conforming to the organization metamodel of the target organizational infrastructure.

As discussed in the Introduction, sometimes the translation from the source organizational model to the target organizational model is not perfect and information is lost. When this occurs, a source organization cannot be completely expressed in the target infrastructure. Consequently, target agents are not able to reason about certain aspects of the organization. The use of special middle-agents called *agent proxies* are proposed to address this problem.

4.2   Agent Proxies

In the ORI layer, agent proxies are components representing agents situated in a remote organizational infrastructure. They serve two basic purposes.

Firstly, they are the starting point of messages forwarded from one infrastructure space to another. When an external agent enters in a MAS, it is expected that it communicates with other agents inside the MAS. However, if the agent that must receive a message is not physically running in the same infrastructure space, there must be a way to route the message to the recipient. In the ORI layer, this is achieved by the agent proxies. For every remote agent, the organizational provider (and the adapters) register an agent proxy. These proxies will be visible to the other agents as being local agents. When a message comes to an agent proxy, the proxy forwards it to the respective provider (or adapter). Then, the provider (or adapter) forwards the message to the adapter (or provider) that is running in the same infrastructure of the real receiver of the message. Finally, the adapter (or provider) sends the message to the receiver.

Secondly, the agent proxies can function as *guides* or *governors* for the remote agents. This occurs only in the case of the proxies in the provider side. Recalling, when the target organizational model cannot represent certain aspects of the source organizational model, the translation source/target loses information. Then, the proxies in the provider side will represent agents that are not able to reason about certain aspects of the organization. To ease this problem the agent proxy can assume the active role of guiding the remote agent in doing what have to be done inside the organization. The exact way of the conversation between remote proxy and external agent will be dictated by the source and target organizational models.

4.3   Organization Life-Cycle

This section describes some very basic events in the life-cycle of an agent organization and how the ORI layer deals with them. A common denominator in all organizational models, is that organizations are structured around roles that can be gathered in groups. In the sequel, it is discussed how the events of role adoption and group creation, which affect the organizational state of the MAS, are propagated along the ORI layer.

Role playing. Each organizational event can be triggered either on the side of the organizational provider or on the side of some adapter. For example, a request to play a role can be issued by an agent that is situated in the source organization or by a remote agent running on a target infrastructure.

In the first case, the protocol followed by the provider and the adapters to synchronize their state will be the following. Firstly, interacting with the infrastructure of the source organization, the organizational provider detects the assignment of a role to an agent on the source organization. Secondly, it gets the new source organizational state and translate it to the integrated format (via M2M layer). Thirdly, it broadcasts the new organizational state (in the integrated format) to all organizational adapters present in the same OrgIntGr. By their time, each adapter receives the new state and transforms it (via M2M layer) to an equivalent new state on top of the target infrastructure. In this manner, each new role assignment in the source organization is propagated from the ORI layer to the the target organizations. And so, every agent running on a target infrastructure gets to know about the new role assignment.

In the second case (when an agent requests to play a role in the adapter side), the protocol is a little more complex. Firstly, the organizational adapter notifies the organizational provider that an agent is requesting to play a role. Then, the provider forwards the request to the underlying organizational infrastructure for validation and execution. Upon receiving the role play request result, the organizational provider communicates it to the issuing adapter. After that, in the case of an accepted request, the organizational provider also broadcasts the new organizational state (translated to the integrated format) to all adapters present in the OrgIntGr. In this manner, each role request from the adapter side is firstly performed in the source organization an then propagated to all target organizations.

Group creation. The group creation event is dealt by the ORI layer in a way similar to that of the role adoption event. To avoid repetition of textual description, the dynamics of the ORI layer during a group creation event is depicted in the diagrams of Figure 5.

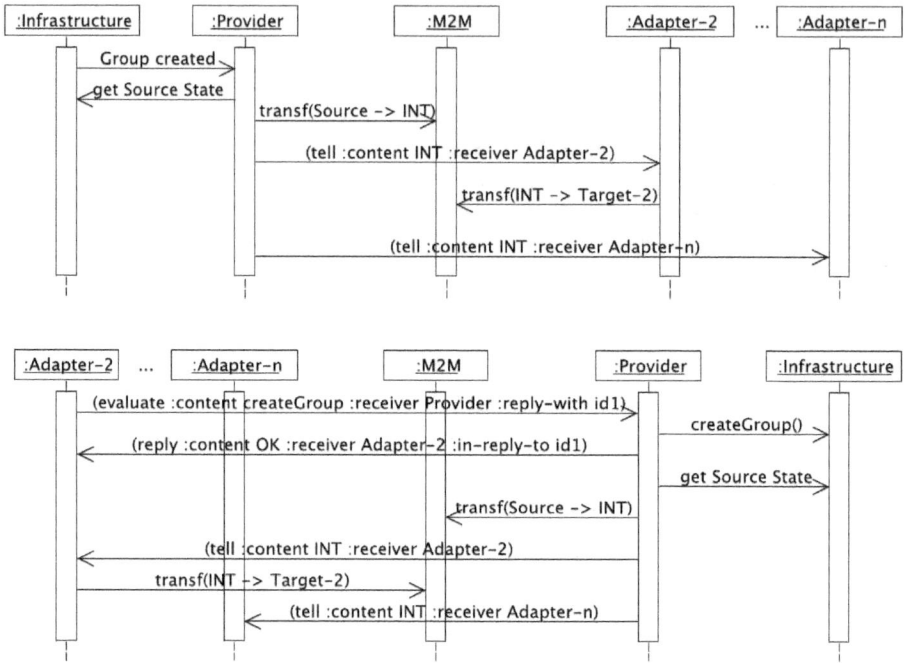

Fig. 5. Group creation event sequences

In the upper diagram, a group creation event happening in the organizational provider side is shown. Below, it is seen a group creation request taking place in the adapter side and its consequences.

The communications between the organizational provider and adapters occurs in the context of the ORISOC and, in the diagram, are expressed as KQML messages. The messages from the provider (or adapter) to the M2M layer are simple method invocation. Finally, the interaction between the organizational infrastructure and the provider (or the adapters) depends on the specific infrastructure. For instance, in the case of the MADKIT platform this interaction can be operationalized by a mechanism called *kernel hooks*. By using this mechanism, the provider (or adapter) can register itself with the kernel of the MADKIT platform and pass to listen/intercept the organizational events. As another example, in the case of S-MOISE+ infrastructure, the organization is controlled by a special agent called *OrgManager*. And, this agent can be contacted via KQML messages for the performance of organizational services.

5   Implementation and Validation

MAORI was fully implemented in the Java programming language. The OMM layer was automatically generated by using the Eclipse Modeling Framework (EMF)[2]. Regarding the M2M layer, it was first prototyped in the Atlas Transformation Language

---

[2] http://www.eclipse.org/modeling/emf/

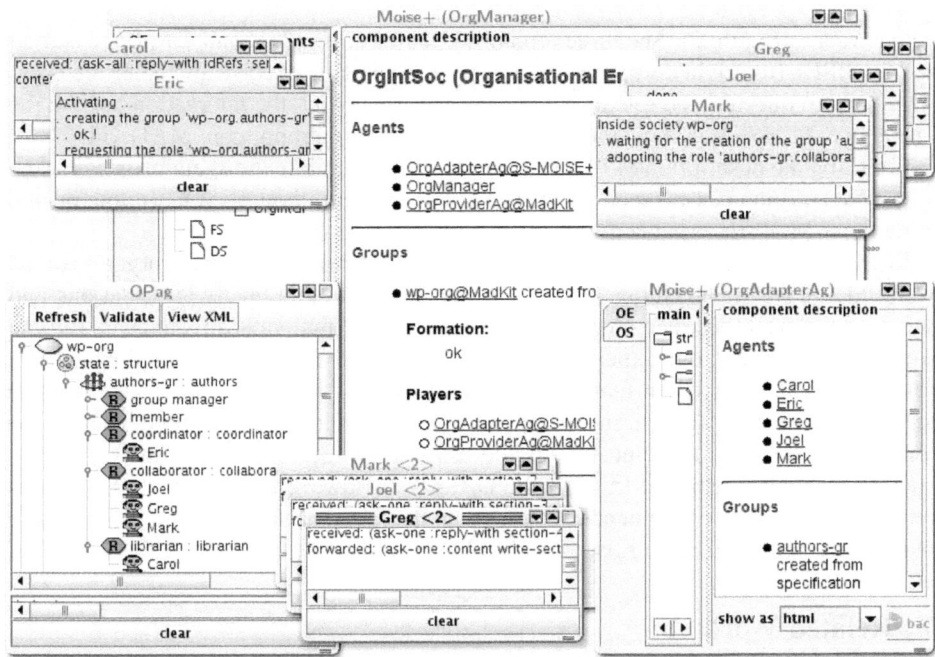

Fig. 6. The write paper agent organization

(ATL)[3] and then ported to Java for performance reasons. The ORI layer is currently implemented for three organizational infrastructures: the MADKIT, the S-MOISE+ and the J-MOISE+ infrastructures[4].

In order to assess the effectiveness and performance of MAORI, some prototype applications are being developed. One is the example of a group of agents that wants to write a paper and use for this purpose an explicit organization to help them to collaborate. The organization consists in a group composed of: one agent in the role of paper coordinator (who controls the process and writes the introduction and conclusion of the paper), one to five agents in the role of collaborators (who writes the paper sections) and one agent in the role of librarian (who compiles the bibliography).

Taking this simple example, some experiments were performed. One of them is illustrated in Figure 6. In this experiment we have an organization composed of five agents – one coordinator (Eric), three collaborators (Greg, Joel and Mark) and one librarian (Carol). Initially the organization is started in the MADKIT platform (the window seen on the bottom left corner of Figure 6). Also in MADKIT, the agents Eric and Carol are started (top left corner of Figure 6). After that, in the S-MOISE+ is started one organizational adapter that imports the organization (the window on the bottom

---

[3] http://www.eclipse.org/m2m/atl/

[4] Both S-MOISE+ and J-MOISE+ are based on the same organizational model, MOISE+ [2]; they differ in the agent platform below the organizational infrastructure; S-MOISE+ runs on an communication infrastructure called SACI; J-MOISE+ is based on the Jason (http://jason.sourceforge.net) interpreter for AgentSpeak. MADKIT uses the AGR model [1].

right corner of Figure 6). The three remaining agents (Greg, Joel and Carol) are started in S-MOISE+ (top right corner of Figure 6). These agents perceive and enter the organization by requesting the role of collaborator. At this point, the interaction begins: the agents in S-MOISE+ are now members of an organization running in MADKIT.

Finishing the description of Figure 6, on the bottom middle the agent proxies for the S-MOISE+ agents can be seen. And, in the background, the ORISOC (implemented using the S-MOISE+ organizational infrastructure) is shown.

Regarding the performance, the following can be noted. For each organizational event, the target organizations have to be updated. And this involve translations and message exchange between adapters and providers. At first sight this appears to be a bottleneck. However, our experiments have shown that the organizational events are not so frequent. They occur mainly during organization setup. The message exchange between the domain agents, on the other hand, are much more frequent. They occur constantly and every time a message is addressed to an agent running in another infrastructure, the message has to traverse the ORI layer. However, this cost can be seen as being inherent to the problem addressed, given the fact that the agents are supposed to be located in different platforms.

6   Related Work

Full interoperability across open MASs boundaries is a complex problem involving several complementary aspects: heterogeneous communication infrastructures, heterogeneous domain ontologies and heterogeneous organizational infrastructures are three of them. While the first two aspects have been discussed in the literature, to the best of our knowledge, we do not find other work that deals explicitly with matters of organizational interoperability.

In [11], the authors present the implementation of an RETSINA-OAA interoperator that to some extent performs a similar function of our ORI layer. However, the focus is different: in [11] the RETSINA-OAA interoperator deals with service location and communication interoperability between agent-centered platforms. Another work that focus on communication interoperability is [14].

Regarding domain interoperability, we can cite the work [15]. The authors propose an extension of the agent-centered platforms with a component called Platform Matcher Service (PMS) responsible for linking one organization to other similar organizations (w.r.t. the domain ontology). To this end, the PMS consults a Federation Directory Service (FDS) where several organizations having similar domain ontologies are registered.

7   Conclusion

In this paper, we approached the problem of making agents to effectively participate in open organizational-centered MASs when these agents and the MASs were conceived with different organizational models/infrastructures. Accordingly, the paper contribution was MAORI - a Model-based Architecture for Organizational Interoperability. MAORI addresses the problem by providing a middleware layer interconnecting organizational infrastructures. By means of MAORI, a running agent organization can be transported to several organizational infrastructures. Therefore, agents interpreting different organizational model can interact and form a large scale organizational-centered MAS.

Currently, MAORI is a prototype supporting the MADKIT, S-MOISE+ and J-MOISE+ organizational infrastructures. Our future work direction include developing agents organizations to test and improve the approach, designing a more efficient mechanism to synchronize the organizational states than the translation of the entire organizational state, and the implementation of MAORI in other organizational infrastructures.

References

1. Ferber, J., Gutknecht, O., Michel, F.: From agents to organizations: an organizational view of multi-agent systems. In: Giorgini, P., Müller, J.P., Odell, J.J. (eds.) AOSE 2003. LNCS, vol. 2935, pp. 214–230. Springer, Heidelberg (2004)
2. Hübner, J.F., Sichman, J.S., Boissier, O.: A model for the structural, functional, and deontic specification of organizations in multiagent systems. In: Bittencourt, G., Ramalho, G.L. (eds.) SBIA 2002. LNCS (LNAI), vol. 2507, pp. 118–128. Springer, Heidelberg (2002)
3. Esteva, M., Padget, J., Sierra, C.: Formalizing a language for institutions and norms. In: Meyer, J.-J.C., Tambe, M. (eds.) ATAL 2001. LNCS (LNAI), vol. 2333, pp. 348–366. Springer, Heidelberg (2002)
4. Dignum, V.: A model for organizational interaction: based on agents, founded in logic. PhD thesis, Utrecht University (2004)
5. Gutknecht, O., Ferber, J.: The MADKIT agent platform architecture. In: Wagner, T.A., Rana, O.F. (eds.) AA-WS 2000. LNCS (LNAI), vol. 1887, pp. 48–55. Springer, Heidelberg (2001)
6. Hübner, J.F., Sichman, J.S., Boissier, O.: S-moise+: A middleware for developing organised multi-agent systems. In: Int. Workshop on Organizations in MAS: From Organizations to Organization Oriented Programming (OOOP 2005), pp. 107–120 (2005)
7. Esteva, M., Rosell, B., Rodríguez-Aguilar, J.A., Arcos, J.L.: AMELI: an agent-based middleware for electronic institutions. In: AAMAS'04., vol. I, pp. 236–243. IEEE Press, Los Alamitos (2004)
8. Boissier, O., Hübner, J.F., Sichman, J.S.: Organisational oriented programming from closed to open organizations. In: O'Hare, G.M.P., Ricci, A., O'Grady, M.J., Dikenelli, O. (eds.) ESAW 2006. LNCS (LNAI), vol. 4457, pp. 86–105. Springer, Heidelberg (2007)
9. Magnin, L., Pham, V.T., Dury, A., Besson, N., Thiefaine, A.: Our guest agents are welcome to your agent platforms. In: ACM Symposium on Applied Computing 2002, pp. 107–114. ACM Press, New York (2002)
10. Davidsson, P.: Categories of artificial societies. In: Omicini, A., Petta, P., Tolksdorf, R. (eds.) ESAW 2001. LNCS (LNAI), vol. 2203, pp. 1–9. Springer, Heidelberg (2002)
11. Giampapa, J.A., Paolucci, M., Sycara, K.: Agent interoperation across multagent system boundaries. In: Fourth International Conference on Autonomous Agents, Agents 2000 (2000)
12. Coutinho, L., Sichman, J., Boissier, O.: Modelling Dimensions for Agent Organizations. In: Handbook of research on multi-agent systems: semantics and dynamics of organizational models. Information Science Reference, pp. 18–50 (2009)
13. Coutinho, L.R., Brandão, A.A.F., Sichman, J.S., Boissier, O.: Model-driven integration of organizational models. In: Luck, M., Gomez-Sanz, J.J. (eds.) AOSE'08. LNCS, vol. 5386, pp. 1–15. Springer, Heidelberg (2009)
14. Suguri, H., Kodama, E., Miyazaki, M., Kaji, I.: Assuring interoperability between heterogeneous multi-agent sytems with a gateway agent. In: 7th IEEE Int. Symp. on High Assurance Systems Engineering, HASE'02 (2002)
15. Erdur, R.C., Dikenelli, O., Seylan, I., Gürcan, Ö.: Semantically federating multi-agent organizations. In: Gleizes, M.-P., Omicini, A., Zambonelli, F. (eds.) ESAW 2004. LNCS (LNAI), vol. 3451, pp. 74–89. Springer, Heidelberg (2005)

A Normative Organisation Programming Language for Organisation Management Infrastructures

Jomi F. Hübner[1,2,*], Olivier Boissier[2], and Rafael H. Bordini[3]

[1] Department of Automation and Systems Engineering
Federal University of Santa Catarina
Florianópolis, Brazil
`jomi@das.ufsc.br`
[2] Ecole Nationale Supérieure des Mines
Saint Etienne, France
`{hubner,boissier}@emse.fr`
[3] Institute of Informatics
Federal University of Rio Grande do Sul
Porto Alegre, Brazil
`R.Bordini@inf.ufrgs.br`

Abstract. The Organisation Management Infrastructure (OMI) is an important component to support and monitor the execution of large-scale open multi-agent organisations whose functioning is described using high-level abstract modelling languages. Their interpretation by the OMI leads to heavy-weight programs, hindering flexibility and evolution. In this paper, we introduce a normative organisation programming language, called NOPL, based on a simple and elegant normative programming language. We show the suitability of these languages for programming the OMI of the $\mathcal{M}$OISE framework; in particular, we show how $\mathcal{M}$OISE's Organisation Modelling Language can be translated into NOPL. We also briefly describe how this all has been implemented on top of **ORA4MAS**, the artifact-based OMI for $\mathcal{M}$OISE.

1 Introduction

The use of organisational and normative concepts is widely accepted as a suitable approach for the design and implementation of Multi-Agent Systems (MAS) [1,5,4,13]. These concepts are useful for the design of MAS, so they are present in various different software engineering methodologies for MAS. However, they are also used at runtime to make agents aware of the organisation in which they take part, on one hand, and to support and monitor their activity to achieve the purpose of the organisation on the other hand. The Organisation Management Infrastructure (OMI) plays an important role in the realisation of the latter aspect. In this paper, we will focus on the OMI.

A recent trend in the development of OMIs is to provide languages that the MAS designer (human or artificial in the case of self-organisation) uses to write a program that will define the *organisational* functioning of the system, complementing agent programming languages that defines the *individual* functioning within the system. The

---

* Supported by the ANR in the ForTrust project (ANR-06-SETI-006).

J. Padget et al. (Eds.): COIN 2009, LNAI 6069, pp. 114–129, 2010.

former type of languages can focus on different aspects of the overall system, for example: structural aspects (roles and groups) [7], dialogical aspects [5], coordination aspects [18], and normative aspects [21,9]. The OMI is then responsible for interpreting such a language and providing corresponding services to the agents. For instance, in the case of $\mathcal{M}\text{OISE}^+$ [13], the designer can program a norm such as "an agent playing the role 'seller' is *obliged* to deliver some goods after being payed by the agent playing role 'buyer'". The OMI is responsible for identifying the activation of that obligation and to enforce the compliance to that norm by the agents playing the corresponding roles.

We are particularly interested in a flexible and adaptable implementation of OMIs. Such implementation is normally coded using an object-oriented programming language (e.g. Java). However, the exploratory stage of current OMI languages often requires changes in the implementation so that one can experiment with new features. The refactoring of the OMI for such experiments is usually an expensive task that we would like to simplify. Our work therefore addresses one of the main missing ingredients for the *practical* development of sophisticated multi-agent systems where the macro-level requires complex organisational and normative structures in the context of so many different views and approaches to such structures still being actively investigated by the MAS research community.

This problem is particularly complex for organisation models that consider elements with different natures such as groups, roles, common goals, and norms. These elements have their own life cycle, are closely related to each other, and are *constrained* by a set of properties (e.g. role compatibility and cardinality). Our proposal aims at expressing these different properties in a unified framework based on *norms*. The OMI is then mainly concerned with providing a uniform mechanism to interpret and manage the status of the normative expressions instead of specific mechanisms for each kind of constraints. However, we do not want to force the MAS designer to program the organisation using only norms. The designer should program their organisation using more suitable constructs. For example, using a role cardinality constructor to state "a classroom has one professor" instead of a norm like "it is prohibited that two agents play the role professor in the same classroom").

The solution presented in this paper is to translate a high-level language into another, simpler language. The problem of implementing the OMI is thereby reduced to a translation problem, which is usually much simpler and less error prone. We start from an organisational modelling language which is then automatically translated into a normative programming language. The language used by the MAS designer has more abstractions available (such as groups, roles, and global plans) than normative languages. More precisely, our starting language is the $\mathcal{M}\text{OISE}$ Organisation Modelling Language (OML — see Sec. 3) and our target language is the Normative Organisation Programming Language (NOPL — Sec. 4). NOPL is a particular class of a normative programming language presented and formalised in this paper (Sec. 2). All of this has been implemented on top of our previous work on OMI where an artifact-based approach, called ORA4MAS, was used (Sec. 5).

The main contributions of this paper are: (i) a normative programming language and its formalisation using operational semantics; (ii) the translation from an organisational language into the normative language; and (iii) an implemented artifact-based OMI that interprets the target normative language. These contributions are better discussed and placed in the context of the relevant literature in Sec. 6.

2   Normative Programming Language

Although several languages for norms are available (e.g. [21,23,9]), for this project we need a language that handles *obligations* and *regimentation*. While agents can have un-fulfilled obligations (and sanctions might take place later), regimentation is a preventive strategy of enforcement: agents are not capable of violating a regimented norm [14]. Regimentation is important for an OMI to allow situations where the designer wants to define norms that must always be followed because their violation represents a se-rious risk to the organisation.[1] Most existing languages consider either obligation or regimentation as enforcement strategies, and do not allow the designers (or the agents) to dynamically choose the best strategy for their application.

The language that we define is based on the following assumptions. (*i*) Permissions are defined by omission, as in the work in [10]. (*ii*) Prohibitions are represented either by regimentation or as an obligation for someone else to decide how to handle the situation. For example, consider the norm "it is prohibited to submit a paper with more than 6 pages". In case of regimentation of this norm, attempts to submit a paper with more than 6 pages will fail. In case this norm is not regimented, the designer has to define a norm such as "when a paper with more than 6 pages is submitted, the chair must decide whether to accept the submission or not". (*iii*) Sanctions are considered as an obligation (i.e. someone else is *obliged* to apply the sanction) and (*iv*) norms are consistent (either the programmer or the program generator are supposed to handle this issue). Thus, the language can be relatively simple, reduced to two main constructs: *obligation* and *regimentation*.

2.1   Syntax

Given the above requirements and simplifications, we introduce below a new Norma-tive Programming Language (NPL) (Fig. 1 contains the definition of its syntax).[2] A normative program *np* is composed of: (*i*) a set of facts and inference rules (following the syntax used in *Jason* [2]); and (*ii*) a set of norms. A NPL norm has the general form norm *id* : φ -> ψ, where *id* is a unique *identifier* of the norm; φ is a formula that determines the *activation condition* for the norm; and ψ is the *consequence* of the activation of the norm. Two types of norm consequences ψ are available:

- *fail* – fail(r): represents the case where the norm is regimented; argument r rep-resents the reason for the failure;

---

[1] The importance of regimentation is corroborated by relevant implementations of OMI, such as Madkit [7], S-$\mathcal{M}$OISE^{+} [12], and AMELI [6], which consider regimentation as a main enforcement mechanism.

[2] The non-terminals not included in the specification, *atom*, *id*, *var*, and *number*, correspond, respectively, to predicates, identifiers, variables, and numbers as used in Prolog.

np	: : = **"np"** *atom* "{" (*rule* | *norm*)* "}"
rule	: : = *atom* ["**:-**" *formula*] "**.**"
norm	: : = **"norm"** *id* "**:**" *formula* "**->**" (*fail* | *obl*) "**.**"
fail	: : = "**fail(**" *atom* "**)**"
obl	: : = "**obligation(**" (*var* | *id*) "**,**" *atom* "**,**" *formula* "**,**" *time* "**)**"

formula : : = *atom* \| "**not**" *formula* \| *atom* ("**&**" \| "**|**") *formula*

time   : : = "ˋ" ("**now**" \| *number* ("**second**" \| "**minute**" \| ...)) "ˋ"
          [("**+**" \| "**-**") *time*]

Fig. 1. EBNF of the NPL

- *obl* – obligation(a, r, g, d): represents the case where an obligation for some agent a is created. Argument r is the reason for the obligation (which has to include the id of the norm from which the obligation has been created); g is the formula that represents the obligation itself (a state of the world that the agent must try to bring about, i.e. a goal it has to achieve); and d is the deadline to fulfil the obligation.

A simple example to illustrate the language is given below; we used source code comments to explain the program.

```
np example {
a(1). a(2).                                        // facts
ok(X) :- a(A) & b(B) & A>B & X = A*B.  // rule
   // note that b/1 is not defined in the program;
   // it is a dynamic fact provided at run-time

// alice has 4 hours to achieve a value of X < 5
norm n1: ok(X) & X > 5
 -> obligation(alice,n1,ok(X) & X<5,`now`+`4 hours`).

// bob is obliged to sanction alice in case X > 10
norm n2: ok(X) & X > 10
 -> obligation(bob,n2,sanction(alice),`now`+`1 day`).

// example of regimented norm; X cannot be > 15
norm n3: ok(X) & X > 15 -> fail(n3(X)).
 }
```

As in other approaches (e.g. [8,22]), we have a static/declarative aspect of the norm (where norms are expressed in NPL resulting in a normative program) and a dynamic/operational aspect (where obligations are created for existing agents). We call the first aspect simply norm and the second obligation. An obligation has thus a run-time lifecycle. It is created when the activation condition φ of some norm n holds. The activation condition formula is used to instantiate the values of variables a, r, g, and d of the obligation to be created. Once created, the initial state of an obligation is *active* (Fig. 2). The state changes to *fulfilled* when agent a fulfils the norm's obligation g before the

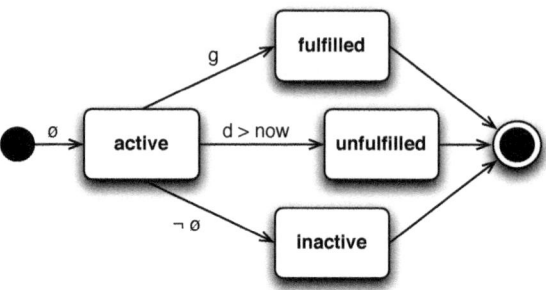

Fig. 2. State Transitions for Obligations

deadline d. The obligation state changes to *unfulfilled* when agent a does not fulfil obligation g before deadline d. As soon as the activation condition (φ) of the norm that created the obligation ceases to hold, the state changes to *inactive*. Note that a reference to the norm that led to the creation of the obligation is kept as part of the obligation itself (the r argument), and the activation condition of this norm must remain true for the obligation to stay active; only an active obligation will become either fulfilled or unfulfilled, eventually. Fig. 2 shows the obligation life-cycle.

2.2   Semantics

We now give semantics to NPL using the well known structural operational semantics approach [17].

A program in NPL is essentially a set of norms where each norm is given according to the grammar in Fig. 1; it can also contain a set of initial facts and inference rules specific to the program's domain (all according to the grammar of the NPL language). The normative system operates in conjunction with an agent execution system; the former is constantly fed by the latter with "facts" which, possibly together with the domain rules, express the current state of the execution system. Any change in such facts leads to a potential change in the state of the normative system, and the execution system checks whether the normative system is still in a sound state before carrying out particular execution steps; similarly, it can have access to current obligations generated by the normative system. The overall system's clock also causes potential changes in the state of the transition system by changing the time component of its configuration.

As we use operational semantics to give semantics to the normative programming language (i.e. the language used to program the normative system specifically), we first need to define a configuration of the transition system that will be defined through the semantic rules presented later. A configuration of our normative system, giving semantics to NPL, is a tuple $\langle F, N, \top, OS, t \rangle$ where:

- F is a set of facts received from the execution system and possibly rules expressing domain knowledge. The former works as a form of input from the OMI to the normative interpreter. Each formula $f \in F$ is, as explained earlier, an atomic first order formula or a Horn clause.

- N is a set of norms, where each norm $n \in N$ is a norm in the syntax defined for *norm* in the grammar in Fig. 1.
- The state of the normative system is either a sound state denoted by $\top$ or a failure state denoted by $\bot$; the latter is caused by *regimentation* through the `fail(_)` language construct within norms. This is accessible to the agent execution system which prevents the execution of the action that would lead to the facts causing the failure state, and rolls back the facts about the state of the execution system.
- OS is a set of obligations, each accompanied by its current state; each element $os \in OS$ is of the form $\langle o, ost \rangle$ where o is an obligation, again according to the syntax for obligations given in Fig. 1, and $ost \in \{$**active, fulfilled, unfulfilled, inactive**$\}$ (the possible states of an obligation). This is also of interest to the agent execution system and thus accessible to it.
- t is the current time which is automatically changed by the underlying execution system, using a discrete, linear notion of time. For the sake of simplicity, it is assumed that all rules that could apply at a given moment in time are actually applied before the system changes the state to the next time.

Given a normative program P — which is, remember, a set of facts and rules (P_F) and a set of norms (P_N) written in NPL — the initial configuration of the normative system (before the system execution starts) is $\langle P_F, P_N, \top, \emptyset, 0 \rangle$.

In the semantic rules, we use the notation T_c to denote the component c of tuple T. The semantic rules are as follows.

Norms. The rule below formalises *regimentation*: when any norm n becomes active — i.e. its *condition* component holds in the current state — and its *consequence* is `fail(_)`, we move to a configuration where the normative state is no longer sound but a failure state ($\bot$). Note that we use n_φ to refer to the condition part of norm n (the formula between "$:$" and "$->$" in NPL's syntax) and n_ψ to refer to the consequence part of n (the formula after "$->$").

$$\frac{n \in N \qquad F \models n_\varphi \qquad n_\psi = \texttt{fail(\_)}}{\langle F, N, \top, OS, t \rangle \longrightarrow \langle F, N, \bot, OS, t \rangle} \quad \textbf{(Regim)}$$

The underlying execution system, after realising a failure state caused by Rule **Regim** above, needs to ensure the facts are rolled back to the previously consistent state, which will make the following rule apply.

$$\frac{\forall n \in N.(F \models n_\varphi \Rightarrow n_\psi \neq \texttt{fail(\_)})}{\langle F, N, \bot, OS, t \rangle \longrightarrow \langle F, N, \top, OS, t \rangle} \quad \textbf{(Consist)}$$

The next rule is similar to Rule **Regim** but instead of failure, the consequence is the creation of an obligation. In the rule, m.g.u. means "most general unifier" as in Prolog-like unification; the notation $t\theta$ means the application of the variable substitution function θ to formula t. Note that we require that the deadlines of newly created obligations are not yet past. The notation $\overset{\text{obl}}{=}$ is used for equality of obligations, which ignores the deadline in the comparison. That is, we define that an obligation $obligation(a, r, g, d)$ is equals to an obligation $obligation(a', r', g', d')$ if and only if $a = a'$, $r = r'$, and $g = g'$. Because of this, Rule **Oblig** does not allow the creation of the same obligation with two different deadlines. Note however that if there already exists an equal obligation but it has become inactive, this does not prevent the creation of the new obligation.

$$\frac{n \in N \quad F \models n_\varphi \quad n_\psi = o \quad o\theta_d > t \\ \neg\exists\langle o', ost\rangle \in OS . (o' \overset{\mathrm{obl}}{=} o\theta \wedge ost \neq \mathbf{inactive})}{\langle F, N, \top, OS, t\rangle \longrightarrow \langle F, N, \top, OS \cup \langle o\theta, \mathbf{active}\rangle, t\rangle} \quad \textbf{(Oblig)}$$

where θ is the m.g.u. such that $F \models o\theta$

Obligations. Recall that an NPL obligation has the general form obligation(a, r, g, d). With a slight abuse of notation, we shall use o_a to refer to the agent that has the obligation o; o_r to refer to the reason for obligation o; o_g to refer to the state of the world that agent o_a is obliged to achieve (the *goal* the agent should adopt); and o_d to refer to the deadline for the agent to do so. An important aspect of the obligation syntax is that the NPL parser always ensures that the programmer used the norm's id as predicate symbol in o_r and so in the semantics, when we say o_r, we are actually referring to the activation condition n_φ of the norm used to create the obligation.

Rule **Fulfil** says that the state of an active obligation o should be changed to **fulfilled** if the state of the world o_g that the agent agent was obliged to achieve has already been achieved (i.e. the domain rules and the facts from the underlying execution system imply g). Note however that such state must have been achieved *within the deadline*.

$$\frac{os \in OS \quad os = \langle o, \mathbf{active}\rangle \quad F \models o_g \quad o_d \geq t}{\langle F, N, \top, OS, t\rangle \longrightarrow \langle F, N, \top, (OS \setminus \{os\}) \cup \{\langle o, \mathbf{fulfilled}\rangle\}, t\rangle} \quad \textbf{(Fulfil)}$$

Rule **Unfulfil** says that the state of an *active obligation* o should be changed to **unfulfilled** if the deadline is already past; note that the rule above would have changed the status to **fulfilled** so the obligation would no longer be active if it had been achieved in time.

$$\frac{os \in OS \quad os = \langle o, \mathbf{active}\rangle \quad o_d < t}{\langle F, N, \top, OS, t\rangle \longrightarrow \langle F, N, \top, (OS \setminus \{os\}) \cup \{\langle o, \mathbf{unfulfilled}\rangle\}, t\rangle} \quad \textbf{(Unfulfil)}$$

Rule **Inactive** says that the state of an active obligation o should be changed to **inactive** if the reason (i.e. motivation) for the obligation no longer holds in the current system state reflected in F.

$$\frac{os \in OS \quad os = \langle o, \mathbf{active}\rangle \quad F \not\models o_r}{\langle F, N, \top, OS, t\rangle \longrightarrow \langle F, N, \top, (OS \setminus \{os\}) \cup \{\langle o, \mathbf{inactive}\rangle\}, t\rangle} \quad \textbf{(Inactive)}$$

Algorithm 1 shows an NPL interpreter, which makes it easier to understand the normative programming language for those not familiar with structural operational semantics.

Algorithm 1. NPL Interpreting Algorithm

```
1: for all norms n in N do
2:    if F ⊨ nᵩ then
3:       if nᵩ = fail {regimentation} then
4:          return fail
5:       else
6:          if nᵩ ∉ OS then
7:             add nᵩθ to OS
8:             where θ is the m.g.u. such that F ⊨ nᵩθ
9: for all obligations ⟨o, ost⟩ ∈ OS do
10:   if ost = active and F ⊨ oₒ and o_d ≥ t then
11:      change ost to fulfilled
12:   if ost = active and o_d < t then
13:      change ost to unfulfilled
14:   if ost = active and F ⊭ oᵣ then
15:      change ost to inactive
16:   if ost = inactive and F ⊨ oᵣ then
17:      change ost to active
```

3 $\mathcal{M}$OISE Organisational Modelling Language

The $\mathcal{M}$OISE framework includes an organisational modelling language (OML) that explicitly decomposes the specification of organisation into structural, functional, and normative dimensions [13]. The structural dimension specifies the *roles*, *groups*, and *links* of the organisation. The definition of roles states that when an agent chooses to play some role in a group, it is accepting some behavioural constraints and rights related to this role. The functional dimension specifies how the *global collective goals* should be achieved, i.e. how these goals are decomposed (within global *plans*), grouped in coherent sets (through *missions*) to be distributed among the agents. The decomposition of global goals results in a goal tree, called *scheme*, where the leaf-goals can be achieved individually by the agents. The normative dimension is added in order to bind the structural dimension with the functional one by means of the specification of the roles' *permissions* and *obligations* within missions. When an agent chooses to play some role in a group, it commits to these permissions and obligations.

As an illustrative and simple example of an organisation specified using $\mathcal{M}$OISE$^+$, we consider agents that aim at writing a paper together and therefore there is an organisational specification to help them collaborate. Due to lack of space, we will focus on the functional and normative dimensions in the remainder of this paper. For the structure of the organisation, it is enough to know that there is only one group (`wpgroup`) where two roles (*editor* and *writer*) can be played. To coordinate the achievement of the goal of writing a paper, a scheme is defined in the functional specification of the organisation (Fig. 3(a)). In this scheme, a draft version of the paper has to be written first (identified by the goal *fdv* in Fig. 3(a)). This goal is decomposed into three sub-goals: writing a title, an abstract, and the section titles; the sub-goals have to be achieved in this very sequence. Other goals, such as *finish*, have sub-goals that can be achieved in parallel. The specification also includes a "time-to-fulfil" (TTF) attribute for goals indicating how much time an agent has to achieve the goal. The goals of this scheme are distributed in three missions which have specific cardinalities (see Fig. 3(c)): the mission $mMan$ is for the general management of the process (one and only one agent must commit to it), mission $mCol$ is for the collaboration in writing the paper's content (from one to five agents can commit to it), and mission $mBib$ is for gathering the references for the paper (one and only one agent must commit to it). A mission defines all goals an agent commits to when participating in the execution of a scheme; for example, a commitment to mission $mMan$ is effectively a commitment to achieve four goals of the scheme. Goals without an assigned mission (e.g. *fdv*) are satisfied by the achievement of their sub-goals.

The normative specification relates roles to missions (see Table 1). For example, norm n2 states that any agent playing the role *writer* has one day to commit to mission $mCol$. Designers can also define their own application-dependent conditions (as in norms n4–n6). Norms n4 and n5 define sanction and reward strategies for conformance and violation of norms n2 and n3 respectively. Norm n5 can be read as "the agent playing role 'editor' has 3 hours to commit to mission mr when norm n3 is fulfilled". Once committed to mission mr, the editor has to achieve the goal *reward*. Note that a norm in $\mathcal{M}$OISE is always an obligation or permission to commit to a mission. Goals are therefore indirectly linked to roles since a mission is a set of goals.

Table 1. Normative Specification for the Paper Writing Example

id	condition	role	type	mission	TTF
n1		editor	per	$mMan$	–
n2		writer	obl	$mCol$	1 day
n3		writer	obl	$mBib$	1 day
n4	violation(n2)	editor	obl	ms	3 hours
n5	conformance(n3)	editor	obl	mr	3 hours
n6	#mc	editor	obl	ms	1 hour

#mc stands for the condition "more agents committed to a mission than permitted by the mission cardinality".

4   Normative Organisation Programming Language

The NOPL is a particular class of NPL programs applied to $\mathcal{M}$OISE. The syntax and semantics are the same as presented in Sec. 2, but the set of facts, rules, and norms are specific to the $\mathcal{M}$OISE model and the organisational artifacts presented in Sec. 5. The main idea is that an Organisational Specification (OS) is translated into various different programs in NOPL; such programs then define the management of norms for groups and schemes. In this section we consider only the programs generated for *schemes*.

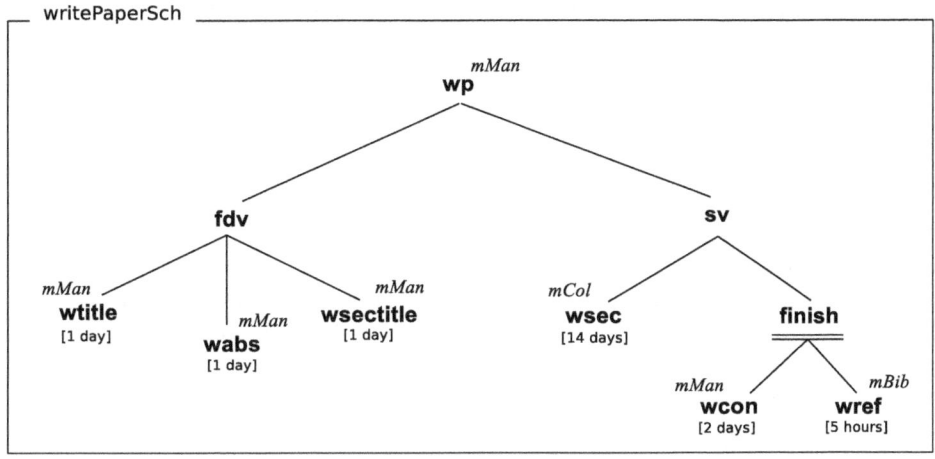

(a) Paper Writing Scheme

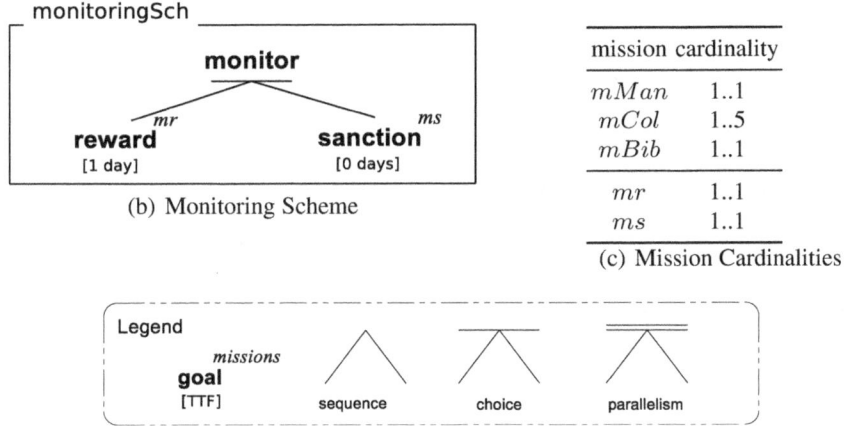

(b) Monitoring Scheme

mission	cardinality
$mMan$	1..1
$mCol$	1..5
$mBib$	1..1
mr	1..1
ms	1..1

(c) Mission Cardinalities

Legend

goal *missions* [TTF]	$\triangle$ sequence	$\overline{\triangle}$ choice	$\overline{\overline{\triangle}}$ parallelism

Fig. 3. Functional Specification for the Paper Writing Example

4.1 Facts

For scheme programs, the following facts, defined in the OS, are considered:

- scheme_mission(m, min, max): is a fact that defines the cardinality of a mission (e.g. scheme_mission(mCol,1,5)).
- goal(m, g, pre-$cond$, 'ttf'): is a fact that defines the arguments for a goal g: its mission, pre-conditions, and TTF (e.g. goal(mMan,wsec,[wcon],'2 days')).

The NOPL also defines some dynamic facts that represent the current state of the organisation and will be provided by the artifact that manages the scheme instance:

- plays(a, ρ, gr): agent a plays the role ρ in the group instance gr.

- responsible(*gr*,*s*): the group instance *gr* is responsible for the missions of scheme instance *s*.
- committed(*a*,*m*,*s*): agent *a* is committed to mission *m* in scheme *s*.
- achieved(*s*,*g*,*a*): goal *g* in scheme *s* has been achieved by agent *a*.

4.2 Rules

Besides facts, we define some rules that are useful for the NOPL programs. The rules are used to infer the state of the scheme (e.g. whether it is well-formed) and goals (e.g. whether it is ready to be achieved or not). Note that the semantics of *well-formed* and *ready to be achieved* are formally given by these rules. As an example, some such rules are listed below. Although the rule well_formed is specific for the paper writing scheme, the others are generic.

```
// number of players of a mission M in scheme S
mplayers(M,S,V)  :- .count(committed(_,M,S),V).

// status of a scheme S
well_formed(S)  :-
 mplayers(mBib,S,V1) & V1 >= 1 & V1 <= 1 &
 mplayers(mCol,S,V2) & V2 >= 1 & V2 <= 5 &
 mplayers(mMan,S,V3) & V3 >= 1 & V3 <= 1.

// ready goals: all pre-conditions have been achieved
ready(S,G)  :-  goal(_, G, PCG, _) & all_achieved(S,PCG).

all_achieved(_,[]).
all_achieved(S,[G|T]) :- achieved(S,G,_) & all_achieved(S,T).
```

4.3 Norms

We have three classes of norms in NOPL: norms for goals, norms for properties, and domain norms (which are explicitly stated in the normative specification). For the first class, we have only the following norm that handles obligations to achieve goals:

```
// agents are obliged to fulfil their ready goals
norm ngoal: committed(A,M,S) & goal(M,G,_,D) &
            well_formed(S) & ready(S,G)
 -> obligation(A,ngoal,achieved(S,G,A),'now' + D).
```

This norm can be read as "when an agent A: (1) is committed to a mission M that (2) includes a goal G, and (3) the mission's scheme is well-formed, and (4) the goal is ready, then agent A is obliged to achieve the goal G before the deadline for the goal". This norm gives precise semantics for the notion of *commitment* in $\mathcal{M}$OISE framework. It also illustrates the advantage of using a translation to implement the OMI instead of an object oriented programming language. For example, if some application or experiment requires a semantics of commitment where the agent is obliged to achieve the goal even if the scheme is not well-formed, it is simply a matter of changing the translation to a norm that does not include the `well_formed(S)` predicate in the activation condition of the norm. One could even conceive an application using schemes being managed by different NOPL programs (i.e. each scheme translated differently).

For the second class of norms, only the mission cardinality property is considered in this paper since other properties are handled in a similar way. In the case of mission cardinality, the norm has to define the consequences of a circumstance where there are more agents committed to a mission than permitted in the scheme specification. As presented in Sec. 2, two kinds of consequences are possible, obligation and regimentation, and the designer chooses one or the other when writing the OS. Regimentation is the default consequence and it is used when there is no norm with condition #mc in the normative specification. Otherwise, as in norm n6 of Table 1, the consequence will be an obligation. The norm for mission cardinality regimentation is:

```
// norm for cardinality regimentation
norm mission_cardinality: scheme_mission(M,_,MMax) &
                          mplayers(M,S,MP) &  MP > MMax
 -> fail(mission_cardinality).
```

and the norm without regimentation is:

```
// norm for cardinality without regimentation
norm mission_cardinality: scheme_mission(M,_,MMax) &
                mplayers(M,S,MP) &  MP > MMax &
                responsible(Gr,S) & plays(A,editor,Gr)
 -> obligation(A,mission_cardinality,committed(A,ms,_),
               'now'+'1 hour').
```

where the agent playing editor is obliged to commit to the mission ms in one hour.

For the third class of norms, each norm in the normative specification of the OML has a corresponding norm in NOPL. Whereas OML obligations refer to roles and missions, NPL requires that obligations are for agents and towards a goal. The NOPL norm thus identifies the agents playing the role in groups responsible for the scheme and, if the number of current players still does not reach the maximum cardinality, the agent is obliged to achieve a state where it is committed to the mission. For example, the NOPL norm for norm n2 in Table 1 is:

```
norm n2: plays(A,writer,Gr) & responsible(Gr,S) &
         mplayers(mCol,S,V) & V < 5
 -> obligation(A,n2,committed(A,mCol,S),'now'+'1 day').
```

5   Artifact-Based Architecture

The approach introduced in this paper has been implemented in an OMI that follows the Agent & Artifact model [15,11]. In this approach, a set of organisational artifacts is available in the MAS environment providing operations and observable properties for the agents so that they can interact with the OMI. For example, each scheme instance is managed by a "scheme artifact". The scheme artifact provides operations like "commit to mission" and "goal x is achieved" (with which agents can act upon the scheme) and observable properties (that agents perceive as the current state of the scheme). We can effortlessly distribute the OMI by deploying as many artifacts as necessary for the application.

Each organisational artifact has an NPL interpreter loaded with (*i*) the NOPL program automatically generated from the OS for the type of the artifact (e.g. the artifact that will manage the writing paper scheme will be loaded with the NOPL program translated from the corresponding scheme specification); and (*ii*) dynamic facts representing the current state of (part of) the organisation (e.g. the scheme artifact will produce dynamic facts related to the current state of the scheme instance). The interpreter is then used to compute: (*i*) whether some operation will bring the organisation into an inconsistent state (where inconsistency is defined by means of regimentations), and (*ii*) the current state of the obligations.

Algorithm 2, implemented on top of CArtAgO [19], shows the general pattern we used to implement every operation (e.g. role adoption and commitment to mission) in the organisational artifacts. Whenever an operation is triggered by an agent, the algorithm first stores a 'backup' copy of the current state of the artifact (line 5). This backup is restored (line 10) if the operation leads to a failure (e.g. when committing to a mission that is not permitted). The overall functioning is that invalid operations do not change the artifact state.[3] A valid operation is thus an operation that changes the state of the artifact to one where no fail is produced by the NPL interpreter. In case the operation is valid, the algorithm simply updates the current state of the obligations (line 13). Although the NPL handles *states* in the norm's conditions, this pattern of integration has allowed us to use NPL to manage agents' *actions*, i.e. the regimentation of operation on artifacts.

Algorithm 2. Artifact Integration with NOPL
_____
1: let *oe* be the current state of the organisation managed by the artifact
2: let *p* be the current NOPL program
3: let *npi* be the NPL interpreter
4: **when** an operation *o* is triggered by agent *a* **do**
5:      $oe' \leftarrow oe$ // creates a "backup" of current *oe*
6:      execute operation *o* to change *oe*
7:      $f \leftarrow$ a list of predicates representing *oe*
8:      $r \leftarrow npi(p, f)$ // runs the interpreter for the new state
9:      **if** $r = $ fail **then**
10:         $oe \leftarrow oe'$ // restore the state backup
11:         **return** fail operation *o*
12:     **else**
13:         update obligations in the observable properties
14:         **return** succeed operation *o*
_____

Notice that the NOPL program is not seen by the agents. They continue to perceive and reason on the scheme specification as defined in the OML. The NOPL is used only inside the artifact to simplify its development.

---

[3] This functioning requires that operations are not executed in parallel, which can be easily configured in CArtAgO.

Given the general pattern of integration proposed in Algorithm 2, organisational artifacts are mostly programmed in NOPL. Only the management of changes in the organisational state remains coded in Java within the organisational artifact.

6   Related Work

This work is based on several approaches to organisation, institutions, and norms (cited throughout the paper). In this section, we briefly relate and compare our main contributions to such work.

The first contribution of the paper, the NPL, should be considered specially for two properties of the language: its simplicity and its formalisation (that led to an available implementation). Similar work has been done by Tinnemeier et al. [21,20], where the operational semantics for a normative language was also proposed. Their approach and ours are similar on certain points. For instance, both consider norms as "declarative" norms (i.e. "ought-to-be" norms) in the sense that obligations and regimentation bear on goals. However our work differs in several aspects. In our approach, the NOPL is for the OMI and not to be used by programmers. The programmer continues to use OML to define both an organisation and the norms that have to be managed within such a structure. Organisation primitives are much richer in the OML than in the normative language. Another clear distinction is that we rely on a dedicated programming model (the Agent & Artifact model) providing a clear connection of the organisation to the environment and allowing us to implement regimentation on physical actions [16]. The artifacts model also simplified the distribution of the management of the state of the organisation with several instances and types of artifacts.

Regarding the second contribution, namely the automatic translation, we were inspired by work on ISLANDER [3,9]. The main difference here is the initial and target languages. While they translate a normative specification into a rule-based language, we start from an organisational language and the target is a normative language. It is simpler to translate OML norms into NPL norms, since we have norms in both sides of the translation, than translate organisational norms into rules.

Regarding the third contribution, the OMI, we started from ORA4MAS [11]. The advantages of the approach presented here are twofold: (i) it is easier to change the translation than the Java implementation of the OMI; and (ii) with the operational semantics of NPL and the formal translation we are taking significant steps towards a formal semantics for $\mathcal{M}$OISE.

7   Conclusion

In this paper, we introduced an approach for translating an organisation specification written in $\mathcal{M}$OISE OML into a normative program that can be interpreted by an artifact-based OMI. Focusing on the translation rather than Java coding, we have brought flexibility to the development of the OMI. We also made the point that such a normative language can be based on only two basic concepts: regimentation and obligation. Prohibitions are considered either as regimentation or as an obligation for someone else to apply sanction. As a consequence, the resulting NPL is elegant and simpler to formalise (only 6 rules in the operational semantics) and implement. Future work will concern the proof of correctness of the translation from OML into NOPL and the exploration of NPL translations for other organisational and institutional languages in order to assess its generality.

References

1. Boissier, O., Hübner, J.F., Sichman, J.S.: Organization oriented programming from closed to open organizations. In: O'Hare, G.M.P., Ricci, A., O'Grady, M.J., Dikenelli, O. (eds.) ESAW 2006. LNCS (LNAI), vol. 4457, pp. 86–105. Springer, Heidelberg (2007)
2. Bordini, R.H., Hübner, J.F., Wooldrige, M.: Programming Multi-Agent Systems in AgentSpeak using Jason. John Wiley & Sons, Chichester (2007)
3. da Silva, V.T.: From the specification to the implementation of norms: an automatic approach to generate rules from norm to govern the behaviour of agents. Journal of Autonomous Agents and Multi-Agent Systems 17(1), 113–155 (2008)
4. Dignum, V., Vazquez-Salceda, J., Dignum, F.: OMNI: Introducing social structure, norms and ontologies into agent organizations. In: Bordini, R.H., Dastani, M.M., Dix, J., El Fallah Seghrouchni, A. (eds.) PROMAS 2004. LNCS (LNAI), vol. 3346, pp. 181–198. Springer, Heidelberg (2005)
5. Esteva, M., de la Cruz, D., Sierra, C.: ISLANDER: an electronic institutions. In: Castelfranchi, C., Lewis Johnson, W. (eds.) Proceedings of the First International Joint Conference on Autonomous Agents and MultiAgent Systems (AAMAS 2002). LNCS (LNAI), vol. 1191, pp. 1045–1052. Springer, Heidelberg (2002)
6. Esteva, M., Rodríguez-Aguilar, J.A., Rosell, B., Arcos, J.L.: AMELI: An agent-based middleware for electronic institutions. In: Jennings, N.R., Sierra, C., Sonenberg, L., Tambe, M. (eds.) Proceedings of the Third International Joint Conference on Autonomous Agents and Multi-Agent Systems (AAMAS'2004), pp. 236–243. ACM, New York (2004)
7. Ferber, J., Gutknecht, O.: A meta-model for the analysis and design of organizations in multi-agents systems. In: Demazeau, Y. (ed.) Proceedings of the 3rd International Conference on Multi-Agent Systems (ICMAS'98), pp. 128–135. IEEE Press, Los Alamitos (1998)
8. Fornara, N., Colombetti, M.: Specifying and enforcing norms in artificial institutions. In: Omicini, A., Dunin-Keplicz, B., Padget, J. (eds.) Proceedings of the 4th European Workshop on Multi-Agent Systems, EUMAS'06 (2006)
9. García-Camino, A., Rodríguez-Aguilar, J.A., Sierra, C., Vasconcelos, W.: Constraining rule-based programming norms for electronic institutions. Journal of Autonomous Agents and Multi-Agent Systems 18(1), 186–217 (2009)
10. Grossi, D., Aldewered, H., Dignum, F.: Ubi Lex, Ibi Poena: Designing norm enforcement in e-institutions. In: Noriega, P., Vázquez-Salceda, J., Boella, G., Boissier, O., Dignum, V., Fornara, N., Matson, E. (eds.) COIN 2006. LNCS (LNAI), vol. 4386, pp. 101–114. Springer, Heidelberg (2007)
11. Hübner, J.F., Boissier, O., Kitio, R., Ricci, A.: Instrumenting multi-agent organisations with organisational artifacts and agents: "giving the organisational power back to the agents". Journal of Autonomous Agents and Multi-Agent Systems (2009)
12. Hübner, J.F., Sichman, J.S., Boissier, O.: S-MOISE+: A middleware for developing organised multi-agent systems. In: Boissier, O., Padget, J., Dignum, V., Lindemann, G., Matson, E., Ossowski, S., Sichman, J.S., Vázquez-Salceda, J. (eds.) ANIREM 2005 and OOOP 2005. LNCS (LNAI), vol. 3913, pp. 64–78. Springer, Heidelberg (2006)
13. Hübner, J.F., Sichman, J.S., Boissier, O.: Developing organised multi-agent systems using the MOISE+ model: Programming issues at the system and agent levels. International Journal of Agent-Oriented Software Engineering 1(3/4), 370–395 (2007)

14. Jones, A.J.I., Sergot, M.: On the characterization of law and computer systems: the normative systems perspective. In: Deontic logic in computer science: normative system specification, pp. 275–307. John Wiley and Sons Ltd., Chichester (1993)
15. Omicini, A., Ricci, A., Viroli, M.: Artifacts in the A&A meta-model for multi-agent systems. Journal of Autonomous Agents and Multi-Agent Systems 17(3), 432–456 (2008)
16. Piunti, M., Ricci, A., Boissier, O., Hübner, J.F.: Embodying organisations in multi-agent work environments. In: Proceedings of International Joint Conferences on Web Intelligence and Intelligent Agent Technologies (WI-IAT 2009), pp. 511–518. IEEE/WIC/ACM (2009)
17. Plotkin, G.D.: A structural approach to operational semantics. Technical report, Computer Science Department, Aarhus University, Aarhus, Denmark (1981)
18. Pynadath, D.V., Tambe, M.: An automated teamwork infrastructure for heterogeneous software agents and humans. Autonomous Agents and Multi-Agent Systems 7(1-2), 71–100 (2003)
19. Ricci, A., Piunti, M., Viroli, M., Omicini, A.: Environment programming in CArtAgO. In: Bordini, R.H., Dastani, M., Dix, J., El Fallah Seghrouchni, A. (eds.) Multi-Agent Programming: Languages, Tools and Applications, ch. 8, pp. 259–288. Springer, Heidelberg (2009)
20. Tinnemeier, N.A.M., Dastani, M., Meyer, J.-J., van der Torre, L.: Programming normative artifacts with declarative obligations and prohibitions. In: Yates, R.B. (ed.) Proceedings of International Joint Conferences on Web Intelligence and Intelligent Agent Technologies (WI-IAT 2009), pp. 145–152. IEEE/WIC/ACM (2009)
21. Tinnemeier, N., Dastani, M., Meyer, J.-J.: Roles and norms for programming agent organizations. In: Sichman, J., Decker, K., Sierra, C., Castelfranchi, C. (eds.) Proc. of AAMAS'09, pp. 121–128 (2009)
22. Vázquez-Salceda, J., Aldewereld, H., Dignum, F.: Norms in multiagent systems: some implementation guidelines. In: Proceedings of the Second European Workshop on Multi-Agent Systems, EUMAS 2004 (2004), http://people.cs.uu.nl/dignum/papers/eumas04.PDF
23. López, F., López, M.L., d'Inverno, M.: Constraining autonomy through norms. In: Proceedings of the first international joint conference on Autonomous agents and multiagent systems, pp. 674–681. ACM Press, New York (2002)

Part II

Social Norms and Semantics

Monitoring Social Expectations in Second Life

Stephen Cranefield and Guannan Li

Department of Information Science
University of Otago
PO Box 56, Dunedin 9054, New Zealand
scranefield@infoscience.otago.ac.nz

Abstract. Online virtual worlds such as Second Life provide a rich medium for unstructured human interaction in a shared simulated 3D environment. However, many human interactions take place in a structured social context where participants play particular roles and are subject to expectations governing their behaviour, and current virtual worlds do not provide any support for this type of interaction. There is therefore an opportunity to adapt the tools developed in the MAS community for structured social interactions between software agents (inspired by human society) and adapt these for use with the computer-mediated human communication provided by virtual worlds.

This paper describes the application of one such tool for use with Second Life. A model checker for online monitoring of social expectations defined in temporal logic has been integrated with Second Life, allowing users to be notified when their expectations of others have been fulfilled or violated. Avatar actions in the virtual world are detected by a script, encoded as propositions and sent to the model checker, along with the social expectation rules to be monitored. Notifications of expectation fulfilment and violation are returned to the script to be displayed to the user. This utility of this tool is reliant on the ability of the Linden scripting language (LSL) to detect events of significance in the application domain, and a discussion is presented on how a range of monitored structured social scenarios could be realised despite the limitations of LSL.

1 Introduction

Much of the research in multi-agent systems addresses techniques for modelling, constructing and controlling open systems of autonomous agents. These agents are taken to be self-interested or representing self-interested people or organisations, and thus no assumptions can be made about their conformance to the design goals, social conventions or regulations governing the societies in which they participate. Inspired by human society, MAS researchers have adopted, formalised and created computational infrastructure allowing concepts from human society such as trust, reputation, expectation, commitment and narrative to be explicitly modelled and manipulated in order to increase agents' awareness of the social context of their interactions. This awareness helps agents to carry out their interactions efficiently and helps preserve order in the society, e.g. the existence of reputation, recommendation and/or sanction mechanisms discourages anti-social behaviour.

As the new 'Web 2.0' style Web sites and applications proliferate, people's use of the Web is moving from passive information consumption to active information sharing

J. Padget et al. (Eds.): COIN 2009, LNAI 6069, pp. 133–146, 2010.
© Springer-Verlag Berlin Heidelberg 2010

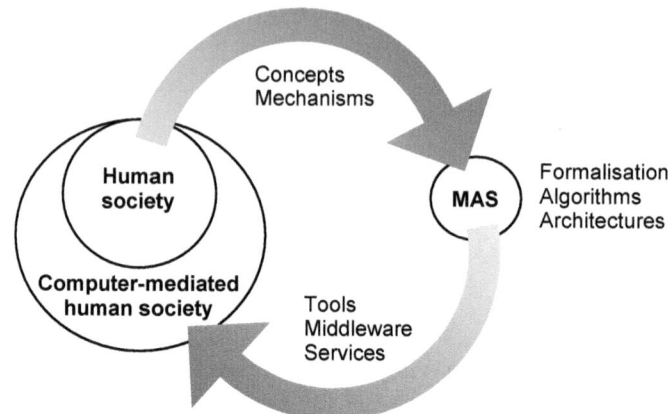

Fig. 1. Feedback from MAS research to computer-mediated human societies

and interaction within virtual communities; in other words, for millions of users, the Web is now a place for social interaction. However, while Web 2.0 applications provide the middleware to enable interaction, they generally provide no support for users to maintain an awareness of the social context of their interactions (other than basic presence information indicating which users in a 'buddy list' online). There is therefore an opportunity for the software techniques developed in MAS research for maintaining social awareness, that were inspired by human society, to be applied in the context of electronically mediated human interaction, as well as in their original context of software agent interaction (see Figure 1).

This paper reports on an investigation into the use of one such social awareness tool in conjunction with the Second Life online virtual world. Second Life is a 'Web 3D' application providing a simulated three dimensional environment in which users can move around and interact with other users and simulated objects [1]. Users are represented in the virtual world by animated avatars that they control via the Second Life Viewer client software. Human interaction in virtual worlds is essentially unconstrained—the users can do whatever they like, subject to the artificial physics of the simulated world and a few constraints that the worlds support, such as the ability of land owners to control who can access their land. However, many human interactions take place in a structured social context where participants play particular roles and there are constraints imposed by the social or organisational context, e.g. participants in a meeting should not leave without formally excusing themselves, and students in an in-world lecture should remain quiet until the end of the lecture. Researchers in the field of multi-agent systems have proposed (based on human society) that the violation of social norms such as these can be discouraged by publishing explicit formal definitions of the norms, building tools that track (relevant) events and detect any violations, and punishing offenders by lowering their reputations or sanctioning them in some other way [2]. Integrating this type of tool with virtual worlds could enhance the support provided by those worlds for social activities that are subject to norms.

In this research we have investigated the use of a tool for online monitoring of 'social expectations' [3] in conjunction with Second Life. The mechanism involves a script running in Second Life that is configured to detect and record particular events of interest for a given scenario, and to model these as a sequence of state descriptions that are sent to an external monitor along with a property to be monitored. The monitor sends notifications back to the script when the property is satisfied. These notifications could be handled in a variety of ways: the information or some consequences of it (such as a reputation adjustment) could be communicated privately to the script's owner via text chat or a "head-up display" object, it could be broadcast on the public chat channel or posted directly to a publicly observable (simulated) in-world notice-board, or the avatar causing a violation could be automatically ejected and/or banned from the script owner's land. However, investigating and evaluating these notification handling techniques is not part of the research reported in this paper.

It is important to note that the monitoring mechanism is not intended to provide a global surveillance mechanism for Second Life, but rather, to allow specific users and communities to model and track the social expectations that apply in particular types of structured interaction ocurring within a single Second Life "land parcel".

The rest of this paper is structured as follows. A brief overview of the Second Life architecture is given in Section 2 and then Section 3 describes how we have used the Linden Scripting Language to detect avatars in Second Life and create a sequence of propositional state models to send to the monitor. The architecture for communication between this script and the monitor is presented in Section 4. Section 5 discusses the concept of conditional social expectations used in this work, and the model checking tool that is used as the expectation monitor. Section 6 presents some simple scenarios of activities in Second Life being monitored, and Section 7 discusses some issues arising from limitations of the Linden Scripting Language and the temporal logic used to express rules. Some related work is described in Section 8, and Section 9 concludes the paper.

2   Second Life Architecture

Second Life is based on a client-server architecture, with each user's viewer communicating with a server that simulates the current 256m × 256m "region" in which the user's avatar is located. The regions are linked in a rectangular mesh and partitioned across multiple servers (known as simulators or "sims"). In 2007 there were 15400 simulator processes updating their regions at a targeted rate of 45 frames per second [4]. Each region can support 100 avatars and 15000 primitive objects (from which in-world structures are built) [5]. A region is divided into "land parcels" of varying sizes, which are the portions of land owned by different users or groups.

There are also a number of centralised databases used by the simulators, e.g. to access user identity information.

3   Detecting Events in Second Life

As shown in Figure 2, the Second Life Viewer provides, by default, a graphical view of the user's avatar and other objects and avatars within the view. The user can control

Fig. 2. The Second Life Viewer

the 'camera' to obtain other views. Avatars can be controlled to perform a range of basic animations such as standing, walking and flying, or predefined "gestures" that are combinations of animation, text chat and sounds. Communication with other avatars (and hence their users) is via text chat, private instant messages, or audio streaming. The user experience is therefore a rich multimedia one in which human perception and intelligence is needed to interpret the full stream of incoming data. However, the Linden Scripting Language (LSL [6]) can be used to attach scripts to objects (e.g. to animate doors), and there are a number of sensor functions available to detect objects and events in the environment. These scripts are run within the Second Life simulator servers, but have some limited ability to communicate with the outside world.

LSL is based on a state-event model, and a script consists of defined states and handlers for events that it is programmed to handle. Certain events in the environment automatically trigger events on a script attached to an object. These include collisions with other objects and with the 'land', 'touches' (when a user clicks on the object), and money (in Linden dollars) being given to the object. Some other types of event must be explicitly subscribed to by calling functions such as `llSensor` and `llSensorRepeat` for scanning for avatars and objects in the current region within a given arc and range (up to 96 metres), `llListen` for detecting chat messages from objects or avatars within hearing range, and `llSetTimerEvent` for setting a timer. These functions take parameters that provide some selectivity over what is sensed, e.g. a particular avatar name or object type can be specified in `llListen`, and `llListen` can be set to listen on a particular channel, for a message from a particular avatar, and even for a particular message.

In this paper we focus on the detection of other avatars via the function `llSensor Repeat`, which repeatedly polls for nearby avatars (we choose not to scan for objects also) at an interval specified in a parameter. A series of `sensor` events are then generated, which indicate the number of avatars (up to a maximum of 16) detected in each sensing operation. A loop is used to get the unique key that identifies each of these avatars (via function `llDetectedKey`) and the avatar's name (via `llDetectedName`). The key can then be used to obtain each avatar's current basic animation (via `llGetAnimation`). Our script can be configured with a filter list specifying which avatar/animation observations should be either recorded or ignored, where the specified avatar and animation can refer to a particular value, or "any". To reduce the computation in subsequent steps, detected avatar animations are filtered through this list sequentially, resulting in a set of $(avatar\_name, animation)$ pairs that comprise a model of the current state of the avatars within the sensor range. Another configuration list specifies the optional assignment of avatars to named groups or roles such as "Friend" or "ClubOfficial". There is currently no connection with the official Second Life concept of a user group (although official group membership can be detected). Group names can also be included in the filter list, with an intended existential meaning, i.e. a pair $(group\_name, animation)$ represents an observation that *some* member of the group is performing the specified animation. The configuration lists provide scenario-specific relevance criteria on the observed events, and are read from a 'notecard' (a type of avatar inventory item that is commonly used to store textual configuration data for scripts), along with the property to be monitored.

When the script starts up, it sends the property to be monitored to the monitor. It then sends a series of state descriptions to the monitor as sensor events occur. However, we choose not to send a state description if there is no change since the previous state, so states represent periods of unchanging behaviour rather than regularly spaced points in time. State descriptions are sets of proposition symbols of the form *avatar_animation* or *group_animation*.

This process can easily be extended to handle other types of Second Life events that have an obvious translation to propositional (rather than predicate) logic, such as detecting that an avatar has sent a chat message (if it is not required to model the contents of the message). Section 7 discusses this further.

4   Communication between Second Life and the Monitor

Second Life provides three mechanisms for communication with entities outside their own server or the Second Life Viewer: scripts can send email messages, initiate HTTP requests, or listen for incoming XML-RPC connections (which must include a parameter giving the key for a channel previously created by the script). To push property and state information to the monitor we use HTTP. However, instead of directly embedding the monitor in an HTTP server, to avoid local firewall restrictions we have chosen to use Twitter [7] as a message channel. An XML-RPC channel key, the property to be monitored and a series of state descriptions are sent to a predefined Twitter account as direct messages using the HTTP API[1]. The Twitter API requires authentication, which can be achieved from LSL only by including the username and password in the URL in the form http://username:password@.....

The monitor is wrapped by a Java client that polls Twitter (using the Twitter4J library [9]) to retrieve direct messages for the predetermined account. These are ignored

---

[1] Twitter messages are restricted to 140 characters and calls to the Twitter API are subject to a limit of 70 requests per hour, which is sufficient for testing our mechanism. For production use an alternative HTTP-accessible messaging service could be used, such as the Amazon Simple Queue Service [8].

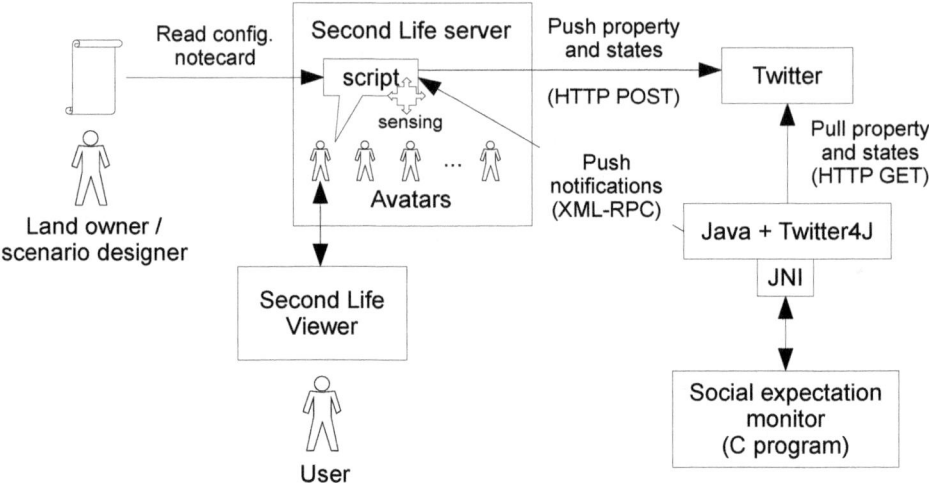

Fig. 3. The communications architecture

until a pair of messages containing an XML-RPC channel key and a property to be monitored (prefixed with "C:" and "P:" respectively) are received, which indicates that a new monitoring session has begun. The monitoring session then consists of a series of messages beginning with "S:", each containing a list of propositions describing a new state. The monitor does not currently work in an incremental 'online' mode—it must be given a complete history of states and restarted each time a new state is received[2]; therefore, the Java wrapper must record the history of states. It also generates a unique name for each state (which the monitor requires).

Each time a state is received, the monitor (which is implemented in C) is invoked using the Java Native Interface (JNI). The rule and state history are written to files and the names passed as command-line arguments. An additional argument indicates the desired name of the output file. The output is parsed and, if the property is determined to be true in any state, that information is sent directly back to the Second Life script via XML-RPC.

Figure 3 gives an overview of the communication architecture.

5   Monitoring Social Expectations

5.1   Modelling Social Expectations

MAS researchers working on normative systems and electronic institutions [2] have proposed various languages for modelling the rules governing agent interaction in open societies, including abductive logic programming rules [10], enhanced finite state machine style models, [11], deontic logic [12], and institutional action description languages based using formalisms such as the event calculus [13].

---

[2] Work is in progress to add an online mode to the monitor.

The monitor used in this work is designed to track rules of *social expectation*. These are temporal logic rules that are triggered by conditions on the past and present, resulting in *expectations* on present and future events. The language does not include deontic concepts such as obligation and permission, but it allows the expression of social rules that impose complex temporal constraints on future behaviour, in contrast to the simple deadlines supported by most normative languages. It can also be used to express rules of social interaction that are less authoritative than centrally established norms, e.g. conditional rules of expectation that an agent has established as its personal norms, or rules expressing learned regularities in the patterns of other agents' behaviour. The key distinction between these cases is the process that creates the rules, and how agents react to detected fulfilments and violations.

Expectations become active when their condition evaluates to true in the current state. These expectations are then considered to be fulfilled or violated if they evaluate to true in a state without considering any future states that might be available in the model[3]. If an active expectation is not fulfilled or violated in a given state, then it remains active in the following state, but in a "progressed" form. Formula progression involves partially evaluating the formula in terms of the current state and re-expressing it from the viewpoint of the next state [14]. A detailed explanation is beyond the scope of this paper, but a simple example is that an expectation $\bigcirc\phi$ (meaning that ϕ must be true in the state that follows) progresses to the expectation ϕ in the next state.

5.2 The Social Expectation Monitor

The monitoring tool we have used is an extension [3] of a model checker for hybrid temporal logics [15]. Model checking is the computational process of evaluating whether a formal model of a process, usually modelled as a Kripke structure (a form of nondeterministic finite state machine), satisfies a given property, usually expressed in temporal logic. For monitoring social expectations in an open system, we cannot assume that we can obtain the specifications or code of all participating agents to form our model. Instead our model is the sequence of system states recorded by a particular observer, in other words, we are addressing the problem of *model checking a path* [16]. The task of the model checker is therefore not to check that the overall system *necessarily* satisfies a given property, but just that the observed behaviour of the system has, to date, satisfied it. The properties we use are assertions that a social expectation exists or has been fulfilled or violated, based on a conditional rule of expectation, expressed in temporal logic.

The basic logic used includes these types of expression, in addition to the standard Boolean constants and connectives (true, false, $\wedge$, $\vee$ and $\neg$):

- Proposition symbols. In our application these represent observations made in Second Life, e.g. *avatar_name_sitting*.
- $\bigcirc\phi$: formula ϕ is true when evaluated in the next state

---

[3] This restriction is necessary, for example, when examing an audit trail to find violations of triggered rules in *any* state. The standard temporal logic semantics would conclude that an expectation "eventually p" is fulfilled in a state s even if p doesn't become true until some later state s'.

- ◇φ: φ is true in the current or some future state
- □φ: φ is true in all states from now onwards
- φ U ψ: ψ is true at the current or some future state, and φ is true for all states from now until just before that state

◇ and □ can be expressed in terms of U and are abbreviations of longer expressions.

The logic also has some features of Hybrid Logic [17], but these are not used in this work except for the use of a *nominal* (a proposition that is true in a unique state) in the output from the model checker to 'name' the state in which a fulfilled or violated rule of expectation became active.

Finally, the logic includes the following operators related to conditional rules of expectation, and these are the types of expression sent from the Second Life script to the model checker:

- ExistsExp($Condition, Expectation$)
- ExistsFulf($Condition, Expectation$)
- ExistsViol($Condition, Expectation$)

where $Condition$ and $Expectation$ can be any formula that does not include ExistsExp, ExistsFulf and ExistsViol.

The first of these operators evaluates to true if there is an expectation existing in the current state that results from the rule specified in the arguments being triggered in the present or past. The other two operators evaluate to true if there is currently a fulfilled or violated expectation (respectively) resulting from the rule.

Formal semantics for this logic can be found elsewhere [3].

The input syntax to the model checker is slightly more verbose than that shown above. In particular, temporal operators must indicate the name of the "next state modality" as it appears in the input Kripke structure. In the examples in this paper, this will always be written as "<next>". Writing "<next>" on its own refers to the operator ○.

6   Two Simple Scenarios

A simple rule of expectation that might apply in a Second Life scenario is that no one should ever fly. This might apply in a region used by members of a group that enacts historical behaviour. To monitor this expectation we can use the following property:

```
ExistsViol<next>(true, !any_flying)
```

This is an unconditional rule (it is triggered in every state) stating the expectation that there will not be any member of the group "Any" (comprising all avatars) flying.

If this is the only animation state to be tracked, the script's filter list will state that the animation "Flying" for group "Any" should be recorded, but otherwise all animations for all avatars and other groups should be discarded. On startup, the script sends the property to be monitored to the monitor, via Twitter, and then as avatars move around in Second Life and their animations are detected, it sends state messages that will either contain no propositions (if no one is flying) or will state that someone is flying:

```
S: any_flying
```

These states are accumulated, and each time a new state is received, the monitor is called and provided with the property to be monitored and the model (state history), e.g. $s_1 : \{\}$, $s_2 : \{\}$, $s_3 : \{\texttt{any\_flying}\}$ (the model is actually represented in XML—an example appears below).

For this model, the monitor detects that the property is satisfied (i.e. the rule is violated) in state s_3 and a notification is sent back to the script. How this is handled is up to the script designer, but one option is for the script to be running in a "head-up-display" object, allowing the user to be informed in a way that other avatars cannot observe.

We now consider a slightly more complex example where there are two groups (or roles) specified in the script's group configuration list: `leader` (a singleton group) and `follower`. We want to monitor for violations of the rule that once the leader is standing, then from the next state a follower must not be sitting until the leader is sitting again. This is expressed using the following property:

```
ExistsViol<next>(
   leader_standing,
   <next>(U<next>(!follower_sitting,
                  leader_sitting))
)
```

The filter list can be configured so that only the propositions occurring in this rule are regarded as relevant for describing the state.

Suppose the scenario begins with the leader sitting and then standing, followed by the follower sitting, and finally the leader sitting again. This causes the following four states to be generated:

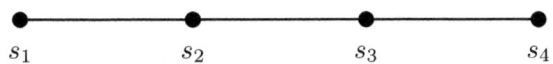

leader_sitting   leader_standing follower_sitting   leader_sitting

$$s_1 \qquad\qquad s_2 \qquad\qquad s_3 \qquad\qquad s_4$$

This is represented in the following XML format to be input to the model checker:

```
<hl-kripke-struct name="M">
   <world label="s1"/>
   <world label="s2"/>
   <world label="s3"/>
   <world label="s4"/>
   <modality label="next">
      <acc-pair to-world-label="s2"
                from-world-label="s1"/>
      <acc-pair to-world-label="s3"
                from-world-label="s2"/>
      <acc-pair to-world-label="s4"
                from-world-label="s3"/>
   </modality>
   <prop-sym label="leader_standing"
```

```
                truth-assignments="s2"/>
   <prop-sym label="leader_sitting"
                truth-assignments="s1 s4"/>
   <prop-sym label="follower_sitting"
                truth-assignments="s3"/>
   <nominal label="s1" truth-assignment="s1"/>
   <nominal label="s2" truth-assignment="s2"/>
   <nominal label="s3" truth-assignment="s3"/>
   <nominal label="s4" truth-assignment="s4"/>
</hl-kripke-struct>
```

The output of the model checker is:

```
s3: (s2, U<next>(!(follower_sitting),
                    leader_sitting))
```

This means that a violation occurred in state s_3 from the rule being triggered in state s_2. The violated expectation (after progression to state s_3) is:

```
U<next>(!(follower_sitting), leader_sitting)
```

This information is sent to the script.

7   Discussion

As mentioned in Section 3, our detection script currently only detects the animations of avatars. This limits the scenarios that can be modelled to those based on (simulated) physical action. However, it is straightforward to add the ability to detect other LSL events, provided that they can be translated to a propositional representation. Thus we could detect that an avatar has sent a chat message, but we cannnot provide a propositional encoding that can express all possible chat message contents. However, the addition of new types of configuration list would allow additional flexibility. For example, regular expressions or other types of pattern could be defined along with a string that can be appended to an avatar or group name to generate a proposition meaning that that avatar (or a member of that group) sent a chat message matching the pattern.

The LSL sensor functions have a limited range (96 metres) and will return a maximum of 16 avatars or objects. For scenarios where this is not sufficient, an array of scripted monitor objects could be pre-positioned in the region, and these could communicate with each other either via a private chat channel or via an external server. Interconnected scripted objects of this sort are already used as 'proximity sensors' for recording land use metrics in Second Life, such as the number and identities of avatars visiting a region over a period of time [18]. There are at least two companies selling proximity sensors in Second Life. Through the use of multiple sensors, large multi-region "estates" can be monitored, which suggests that there are no inherent limitations in the use of LSL sensors that would prevent an extension of our approach from being applied to large land areas. However, when multiple sensors are running and many avatars are detected, the communication with the external model checker may become a bottleneck. In this case, real-time notification of social expectation fulfilments and violations may not be possible, but it would still be useful to collect audit trails that could be used as evidence to support claims of antisocial behaviour.

As LSL scripts are run on the Second Life simulator servers, a Second Life region can suffer from "lag"—a noticeable drop in response time—when too many complex scripts are running simultaneously [19]. It is important to note, therefore, that we are not proposing that our monitoring technique will be used by numerous participants in a scenario. Rather, we expect that in many scenarios there would be a single avatar (e.g. the land owner or a group leader) running the monitor script. Even if many avatars choose to run a monitor, this is not necessarily infeasible. In 2007 it was reported that the Second Life grid was running 30 million concurrent scripts at any time, with an average of 2000 per simulator (although most of these may be waiting for input) [4]. Furthermore, ongoing research into more scalable virtual world architectures should result in the ability to support higher levels of scripting. For example, Cox and Crowther [19] suggest that sensor data feeds could be sent to clients to be analysed by client-side listeners. While Second Life is a proprietary system that may not evolve in this direction, this type of architecture could be investigated using open source virtual world implementations such as OpenSimulator [20] and Wonderland [21].

A significant limitation of the Linden Scripting Language is that the events that a script can detect are focused on the scripted object's own interactions with the environment—there is no facility for observing interactions between other agents, except for what can be deduced from their animations and chat. For many scenarios, it would be desirable to detect these interactions, for example, passing a certain object or sending money from one avatar to another might be a significant event in a society. One way around this problem would be to add additional scripted objects to the environment and set up the social conventions that these objects must be used for certain purposes. For example, an object in the middle of a conference table might need to be touched in order to request the right to speak next. These objects would generate appropriate propositions and send them to the main script via a private link.

When defining expectations on avatar actions, rather than relying on potentially complex rules expressed in terms of basic animations, it would be useful to be able to define more complex behaviours that scripts could detect and rules could refer to. Artikis and Paliouras [22] have investigated the recognition of "long-term behaviours" such as fighting, taking as input a set of basic "short-term" behaviours detected in surveillance video frames. This work could be applied to extend the monitoring mechanism described here.

The logic used currently is based on a discrete model of time, which can cause problems in some scenarios. For example, in the leader/follower scenario, it would be reasonable to allow the follower some (short) amount of time to stand after the leader stands. However, if a follower stands and another does not stand within the granularity of the same sensor event, then that second follower will be deemed in violation. It would be useful to be able to model some aspects of real time. This could be done by moving to a real-time temporal logic (which would involve some theoretical work on extending the model checker), or by some pragmatic means such as allowing the configuration parameters to define a frequency for regular "tick" timer events.

8 Related Work

There seems to be little prior work that has explored the use of social awareness technology from multi-agent systems or other fields to support human interaction on the Internet in general, and in virtual worlds in particular.

A few avatar rating and reputation systems have been developed [23] to replace Second Life's own ratings system, which was disestablished in 2007. These provide various mechanisms to allow users to share their personal opinions of avatars with others.

Closer to our own work, Bogdanovych et al. [24,25] have linked the AMELI electronic institution middleware [26] with Second Life. However, their aim is not to provide support for human interactions within Second Life, but rather to provide a rich interface for users to participate in an e-institution mediated by AMELI (in which the other participants may be software agents). This is done by generating a 3D environment from the institution's specification, e.g. *scenes* in the e-institution become rooms and transitions between scenes become doors. As a user controls their avatar to perform actions in Second Life, this causes an associated agent linked to AMELI to send messages to other agents, as defined by an action/message mapping table. Moving the avatar between rooms causes the agent to make a transition between scenes, but doors in Second Life will only open when the agent is allowed to make the corresponding scene transition according the rules of the institution.

This approach could be used to design and instrument environments that support structured human-to-human interaction in Second Life, but the e-institution model of communication is highly stylised and likely to seem unnatural for human users. In our work we are aiming to provide generic social awareness tools for virtual world users while placing as few restrictions as possible on the forms of interaction that are compatible with those tools. However, as discussed in Section 7, the limitation of the sensing functions provided by virtual world scripting languages may mean that some types of scenario cannot be implemented without providing specific scripted coordination objects that users are required to use, or the use of chat messages containing precise prespecified words or phrases.

9 Conclusion

This paper has reported on a prototype application of a model checking tool for social expectation monitoring applied to monitoring social interactions in Second Life. The techniques used for monitoring events in Second Life and allowing communication between a Second Life script and the monitor have been described, and these have been successfully tested on some simple scenarios. A discussion was presented on some of the limitations imposed by the LSL language and the logic used in the model checker, along with some suggestions for resolving these issues. Further work is needed to explore more complex scenarios and to test the scalability of the approach.

References

1. Linden Lab.: Second Life home page (2008), `http://secondlife.com/`
2. Boella, G., van der Torre, L., Verhagen, H.: Introduction to normative multiagent systems. In: Boella, G., van der Torre, L., Verhagen, H. (eds.) Normative Multi-agent Systems. Dagstuhl Seminar Proceedings, Internationales Begegnungs- und Forschungszentrum für Informatik (IBFI), Schloss Dagstuhl, Germany, vol. 07122 (2007)
3. Cranefield, S., Winikoff, M.: Verifying social expectations by model checking truncated paths. In: Hübner, J.F., Matson, E., Boissier, O., Dignum, V. (eds.) COIN@AAMAS 2008. LNCS, vol. 5428, pp. 204–219. Springer, Heidelberg (2009)
4. Wilkes, I.: Second Life: how it works (and how it doesn't). Presentation video and slides from QCon San Francisco 2007 (2007), `http://www.infoq.com/presentations/Second-Life-Ian-Wilkes`
5. Linden Lab: Land. Article on Second Life wiki (2009), `http://wiki.secondlife.com/wiki/Land`
6. Linden Lab: LSL portal (2008), `http://wiki.secondlife.com/wiki/LSL_Portal`
7. Twitter: Twitter home page (2008), `http://twitter.com/`
8. Amazon Web Services: Amazon simple queue service (2008), `http://aws.amazon.com/sqs/`
9. Yamamoto, Y.: Twitter4j (2008), `http://yusuke.homeip.net/twitter4j/en/`
10. Alberti, M., Chesani, F., Gavanelli, M., Lamma, E., Mello, P., Torroni, P.: Compliance verification of agent interaction: a logic-based software tool. In: Trappl, R. (ed.) Cybernetics and Systems 2004. Austrian Society for Cybernetics Studies, vol. II, pp. 570–575 (2004)
11. Esteva, M., de la Cruz, D., Sierra, C.: ISLANDER: an electronic institutions editor. In: Proceedings of the 1st International Joint Conference on Autonomous Agents and Multiagent Systems, pp. 1045–1052. ACM, New York (2002)
12. Vázquez-Salceda, J., Aldewereld, H., Dignum, F.: Implementing norms in multiagent systems. In: Lindemann, G., Denzinger, J., Timm, I.J., Unland, R. (eds.) MATES 2004. LNCS (LNAI), vol. 3187, pp. 313–327. Springer, Heidelberg (2004)
13. Farrell, A.D.H., Sergot, M.J., Sallé, M., Bartolini, C.: Using the event calculus for tracking the normative state of contracts. International Journal of Cooperative Information Systems 14(2&3), 99–129 (2005)
14. Bacchus, F., Kabanza, F.: Using temporal logics to express search control knowledge for planning. Artificial Intelligence 116(1-2), 123–191 (2000)
15. Dragone, L.: Hybrid logics model checker (2005), `http://luigidragone.com/hlmc/`
16. Markey, N., Schnoebelen, P.: Model checking a path. In: Amadio, R.M., Lugiez, D. (eds.) CONCUR 2003. LNCS, vol. 2761, pp. 251–265. Springer, Heidelberg (2003)
17. Blackburn, P., de Rijke, M., Venema, Y.: Modal Logic. Cambridge University Press, Cambridge (2001)
18. Kezema, K.: Further analysis of parcel data collection. Blog post (2009), `http://jeffkurka.blogspot.com/2009/03/further-analysis-of-parcel-data.html`
19. Cox, R.J., Crowther, P.S.: A review of Linden Scripting Language and its role in Second Life. In: Purvis, M., Savarimuthu, B.T.R. (eds.) Computer-Mediated Social Networking. First International Conference, ICCMSN 2008. LNCS (LNAI), vol. 5322, pp. 35–47. Springer, Heidelberg (2009)
20. opensimulator.org: Open simulator wiki (2009), `http://opensimulator.org/wiki/Main_Page`

21. Sun Microsystems, CollabNet and O'Reilly Media: Project Wonderland: Toolkit for building 3D virtual worlds (2009), https://lg3d-wonderland.dev.java.net/
22. Artikis, A., Paliouras, G.: Behaviour recognition using the event calculus. In: Artificial Intelligence Applications and Innovations III. IFIP Advances in Information and Communication Technology, vol. 296, pp. 469–478. Springer, Heidelberg (2009)
23. Second Life: Removal of ratings in beta (2007),http://blog.secondlife.com/2007/04/12/removal-of-ratings-in-beta/
24. Bogdanovych, A., Berger, H., Sierra, C., Simoff, S.J.: Humans and agents in 3D electronic institutions. In: Proceedings of the 4rd International Joint Conference on Autonomous Agents and Multiagent Systems, pp. 1093–1094. ACM, New York (2005)
25. Bogdanovych, A., Esteva, M., Simoff, S.J., Sierra, C., Berger, H.: A methodology for 3D electronic institutions. In: Proceedings of the 6th International Joint Conference on Autonomous Agents and Multiagent Systems, pp. 358–360. IFAAMAS (2007)
26. Esteva, M., Rosell, B., Rodrguez-Aguilar, J.A., Arcos, J.L.: AMELI: An agent-based middleware for electronic institutions. In: Proceedings of the 3rd International Joint Conference on Autonomous Agents and Multiagent Systems, vol. 1, pp. 236–243. IEEE Computer Society, Los Alamitos (2004)

Towards a Logical Model of Social Agreement
for Agent Societies

Emiliano Lorini[1] and Mario Verdicchio[2]

[1] Université de Toulouse, CNRS, Institut de Recherche en Informatique de Toulouse, France
[2] Università degli studi di Bergamo, Italy

Abstract. Multi-agent systems (MASs), comprised of autonomous entities with
the aim to cooperate to reach a common goal, may be viewed as computational
models of distributed complex systems such as organizations and institutions.
There have been several model proposals in the agent literature with the aim to
support, integrate, substitute human organizations, but no attempt has gone beyond the boundaries of this research context to become a mainstream software
engineering implementation guideline, nor has it been adopted as a universal
model of multi-agent interaction in economics or social sciences. In this work we
counter top-down, operational organization specifications with a logical model
of a fundamental concept: agreement, with the long-term aim to create a formal
model of multi-agent organization that can serve as a universally accepted basis
for implementation of collaborative distributed systems.

1 Introduction

Multi-agent systems (MASs) can provide an effective computational model of autonomous individuals interacting in a complex distributed system. The models that simulate
the operations of multiple entities can show how agent technology can be exploited in
economics and social sciences. The lack of a breakthrough so far is possibly paralleled
by some lack of generality in the proposed MAS implementations. Several research
works aim at proposing operational models of multi-agent organizations in the form of
templates of norms, roles, interaction patterns, and so on, that have a significant impact
on the agent community, but whose adoption by a wider audience may be hindered by a
discrepancy between how organizations are conceived in this research context and how
they actually emerge in the real world.

In this work we begin our attempt to formalize the concept of organization starting
from what we consider its most fundamental component: agreement. We see an organization as a way to coordinate agent interaction that starts from an agreement between
the relevant agents. Moreover, we adopt a bottom-up, formal approach to keep our analysis as general as possible, and, as a consequence, the application field of our current
and future results as wide as possible.

The paper is organized as follows: Section 2 illustrates more in detail the motivations
to our efforts; Section 3 presents the syntax and the semantics of our logical model, and
some choices made in the model are discussed in Section 4, while Section 5 presents
some theorems; Sections 6 and 7 illustrate how agreements are formed and how commitments and norms can be grounded on them, respectively; Section 8 provides some
pointers to significant related literature, and, finally, Section 9 concludes.

J. Padget et al. (Eds.): COIN 2009, LNAI 6069, pp. 147–162, 2010.

2   Motivation

MASs can be seen as conceived with two distinct purposes. In the scenarios envisioned by the pioneers of this field, whose hopes were boosted also by the unprecedented success of Internet technologies, agents were viewed as a further development of the object-oriented paradigm, leading to the implementation of goal-driven, mobile programs that could cooperate with each other autonomously to reach a common objective. In a broader interpretation including social, economic, legal aspects, MASs are seen as a computational model of groups of interacting entities: Agents are programs that simulate a real-life complex system whose properties are to be analyzed by means of a computer system.

The lack (so far) of a so-called 'killer application' based on MAS technology does not mean that the latter interpretation traces the only viable path for agent researchers. Nevertheless, in our opinion, significant achievements in the simulation-oriented MAS research are a necessary step to finally reach a breakthrough also in mainstream software development. We agree with DeLoach [5]: MAS researchers have not yet demonstrated that the agent approach can yield competitive or even better solutions than other programming paradigms by providing reliable, complex, distributed systems.

We refer to virtual organizations, and think that the relevance of MAS technologies can be shown by a believable agent-based simulation of real-life, human organizations. Once agents are proven to be capable of delivering detailed models of complex organizations, then they can become a very appealing candidate for cutting-edge software solutions aiming at supporting, or even substituting, their human counterparts.

Several models of virtual organizations have been proposed in the literature [19], [8]. In particular, Electronic Institutions [17] have been introduced to regulate agent interaction in open environments. We see some issues rising from this research line: How really open are these environments with respect to the constraints introduced by the proposed organizational models? How does the operational nature of these models (as opposed to logical) affect their impact on the potential adopters? These questions are facets of our main concern: The affinity of virtual organizations with real ones is a key factor in MAS technology's shift from research to practice. Although we can provide detailed specifications of virtual organizations in terms of roles, scenarios, interaction patterns, communication protocols and so on, we think that such approach inevitably narrows down the scope of a proposal to the researchers' working hypotheses. The top-down specification of a predefined template is not the way organizations are born in the real world, and this distance between theoretical research and actual organizational dynamics might correspond to the gap between the agent-based proposals and the solutions adopted in the industry.

Our work has a rather different, if not opposite, starting point. We intend to provide a logical model (as opposed to operational) that allows for the formalization of the creation of organizations in a bottom-up fashion (as opposed to top-down). It might seem surprising that researchers who call for the elimination of the gap between theory and practice opt for a logic-based approach. However, this is a research field where universal models for basic concepts, including the very concept of 'agent', are still missing. We think that theoretical definitions of general concepts might work as wider and more solid foundations for the construction of a model of organizations that can eventually provide effective implementation guidelines. This is also the idea behind the choice of a bottom-up approach: To keep a model of organizations as general as possible, instead of trying to impose a standard template, which is a surely successful approach only in monopoly contexts, we aim at shedding some light on the basic mechanisms that lead a group of independent individuals (or autonomous agents) to form an organization.

In a top-down approach, agents join an organization with pre-established rules. In our bottom-up approach, we see an organization as the product of the agreement of several agents on how their future interactions should be regulated. Thus, the aim of this work is to formally define 'agreement' as a fundamental concept for the creation of multi-agent organizations, that is, we intend to propose a logic of social agreement.

3   A Modal Logic of Social Agreement

We present in this section the syntax and semantics of the modal logic $\mathcal{SAL}$ (*Social Agreement Logic*). The logic $\mathcal{SAL}$ specifies the conditions under which agreements are established and annulled. The main idea behind the formalism is to take *agreement* as a primitive object and to clarify its relationships with the concept of *preference* (i.e. how agreement formation depend on agents' preferences). We make a general assumption about rationality of agents in our logical approach to agreement. In particular, we suppose that the agents in a group I agree about a certain issue φ only if φ is something satisfactory for the agents in I. In other words, an agreement between certain agents is formed only if the content of agreement is something good for every agent.

3.1   Syntax

Let $ATM = \{p, q, \ldots\}$ be a nonempty set of atomic formulas, $AGT = \{i, j, \ldots\}$ a nonempty finite set of agents, and $ACT = \{\alpha, \beta, \ldots\}$ a nonempty set of atomic actions. We note $2^{ACT*} = 2^{ACT} \setminus \emptyset$ the set of all non-empty sets of actions, and $2^{AGT*} = 2^{AGT} \setminus \emptyset$ the set of all non-empty sets of agents.

We introduce a function REP that associates to every agent i in AGT a non-empty set of atomic actions called *action repertoire* of agent i:

$$REP : AGT \longrightarrow 2^{ACT*}.$$

For every agent $i \in AGT$ we define the set of i's *action tokens* of the form $i{:}\alpha$, that is,

$$\Delta_i = \{i{:}\alpha \mid \alpha \in REP(i)\}.$$

That is, $i{:}\alpha$ is an action token of agent i only if α is part of i's repertoire. We note

$$\Delta = \bigcup_{i \in AGT} \Delta_i$$

the pointwise union of the sets of possible action tokens of all agents.

The following abbreviations are convenient to speak about joint actions of groups of agents. For every non-empty set of agents I we note $JACT_I$ the set of all possible *combinations of actions* of the agents in I (or *joint actions* of the agents in I), that is,

$$JACT_I = \prod_{i \in I} \Delta_i.$$

For notational convenience we write $JACT$ instead of $JACT_{AGT}$. Elements in every $JACT_I$ are tuples noted δ_I, δ_I', δ_I'',.... Elements in $JACT$ are simply noted δ, δ', δ'',... For example suppose that $I = \{1, 2, 3\}$ and $\delta_I = \langle 1{:}\alpha, 2{:}\beta, 3{:}\gamma \rangle$. This means that δ_I is the joint action of the agents $1, 2, 3$ in which 1 does action α, 2 does action β and 3 does action γ. For notational convenience, we write δ_i instead of $\delta_{\{i\}}$ for every $i \in AGT$.

The language of $\mathcal{SAL}$ is the set of formulas defined by the following BNF:

$$\varphi ::= p \mid \bot \mid \neg\varphi \mid \varphi \vee \varphi \mid \texttt{Agree}_I\varphi \mid \texttt{Do}_{i:\alpha}\varphi$$

where p ranges over ATM, i ranges over AGT, $i{:}\alpha$ ranges over Δ_i, and I ranges over 2^{AGT*}.

The classical Boolean connectives $\wedge$, $\rightarrow$, $\leftrightarrow$ and $\top$ (tautology) are defined from $\bot$, $\vee$ and $\neg$ in the usual manner.

The operators of our logic have the following reading.

- $\texttt{Agree}_I\varphi$: 'the agents in the group I agree that φ'.
- $\texttt{Do}_{i:\alpha}\varphi$: 'agent i is going to do α and φ will be true afterwards' (therefore $\texttt{Do}_{i:\alpha}\top$ is read: 'agent i is going to do α').

Operators of the form $\texttt{Agree}_I$ enable one to express those issues on which the agents in I agree, while forming a coalition. For example, $\texttt{Agree}_I\neg smokePublic$ expresses that the agents in I agree that people should not smoke in public spaces.

The formula $\texttt{Agree}_I\bot$ literally means that 'the agents in I agree on a contradiction'. We assign a special meaning to this formula by supposing that 'agreeing on a contradiction' means 'not being part of the same group' (or 'not forming a coalition'). This is because we assume that functioning as members of the same coalition is (at least in a minimal sense) a rational activity, and a rational group of agents cannot agree on a contradiction. Thus, $\texttt{Agree}_I\bot$ should be read 'the agents in I do not function as members of the same group' or 'the agents in I do not form a coalition' or 'the agents in I do not constitute a group'. Conversely, $\neg\texttt{Agree}_I\bot$ has to be read 'the agents in I function as members of the same group' or 'the agents in I form a coalition' or 'the agents in I constitute a group'. This concept of constituted group is expressed by the following abbreviation. For every $I \in 2^{AGT*}$:

$$\texttt{Group}(I) \stackrel{\text{def}}{=} \neg\texttt{Agree}_I\bot.$$

Note that this definition of group demands for some form of agreement, in particular if the agents in I form a coalition (i.e. $\texttt{Group}(I)$) then the agents in I agree that they form a coalition (i.e. $\texttt{Agree}_I\texttt{Group}(I)$). Indeed, as we will show in Section 3.3, our agreement operators satisfy the axiom $\neg\texttt{Agree}_I\varphi \rightarrow \texttt{Agree}_I\neg\texttt{Agree}_I\varphi$.

If I is a singleton then $\texttt{Agree}_I$ is used to express the individual preferences of agent i. That is, for every $i \in AGT$:

$$\texttt{Pref}_i\varphi \stackrel{\text{def}}{=} \texttt{Agree}_{\{i\}}\varphi.$$

Formula $\texttt{Pref}_i\varphi$ has to be read 'agent i prefers that φ is possible' (semantically this means that 'φ is true in all states that are preferred by agent i').

The following additional abbreviations will be useful to make more compact our notation in the sequel of the article. For every $i \in AGT$:

$$\text{Sat}_i \varphi \stackrel{\text{def}}{=} \neg \text{Pref}_i \neg \varphi.$$

Formula $\text{Sat}_i \varphi$ has to be read 'φ is a satisfactory state of affairs for agent i' (semantically this means that 'there exists at least one preferred state of agent i in which φ is true').

For every $I \in 2^{AGT*}$ and $\delta_I \in JACT_I$:

$$\text{Do}_{\delta_I} \varphi \stackrel{\text{def}}{=} \bigwedge_{j \in I} \text{Do}_{\delta_j} \varphi.$$

Formula $\text{Do}_{\delta_I} \varphi$ has to be read 'the agents in I execute in parallel their individual actions δ_i in the vector δ_I and φ will be true after this parallel execution'. We shorten this to 'the joint action δ_I is going to be performed by group I and φ will be true afterwards'. In other words, we consider a weak notion of joint action δ_I as the parallel execution of the individual actions δ_i by every agent in I.

For every $I \in 2^{AGT*}$:

$$\text{Pref}_I \varphi \stackrel{\text{def}}{=} \bigwedge_{j \in I} \text{Pref}_j \varphi;$$
$$\text{Sat}_I \varphi \stackrel{\text{def}}{=} \bigwedge_{j \in I} \text{Sat}_j \varphi.$$

Formula $\text{Pref}_I \varphi$ has to be read 'every agent in I prefers that φ is true', whilst $\text{Sat}_I \varphi$ has to be read 'φ is satisfactory for every agent in I'.

3.2 Semantics

Frames of the logic $\mathcal{SAL}$ ($\mathcal{SAL}$-frames) are tuples $F = \langle W, R, A \rangle$ defined as follows.

- W is a non empty set of possible worlds or states.
- $R : \Delta \longrightarrow W \times W$ maps every possible action token $i{:}\alpha$ to a deterministic relation $R_{i{:}\alpha}$ between possible worlds in W.[1]
- $A : 2^{AGT*} \longrightarrow W \times W$ maps every non-empty set of agents I to a transitive[2] and Euclidean[3] relation A_I between possible worlds in W.

It is convenient to view relations on W as functions from W to 2^W; therefore we write $A_I(w) = \{w' : (w, w') \in A_I\}$ and $R_{i{:}\alpha}(w) = \{w' : (w, w') \in R_{i{:}\alpha}\}$. If $A_I(w) \neq \emptyset$ and $R_{i{:}\alpha}(w) \neq \emptyset$ then we say that A_I and $R_{i{:}\alpha}$ are defined at w.

Given a world $w \in W$, $A_I(w)$ is the set of worlds which are compatible with group I's agreements at world w. If I is a singleton $\{i\}$ then $A_{\{i\}}(w)$ is the set of worlds that agent i prefers. If $(w, w') \in R_{i{:}\alpha}$ then w' is the unique actual *successor* world of world w, that will be reached from w through the occurrence of agent i's action α at w. (We might also say that $R_{i{:}\alpha}$ is a partial function). Therefore, if $R_{i{:}\alpha}(w) = \{w'\}$ then at w agent i performs an action α resulting in the next state w'.

---

[1] A relation $R_{i{:}\alpha}$ is deterministic iff, if $(w, w') \in R_{i{:}\alpha}$ and $(w, w'') \in R_{i{:}\alpha}$ then $w' = w''$.

[2] A relation A_I is transitive iff for every $w \in W$, if $(w, w') \in A_I$ and $(w', w'') \in A_I$ then $(w, w'') \in A_I$.

[3] A relation A_I is Euclidean iff for every $w \in W$, if $(w, w') \in A_I$ and $(w, w'') \in A_I$ then $(w', w'') \in A_I$.

It is convenient to use $R_{\delta_I} = \bigcap_{i \in I} R_{\delta_i}$. If $R_{\delta_I}(w) \neq \emptyset$ then coalition I performs joint action δ_I at w. If $w' \in \bigcap_{i \in I} R_{\delta_i}(w)$ then world w' results from the performance of joint action δ_I by I at w.

Frames will have to satisfy some other constraints in order to be legal $\mathcal{SAL}$-frames. For every $i, j \in AGT$, $\alpha \in REP(i)$, $\beta \in REP(j)$ and $w \in W$ we have:

S1   if $R_{i:\alpha}$ and $R_{j:\beta}$ are defined at w then $R_{i:\alpha}(w) = R_{j:\beta}(w)$.

Constraint S1 says that if w' is the *next* world of w which is reachable from w through the occurrence of agent i's action α and w'' is also the *next* world of w which is reachable from w through the occurrence of agent j's action β, then w' and w'' denote the same world. Indeed, we suppose that every world can only have one *next* world. Note that S1 implies the determinism of every $R_{i:\alpha}$. Moreover, note that constraint S1 justifies the reading of formula $\mathrm{Do}_{i:\alpha}\varphi$ as 'agent i is going to do α and φ will be true afterwards'. Indeed, we intend to express in our logic what agents *will do* as the result of their agreement on what to do together, rather than what agents *will possibly do*.

We also suppose that every agent can perform at most one action at each world. That is, for every $i \in AGT$ and $\alpha, \beta \in REP(i)$ such that $\alpha \neq \beta$ we have:

S2   if $R_{i:\alpha}$ is defined at w then $R_{i:\beta}$ is not defined at w.

We impose the following semantic constraint for individual preferences by supposing that every relation $A_{\{i\}}$ is serial, i.e. an agent has always at least one preferred state. For every $w \in W$ and $i \in AGT$:

S3 $A_{\{i\}}(w) \neq \emptyset$.

The following semantic constraint concerns the relationship between agreements and individual preferences. For every $w \in W$ and $I, J \in 2^{AGT*}$ such that $J \subseteq I$:

S4   if $w' \in A_I(w)$ then $w' \in A_J(w')$.

According to the constraint S4, if w' is a world which is compatible with I's agreements at w and J is a subgroup of group I, then w' belongs to the set of worlds that are compatible with J's agreements at w'.

The last two semantic constraints we consider are about the relationships between preferred states of an agent and actions. For every $w \in W$, $i \in AGT$ and $\delta_i \in \Delta_i$:

S5   if R_{δ_i} is defined at w' for every $w' \in A_{\{i\}}(w)$ then R_{δ_i} is defined at w.

According to the constraint S5, if action δ_i of agent i occurs in every state which is preferred by agent i, then the action δ_i occurs in the current state.

For every $w \in W$ and $i \in AGT$:

S6   if R_{δ_i} is defined at w then there exists $I \in 2^{AGT*}$ such that $i \in I$ and R_{δ_i} is defined at w' for every $w' \in A_I(w)$.

According to the constraint S6, if agent i's action δ_i occurs at world w then there exists a group I to which i belongs such that, for every world w' which is compatible with I's agreements at w, i's action δ_i occurs at w'.

Models of the logic $\mathcal{SAL}$ ($\mathcal{SAL}$-models) are tuples $M = \langle F, V \rangle$ defined as follows.

- F is a $\mathcal{SAL}$-frame.
- $V : W \longrightarrow 2^{ATM}$ is a valuation function.

Given a model M, a world w and a formula φ, we write $M, w \models \varphi$ to mean that φ is true at world w in M. The rules defining the truth conditions of formulas are just standard for p, $\bot$, $\neg$ and $\vee$. The following are the remaining truth conditions for $\mathtt{Agree}_I\varphi$ and $\mathtt{Do}_{i:\alpha}$.

- $M, w \models \mathtt{Agree}_I\varphi$ iff $M, w' \models \varphi$ for all w' such that $w' \in A_I(w)$
- $M, w \models \mathtt{Do}_{i:\alpha}\varphi$ iff there exists $w' \in R_{i:\alpha}(w)$ such that $M, w' \models \varphi$

Note that $\mathtt{Agree}_I$ is a modal operator of type necessity, whilst $\mathtt{Do}_{i:\alpha}$ is of type possibility. The following section is devoted to illustrate the axiomatization of $\mathcal{SAL}$.

3.3 Axiomatization

The axiomatization of the logic $\mathcal{SAL}$ includes all tautologies of propositional calculus and the rule of inference *modus ponens* (**MP**).

(MP)   From $\vdash_{\mathcal{SAL}} \varphi$ and $\vdash_{\mathcal{SAL}} \varphi \to \psi$ infer $\vdash_{\mathcal{SAL}} \psi$

We have the following four principles for the dynamic operators $\mathtt{Do}_{i:\alpha}$.

($\mathbf{K_{Do}}$) $(\mathtt{Do}_{i:\alpha}\varphi \wedge \neg\mathtt{Do}_{i:\alpha}\neg\psi) \to \mathtt{Do}_{i:\alpha}(\varphi \wedge \psi)$

($\mathbf{Alt_{Do}}$) $\mathtt{Do}_{i:\alpha}\varphi \to \neg\mathtt{Do}_{j:\beta}\neg\varphi$

(Single) $\mathtt{Do}_{i:\alpha}\top \to \neg\mathtt{Do}_{i:\beta}\top$ if $\alpha \neq \beta$

($\mathbf{Nec_{Do}}$)   From $\vdash_{\mathcal{SAL}} \varphi$ infer $\vdash_{\mathcal{SAL}} \neg\mathtt{Do}_{i:\alpha}\neg\varphi$

Dynamic operators of the form $\mathtt{Do}_{i:\alpha}$ are modal operators which satisfy the axioms and rule of inference of the basic normal modal logic K (Axiom $\mathbf{K_{Do}}$ and rule of inference $\mathbf{Nec_{Do}}$). Moreover, according to Axiom $\mathbf{Alt_{Do}}$, if i is going to do α and φ will be true afterwards, then it cannot be the case that j is going to do β and $\neg\varphi$ will be true afterwards. According to Axiom **Single**, an agent cannot perform more than one action at a time. This axiom makes perfectly sense in simplified artificial settings and in game-theoretic scenarios in which actions of agents and joint actions of groups never occur in parallel.

    We have the following principles for the agreement operators and the preference operators, and for the relationships between agreement operators, preference operators and dynamic operators.

($\mathbf{K_{Agree}}$) $(\mathtt{Agree}_I\varphi \wedge \mathtt{Agree}_I(\varphi \to \psi)) \to \mathtt{Agree}_I\psi$

($\mathbf{D_{Pref}}$) $\neg\mathtt{Pref}_i\bot$

($\mathbf{4_{Agree}}$) $\mathtt{Agree}_I\varphi \to \mathtt{Agree}_I\mathtt{Agree}_I\varphi$

($\mathbf{5_{Agree}}$) $\neg\mathtt{Agree}_I\varphi \to \mathtt{Agree}_I\neg\mathtt{Agree}_I\varphi$

($\mathbf{Subgroup_{Agree}}$) $\mathtt{Agree}_I(\varphi \to \neg\mathtt{Agree}_J\neg\varphi)$ if $J \subseteq I$

($\mathbf{Int1_{Pref,Do}}$) $\mathtt{Pref}_i\mathtt{Do}_{\delta_i}\top \to \mathtt{Do}_{\delta_i}\top$

($\mathbf{Int2_{Pref,Do}}$) $\mathtt{Do}_{\delta_i}\top \to \bigvee_{i \in I} \mathtt{Agree}_I\mathtt{Do}_{\delta_i}$

($\mathbf{Nec_{Agree}}$)   From $\vdash_{\mathcal{SAL}} \varphi$ infer $\vdash_{\mathcal{SAL}} \mathtt{Agree}_I\varphi$

Operators for agreement of the form $\mathtt{Agree}_I$ are modal operators which satisfy the axioms and rule of inference of the basic normal modal logic K45 [4] (Axioms $\mathbf{K}_{\mathtt{Agree}}$, $\mathbf{4}_{\mathtt{Agree}}$ and $\mathbf{5}_{\mathtt{Agree}}$, and rule of inference $\mathbf{Nec}_{\mathtt{Agree}}$). It is supposed that the agents in a coalition always agree on the contents of their agreements and on the contents of their disagreements (Axioms $\mathbf{4}_{\mathtt{Agree}}$ and $\mathbf{5}_{\mathtt{Agree}}$). That is, if the agents in I agree (resp. do not agree) that φ should be true then, they agree that they agree (resp. do not agree) that φ should be true.

We add a specific principle for individual preferences by supposing that an agent cannot have contradictory preferences (Axiom $\mathbf{D}_{\mathtt{Pref}}$).

Axiom $\mathbf{Subgroup}_{\mathtt{Agree}}$ is about the relationship between the agreements of a group and the agreements of its subgroups. The agents of a group I agree that φ should be true only if there is no subgroup J of I such that J agree that φ should be false. A specific instance of Axiom $\mathbf{Subgroup}_{\mathtt{Agree}}$ is $\mathtt{Agree}_I(\varphi \rightarrow \mathtt{Sat}_i\varphi)$ if $i \in I$. This means that the agents of a group I agree that φ should be true only if φ is satisfactory for every agent in I. A more detailed explanation of the logical consequences of Axiom $\mathbf{Subgroup}_{\mathtt{Agree}}$ is given in Section 5.

Axiom $\mathbf{Int1}_{\mathtt{Pref,Do}}$ and Axiom $\mathbf{Int2}_{\mathtt{Pref,Do}}$ are general principles of intentionality describing the relationship between an agent's action, his preferences, and the agreements of the group to which the agent belongs. According to Axiom $\mathbf{Int1}_{\mathtt{Pref,Do}}$, if agent i prefers that he performs action δ_i (δ_i occurs in all states that are preferred by agent i) then agent i starts to perform action δ_i. A similar principle for the relationship between individual intentions and action occurrences has been studied in [15]. According to Axiom $\mathbf{Int2}_{\mathtt{Pref,Do}}$, if an agent i starts to perform a certain action δ_i then it means that either agents i prefers to perform this action or there exists some group I to which agent i belongs such that the agents in I agree that i should perform action δ_i. In other terms, an agent i's action δ_i is intentional in a general sense: either it is driven by i's intention to perform action δ_i or it is driven by the collective intention that i performs action δ_i of a group I to which agent i belongs.

We call $\mathcal{SAL}$ the logic axiomatized by the axioms and rules of inference presented above. We write $\vdash_{\mathcal{SAL}} \varphi$ if formula φ is a theorem of $\mathcal{SAL}$ (i.e. φ is the derivable from the axioms and rules of inference of the logic $\mathcal{SAL}$). We write $\models_{\mathcal{SAL}} \varphi$ if φ is *valid* in all $\mathcal{SAL}$-models, i.e. $M, w \models \varphi$ for every $\mathcal{SAL}$-model M and world w in M. Finally, we say that φ is *satisfiable* if there exists a $\mathcal{SAL}$-model M and world w in M such that $M, w \models \varphi$. We can prove that the logic $\mathcal{SAL}$ is *sound* and *complete* with respect to the class of $\mathcal{SAL}$-frames. Namely:

Theorem 1. *$\mathcal{SAL}$ is determined by the class of $\mathcal{SAL}$-frames.*

Proof. It is a routine task to check that the axioms of the logic $\mathcal{SAL}$ correspond one-to-one to their semantic counterparts on the frames. In particular, Axioms $\mathbf{4}_{\mathtt{Agree}}$ and $\mathbf{5}_{\mathtt{Agree}}$ correspond to the transitivity and Euclideanity of every relation A_I. Axiom $\mathbf{D}_{\mathtt{Pref}}$ corresponds to the seriality of every relation $A_{\{i\}}$ (constraint S3). Axiom $\mathbf{Alt}_{\mathtt{Do}}$ corresponds to the semantic constraint S1. Axiom $\mathbf{Single}$ corresponds to the semantic constraint S2. Axiom $\mathbf{Subgroup}_{\mathtt{Agree}}$ corresponds to the semantic constraint S4. Axiom $\mathbf{Int1}_{\mathtt{Pref,Do}}$ corresponds to the semantic constraint S5. $\mathbf{Int2}_{\mathtt{Pref,Do}}$ corresponds to the semantic constraint S6.

It is routine, too, to check that all of our axioms are in the Sahlqvist class. This means that the axioms are all expressible as first-order conditions on frames and that they are complete with respect to the defined frames classes, cf. [2, Th. 2.42].   □

4   Discussion

One might wonder why we did not include a principle of monotonicity of the form $\text{Agree}_I\varphi \rightarrow \text{Agree}_J\varphi$ for $J \subseteq I$ in our logic of agreement: for every sets of agents I and J such that $J \subseteq I$, if the agents in I agree that φ should be true then the agents in the subgroup J agree that φ should be true as well. We did not do include this principle because we think that it is not sufficiently general to be applied in all situations. Indeed, a minority group J of a larger group I might exist which does not have the same view than the larger group. For example, imagine I is the group of members of a political party who are choosing the leader of the party for the next years. All agents in I agree that a certain member of the party called Mr. Brown should be the leader for the next years. This is the official position of the party. At the same time, a small minority of I in conspiracy agree that Mr. Black should be the leader.

Consider now the following principle $\text{Agree}_I(\varphi \rightarrow \bigwedge_{i \in I} \text{Pref}_i\varphi)$ and even the weaker $\text{Agree}_I(\varphi \rightarrow \bigvee_{i \in I} \text{Pref}_i\varphi)$: every group of agents I agree that φ should be true only if all of them prefer φ, and every group of agents I agree that φ should be true only if some of them prefers φ. These two principles are also too strong. Indeed, the agents in a group I might agree that φ should be true, without claiming that φ must be preferred by every agent in I and without claiming that φ must be preferred by some agent in I. For example, the members of a community I might agree that taxes should be payed by every agent in I without claiming and agreeing that tax payment must be preferred by every agent in I, and without claiming and agreeing that tax payment must be preferred by some agent in I. The members of the community just agree that tax payment must be something preferable by the whole community.

Finally, let us explain why we did not include stronger versions of Axiom $\textbf{Int1}_{\text{Pref,Do}}$ and Axiom $\textbf{Int2}_{\text{Pref,Do}}$ of the form $\text{Agree}_I\text{Do}_{\delta_I}\top \rightarrow \text{Do}_{\delta_I}\top$ and $\text{Do}_{\delta_I}\top \rightarrow \text{Agree}_I\text{Do}_{\delta_I}\top$ in the axiomatization of our logic $\mathcal{SAL}$ for every $I \in 2^{AGT*}$. On the one hand $\text{Agree}_I\text{Do}_{\delta_I}\top \rightarrow \text{Do}_{\delta_I}\top$ is too strong because autonomous agents should be capable to violate norms and to decide not to conform to agreements with other agents (see Section 7). For example, agents might agree at the public level that each of them should pay taxes (i.e. $\text{Agree}_{\{1,...,n\}}\text{Do}_{\langle 1:payTaxes,...,n:payTaxes\rangle}\top$) but, in private, some of them does not pay taxes (i.e. $\neg\text{Do}_{\langle 1:payTaxes,...,n:payTaxes\rangle}\top$). On the other hand, $\text{Do}_{\delta_I}\top \rightarrow \text{Agree}_I\text{Do}_{\delta_I}\top$ is too strong because there are situations in which the agents in a set I perform a joint action δ_I without agreeing that such a joint action should be performed. Each agent in I is doing his part in δ_I without caring what the other agents in I do. For example, i might be cooking while j is reading a book without reciprocally caring what the other does, and without agreeing that the action of cooking performed by i and the action of reading performed by j should occur together. One might say that i and j do not have *interdependent reasons* for jointly preferring that i cooks while j reads a book.

5 Some $\mathcal{SAL}$-Theorems

Let us now discuss some $\mathcal{SAL}$-theorems. The first group of theorems present some generalizations of Axioms **Alt$_{Do}$** and **Single** for joint actions of groups.

Proposition 1. *For every $I, J \in 2^{AGT*}$ and $\delta_I, \delta'_I, \delta_J$ such that $\delta_I \neq \delta'_I$:*

(1a) $\vdash_{\mathcal{SAL}} \mathrm{Do}_{\delta_I}\varphi \rightarrow \neg\mathrm{Do}_{\delta_J}\neg\varphi$

(1b) $\vdash_{\mathcal{SAL}} \mathrm{Do}_{\delta_I}\top \rightarrow \neg\mathrm{Do}_{\delta'_I}\top$

According to Theorem 1a, if group I is going to perform the joint action δ_I and φ will be true afterwards, then it cannot be the case that group J is going to perform the joint action δ_J and φ is going to be false afterwards. According to Theorem 1b, every group of agents can never perform more than one joint action at a time.

The second group of theorems present some interesting properties of agreement. Theorems 2a and 2b are derivable from Axioms **4$_{Agree}$**, **5$_{Agree}$** and **D$_{Pref}$**. According to these two theorems, the agents in I agree (resp. do not agree) that φ if and only if they agree that they agree (resp. do not agree) that φ. According to Theorem 2c, a group of agents I can intend to perform at most one joint action. Theorem 2d expresses a unanimity principle for agreement: for every set of agents I, the agents in I agree that if each of them prefers φ then φ should be the case. Theorem 2e expresses an interesting property about coalition formation and coalition disintegration: if the agents in I agree that a minority part J of I agrees that φ and another minority part J' of I agrees that $\neg\varphi$, then the agents in I do not form a coalition (i.e. I is not a constituted group).

Proposition 2. *For every $I, J, J' \in 2^{AGT*}$ and δ_I, δ'_I such that $\delta_I \neq \delta'_I$ and $J, J' \subseteq I$:*

(2a) $\vdash_{\mathcal{SAL}} \mathrm{Agree}_I\varphi \leftrightarrow \mathrm{Agree}_I\mathrm{Agree}_I\varphi$

(2b) $\vdash_{\mathcal{SAL}} \neg\mathrm{Agree}_I\varphi \leftrightarrow \mathrm{Agree}_I\neg\mathrm{Agree}_I\varphi$

(2c) $\vdash_{\mathcal{SAL}} \mathrm{Agree}_I\mathrm{Do}_{\delta_I}\top \rightarrow \neg\mathrm{Agree}_I\mathrm{Do}_{\delta'_I}\top$

(2d) $\vdash_{\mathcal{SAL}} \mathrm{Agree}_I(\bigwedge_{i\in I}\mathrm{Pref}_i\varphi \rightarrow \varphi)$

(2e) $\vdash_{\mathcal{SAL}} \mathrm{Agree}_I(\mathrm{Agree}_J\varphi \wedge \mathrm{Agree}_{J'}\neg\varphi) \rightarrow \neg\mathrm{Group}(I)$

At the current stage, our logic does not allow to deal with situations in which I is a constituted group, the agents I agree about a certain fact φ and, at the same time, they agree that some agents in I prefer $\neg\varphi$. Formally, by Theorem 2e and Axiom **4$_{Agree}$**, we can prove that formula $\mathrm{Agree}_I\varphi \wedge \mathrm{Agree}_I\mathrm{Pref}_i\neg\varphi$ implies $\neg\mathrm{Group}(I)$, if $i \in I$. This means that at the current stage our logic $\mathcal{SAL}$ does not allow to handle collective decisions based on special procedures like majority voting in which certain agents might find a collective agreement about something while agreeing that it is not based on unanimous preferences. For example, the agents in I might be the members of the Parliament of a certain country and form a coalition (i.e. $\mathrm{Group}(I)$). They might collectively decide by majority voting to declare war upon another country (i.e. $\mathrm{Agree}_I war$), although they agree that there is a (pacifist) minority $i, j \in I$ preferring that war is not declared upon another country (i.e. $\mathrm{Agree}_I(\mathrm{Pref}_i\neg war \wedge \mathrm{Pref}_j\neg war)$). Although we are aware that this is a limitation of our proposal, we think that our logic of agreement is still sufficiently general to model informal and non-structured groups in which there are no special voting procedures nor special roles (e.g. legislators, officials of the law, etc.) which are responsible for agreement creation. In fact, in such a kind of groups agreements are often about solutions to coordination (or cooperation) problems which are satisfactory for all agents in the group (e.g. some agents find an agreement to have dinner together at a Japanese restaurant rather than at an Indian restaurant).

6   Reaching an Agreement on What to do Together

We can provide in our logic $\mathcal{SAL}$ the formal specification of some additional principles explaining how some agents might reach an agreement on what to do together starting from their individual preferences. We do not intend to add these principles to the axiomatization of $\mathcal{SAL}$ presented in Section 3.3. We just show that $\mathcal{SAL}$ is sufficiently expressive to capture them both syntactically and semantically so that they can be easily integrated into our formal framework. The principles we intend to characterize are specified in terms of agreements about the conditions under which a certain joint action should be performed.

In certain circumstances, it is plausible to suppose that a group of agents I agree that if there exists a unique satisfactory joint action δ_I for all agents in I, then such a joint action should occur. In other terms, the agents in a group I agree on the validity of the following general principle: 'Do together the joint action δ_I, if it is the only joint action that satisfies every agent in I!'. This criteria is often adopted by groups of agents in order to find cooperative solutions which are satisfactory for all them. For example, in a Prisoner Dilemma scenario with two agents i and j the joint action $\langle i{:}cooperate, j{:}cooperate \rangle$ is the only satisfactory solution for both agents. If the two agents i and j agree on the previous principle and face a PD game, then they will agree that $\langle i{:}cooperate, j{:}cooperate \rangle$ is the joint action that they should perform. The previous principle of agreement creation is formally expressed in our logic as follows. For every $I \in 2^{AGT*}$ and $\delta_I \in JACT_I$:

(*) $\mathtt{Agree}_I((\mathtt{Sat}_I\mathtt{Do}_{\delta_I}\top \land \bigwedge\limits_{\delta_I' \neq \delta_I} \neg\mathtt{Sat}_I\,\mathtt{Do}_{\delta_I'}\top) \rightarrow \mathtt{Do}_{\delta_I}\top)$

Principle * corresponds to the following semantic constraint over $\mathcal{SAL}$-frames. For every $w \in W$, $I \in 2^{AGT*}$ and $\delta_I \in JACT_I$:

S6   if $w' \in A_I(w)$ and $A_{\{i\}} \circ R_{\delta_I}(w') \neq \emptyset$ for all $i \in I$ and, for all $\delta_I' \neq \delta_I$ there exists $i \in I$ such that $A_{\{i\}} \circ R_{\delta_I'}(w') = \emptyset$ then, $R_{\delta_I}(w') \neq \emptyset$

where $A_{\{i\}} \circ R_{\delta_I}(w')$ is defined as $\bigcup\{R_{\delta_I}(v) \mid v \in S_i(w')\}$.

If we suppose that the Principle * is valid then the following consequence is derivable for every $I \in 2^{AGT*}$ and $\delta_I \in JACT_I$:

(3) $\mathtt{Agree}_I(\mathtt{Sat}_I\mathtt{Do}_{\delta_I}\top \land \bigwedge\limits_{\delta_I' \neq \delta_I} \neg\mathtt{Sat}_I\,\mathtt{Do}_{\delta_I'}\top) \rightarrow \mathtt{Agree}_I\mathtt{Do}_{\delta_I}\top$

REMARK. Note that in the previous Principles * and 3 of agreement creation *mutual trust* between the agents in the group is implicitly supposed, that is, it is supposed that every agent i in I thinks it possible that the other agents in I will do their parts in the joint action δ_I. Indeed, trust between the members of the group is a necessary condition for agreement creation (on this point, see [1] for instance). We postpone to future work a formal analysis of the relationships between trust and agreement. To this aim, we will have to extend our logic $\mathcal{SAL}$ with doxastic modalities to express agents' beliefs.

Example 1. Imagine a situation of exchange of goods in EBay between two agents i and j. Agent i is the buyer and agent j is the seller. They have to perform a one-shot trade transaction. We suppose $AGT = \{i, j\}$. Agent i has the following two actions available: *pay* and *skip* (do nothing). Agent j has the following two actions available: *send* and *skip* (do nothing). That is, $\Delta_i = \{i{:}send, i{:}skip\}$ and $\Delta_j = \{j{:}pay, j{:}skip\}$. Therefore, the set of possible joint actions of the two agents is

$JACT = \{\langle i{:}skip, j{:}skip \rangle, \langle i{:}send, j{:}skip \rangle, \langle i{:}skip, j{:}pay \rangle, \langle i{:}send, j{:}pay \rangle\}.$

The two agents i and j agree that the situation in which i sends the product and j pays is satisfactory for both of them.

(A) $\texttt{Agree}_{\{i,j\}} \texttt{Sat}_{\{i,j\}} \texttt{Do}_{\langle i{:}send, j{:}pay \rangle} \top.$

Moreover, agent i and agent j agree that the situation in which i does nothing and j pays the product, the situation in which i sends the product and j does not nothing, and the situation in which i and j do nothing, always leave one of them unhappy. Thus we have that agent i and agent j agree that there is no other situation different from $\langle i{:}send, j{:}pay \rangle$ that is a satisfactory situation for both of them:

(B) $\texttt{Agree}_{\{i,j\}} \bigwedge_{\delta'_{\{i,j\}} \neq \langle i{:}send, j{:}pay \rangle} \neg\texttt{Sat}_{\{i,j\}} \texttt{Do}_{\delta'_I} \top.$

From items A and B, by using Principle 3, we infer that agent i and agent j agree that they should perform the joint action $\langle i{:}send, j{:}pay \rangle$:

(C) $\texttt{Agree}_{\{i,j\}} \texttt{Do}_{\langle i{:}send, j{:}pay \rangle} \top.$

Other conditions under which the agents in a group can reach an agreement on what to do together could be studied in our logical framework. For instance, one might want to have general principles of the following form which can be used to find a solution in coordination problems. Suppose that δ_I and δ'_I are both satisfactory joint actions for all agents in group I. Moreover, there are no joint actions δ''_I different from δ_I and δ'_I which are satisfactory for all agents in I. Then, either the agents in I agree that δ_I should be performed or they agree that δ'_I should be performed. In other terms, if the agents in a group I face a coordination problem then they strive to find a solution to this problem.

7 Grounding Norms and Commitments on Agreements

The logic of agreement $\mathcal{SAL}$ presented in the previous section provides not only a formal framework in which the relationships between individual preferences of agents in a group and group agreements can be studied, but also it suggests a different perspective on concepts traditionally studied in the field of deontic logic.

Consider for instance deontic statements of the following form "within the context of group I it is required that agent i will perform action δ_i," or "within the context of group I it is required that agent i will perform his part in the joint action δ_I together with the other agents in I". These statements just say that i has a *directed obligation* towards his group I to do a certain action as part of a joint plan of the group I (see e.g. [13,14] for a different perspective on directed obligations). By way of example, imagine the situation in which agent i and agent j are trying to organize a party together. After a brief negotiation, they conclude that i will prepare the cake, while j will buy drinks for the party. In this situation, "within the context of group $\{i, j\}$ it is required that agent i will prepare the cake for the party and it is required that agent j will buy drinks for the party". The following abbreviation expresses the classical deontic notion of directed obligation in terms of the concept of agreement. For every $I \in 2^{AGT*}$, $i \in I$ and $\delta_i \in \Delta_i$:

$$\texttt{Oblig}_i(\delta_i, I) \stackrel{\text{def}}{=} \texttt{Agree}_I \texttt{Do}_{\delta_i} \top.$$

Formula $\texttt{Oblig}_i(\delta_i, I)$ has to be read 'within the context of group I it is required that agent i will perform action δ_i'.[4] It is to be noted that the notion of directed obligation represents an essential constituent of the notion of *social commitment*. Thus, in our approach, an essential aspect of an agent i's commitment with respect to his group I to do a certain action δ_i is the fact that all agents in I agree that i should perform action δ_i. Since all agents in the group I agree on this, they are entitled to require agent i to perform this action. Moving beyond the notion of directed obligation as an essential constituent of social commitment, our logic $\mathcal{SAL}$ can be used to provide a a formal characterization of the notion of *mutual (directed) obligation* in a group I, as 'every agent in I is required to perform his part in a joint action δ_I of the group'. Formally, for every $I \in 2^{AGT*}$ and $\delta_I \in JACT_I$:

$$\texttt{MutualObg}_I(\delta_I) \stackrel{\text{def}}{=} \bigwedge_{i \in I} \texttt{Oblig}_i(\delta_i, I).$$

Formula $\texttt{MutualObg}_I(\delta_I)$, which is equivalent to $\texttt{Agree}_I \texttt{Do}_{\delta_I} \top$, has to be read 'the agents in the group I are mutually obliged to perform their parts in the joint action δ_I'. This notion of mutual (directed) obligation is an essential constituent of the notion of *mutual (social) commitment*. As already emphasized in Section 4, in our logic agents can violate obligations assigned to them (breaking their social commitments). Violation of a directed obligation is expressed in our logic by the construction $\texttt{Oblig}_i(\delta_i, I) \wedge \neg \texttt{Do}_{\delta_i} \top$: within the context of group I it is required that agent i will perform action δ_i, but agent i does not perform action δ_i. The discussion on the notion of commitment will be extended in Section 8 where our approach will be compared with some formal approaches to agreement recently proposed in the MAS area.

8   Related Work

The literature on agents, organizations, agreements is too vast to be given an exhaustive overview here: let us provide pointers to some significant works that relate to our effort

---

[4] Note that $\texttt{Oblig}_i(\delta_i, I)$ captures a specific notion of obligation based on agreement. We are aware that other forms of obligations exist in social life like legal obligations or moral obligations (an agent may feel obliged to do something for his own moral reasons).

or that are set against it in a way that stimulates discussion. We take inspiration from Garcia et al. [10] to determine the dimensions along which multi-agent organizational concepts are developed: structural, functional, dynamic, and normative.

From a conceptual perspective, the formalization of agreements comes before any structural consideration. As an example, Dignum et al. [7] propose an attempt to describe minimum requirements for agents to be organized into an institution. The minimum requirements rely on an existing institution designed with the ISLANDER tool [8], and call for a middle agent. ISLANDER is probably the most complete tool to date for the specification of institutions in terms of roles and scenes. The tool is kept as general as possible to allow for the widest possible variety of definable institutions. Nevertheless, the specification of an institution is entirely performed by a human designer, and agents join an institution by assuming one or more roles, with no account of the process by which individuals look for and reach agreements that give rise to an institution. Thus, the platform is an effective means to translate an existing institution into a MAS, but the automatization of the creation of organizations is out of scope.

With respect to the functional dimension of organizations, that is, their goals and how to achieve them, we adopt the conceptual distinction drawn by Griffiths and Luck [12] between teamwork and coalition formation. The former is seen as focused on task assignment and action coordination among agents in the short term, whereas the latter is said to be dealing with the establishment in the long term of a group of agents with a common aim or goal. Although agreeing with the authors in viewing multi-agent organizations as a means to achieve long-termed objectives and in considering trust as a key concept for an organization that influences an agent's decisions on undertaking cooperations, our focus is slightly different in the context of this research: we consider an organization to be born when an agreement is made, so our efforts are on the formalization of agreements. An investigation on the relationship between trust and agreements lies ahead in our research path. Nevertheless, we share the authors' aim to determine the basic principles that lead to the creation of organizations, as opposed to several coalition formation research works optimizing match-making algorithms between a set of tasks and a set of agent capabilities (e.g.: [18]).

We can consider dynamic and normative dimensions as intrinsic to any attempt to formalize a concept like a multi-agent organization. Dynamic aspects include the formation and the evolution of coalitions of agents and, on a smaller scale, the preconditions and the consequences of an agent's action. When these conditions deal with deontic concepts the MAS is characterized also by a normative dimension. An important question is which normative concept or set of concepts to choose as the fundamental basis for the formalization of organizations. Dignum et al., for instance, choose violation as a fundamental concept to define deadlines in a MAS [6]. Violation is surely a very important concept in any normative context, and especially in those where deadlines are the central focus. Nevertheless, we argue that it does not play a primary role when one wants to deal with a more general overview of organizations, especially electronic ones. As pointed out by Cardoso et al. [3], while in real life a coercive action is eventually enforced against individuals not able or willing to abide by a sanction deriving by some misdemeanor, such coercions are not (yet?) implementable in a distributed information system, so that effectiveness of violations and relevant sanctions is somehow diminished. Boella and van der Torre [9] propose contracts, defined as a special type of beliefs ascribed to a group of agents, as a foundational means for the creation of legal institutions. We follow a similar approach, but consider agreement as a more basic concept that precedes contracts.

In [20] a formal approach to multiparty agreement between agents is proposed based on the notion of social commitment: A multiparty agreement among the agents in $\{1, \ldots, n\}$ is given by a set of commitments $\{C_1, \ldots, C_n\}$ where C_i the commitment that agent i has towards the other agents. In this approach the notion of commitment is taken as a primitive concept and the notion of agreement is built on it, which we counter by starting from a primitive notion of agreement in a group I (which depends on the individual preferences of the agents in I), on the top of which we built a notion of directed obligation, the essential constituent of the notion of social commitment. The logic of agreement $\mathcal{SAL}$ has some similarities with the logical framework based on the concept of acceptance we presented in [16] and [11], in which a logical analysis of the relationships between the rules and norms of an institution and the *acceptances* of these rules and norms by the members of the institution has been provided. However, these works do not analyze the relationships between individual preferences of agents and collective acceptances (or agreements) which we presented in this paper.

9   Conclusions

This work is a starting point of a long enterprise. Our long-term aim is to provide a formal specification of all the basic notions that characterize organizations in general, including those in the real world, and we started with what we consider to be a fundamental concept: agreement. The formalization of this concept with a logical approach aims at analyzing in detail both its static characteristics and its dynamic properties, that is, what is meant by the term agreement and how it is supposed to influence agents' behavior when cooperation is the common goal. Once a model is universally established which is formal and general enough to abstract from particular types of organizations or specific operational details, such a model may be used as a sound basis for an agent-based implementation that can really have a significant impact on economic or social scientific contexts. The relations between our formalization of agreement and the notions of norms and commitments have been investigated in this work, but other dimensions of multi-agent interaction, such as trust, are still to be tackled, which is what we intend to pursue in the future.

Acknowledgements

Emiliano Lorini is supported by the project ForTrust "Social trust analysis and formalization" ANR-06-SETI-006 financed by the French ANR.

References

1. Andrighetto, G., Tummolini, L., Castelfranchi, C., Conte, R.: A convention or (tacit) agreement between us. In: van Benthem, V.F., Hendricks, J., Symons, J., Pedersen, S.A. (eds.) Between Logic and Intuition: David Lewis and the Future of Formal Methods, Philosophy Synthese Library. Springer, Heidelberg (to appear)

2. Blackburn, P., de Rijke, M., Venema, Y.: Modal Logic. Cambridge University Press, Cambridge (2001)
3. Cardoso, H.L., Rocha, A.P., Oliveira, E.: Supporting virtual organizations through electronic institutions and normative multi-agent system. In: Rennard, J.P. (ed.) Handbook of Research on Nature Inspired Computing for Economy and Management. Idea Group, USA (2006)
4. Chellas, B.F.: Modal logic: an introduction. Cambridge University Press, Cambridge (1980)
5. DeLoach, S.A.: Moving multiagent systems from research to practice. In: Future of Software Engineering and Multi-Agent Systems, FOSE-MAS (2008)
6. Dignum, F., Broersen, J., Dignum, V., Meyer, J.J.: Meeting the deadline: Why, when and how. In: Hinchey, M.G., Rash, J.L., Truszkowski, W.F., Rouff, C.A. (eds.) FAABS 2004. LNCS (LNAI), vol. 3228, pp. 30–40. Springer, Heidelberg (2004)
7. Dignum, F., Dignum, V., Thangarajah, J., Padgham, L., Winikoff, M.: Open agent systems??? In: Luck, M., Padgham, L. (eds.) Agent-Oriented Software Engineering VIII. LNCS, vol. 4951, pp. 73–87. Springer, Heidelberg (2008)
8. Esteva, M., de la Cruz, D., Sierra, C.: Islander: an electronic institutions editor. In: Proceedings of AAMAS '02, pp. 1045–1052. ACM Press, New York (2002)
9. Boella, G., van der Torre, L.: Contracts as legal institutions in organizations of autonomous agents. In: Proceedings of AAMAS '04, pp. 948–955. ACM Press, New York (2004)
10. Garcia, E., Argente, E., Giret, A., Botti, V.: Issues for organizational multiagent systems development. In: Sixth International Workshop From Agent Theory to Agent Implementation (AT2AI-6), pp. 59–65 (2008)
11. Gaudou, B., Longin, D., Lorini, E., Tummolini, L.: Anchoring institutions in agents' attitudes: Towards a logical framework for autonomous mas. In: Proceedings of AAMAS '08, pp. 728–735. ACM Press, New York (2008)
12. Griffiths, N., Luck, M.: Coalition formation through motivation and trust. In: Proceedings of AAMAS '03, pp. 17–24. ACM Press, New York (2003)
13. Kanger, S., Kanger, H.: Rights and parliamentarism. Theoria 6(2), 85–115 (1966)
14. Lindahl, L.: Stig Kanger's theory of rights. In: Holmström-Hintikka, G., Lindström, S., Sliwinski, R. (eds.) Collected Papers of Stig Kanger with Essays on his Life and Work, vol. 2, pp. 151–171. Kluwer, Dordrecht (2001)
15. Lorini, E., Herzig, A.: A logic of intention and attempt. Synthese 163(1), 45–77
16. Lorini, E., Longin, D., Gaudou, B., Herzig, A.: The logic of acceptance: Grounding institutions on agents' attitudes. Journal of Logic and Computation (to appear)
17. Noriega, P., Sierra, C.: Electronic institutions: Future trends and challenges. In: Klusch, M., Ossowski, S., Shehory, O. (eds.) CIA 2002. LNCS (LNAI), vol. 2446, pp. 14–17. Springer, Heidelberg (2002)
18. Shehory, O., Sycara, K.P., Jha, S.: Multi-agent coordination through coalition formation. In: Rao, A., Singh, M.P., Wooldridge, M.J. (eds.) ATAL 1997. LNCS, vol. 1365, pp. 143–154. Springer, Heidelberg (1998)
19. Sycara, K., Paolucci, M., van Velsen, N., Giampapa, J.A.: The Retsina MAS infrastructure. Autonomous Agents and MAS 7(1-2) (2003)
20. Wan, F., Singh, M.P.: Formalizing and achieving multiparty agreements via commitments. In: Proceedings of AAMAS '05, pp. 770–777. ACM Press, New York (2005)

Promotion of Selfish Agents
in Hierarchical Organisations

Suzanne Sadedin[1] and Christian Guttmann[2]

[1] Clayton School of Information Technology
Monash University, Melbourne, Australia
suzanne.sadedin@infotech.monash.edu.au
[2] Department of General Practice
Faculty of Medicine, Nursing and Health Sciences
Monash University, Melbourne, Australia
christian.guttmann@gmail.com

Abstract. In hierarchical organisations, a preferred outcome is to promote a more productive worker to a more influential status. However, productivity is rarely directly measurable, so an individual worker often has both motive and opportunity to misrepresent his productivity. This leads to an alternative possibility: the promotion of selfish individuals. We use an agent-based model to study how selfishness and competency of agents influence their promotion in hierarchical organisations. We consider the case where selfish agents can overstate their productivity and thus obtain undeserved promotions. Our results suggest that more productive agents reach positions of power most of the time. However, even under ideal conditions, selfish agents occasionally dominate the higher levels of a hierarchical organisation, which in turn has a dramatic effect on all lower levels. For organisations of around 100-10,000 employees with 3-4 hierarchy levels, on average, the promotion of selfish agents is minimized and the promotion of competent agents is maximized. Finally, we show that judging the productivity of an individual agent has a greater impact on promoting selfish behaviour than judging the productivity of an individual's team. These results illustrate that agent-based models provide a powerful framework for examining how local interactions contribute to the large-scale properties of multi-layered organisations.

1 Introduction

In hierarchical organisations, high-achieving individuals are often rewarded with promotions that provide money and power [Stumpf and London 1981]. Promotions thus might serve as an iterated filtration process, where at each step the most productive individual is promoted, so that the most useful and competent individuals attain the greatest influence. This ideal is captured by the proverb "the cream floats to the top". However, an individual's true contribution to their organization can rarely be accurately measured [Kanter and Summers 1987, Jensen and Murphy 1990, Guest 1997, Bourne et al. 2000]. Consequently, the rewards of power may encourage selfish individuals to cheat by misrepresenting their productivity and thereby attain undeserved promotions [Dess and Robinson

J. Padget et al. (Eds.): COIN 2009, LNAI 6069, pp. 163–178, 2010.
© Springer-Verlag Berlin Heidelberg 2010

1984, Jensen and Murphy 1990, Guest 1997]. If so, the hierarchy might promote the most selfish individuals instead of the most productive. The likelihood of these opposing possibilities has not been formally investigated. Here, we use an agent-based model to explore how hierarchical organisations evolve when individuals in the hierarchy have varying degrees of selfishness and competency.

Developing efficient and effective organisational structures has been a prominent issue for decades. Within this field, a major concern has been how to structure incentives and monitor individuals to obtain optimal performance in the face of conflicting interests [Jensen and Murphy 1990, Guest 1997, Bourne et al. 2000]. However, researchers have only just begun to examine the topic from a computational viewpoint that treats individuals as autonomous and interacting entities. The first agent based organisational models were developed in the 1980s [Bond and Gasser 1988]. Following this work, formal representations of organisations, including roles, obligations, capabilities, from both agent and organisational perspectives were developed [Dignum et al. 2002, Dastani et al. 2002, Matson and DeLoach 2005]. Many of these models focus on formally defining interactions and roles [Dignum et al. 2002]. However, the possibility that agents may have a direct conflict of interest with their organisation has not been previously considered. Thus, this paper is the first to study the possible impact of selfishness and cheating on organisational function in an agent-based model.

Because the interests of organisations and individuals are not identical, and performance can rarely be directly measured [Guest 1997], there is often an opportunity for individuals to "cheat": that is, to maximize others' impression of their contribution, rather than their actual contribution. For example, if academic performance measures emphasise the number of publications, academics may write endless trivial papers. If they emphasise journal prestige, academics may abandon creativity to conform to fashion. If citations are counted, academics may focus on advertising. Thus, each measure of academic performance can be maximized by a behaviour that actually reduces an academic's overall contribution. While for some industries performance measures may be easier than in academia, measuring the performance of managers in general is notoriously problematic [Dess and Robinson 1984, Kanter and Summers 1987, Jensen and Murphy 1990, Guest 1997]. To the extent that performance measures do not directly correspond to performance, there is temptation for individuals to optimize the measure, not the performance. Individuals vary in orientation toward collectivist versus individual goals, and this orientation impacts their reactions to management practices substantially [Ramamoorthy and Carroll 1998].

Individuals who do not cheat given the opportunity are, in a sense, displaying altruism. The evolution and maintenance of selfishness and altruism are a major topic of game theory research [Axelrod 1988]. Recently, research has shifted to consider the evolutionary dynamics of altruism on networks, where agents interact repeatedly with the same agent (e.g., Jansen and van Baalen [2006]). However, these networks have so far used random or lattice structures rather than hierarchies, and agents are typically confined to a fixed position on the network. Here, we consider the more constrained (but socially relevant) scenario of an organisational hierarchy where a high "score" - obtained either by honest performance or selfish deception – is likely to lead to promotion to a higher tier.

Models of opinion formation can also reveal complex dynamics, including rapid state transitions in simple lattice and random Boolean networks [Green et al. 2006]. The complex dynamics observed in even simple models suggest that self-organisation in agent hierarchies may have non-intuitive features. Will genuinely competent and altruistic individuals naturally rise to power in hierarchies, or will hierarchies often be dominated by cheats? Can features of the hierarchy influence the power of dishonesty? Is heavy-handed regulation necessary to moderate the impact of selfishness, and if so, how should cheats be punished? These questions are sufficiently complex that analytical solutions are currently intractable.

Agent-based models provide a means to clarify such difficult questions. Simulating the interactions between large numbers of agents in complex networks often yields outcomes at the system level that are non-intuitive from an individual perspective (emergent). Such models have been used to examine a wide variety of related problems such as opinion formation and cultural dynamics [Kacperski and Holyst 2000, Plewczynski 1998] as well as the dynamics of co-operation and selfishness [Jansen and van Baalen 2006]. Because the properties of the system emerge from local interactions among its components (agents) rather than from an external controlling force, such systems are said to be self-organizing (see review by Green et al. [2008]).

Here, we use a novel agent-based model to study how the distribution of selfishness and competency self-organise in hierarchical organisations. This paper addresses the following issues.

- **Under what conditions do hierarchical structures favour selfish or altruistic agents, and competent or incompetent agents?** In particular, we examine how selfishness, competency and status are related in organisations where selfishness can positively or negatively influence an agent's overall productivity.
- **How do competency and selfishness of high-ranked agents changes in response to organisation size and structure?** If multi-tiered hierarchies act as an effective filtration system for unproductive agents, we might expect that hierarchies with more tiers would promote more competent leaders. However, if deception propagates as agents are promoted, leaders may also be more selfish and, potentially, less productive.
- **How do promotions influence selfishness and competency at high ranks?** The performance of an individual is often difficult to separate from that of a team. We examine the impact of this lack of clarity on the promotion of selfishness. We also study the effects of punishing agents for selfish behaviour to test whether selfishness can be effectively suppressed without reducing competency.

In the following sections, we first describe the simulation model in detail, and our experiments. We present results from two experiments. In the first experiment, we explore the impact of organization size and complexity on selfishness and competency at different levels. In the second experiment, we consider the influence of punishment and opportunity on cheating behaviour. Finally, we discuss some case studies of how the observed processes might impact productivity at the organisational scale using data from real-life domains, and suggest some future directions for research.

2   Model

2.1   Overview

We developed an agent-based model for the evolution over time of a hierarchically structured organisation (tree). The hierarchy consists of L tiers, with each node giving rise to G branches. Thus, the total number of nodes, $N = \sum_{i=0}^{i=L-1} G^i$. We tested the simulation for most values of L and G that yield $N < 10,000$.

Each agent occupies a node in the hierarchy and provides a yield, Y, to the organisation. Agent status is scaled between 0 and 1, with 0 indicating an agent on the bottom tier and 1 indicating an agent on the top tier. There is only one agent with status 1, which we refer to as the Chief Executive Officer (CEO). Each agent with a non-zero status (manager) monitors the G agents immediately below him (his subordinates) and has a perception U_P about the yield of each subordinate.

At each iteration, a randomly chosen manager leaves the organisation. The subordinate perceived by this manager to have the highest yield from the level below is promoted to take place of each departing manager. Promotion creates a line of vacancies to the base of the hierarchy, which are filled progressively in the same way, with a random new agent introduced at the bottom.

2.2   Agent Traits and Behaviour

Agents have two quantitative traits, competency and selfishness, with randomly chosen Gaussian-distributed values between 0 and 1 ($\mu = 0.5, \sigma = 0.1$).

Definition 1. *An agent's yield to the organisation is*

$$Y = C + SI, \text{ where}$$

· *Competency, C, determines how much an agent can contribute to the organisation.*
· *Selfishness, S, determines how likely it is that an agent "cheats" by overstating its productivity when it has the opportunity.*
· *I is a parameter that influences the impact of selfishness on productivity. We consider both negative (-1) and positive (1) values of I to allow for the possibility that selfishness increases or decreases productivity, giving yield in the range $[-1, 2]$.*

To examine the impact of the difficulty of separating individual and team performance, we consider two possible ways of determining perceived yield U_P. In both cases, U_P has the range [-1,2].

Table 1. Model parameters and their experimental values (* indicates default values)

Parameter	Symbol	Values
Tiers in the hierarchy	L	2-10, *5
Size of groups (branches)	G	2-9000, *5
Impact of selfishness	I	-1, 0, 1
Duration of punishment	P_I	*0, 10
Opportunity to cheat	P_C	*0.25, 0.5, 0.75
Detectability of cheating	P_D	*0.25, 0.5, 0.75

- **Alone scenario.** Perceived yield U_P is normally determined by the agent's yield ($U_P = U_Y$, where U_Y denotes the agent's actual yield).
- **Team scenario.** Perceived yield U_P is normally half the agent's yield ($U_Y/2$) multiplied by the mean perceived yield of its subordinates. This value gives 50% weight each to individual and team performance; teams can impact an agent's perceived yield either positively or negatively.

If the subordinate cheats, U_P is further modified. The probability that a subordinate cheats is the subordinate's selfishness U_S multiplied by parameter P_C, the probability of an opportunity to cheat.

When a subordinate cheats, it is detected by the manager with probability $M_Y \times P_D$, the yield of the manager multiplied by the detectability of cheating (truncated to 1 if greater than 1). A subordinate that is detected cheating is punished with a zero perceived yield that iteration and for the next P_I iterations. However, if the subordinate is not detected, its perceived yield is given by $U_P = U_Y + 2U_S$. (Doubling U_S allows selfishness to enhance perceived yield even when the impact of selfishness, I, is negative). In this way, agents who cheat risk missing promotions if they are caught, but can also gain extra promotions, especially if their manager is itself selfish or incompetent.

2.3   Experiments

We ran the simulation for 40 replicates, each of 40,000 iterations, recording the distribution of selfishness and competency in the hierarchy every 2,000 iterations for each parameter value. In particular, we are interested in the traits of the agent who rises to the top of the hierarchy. For clarity, we term this agent the CEO of the organisation.

Two simulation experiments were completed.

- In Experiment 1, we varied L, G and I and considered both *Team* and *Alone* scenarios to explore how organisation size and structure influence the promotion of competency and selfishness.
- In Experiment 2, L and G were constant and I, P_I, P_C and P_D were varied to examine the impact of punishment and opportunity. Each experiment was run as a fully crossed design. See Table 1 for parameter values.

3   Results

3.1   Experiment 1 - Structure and Size of Organisations

In many situations studied, agents who rose in the hierarchy were more productive (Figure 1), supporting the idea that "the cream rises to the top" due to the
agents' competency. That is, high-ranked agents were less selfish than the average agent if selfishness decreased productivity, and more selfish than the average
agent if selfishness increased productivity. However, this effect was observed
only when the number of tiers in the hierarchy was small: as the complexity
of the hierarchy increased, mediocrity prevailed. The impact of selfishness on
productivity also obscured general competency: when productivity was related
to selfishness either positively or negatively, less competent agents were usually
promoted (Figure 2).

Organisation size and structure had substantial implications for competency
and selfishness at high ranks. Figure 3 shows the effect on the CEO of the number
of tiers and number of employees. In general, as the number of tiers increased, so
did the selfishness and incompetence of the CEO. In small organisations ($N <$
100), a hierarchy with only two tiers was ideal. However, in larger organisations
($N > 100$), hierarchies with 3-4 tiers promoted the least selfish and incompetent
CEOs.

We observed a subtle impact of the way in which agent performance is judged,
by the individual's traits or the collective contribution of their team. In small

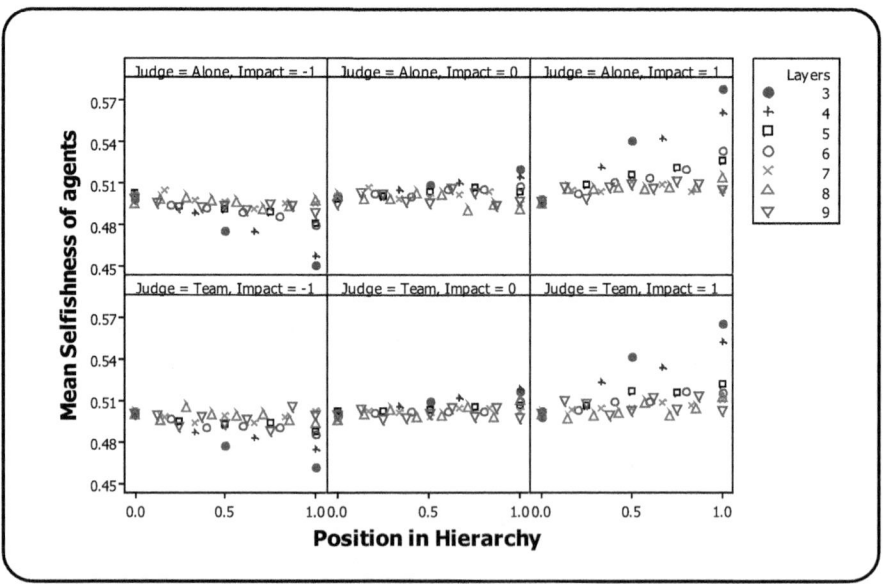

Fig. 1. Mean selfishness of agents at different levels in hierarchies (Experiment 1).
Symbols indicate the number of tiers in the organization L. Panels show experimental
condition; alone or team (rows) and impact of selfishness I (columns).

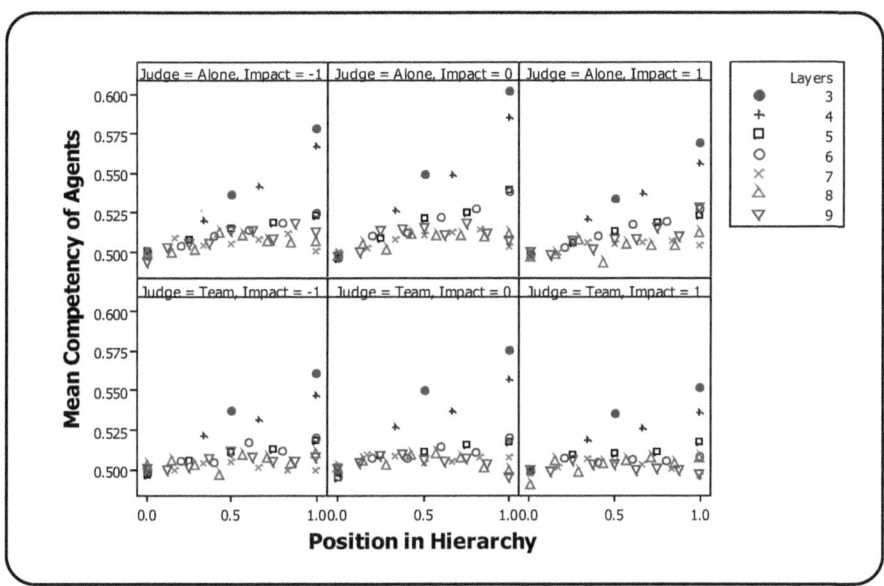

Fig. 2. Mean competency of agents at different levels in hierarchies (Experiment 1). Results grouped as in Figure 1.

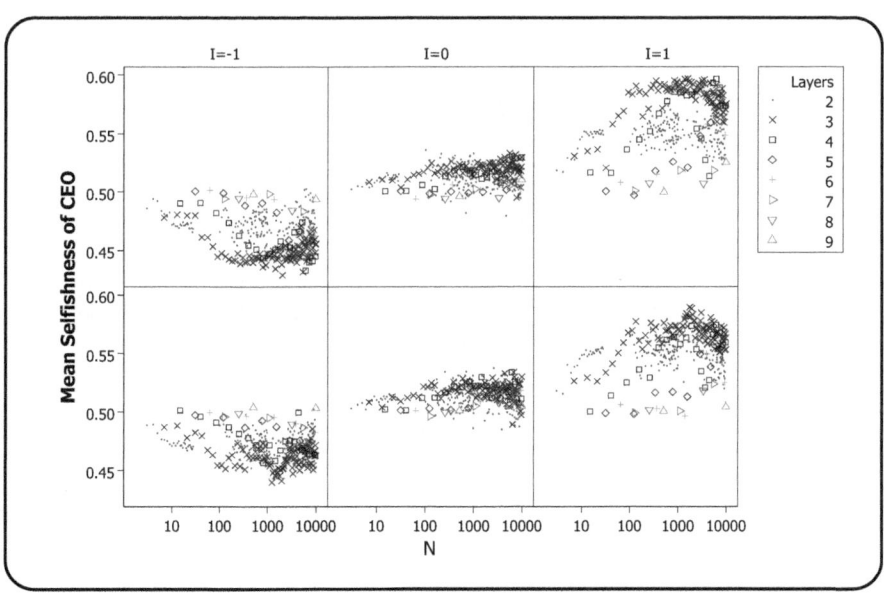

Fig. 3. CEO selfishness plotted against number of employees N. Results are grouped as in Figure 1.

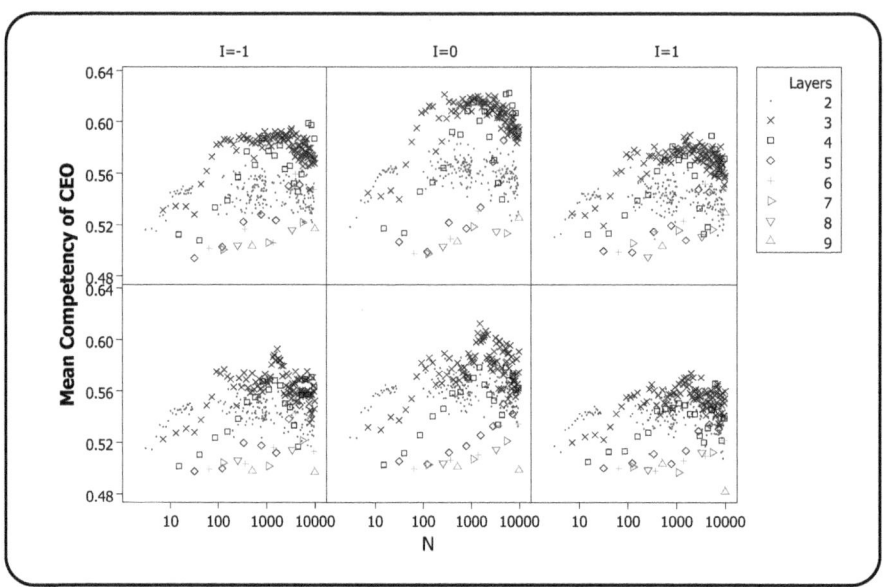

Fig. 4. CEO competency plotted against number of employees N. Results are grouped as in Figure 1.

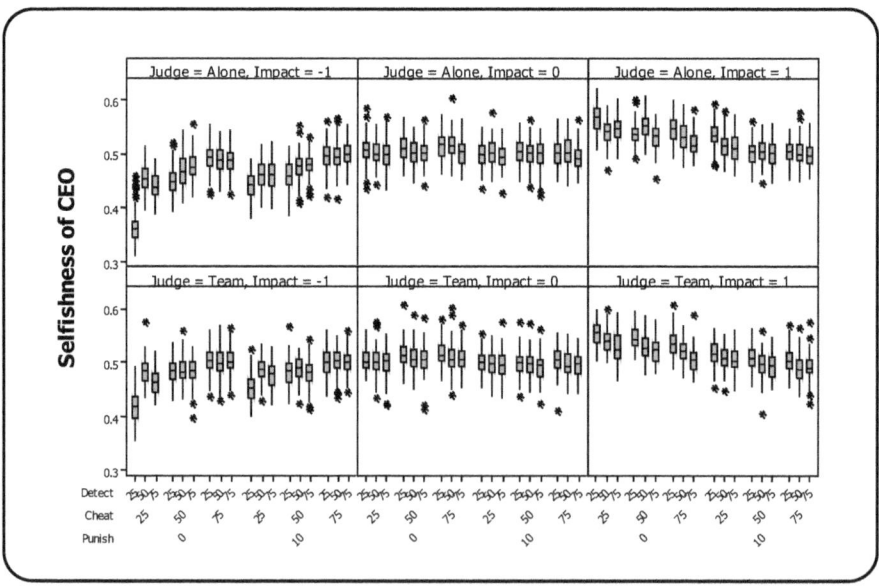

Fig. 5. Boxplots of CEO selfishness under different detection, cheating and punishment conditions in Experiment 2. Panels as for Figure 1.

organisations ($N < 100$), judging performance by teams impaired promotion of the least selfish and incompetent. However, in larger organisations, judging by teams enhanced promotion of unselfish and competent agents (Figures 3 and 4). The strength of this effect increased with the number of tiers in the hierarchy.

3.2 Experiment 2 - Opportunity, Detection and Punishment of Cheating

Figures 5 and 6 show boxplots of CEO selfishness and competency under different conditions. CEOs who possessed the most extreme traits were promoted when punishment was light, and both opportunities for, and detection of cheating were rare. CEOs who were both the least selfish and most competent of all were seen when selfishness decreased productivity in this situation. However, when selfishness increased productivity, the same conditions led to promotion of the most selfish CEOs. These selfish CEOs were moderately competent.

Analysis of variance using a general linear model showed significant effects of all independent variables (Table 2) for both selfishness and competency. Although effects were significant, variance was high within conditions, reflecting the unpredictable state of the model at any time; thus, we obtained small overall correlations of $r^2 = 13.08\%$ and $r^2 = 44.42\%$ for selfishness and competency respectively. In general, as expected, more severe punishments and increased detection led to reduced selfishness. However, frequent detection and severe punishment of selfishness also strongly repressed competency of CEOs. Frequent opportunities

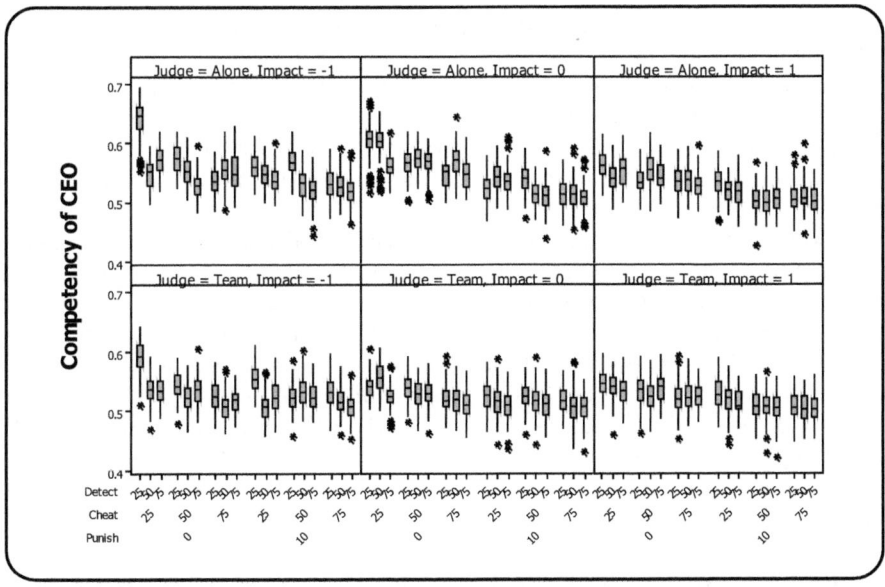

Fig. 6. Boxplots of CEO competency under different detection, cheating and punishment conditions in Experiment 2. Panels as for Figure 1.

Table 2. Analysis of variance for competency and selfishness with degrees of freedom DF, F-test statistic F and probability P

Trait	.	Selfishness	.	Competency	.
Parameter	DF	F	P	F	P
Alone/Team	1	33.30	< 0.001	584.65	< 0.001
I	2	3559.55	< 0.001	470.69	< 0.001
P_I	1	506.86	< 0.001	3064.50	< 0.001
P_C	2	210.8	< 0.001	1035.08	< 0.001
P_D	2	26.17	< 0.001	274.32	< 0.001
Error	53987				

to cheat led to increased selfishness when cheating reduced productivity, but decreased selfishness when selfishness increased productivity. Opportunities to cheat uniformly led to the promotion of less competent CEOs.

3.3 Analysis

Our results show that for moderate-sized organisations with 100-10000 employees, hierarchies with 3-4 tiers promote leaders who contribute the most to productivity of the organisation. This was observed whether cheating enhances or detracts from productivity. However, when hierarchies had more than 4 tiers, performance of leaders declined as the number of tiers increased: in hierarchies with 7 or more tiers, top-ranked agents were no more productive than agents at the third tier. This observation is interesting in the light of historical studies showing that long-lived hierarchical organisations (such as the Catholic Church) rarely have more than 4 tiers; however, simple organisational structures also offer other benefits such as facilitating information flow. The current data suggest that the benefits of repeated filtration offered by numerous hierarchical tiers are outweighed (at least for the parameter ranges tested) by the cost of long path length: the most competent and altruistic individuals often leave the organisation before they attain high status.

A second key observation is that agents with ideal traits were more likely to be promoted when punishment was light, opportunities to cheat were rare, and detection of cheating was also rare. In particular, while detection and punishment of cheating was effective in reducing the selfishness of CEOs, competency was also strongly suppressed by these factors. Across all conditions, the more opportunities there were for cheating, the less competent the CEO. Opportunities to cheat exacerbated the CEO's selfishness when cheating damaged productivity, but suppressed it when cheating enhanced productivity. We attribute this to frequent cheating creating a noisy environment where genuine productivity could not be detected.

4   Discussion and Related Research

The model presented here is basic and preliminary in many respects: further research is required to investigate the applicability of these suggestions in more realistic scenarios. In the following sections, we discuss these limitations in the context of related research, and how possible extensions could address these concerns. Note that the introduction discussed primary related research on agent organisations, selfishness in game theoretic research and evolutionary dynamics.

4.1 Organisational Cost of Promoting Incompetent Employees

The current model has focused on understanding how individuals are promoted to certain positions based on their degree of selfishness and competency. However, from an economical point of view, it is of primary importance to know how agent selfishness and competency influence productivity at the level of the entire organisation.

We assume that higher ranked employees have a higher influence on the organisation. Reliable data quantifying the actual influence of employees at different organisational tiers are unavailable. This makes it difficult to measure precisely the overall productivity. However, we have reliable data of the costs of ranked employees in many organisations, particularly regulated organisations, including universities and public offices. Such costs are often assumed to be proportional to influence. Given that we have a value for individual competency, this measure for cost allows us to calculate a rank/cost ratio.

Costs for ranked employees are readily available. For example, Monash University has a salary scale of employees at five different levels.[1]

Rank	Income	Normalised Value (approximate)
Level A (Assistant Lecturer)	$66,360	1.0
Level B (Lecturer)	$82,951	1.25
Level C (Senior Lecturer)	$98,667	1.49
Level D (Associate Professor)	$113,509	1.71
Level E (Professor)	$132,722	2.0

For illustrative purposes we show a simple way to calculate the rank/cost (RC) ratio of the organisation. We multiply each agent's competency with the normalised value associated to each agent's rank, and add all resulting values. So, for example, consider a university department. If we have one professor at level E with a competency of 0.72, and two employees at Level C with competency 0.8 and 0.5, we have the following overall value for RC: 2.0 * 0.72 + 1.49 * (0.8+0.5) = 3.38. A better allocation of resources would be if the professor is at 0.8, and one of the senior lecturer is at 0.72, as this yields the following value for RC: 2.0 * 0.8 + 1.49 * (0.72+0.5) = 3.46. So, a lower value of RC indicates a worse allocation of money to individuals. Knowing the underlying, and controllable conditions that increase or decrease this ratio value is a guide to reduce costs to an organisation.

---

[1] These levels are subdivided into steps, but we have taken the highest step for the year 2008. Table taken from URL:http://www.adm.monash.edu.au/enterprise-agreements/academic-general-2005/salary-academic.html. Such income scales vary little between different universities in Australia.

4.2   Panel Decisions

In our current model, the decision of promoting an employee remains with one manager. However, in many organisations, promotion decisions are made by a panel. Such a panel may consist of many managers at the same hierarchical level, managers at different hierarchical levels, and external agents. One immediate implication of panel decisions in our model is that a cheating agent is more likely to be detected as it will be assessed by many managers with varying degrees of "cheating detection" ability. However, if the impact of cheater-detection is often negative, as suggested by our model results, this might lead to panels making worse decisions than individual managers. Panel decision making raises many complex issues, including the information available to each decision-maker, their relative power, and costs of panel involvement.

For example, at Australian universities, an application for a promotion from lecturer to professor would be decided by a panel consisting of various actors, including the head of department and the dean of the faculty (both are at different hierarchical levels).

4.3   Agents That Model the Behaviour of Other Agents

Early research on multi-agent systems recognised that the coordination of agents will be problematic if they are not able to predict their own behaviour and that of others [Bond and Gasser 1988], particularly when they predict other agents' roles and capabilities in organisational settings [Dignum et al. 2002]. Significant research contributions have been made towards understanding the role of "modelling other agents" in the coordination of agents [Smith 1980, Stone et al. 2000, Garrido et al. 2000, Gmytrasiewicz and Durfee 2001, Kok and Vlassis 2001, Vassileva et al. 2003]. In particular, agent models are used to predict the decisions of collaborators [Gmytrasiewicz and Durfee 2001], match students with tutors in collaborative support environments [Vassileva et al. 2003], schedule meetings based on the availability of agents [Garrido et al. 2000], and predict the performance of soccer-agents in RoboCup [Stone et al. 2000, Kok and Vlassis 2001]. Different research initiatives make distinct assumptions that influence what to model, how to model it, and how to use and refine models. Recently this research has been extended to ensure that coordination is improved by collective contributions of a group of knowledgeable agents as opposed to "isolated" contributions by individuals [Guttmann 2008]. This approach is called Collective Iterative Allocation (CIA) and involves a group of agents that collectively refine allocations of a team to a task (or in this case, a promotion to an employee). In the current model, managers maintain a simple model of subordinates' short-term productivity; subordinates do not model their managers at all. Extending the model, managers might retain or exchange information about subordinates, and subordinates might model managers or even themselves, and adapt their behaviour according to these models.

4.4   Selfishness

Agents are often assumed to behave "as they are supposed to behave", that is, according to the design intentions of a system [Nisan 1999, Zambonelli et al. 2001, Horling and Lesser 2005]. In many domains, this assumption is simplistic as agents often aim to optimise their own criteria [Sergot 2005], particularly when opportunistic behaviour is promoted [Castelfranchi 2001; 2002]. Selfish agents exhibit behaviour that places their own needs and desires above the needs and desires of others. This is an issue in applications such as resource and task allocation, routing and electronic trade [Nisan 1999, Ronen 2000, Anshelevich et al. 2003, Anderegg and Eidenbenz 2003, Guttmann 2008]. In our framework, a selfish agent can behave such that it is perceived as being more productive than its actual competency, hence having an unfair advantage over others in the promotion process.

4.5   Agent Learning and Demography

Our model assumes that individuals have fixed traits for their entire lifespans; that they enter and leave organisations at random with respect to age, status, their manager's opinion of them, and their own traits; and that selfishness and competency are Gaussian-distributed traits. All of these assumptions could be refined to provide quantitative predictions more applicable to specific scenarios. For example, some groups (such as graduates newly recruited to an organisation) might have specific trait distributions which change over time. Employees who have remained with the organisation for longer might develop increased loyalty, reducing cheating; alternatively, ability to exploit the system undetected may increase with experience. Appropriate parameter choices for such extensions require empirical data and are likely to be specific to the particular organisation in question.

5   Conclusion

We have used a simple model of organisational hierarchy to address some basic questions about how promotion decisions and the structure of the hierarchy can influence the distribution of individual traits in the hierarchy. In summary, our results suggest that organisations wishing to promote the most productive workers should consider the following guidelines.

- **Have few tiers.** In the conditions studied, organisations with 3-4 tiers optimize promotion of competent CEOs for organisations with 100-10000 employees; 2 layers are better for organisations with < 100 employees.
- **Minimise opportunities to cheat.** Opportunities to cheat obscure the genuine productivity of individuals and are therefore damaging regardless of whether selfishness is productive or costly to the organisation. In our model, minimising opportunities to cheat equates to measuring performance accurately.

- **In small organisations, judge individuals separately; in large organisations, judge individuals by their teams** Judging by teams in a large organisation reduces cheating because unproductive individuals more often promote unproductive subordinates.
- **Disregard cheating when it happens.** In our model, punishment suppresses competency because when cheating is frequent, highly competent agents are likely to be punished. However, the model excludes psychological consequences of punishment. To the extent that individuals are less likely to consider cheating if they fear being caught, punishment may effectively reduce cheating opportunities and thus enhance competency of high-ranked individuals.

The generality of these conclusions is limited by the simplicity of the model. Further work is required to assess the implications of complex promotion dynamics, agent psychology, demographic characteristics and change over time.

Acknowledgements

We thank G. Paperin, D. G. Green and E. A. Duenez-Guzman.

References

Anderegg, L., Eidenbenz, S.: Ad hoc-VCG: A truthful and cost-efficient routing protocol for mobile ad hoc networks with selfish agents. In: Proceedings of the nineth annual international conference on Mobile computing and networking, pp. 245–259 (2003)

Anshelevich, E., Dasgupta, A., Tardos, E., Wexler, T.: Near-optimal network design with selfish agents. In: Proceedings of the thirty-fifth annual ACM symposium on Theory of computing, pp. 511–520 (2003)

Axelrod: The Evolution of Cooperation. Basic Books, New York (1988)

Bond, A.H., Gasser, L.: Distributed Artificial Intelligence. Morgan Kaufmann publishers Inc., San Francisco (1988)

Bourne, M., Mills, J., Wilcox, M., Neely, A., Platts, K.: Designing, implementing and updating performance measurement systems. International Journal of Operations and Production Management, 754–771 (2000)

Castelfranchi, C.: Trust and Deception in Virtual Societies. Kluwer Academic Publishers, Dordrecht (2001)

Castelfranchi, C.: The Role of Trust and Deception in Virtual Societies. International Journal of Electronic Commerce 6(3), 55–70 (2002)

Dastani, M., Dignum, V., Dignum, F.: Organizations and normative agents. LNCS, pp. 982–989. Springer, Heidelberg (2002)

Dess, G.G., Robinson, R.B.J.: Measuring Organizational Performance in the Absence of Objective Measures: The Case of the Privately-Held Firm and Conglomerate Business Unit. Strategic Management Journal, 265–273 (1984)

Dignum, V., Meyer, J., Weigand, H., Dignum, F.: An organization-oriented model for agent societies. In: Proceedings of RASTA, at AAMAS02 (2002)

Garrido, L., Sycara, K., Brena, R.: Quantifying the utility of building agents models: An experimental study. In: Agents-00/ECML-00 Workshop on Learning Agents, Barcelona, Spain (2000)

Gmytrasiewicz, P.J., Durfee, E.H.: Rational communication in multi-agent environments. Autonomous Agents and Multi-Agent Systems 4(3), 233–272 (2001)

Green, D., Leishman, T., Sadedin, S.: The emergence of social consensus in simulation studies with boolean networks. In: PAAA World Congress on Social Simulation, Kyoto, Japan (2006)

Green, D., Sadedin, S., Leishman, T.: Systems theory - self-organization. Encyclopedia of Ecology 4, 3195–3203 (2008)

Guest, D.E.: Human resource management and performance: a review and research agenda. The International Journal of Human Resource Management 8, 263–276 (1997)

Guttmann, C.: Collective Iterative Allocation. PhD thesis, Monash University (2008)

Horling, B., Lesser, V.: A survey of multi-agent organizational paradigms. The Knowledge Engineering Review 19(04), 281–316 (2005)

Jansen, V.A.A., van Baalen, M.: Altruism through beard chromodynamics. Nature 440, 663–666 (2006)

Jensen, M., Murphy, K.: Performance pay and top-management incentives. J. Political Economy 98(1), 225 (1990)

Kacperski, K., Holyst, J.: Phase transitions as a persistent feature of groups with leaders in models of opinion formation. Physica A 287, 631 (2000)

Kanter, R.M., Summers, D.: Doing Well While Doing Good: Dilemmas of Performance Measurement in Nonprofit Organizations and the Need for a Multipleconstituency Approach. In: McKevitt, D., Lawton, A. (eds.) Public Sector Management: Theory, Critique and Practice, New York State, United States of America, pp. 261–262. Open University Press, Stony Stratford (1987)

Kok, J.R., Vlassis, N.: Mutual modeling of teammate behavior. Technical Report UVA-02-04, Computer Science Institute, University of Amsterdam, Netherland (2001)

Matson, E., DeLoach, S.: Formal transition in agent organizations. In: Integration of Knowledge Intensive Multi-Agent Systems, 2005, pp. 235–240 (2005)

Nisan, N.: Algorithms for Selfish Agents Mechanism Design for Distributed Computation. In: Meinel, C., Tison, S. (eds.) STACS 1999. LNCS, vol. 1563, p. 1. Springer, Heidelberg (1999)

Plewczynski, D.: Landau theory of social clustering. Physica A 261, 608 (1998)

Ramamoorthy, N., Carroll, S.: Individualism/Collectivism Orientations and Reactions Toward Alternative Human Resource Management Practices. Human Relations 51, 571–588 (1998)

Ronen, A.: Solving Optimization Problems among Selfish Agents. PhD thesis, Hebrew University in Jerusalem, Israel (2000)

Sergot: Modelling unreliable and untrustworthy agent behaviour. In: Keplicz, B.D., Jankowski, A., Skowron, A., Szczuka, M. (eds.) International workshop on monitoring, security, and rescue technique in multiagent systems, Plock, Poland, pp. 161–177. Springer, Berlin (2005)

Smith, R.G.: The contract net protocol: High-level communication and control in a distributed problem solver. IEEE Transactions on Computers 29(12), 1104–1113 (1980)

Stone, P., Riley, P., Veloso, M.M.: Defining and using ideal teammate and opponent agent models. In: Proceedings of the Innovative Applications of Artificial Intelligence Conference (IAAI), pp. 1040–1045 (2000)

Stumpf, S., London, M.: Management promotions: Individual and organizational factors influencing the decision process. The Academy of Management Review 6(4), 539–549 (1981)

Vassileva, J., McCalla, G.I., Greer, J.E.: Multi-agent multi-user modeling in I-Help. User Modeling and User-Adapted Interaction 13(1-2), 179–210 (2003)

Zambonelli, F., Jennings, N., Wooldridge, M.: Organizational abstractions for the analysis and design of multi-agent systems. In: Ciancarini, P., Wooldridge, M.J. (eds.) AOSE 2000. LNCS, vol. 1957, pp. 235–251. Springer, Heidelberg (2001)

The SIOC Project: Semantically-Interlinked Online Communities, from Humans to Machines

Alexandre Passant[1], Uldis Bojārs[1], John G. Breslin[1,2], and Stefan Decker[1]

[1] Digital Enterprise Research Institute,
National University of Ireland, Galway, Ireland
{firstname.lastname}@deri.org
[2] School of Engineering and Informatics,
National University of Ireland, Galway, Ireland
john.breslin@nuigalway.ie

Abstract. The SIOC project — Semantically-Interlinked Online Communities — is aimed at expressing information about the nature, structure and content of online communities using Semantic Web technologies. Then, information created and maintained *via* human-centric social interactions becomes processable by autonomous software agents for advanced purposes, such as enabling interoperability between applications from the Social Web. In this paper, we describe the various components of the SIOC project (*i.e.* the SIOC Core ontology and its different modules as well as the SIOC ecosystem and some related applications) in this context of online communities, both on the Web and in more restricted virtual environments, also taking into account human-agent communications in such environments.

1 Introduction

While the new paradigms, tools and services introduced by the Social Web — also referred to as Web 2.0 [20] — are now widely accepted in both public and scientific communities (for instance blogs, wikis, tagging practices, etc.), their popularity has also led to various issues. Indeed, due to the heterogenous nature of data models used to represent Social Media Contributions (for instance various APIs or database structures, generally depending on the application provider), finding, interlinking and querying such data within and between online communities is a complex issue. Moreover, such tools generally act as independent data silos where the information is being locked with a lack of machine-readable meta-data; hence, reusing information from these applications is not straightforward, and most of Web 2.0 services can be seen as *"walled gardens"* where information cannot be extracted and reused by users nor software agents.

However, online communities would greatly benefit from better ways to provide machine-readable description of their nature, content and structure, enabling among others interoperability in and between various distinct online communities. For example, it would allow to retrieve content created in different communities but sharing a similar topic, enabling a way to follow and navigate

J. Padget et al. (Eds.): COIN 2009, LNAI 6069, pp. 179–194, 2010.

through distributed conversations across the Social Web — such as following a discussion starting on a bulletin board and continuing on a separated forum.

To that extent, another recent trend with regards to Web technologies concerns the Semantic Web [3], which provide standards and models to build a *Web of Data*, with unified models to represent typed and interlinked data from different sources, where we are currently browsing a *Web of Documents*, with simple pages and hyperlinks. Hence, the vision that we follow consists in combining Semantic Web technologies and paradigms from the Social Web. This leads to *"Social Semantic Information Spaces"* (Figure 1) [8], where information from online communities is created and maintained through social interactions but is at the same time interlinked and machine-readable. Thus, new ways to exploit these online communities can be envisioned, for example using SPARQL to uniformly query data from different communities (Section 5). Such integration of these two fields would thus lead to a Social Semantic Web [10], a vision that has been researched during the past few years [1] and defended by Tim Berners-Lee himself [2].

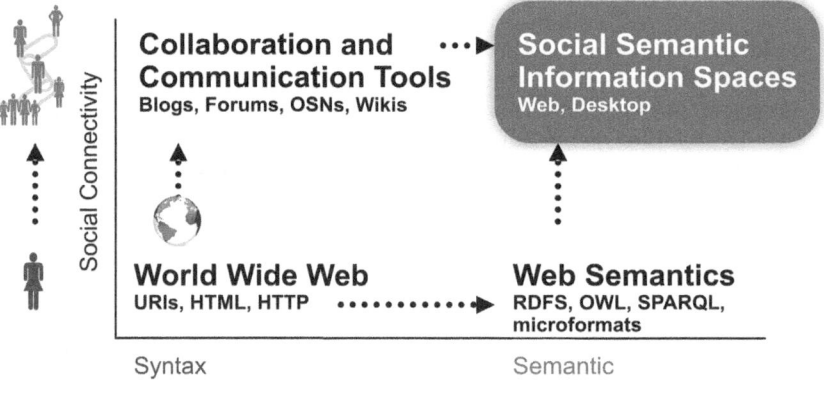

Fig. 1. Social Semantic Information Spaces

Focusing on that integration, the SIOC project[1] — Semantically-Interlinked Online Communities [9] — aims to be a building block of these Social Semantic Information Spaces, solving the aforementioned issues by providing a comprehensive data model (as well as related tools and applications) used to represent online communities and their activities in an homogenous way. To achieve this vision, the SIOC project relies on two main components that are to be discussed in this paper: (1) the SIOC Ontology, composed of the SIOC Core Ontology and various modules; and (2) a set of applications, covering the creation, integration and use of SIOC data in online communities, and that form a SIOC eco-system.

---

[1] http://sioc-project.org

In the next section of this paper, we will detail the SIOC Ontology, *i.e.* the SIOC Core Ontology and its related modules. Then, we will discuss the uptake of SIOC on the Web and describe the SIOC Eco-system. We will continue by presenting various initiatives and applications using SIOC, in online communities. In that section, we will also focus on the ability to use SIOC to represent communities formed not only by humans, but also comprised of both humans and software agents (such as bots on IRC — Internet Relay Chat). We will then present how such data can be queried and reused in order to make sense of online communities thanks to SIOC data, before concluding this paper.

2   The SIOC Ontology

In order to allow agents to process machine-readable data uniformly across different applications, the Semantic Web vision relies on the use of ontologies [13] as models to provide shared semantics between applications on the Web. Hence, to achieve the aforementioned goal of the SIOC project, *i.e.* making information from online communities available to software agents, the first requirement is to provide a comprehensive ontology covering the various artifacts and actions that are created and that happen in these communities.

The SIOC Ontology [4] is composed of a Core Ontology and of a set of modules. The main motivation that lead to splitting the ontology in several parts is to provide an easy integration of SIOC in existing applications by Web developers, that consequently do not have to apprehend a complex schema but can focus on simple models, generally considering first the use of the SIOC Core Ontology, and then using additional modules if required.

In July 2007, the SIOC Ontology was published as a W3C Member Submission[2]. This submission ensures higher visibility of the ontology as a format for representing online communities and offers a way to bootstrap the model and consequently provide more content using it on the Web, as we will see in Section 3. That way, it creates a network of interlinked Social Data at Web scale, augmenting its global value as also discussed in [15].

A comprehensive overview of the SIOC ontology is provided in [7]. We shall also mention that, while being a mature model, the SIOC Ontology still evolves based on the needs of the community and some particular applications that emerge and require new features in the ontology, for instance the concept of *followers* in microblogging applications.

2.1   The SIOC Core Ontology

The main classes and properties in the SIOC Core Ontology[3] are shown in Figure 2. As we introduced earlier, while relatively small and simple, this model is yet powerful enough to represent the content produced and exchanged within online communities. For instance, a `Forum` represents a space in which discussion

---

[2] http://www.w3.org/Submission/2007/02/
[3] http://rdfs.org/sioc/spec

happen (not necessarily a bulletin board, in spite of its name, but any virtual space that hosts discussion), and contains different (instances of) `Posts`, written by (instances of) `UserAccounts`. In order to represent more abstract containers (such as a personal information space that to not necessarily hold discussions), the more general `Container` and `Space` classes can be used. Based on the SIOC Core Ontology, the following example (using RDF N3 serialization[4]) describes how we represent that Alice has created a post in a particular forum (*i.e.* an area of discussion) and that Bob replied to it. In addition, we shall mention that with an emphasis on standardized Semantic Web technologies since its beginning (*i.e.* relying on W3C specifications), the whole ontology has been designed using RDFS and recently was adapted as an OWL-DL model.

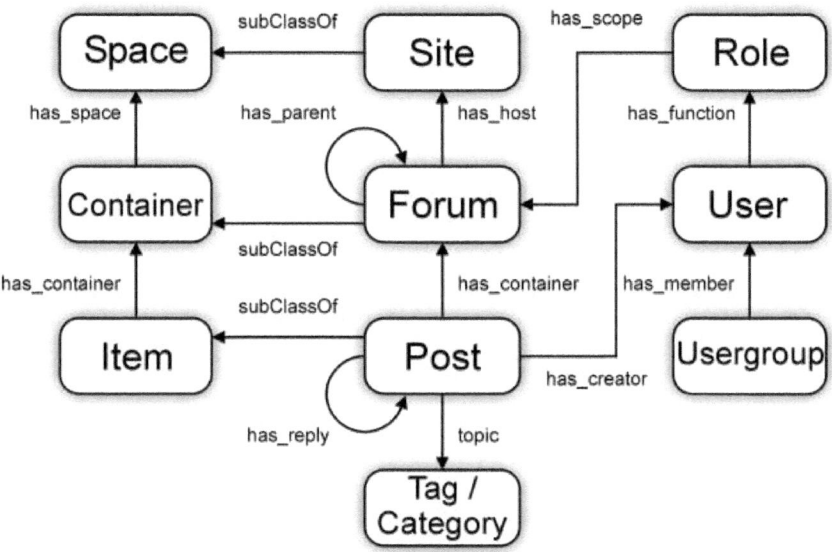

Fig. 2. Main classes and properties in the SIOC ontology

In addition to the ones represented in Figure 2, other classes and properties are provided in the SIOC Core Ontology. For instance, the `previous_version` and `next_version` properties can be used to link versioned items (which is particularly useful in wiki communities), while the `has_modifier` one is used to identify the modifier(s) of any content. Considering once again the use-case of wikis, this property can be used to represent modifiers that are both humans, *i.e.* people editing wiki pages, and autonomous agents, such as both automatically reverting pages edited by vandalism. To that extent, SIOC is then suited not only to human-human online interactions but to any community involving agents, either they are human or machines.

---

[4] Prefixes omitted for space reasons.

```
:post a sioc:Post ;
  sioc:has_creator :alice ;
  sioc:has_container :forum ;
  sioc:has_reply :reply .
:forum a sioc:Forum .
:reply a sioc:Post ;
  sioc:has_creator :bob .
:alice a sioc:UserAccount .
:bob a sioc:UserAccount .
```

Listing 1.1. Example of RDF data modeling a post and its reply using SIOC

2.2 The SIOC Modules

Several SIOC modules have been defined (i) on the one hand to extend some terms from the SIOC Core Ontology (and to avoid making it too complex to apprehend) and (ii) on the other hand to focus on particular features of online communities. Among its different modules, SIOC provides[5]:

- **SIOC Access module:** In order to define access control in online communities and in particular discussion spaces, the SIOC Access module[6] provides simple classes and properties regarding the notions of Role and Permission. Such properties could be combined with authentication schemes relying on Semantic Web technologies, especially FOAF-SSL [28] that provides a decentralized and user-owned authentication scheme based on FOAF, which complements well with the use of SIOC. In addition, one could rely on SIOC-related initiatives, such as the concept of *Faceted Online Presence* [27], as well as work based on policies presented in [25] to enable the management of norms and responsibilities in online communities;
- **SIOC Argument module:** As many people in online communities not only share data but also agree and disagree between them, there is a need to represent these argumentations in a machine-readable way. The SIOC Argument module[7] defines classes and properties to represent simple argumentative discussions in online communities websites [17]. Another fine-grained module aims at representing argumentative discussion is the SWAN/SIOC module, describe later in that section;
- **SIOC Types module:** The SIOC Types module[8] defines advanced content-types to be used when defining user-generated content from online-communities. While the Core Ontology simply defines classes such as sioc:Post/ sioc:Item to represent online contributions and sioc:Forum / sioc:Container to defines online communication spaces, the Types module goes further to provide

---

[5] See http://rdfs.org/sioc/spec/#sec-modules for an up-to-date list of modules, since new ones are regularly designed to enable the use of SIOC in new applications or domain-areas.

[6] http://rdfs.org/sioc/access

[7] http://rdfs.org/sioc/args

[8] http://rdfs.org/sioc/types

more accurate descriptions of the items that are shared. For instance, it includes classes such as `sioct:BlogPost` and `sioct:WikiArticle` to represent the shared items as well as `sioct:Blog` or `sioct:Wiki` for the container, that respectively subclass the `sioc:Post` and `sioc:Forum` classes discussed previously. That way, using the SIOC Types module, the previous example can be refined as depicted in Listing 1.2.

- **SIOC Services module:** Another feature of main Web 2.0 applications is the way they provide access to their content for developers, so that they can build mash-ups, etc. The SIOC Services module[9] defines classes and properties to represent Web services related to online communuties (*e.g.* API endpoint and return format, etc.). We shall note that it aims to be and stay lightweight, and do not compare with webservices description languages and ontologies such as WSDL[10]. However, thanks to this module, agents could figure out how to access an endpoint to retrieve machine-readable description of the community.

- **The SIOC/SWAN module:** Finally, one of the recent development of SIOC is a module defining alignments between SIOC and the SWAN — Semantic Web Applications in Neuromedicine — ontology [11][11], providing a complete model for fine-grained argumentative discussions in online scientific communities through the SWAN/SIOC module [24].

```
:post a sioct:BlogPost ;
  sioc:has_creator :alice ;
  sioc:has_container :forum ;
  sioc:has_reply :reply .
:forum a sioct:Blog .
:reply a sioct:Comment ;
  sioc:has_creator :bob .
:alice a sioc:User .
:bob a sioc:User .
```

Listing 1.2. Example of RDF data to model a post and its reply using the SIOC Core Ontology and the SIOC Types module

2.3   Relationships with Other Vocabularies

SIOC reuses and aligns with various ontologies from the Web. The main goal of such approach is to avoid reinventing new classes and properties, and to benefit from past work from other communities in terms of ontology engineering. Especially, SIOC reuses the Dublin Core model to define various attributes of created content (such as the creation date of an item, using `dcterms:created`),

---

[9] http://rdfs.org/sioc/services
[10] http://www.w3.org/TR/wsdl
[11] http://rdfs.org/sioc/swan

FOAF — Friend Of A Friend [12] — to model personal identity and related attributes and has ties with SKOS — Simple Knowledge Organization System[13] — to model discussion topics (Figure 3). By interlinking FOAF and SIOC, one can have different user profiles on different websites (represented as instances of sioc:UserAccount), all related to the same physical person (foaf:Person) using the foaf:account property. Moreover, we shall note more precisely that each sioc:UserAccount is actually related to the Agent class from FOAF (and not directly to a foaf:Person). Consequently, an instance of sioc:UserAccount can be associated with both software agents and human users, which may be useful when dealing with wikis or IRC bots.

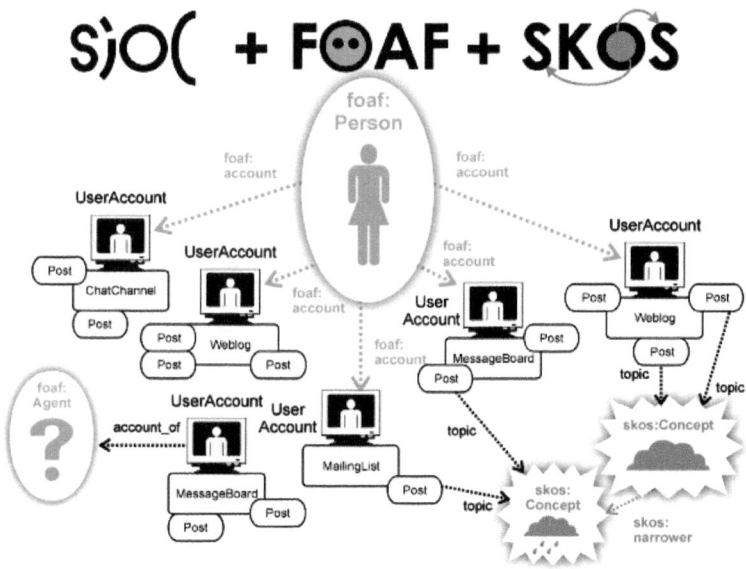

Fig. 3. Combining SIOC with FOAF and SIOC in online communities

3   Current Status and Uptake of SIOC

Since the goal of SIOC is to provide interoperability between communities on the Social Web, one way to evaluate it is to consider its uptake on the Web. To illustrate the amount of SIOC data on the Web, according to the PingTheSemanticWeb (PTSW) service[14] there were 132'475 documents which contain data described using the SIOC ontology by June 2009[15] (Figure 4). Large amounts of

---

[12] http://foaf-project.org

[13] http://www.w3.org/2004/02/skos/

[14] http://pingthesemanticweb.com

[15] The full amount of SIOC information on the Web is larger than described here as PTSW indexes only a part of available RDF data.

SIOC data are provided by wrappers to existing Social Web sites (*e.g.* wrappers for Flickr[16] or MediaWiki[17]). Thus, the Billion Triple Challenge 2009 dataset [18] contains more than 15 million RDF resources described using SIOC. In addition, SIOC is now widely accepted as a core ontology to describe Social Web communities using Semantic Web technologies, alongside with FOAF. Hence, the use of SIOC is suggested by the Yahoo! SearchMonkey developer documentation[19] (SIOC data being indexed by SearchMonkey to improve presentation of search results) and by various best practices documents describing data publishing on the Semantic Web such as [5].

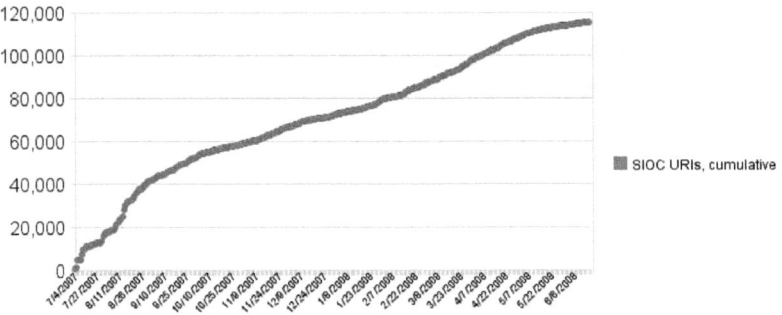

Fig. 4. The amount of SIOC data on the Web (PingTheSemanticWeb data)

Moreover, we shall mention recent initiatives using SIOC that should help sustain its growth, notably its integration as a core vocabulary in Drupal 7, that supports native RDF output *via* RDFa annotations embedded in web pages[20].

3.1 The SIOC Eco-system

Various SIOC-enabled services have been created[21], forming an *eco-system* of applications (Figure 5) that implement the SIOC ontology and that participate in various stages of SIOC information life cycle (from data creation and integration through to its storage and use). The creation of an application ecosystem around an ontology helps to overcome the *"chicken and egg"* problem of the Semantic Web and to facilitate the uptake of the ontology on the Web.

These applications typically belong to one of the following types:

– *data producers* — that allow us to generate SIOC RDF data from various applications;

---

[16] http://apassant.net/home/2007/12/flickrdf/
[17] http://ws.sioc-project.org/mediawiki
[18] http://vmlion25.deri.ie/
[19] http://developer.yahoo.com/searchmonkey/smguide/profile_vocab.html
[20] http://groups.drupal.org/node/16597
[21] http://rdfs.org/sioc/applications/

- *data collectors* — that help with the discovery, crawling and indexing of this data;
- *data consumers* — that allow to browse and analyze the knowledge contained in SIOC data, to visualize and to reuse this data;
- *libraries and utilities* — for supporting the SIOC applications described above.

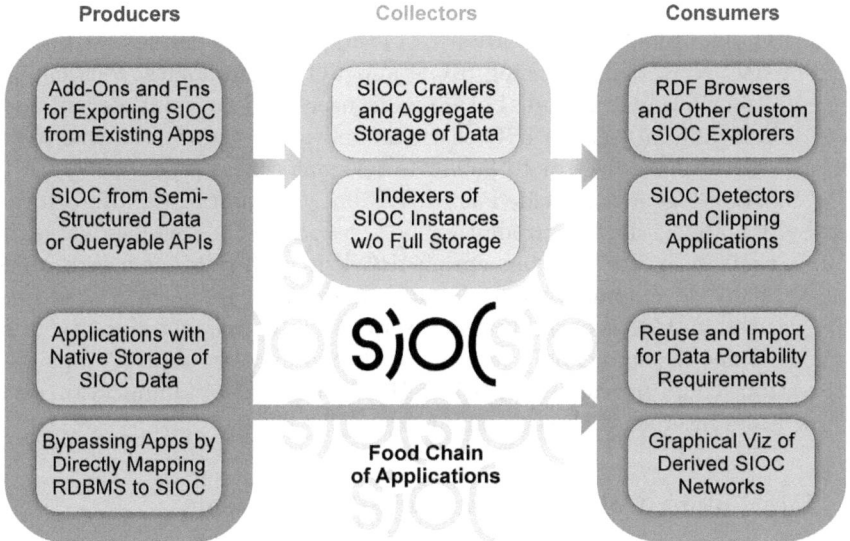

Fig. 5. The SIOC eco-system

In order to bootstrap usage of SIOC and to facilitate its adoption we initially created a small set of *"seed"* applications covering main areas of the ontology ecosystem. Examples of initial SIOC applications include the WordPress SIOC export plugin[22], the Semantic Radar extension for Firefox[23] and various applications for exploring SIOC data. Then, thanks to contributions from the developer community, outside the core team, the size of the SIOC eco-system has grown to over 50 applications. To aid with the production and use of SIOC data in Social Semantic Web applications by the community, reusable APIs, covering various parts of SIOC data life-cycle, have been created for languages such as PHP, Ruby on Rails and Java.

4   Initiatives Using SIOC

Since the goal of SIOC is to enable interoperability of social data on the Web, having applications that address different system and communities is a mean to

---

[22] http://sioc-project.org/wordpress
[23] https://addons.mozilla.org/en-US/firefox/addon/3886

achieve this goal. Thus, within the aforementioned ecosystem, various applications have been developed either to produce, collect and consume SIOC data[24] and we describe some of them in this section.

4.1   Expressing IRC Conversations

Instant messaging is one major form of social interaction and online collaboration, but it is traditionally disconnected from the Web, especially when happening on IRC. The SiocLog application[25] [14] addresses this issue and provides a record of IRC conversations using SIOC and FOAF ontologies. Participants of these conversations may include both human users and automatic agents (called *bots*). Bots are often used on IRC channels for various administrative tasks, to interface with web services or to facilitate teleconferences [12].

The SiocLog logger is provided as in IRC bot. The linked data interface provided by it may use data from another bot — *mttlbot*[26] — which enables users to define their Web IDs and thus enrich IRC logs with relevant user profiles. In terms of future developments, a useful addition to this application would be the ability to identify bots separately from users and to define metadata for describing them. Since users and bots interact with one another on IRC, logs of such conversations could provide insights into the patterns of communication on IRC, *i.e.* how users interact with such bots.

4.2   Interlinking Collaborative Work Environments

The Ecospace Integrated Project[27] is addressing issues of interoperability in the area of Collaborative Work Environments (CWE) like Lotus Notes, Microsoft SharePoint and BSCW. The SIOC ontology has been adopted in the project[28] to provide the basis for the much-needed multi-platform integration and to allow cross-project querying and access to this semantically-interlinked information [19]. This was achieved in three stages: (1) concepts that exist in the CWE domain and that appear in the platforms involved in the project namely, BSCW and Business Collaborator (BC) were mapped to the SIOC ontology; (2) SIOC exporters were developed for these platforms. These tools, based on the conceptual mappings created in the previous stage, annotate the internal data and export them as SIOC RDF data; and (3) a specialized SIOC4CWE explorer was developed for navigating and querying aggregated SIOC data from heterogeneous shared workspaces in a unified way.

Another similar effort, focused more on interoperability issues between Enterprise 2.0 [18] applications (combining blogs, wikis, tagging, RSS feeds) is the

---

[24] An up-to-date list is available at
     http://wiki.sioc-project.org/index.php/Category:Applications
[25] http://github.com/tuukka/sioclog
[26] http://buzzword.org.ok/2009/mttlbot/#project
[27] http://www.ip-ecospace.org/
[28] http://www.ami-communities.eu/wiki/ECOSPACE/SIOC

SemSLATES proposal, in which SIOC has been deployed to provide a foundational layer of integration between these applications, in combination with other services such as semantic wikis and a semantic tagging platform [22]. Figure 6 exemplifies how data from various applications from an Enterprise 2.0 ecosystem (blogs, wikis, RSS feeds) is automatically translated to SIOC to provide a unified representation of social content from these various services in enterprise settings that can be then reused for advanced and cross-application querying purposes.

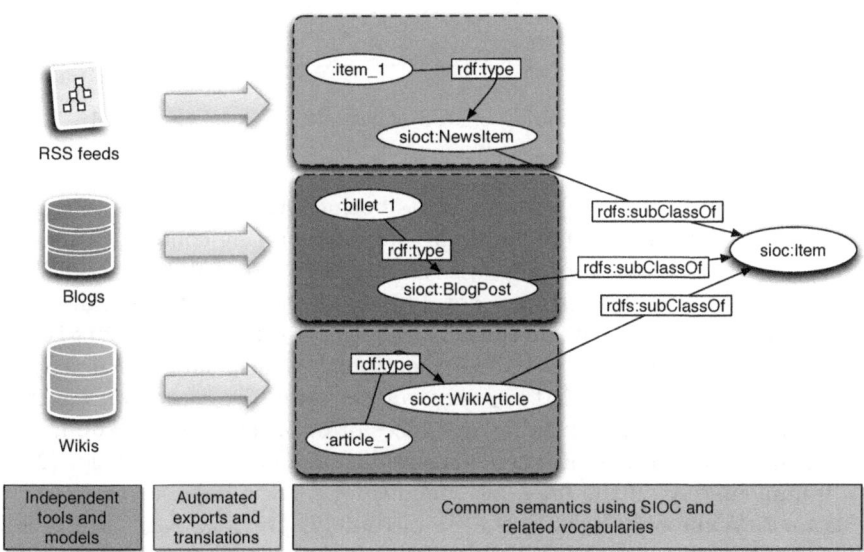

Fig. 6. Using SIOC to unify information from corporate online communities

4.3 Exposing Wiki Structure with SIOC

Another recent area in which SIOC was introduced is the modeling of wiki features, especially with regards to versioning and multi-authoring. To that extent, new properties were introduced in the SIOC ontology and we also developed a SIOC exporter (available as a Web service[29]) for any MediaWiki instance, hence being able to provide a complete SIOC export of popular wikis such as Wikipedia including pages revisions, internal and external links, etc. [21][30] Moreover, once wiki data is exposed to SIOC, it allows to interlink various wikis together, and also to combine wiki data with other SIOC-enabled content (such as blog data or the aforementioned IRC conversations).

---

[29] http://ws.sioc-project.org/mediawiki
[30] The majority of information in the billion triples challenge dataset (including 14,133,700 instances of sioct:WikiArticles) is generated by this wrapper applied to WikiPedia.

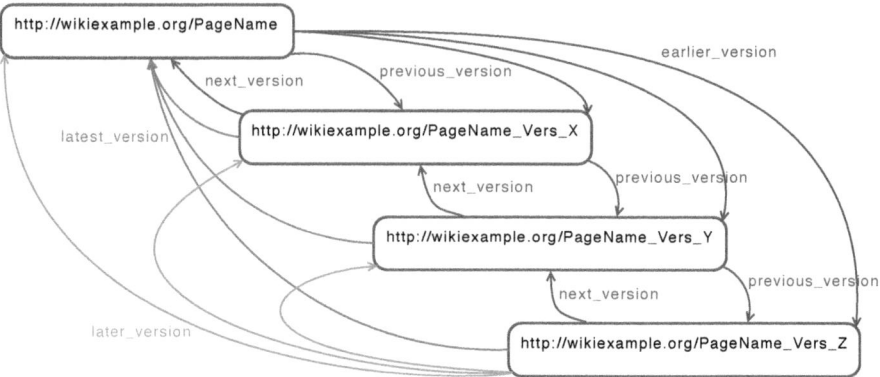

Fig. 7. Modeling versioning of wiki pages with SIOC — From [21]

Interestingly, this SIOC exporter exports both contributions from real people as well as from bots (*e.g.* agents automatically moderating content) while there is unfortunately no way to formally differentiate both (since Wikipedia API does not provide this information) from users. This exporter also features relationships between different versions of the same Wiki page, using the `next_version` and `previous_version` properties that we mentioned earlier. These properties are defined as subproperties of `later_version` and `earlier_version`, which are transitive properties (*i.e.* defined as instances of `owl:TransitiveProperty`). It allows agents that can exploit these transitivity axioms, such as Pellet [26], to identify immediately all the previous versions for a given page, as we can see in the Figure 7. While only links to the (immediately) previous pages are present, new information about online communities are discovered thanks to inference capabilities, consequently augmenting their value for querying and integration purposes.

4.4   Semantic Microblogging

Another important trend in the Web 2.0 world is the use of microblogging, in order to exchange status updates to an update audience, notably using Twitter[31]. In addition to several initiatives that provide SIOC export of microblogging data, such as the Chisimba Tweet aggregator[32], we developed the SMOB framework (for Semantic MicrOBlogging [23]), another example of how Semantic Web technologies can enhance applications from the Social Web. SMOB provides an open platform for decentralized and distributed publishing and aggregating of microblog content, using notably FOAF and SIOC, as well as standards protocols to exchange and query information between publishers and aggregators.

Any content generated with SMOB is available in RDF using the aforementioned vocabularies, and can be combined with other SIOC data, such as blog

---

[31] `http://twitter.com`
[32] `http://tweetgator.peeps.co.za/`

posts and wiki pages, in order to get a real-time overview of activity around a particular topic. Indeed, SMOB also provides interlinking capabilities with other Linking Open Data sources, enabling real-time object-centred sociality [16] for microblogs.

5   Querying and Browsing SIOC Data

Since SIOC data is RDF data, one can simply relies on existing standards to query it, especially SPARQL[33]. The main interest of such approach is that, by exposing data from online communities as SIOC data, the same query pattern can be applied by software agents to any community data. Thus, retrieving the last contributions in Forum X can be done similarly as retrieving the last ones from Wiki Y. In addition, by exposing this data openly on the Web, agents can benefit from Semantic Search engines such as Sindice[34] to find this information, originally distributed on the Web, in a single place.

```
SELECT ?post ?creator ?agent
WHERE {
    ?post a sioc:Post ;
      sioc:has_creator ?creator .
    ?agent foaf:holds_account ?creator .
    !BOUND(?creator rdfs:type foaf:Person)
}
```

Listing 1.3. Example of SPARQL query using SIOC data

Focusing on human-agent conversations, Listing 1.3 shows a SPARQL query retrieving posts created by agents that are not defined as persons, relying on the principles of negation as failure, due to the Open World Assumption of the Semantic Web[35].

To enable human navigation of SIOC data, hence providing a complete human-machine-human chain for information management in online communities, various applications have been built, such as the SIOC browsers defined in [6]. One of them is depicted in Figure 8, representing how SIOC information has been used to identify social networks across distributed conversations, based on the reply patterns of users. It shows once again how common semantics to represent data from online communities can be used to extend the usages we can get from them.

---

[33] http://www.w3.org/TR/rdf-sparql-query/

[34] http://sindice.com

[35] Hence, that query cannot ensure that the identified agent is not a person, which would require a specific class subclass of foaf:Agent, being disjoint of foaf:Person, for instance ex:Bot.

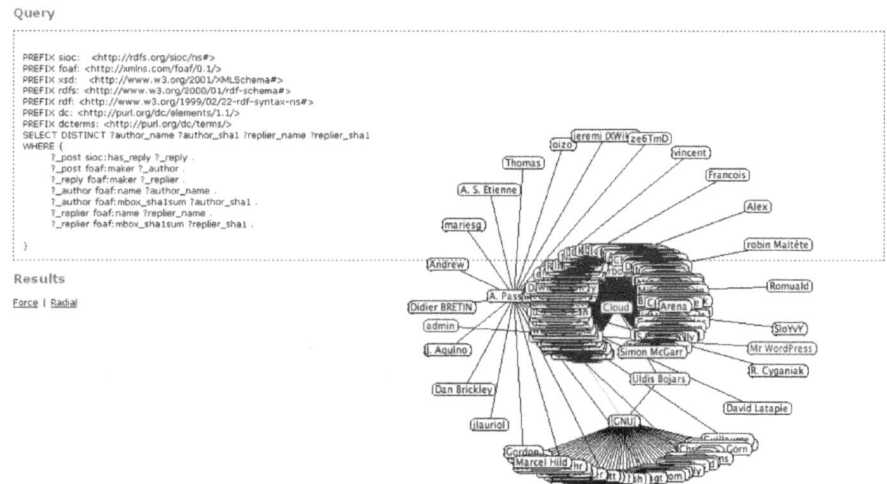

Fig. 8. Identifying social networks from SIOC-based information

6   Conclusion

In this paper, we described the SIOC project, its goals and means as well as related uptake and overview of some of the services exposing or using SIOC information. We detailed the SIOC ontology (both the Core and its modules) as well
as various applications and initiatives using SIOC, describing how they provide
machine processable data from online interactions in various contexts, ranging
from wikis, IRC conversations and microblogging applications. Our current work
focuses on extending the ontology for specific domains and use-cases, as we have
described in this paper in the context of Wikis and microblogging applications.
Indeed, as new Web 2.0 services appear, with new paradigms and features, there
is a need to provide new modules (or enhance the SIOC Core Ontology) to represent interactions happening within these services in a machine-readable way,
so that data can be processed and integrated with other SIOC data.

Acknowledgements

The work presented in this paper has been funded in part by Science Foundation
Ireland under Grant No. SFI/08/CE/I1380 (Líon-2).

References

1. Ankolekar, A., Krötzsch, M., Tran, D.T., Vrandecic, D.: The Two Cultures: Mash-
   ing up Web 2.0 and the Semantic Web. Journal of Web Semantics 6(1), 70–75
   (2008)

2. Berners-Lee, T.: Tim Berners-Lee Podcast at ISWC 2005 (November 2005),
   `http://esw.w3.org/topic/IswcPodcast`
3. Berners-Lee, T., Hendler, J.A., Lassila, O.: The Semantic Web. Scientific American 284(5), 34–43 (2001)
4. Berrueta, D., Brickley, D., Decker, S., Fernández, S., Görn, C., Harth, A., Heath, T., Idehen, K., Kjernsmo, K., Miles, A., Passant, A., Polleres, A., Polo, L., Sintek, M.: SIOC Core Ontology Specification. W3C Member Submission June 12, World Wide Web Consortium (2007),
   `http://www.w3.org/Submission/sioc-spec/`
5. Bizer, C., Cyganiak, R., Heath, T.: How to Publish Linked Data on the Web. Technical report (2007),
   `http://www4.wiwiss.fu-berlin.de/bizer/pub/LinkedDataTutorial/`
6. Bojārs, U., Breslin, J.G., Passant, A.: SIOC Browser – Towards a Richer Blog Browsing Experience. In: Proceedings of the 4th Blogtalk Conference (Blogtalk Reloaded), Books on demand (2006)
7. Bojārs, U., Breslin, J.G., Peristeras, V., Tummarello, G., Decker, S.: Interlinking the Social Web with Semantics. IEEE Intelligent Systems 23(3), 29–40 (2008)
8. Breslin, J.G., Decker, S.: Semantic Web 2.0: Creating Social Semantic Information Spaces. In: Tutorial at the 15th International World Wide Web Conference, WWW 2006 (2006)
9. Breslin, J.G., Harth, A., Bojārs, U., Decker, S.: Towards Semantically-Interlinked Online Communities. In: Gómez-Pérez, A., Euzenat, J. (eds.) ESWC 2005. LNCS, vol. 3532, pp. 500–514. Springer, Heidelberg (2005)
10. Breslin, J.G., Passant, A., Decker, S.: The Social Semantic Web. Springer, Heidelberg (2009)
11. Ciccarese, P., Wu, E., Wong, G., Ocana, M., Kinoshita, J., Ruttenberg, A., Clark, T.: The SWAN biomedical discourse ontology. Journal of Biomedical Informatics 41(5), 739–751 (2008)
12. Froumentin, M.: Zakim — A Multimodal Software System for Large-Scale Teleconferencing. In: Bengio, S., Bourlard, H. (eds.) MLMI 2004. LNCS, vol. 3361, pp. 46–55. Springer, Heidelberg (2005)
13. Gruber, T.R.: Towards Principles for the Design of Ontologies Used for Knowledge Sharing. International Journal Human-Computer Studies 43(5-6), 907–928 (1995)
14. Hastrup, T., Bojars, U., Breslin, J.G.: SiocLog: Providing IRC discussion logs as Linked Data. In: 2nd Social Data on the Web (SDoW 2009) Workshop at the 8th International Semantic Web Conference, vol. 520 (2009)
15. Hendler, J.A., Golbeck, J.: Metcalfe's law, Web 2.0, and the Semantic Web. Journal of Web Semantics 6(1), 14–20 (2008)
16. Knorr-Cetina, K.D.: Sociality with objects: Social relations in postsocial knowledge societies. Theory, Culture and Society 14(4), 1–30 (1997)
17. Lange, C., Bojars, U., Groza, T., Breslin, J., Handschuh, S.: Expressing argumentative discussions in social media sites. In: First International Workshop on Social Data on the Web (SDOW 2008), vol. 405. CEUR-ws.org. (2008)
18. Mcafee, A.P.: Enterprise 2.0: The Dawn of Emergent Collaboration. MIT Sloan Management Review 47(3), 21–28 (2006)
19. Ning, K., Peristeras, V., Bojārs, U., Breslin, J.G.: A SIOC Enabled Explorer of Shared Workspaces. In: CSCW and Web 2.0 Workshop at the 10th European Conference on CSCW, Limerick, Ireland (2007)
20. O'Reilly, T.: O'Reilly Network: What Is Web 2.0: Design Patterns and Business Models for the Next Generation of Software (September 30, 2005),
   `http://www.oreillynet.com/lpt/a/6228`

21. Orlandi, F., Passant, A.: Enabling cross-wikis integration by extending the SIOC ontology. In: Proceedings of the Fourth Workshop on Semantic Wikis, SemWiki 2009 (2009)
22. Passant, A.: Technologies du Web Sémantique pour l'Entreprise 2.0 (Semantic Web technologies for Enterprise 2.0). PhD thesis (2009)
23. Passant, A., Bojars, U., Breslin, J.G., Hastrup, T., Stankovic, M., Laublet, P.: An Overview of SMOB 2: Open, Semantic and Distributed Microblogging. In: 4th International Conference on Weblogs and Social Media, ICWSM 2010 (2010)
24. Passant, A., Ciccarese, P., Breslin, J., Clark, T.: SWAN/SIOC: Aligning Scientific Discourse Representation and Social Semantics. In: Workshop on Semantic Web Applications in Scientific Discourse (co-located with the 8th International Semantic Web Conference), vol. 523. CEUR-ws.org (2009)
25. Passant, A., Kärger, P., Hausenblas, M., Olmedilla, D., Polleres, A., Decker, S.: Enabling Trust and Privacy on the Social Web. In: W3C Workshop on the Future of Social Networking (2009)
26. Sirin, E., Parsia, B., Grau, B.C., Kalyanpur, A., Katz, Y.: Pellet: A practical OWL-DL reasoner. Journal of Web Semantics 5(2), 51–53 (2007)
27. Stankovic, M., Passant, A., Laublet, P.: Directing status messages to their audience in online communities. In: Multi-Agent Logics, Languages, and Organisations Federated Workshops, vol. 494, CEUR-ws.org (2009)
28. Story, H.: FOAF & SSL: creating a global decentralised authentication protocol. In: W3C Workshop on the Future of Social Networking (2009)

Directing Status Messages to Their Audience in Online Communities

Milan Stankovic[1,2], Alexandre Passant[3], and Philippe Laublet[1]

[1] LaLIC, Université Paris–Sorbonne, 28 rue Serpente, 75006 Paris, France
[2] Hypios, 187, rue du Temple, 75003 Paris, France
[3] Digital Enterprise Research Institute, National University of Ireland UI-Galway, Galway, Ireland
milan.stankovic@hypios.com, alexandre.passant@deri.org, philippe.laublet@paris-sorbonne.fr

Abstract. Social interactions have become an important element of today's Web through sites like Social Networks and other online communities. In this paper we focus on a particular aspect of the "Social Web" – the exchange of status messages (short text messages usually broadcasted to a large audience). We investigate the nature of the status message sharing phenomenon and the issues that surround it by the means of a qualitative user study. The results suggest the need to introduce the notion of audience of a status message in the broadcasting in order to prevent the issues of "Gap of Understanding", "Lack of Significance" and "Privacy". In the second part of the paper we present the requirements for a system that would overcome those issues, and seek the concrete solutions in the emerging "Semantic Web" technologies. We present a way how "Semantic Web" ontologies and rules could be used to address the problem of directing status messages to their intended audience. Particularly we show how semantic descriptions of status messages and their intended audiences can be beneficially coupled with the existing distributed data about users to direct status messages to their intended recipients.

Keywords: Online Presence, Virtual Social Networks, Semantic Web.

1 Introduction

Status messages are short textual expressions that describe the state of a user's presence in the online world, i.e. generally on the Web. Sharing status messages on different social services on the Web (Microblogging services, Instant Messaging platforms, Social Networks) became a common practice for people to share thoughts, feelings of the moment, announce one's presence in the online world and broadcast information. However, as more and more users take part in status message sharing, it becomes obvious that the audience of status messages is an important issue. The recently generated overload of status messages on sharing services has brought to light many problems. Firstly, confidentiality of status messages in open communities is a significant question, since not all status messages are meant for general public. Some should be kept private from certain contacts that might use them in an inappropriate way. An

J. Padget et al. (Eds.): COIN 2009, LNAI 6069, pp. 195–210, 2010.

example could be a status message revealing somebody's drinking habits, meant to amuse personal friends, but the same status message could be a source of inconvenience if shown to work colleagues.

Apart from private nature of some status messages there are other reasons why a particular status message might not be suitable for a certain audience. For example, some status message updates may have no significance for certain groups of contacts that consider them as information noise. It is a common case that we subscribe to someone's statuses because of the interest in professional news she/he is sharing, but aside we get a lot of postings about the person's personal life that don't interest us. Problems like those limit in a great deal, the usefulness of today's status sharing services (mostly microblogging services and Social Networks).

Although the notion of audience design has already been studied in sociolinguistics [1] our intention was to complement this work by deepening the understanding of audience-related issues in status message sharing communities on the Social Web. Thus we conducted a qualitative user study with subjects who are using status messages for different purposes and in different contexts on a daily basis. The goal of the study was to develop understanding of the key problems, factors that make a status message open or confidential – that determine its intended audience. Apart from understanding the problems, the outcomes of the study allowed us to explore the space of possible technical solutions to these issues. Thus the second part of our work consists in designing a Semantic Web-based approach for dealing with audience-related issues in status message sharing. The reminder of the paper is organized as follows: in Section 2 we present our user study and its results. Section 3 presents the Presence Diamond, a notion for the study of presence online as a faceted phenomenon. Section 4 lists currently available solutions for problems identified in the study. In Section 5 we synthesize the requirements for an advanced status message publishing system. Section 6 follows with investigation how Semantic Web could help build such a system. In this section, we introduce a way to direct status messages to their intended audience using Semantic Web technologies, and we show how those technologies are flexible enough to support even dynamic audience definitions (where members of the audience change frequently based on various contextual properties). Section 7 presents related work and we finally conclude the paper in Section 8.

2 The User Study

The user study was conducted through a series of interviews with ten users of social networks and microblogging platforms who have been using them for status message sharing for some time (a year in average). The 30-35 minute interviews were field-noted and audio recorded for further reference. Users' age ranged from 22 to 35. This choice proved to correspond well to demographics of users of the most active microblogging services (documented in a statistical report done by Pew Internet [2]). Equal number of female and male subjects, from France and Ireland, with different origins and backgrounds, took part in the interviews.

After a couple of questions about users' background, users were asked to tell their status message publishing experiences. The main goal was to identify their context in the time of publishing, nature of the status message content and the intended audience.

The inconveniences and the inability of microblogging tools and social networks to meet their status message sharing needs were also explored.

Once we collected the user stories, we relied on Grounded Theory inspired approach to extract relevant categories from them, and further generalize the categories to super-categories that we call – major issues. Grounded Theory was introduced by Glaser and Strauss [3] and has served ever since for analysis of results in qualitative research in Social Sciences. Grounded Theory is an approach to looking systematically at qualitative data to derive codes and group them into relevant categories that will further be generalized into concepts that make the ground for generating a theory. Generalizations are derived by thinking efforts of researchers. Due to a space limit, in this paper we present only a part of our findings - the highest level generalizations, and we briefly describe them with some of the lower level generalizations that we find the most relevant to our intended readers. In particular, two features of the Grounded Theory, Open and Axial coding, were conducted by two researchers who reached an agreement about the codes in order to reduce the impact of subjectivity. For more detailed study report we refer the reader to [4].

The chosen research method and the size of the sample correspond to our particular needs that are exploratory in nature, as the study's purpose is to create a ground for further development of a technical solution, and help understand the advantages and disadvantages of a particular technology – Semantic Web in directing status messages to their audience.

Generally, we discovered that many times when users publish a status message, they have a certain audience in mind. The status message is intended for a particular audience either because of its ability to understand the message (or the inability of others to understand it properly) either because of significance of the message for a certain group (and insignificance for others) or because of the confidential nature of the status message content. The next three sections present those major issues, i.e. the main reasons why a status message has its particular audience. Those reasons will be used later to design a Semantic Web approach for dealing with audience issues.

2.1 Gap of Understanding

In many cases where a certain status message is not meant for a certain group of people it is because of their inability to understand, properly interpret and maybe even reply to the content of the message. Sometimes the inability arises from **shallow acquaintance** like in cases where the user publishing a status message knows a certain group of people for a short time. The shallowness of acquaintance can be an obstacle for this group of people to understand jokes, metaphors and properly interpret the intended meanings of status messages. Sometimes the gap of understanding results from **lack of competence** like in cases where users use status messages to ask for advice, or provoke professional discussions. This problem is also present in scenarios of automatic postings of status messages across services (e.g. automatic forwarding from Twitter to Facebook) where mostly different audiences are present on different services. Quite often personal friends from one service (Facebook in our case) don't understand and find irrelevant the profession-related status messages posted on another service (Twitter).

Some status messages bear a **socially established meaning**, understood by a small community of people, like those containing internal jokes, or internal aliases and metaphors. Such status messages may be misinterpreted by people outside that small community and may be source of misunderstandings, inappropriate comments and other inconveniences. This phenomenon is just a reflection of the phenomenon of a speech community that exists in the real world scenarios and is well studied in the field of sociolinguistics [1].

2.2 Lack of Significance

In other cases, a status message is not intended for some people simply because they have no interest in it. This is the case when a status message relates to a certain domain and thus can be of significance only to people with an **interest in the domain**. This case is common when people make connections based on a shared interest, stay in touch and then use status messages to spread domain related news, announce events and provoke discussions. In some cases it is the interest in the domain that makes a certain group of people not interested in other non domain-related status messages of a user. For people who are not familiar with the domain such messages can represent noise.

In other cases some groups of people might not be able to **make use of the information** in the status message, which has an informative purpose. This is the case with status messages highly dependent on location – like those containing invitations to local parties and announcements of local events. In both cases such status messages are irrelevant to people from other locations that could not make use of the announcement, since it relies on a geographical context which they do not belong to.

2.3 Privacy

Privacy is an issue that occurs when a user wants to explicitly restrict access to some groups of contacts for some types of status message or even only for a particular status message. It is usually related to groups of higher granularity, like the case of separating status messages for work and private contacts. People usually perceive some content types (like feelings and moods or travel experiences) to be suitable only for closer contacts or contacts of a more private nature, while those status messages should be kept private from some other (more professional) groups of contacts.

Some users, on the other hand express concern about the **possibilities to track** their status messages to the past and draw conclusions about their personality that would be out of their control. The concern is expressed about the uncontrolled data integration possibilities across services and attempts to integrate status messages with other content about the user and thus perform some spy-like behavior.

3   The Presence Diamond

Once we acknowledge that many status messages have an intended audience and that access to these messages should in some cases be restricted to that particular audience (in case of confidential messages for instance), it becomes clear that one user might want to have different status messages for different audiences at the same time.

In fact, emitting different information (appearances) to different groups of observers is not restricted to status messages, but spans the whole notion of online presence.

By the term online presence we refer to the totality of information that allows perceiving one's presence in online communities. Apart from status messages as an element of presence, availability for interaction might also have a faceted nature and be different for different groups at different times. One can easily imagine a working situation where a user is available for interaction only with his work colleagues and busy for all the others. That can be observed for instance on the status message of instant messaging client of some users, such as "Available for work purposes only". Access to different presence information might also be given only to specific groups of contacts (like in the case of sharing the current location only with closest friends). In the case of online status messages, we can imagine a user feeling to disclose "waiting for tonight's party" to his close friend and "working on a project deliverable" to his colleague at the same time.

Therefore, there is a need to look at the notion of online presence as a faceted phenomenon. For this reason we introduce the notion of the presence diamond (Figure 1.) to capture the faceted nature of presence and the need to appear differently to different groups of people.

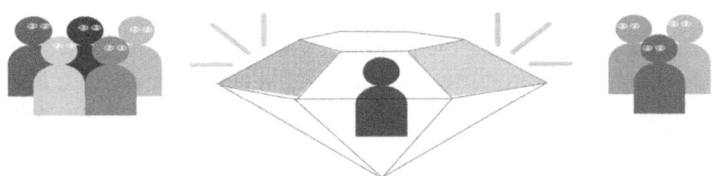

Fig. 1. The Presence Diamond[1]

The notion of presence diamond allows us to look at a person's online presence as a diamond whereby different observers are introduced to different facets of the diamond. Facets differ among themselves in **different types of presence data** that is accessible by observers of a facet (like in cases where one group of observers can access a person's location, availability and a status message, and another group can access only the status message), **different granularity of data** (like in the case of sharing the exact location with closest friends and only the current city/country with strangers), and even in **different data** that is emitted to different observers (like having different status messages and different availability for different groups of contacts, as in our previous example).

The notion of appearing differently to different groups of observers might find its counterpart in the sociolinguistic research. According to [1] style shift in speech occurs as a response to different audiences. The notion of presence diamond brings a similar phenomenon to light, but applied to the different categories (type of presence data, granularity, different data) instead of speech style.

Although the presence diamond does not bring a fundamentally new view on the world it provides a very practical way to think of the space of user's contacts and slice

---

[1] The figure and the notion of the Presence Diamond are strongly inspired by the notion of the diamond of digital identity, that Mike Roch, Director of IT Services at University of Reading, introduced at the Eduserv Digital Identity Workshop in London, January 08, 2009.

that space in groups according to the properties of group members. Further on, the presence diamond slices the space of user's acquaintances from the perspective of the user and his/her publishing needs.

Even though we focus on the particular case of status messages in this paper, we will look at the problem of directing status messages to their intended audience as a sub-problem of enabling faceted online presence (and even online identity), and will therefore favor solutions that are general enough to address the faceted nature of presence as a whole on the Web.

4   Incomplete Ways to Deal with Status Message Directing

Some ways to direct status message updates to a particular audience already exist. In this section we present the workarounds found and applied by users, as well as solutions developed as features of existing and popular Social Web sites. For each of these solutions we discuss their advantages but also their incompleteness.

4.1   User Workarounds

Some users manage to separate their contacts on different Social Web services, by taking into account the nature of relationship with a particular contact. For example, a number of users maintain a list of work-related contacts on Twitter while having a more personal network of friends on Facebook and professional contacts on LinkedIn, then sharing different status message updates for the different audiences. This way, status messages related to private life can be kept confidential from work colleagues, and personal friends don't have to be bothered by work related postings. However, the fact that some contacts use only one social network stands in the way of such a separation. If some of the user's work colleagues use only Facebook, then maintaining the separation would mean not connecting at all with those persons. Apart from this limitation, if the separation by purpose is not done at the start, it is hard to impose it once the user has accepted different types of contacts to his/her social network.

Another way to deal with the identified issues is just to restrict oneself to publishing only status messages acceptable for the wide audience. Some users choose not to publish too personal status messages because work-related contacts might see them, and not to publish work-related status messages because they might not be of interest to their friends. This approach limits the potential of status message sharing in a great deal excluding many professional and staying-in-touch use cases.

4.2   Solutions Developed by Social Web Sites

Solutions for niche microblogging and micro-broadcasting (broadcasting status messages in small communities as opposed to the open nature of Twitter and similar services) began to emerge recently. Those Social Web sites allow for broadcasting of status messages in closed communities (like in ShoutEm[2]) or to people gathered around a certain interest (like in Static[3]). However they mostly require intended

---

[2] http://www.shoutem.com/
[3] http://www.static.com/

recipients of the status message updates to join each closed community, which can get quite complicated having in mind the number of intended audiences a user might have. This approach certainly leads to *social network fatigue* – a phenomenon of loss of motivation to participate in yet another social network when confronted with joining many social networks and building identities on them[4].

The new service E[5] can be used to manage adding different people to different social networks according to the nature of the acquaintance (e.g. adding friends to Facebook and business contacts to MySpace). However, it is hard to enforce this separation since not all users are present on each of those networks and therefore some of connections might be lost if they do not meet the purpose one user has given to his/her social network account.

5 Requirements for an Advanced Status Message Publishing Service

Based on the limitations of current systems discussed in the previous section and the user workarounds disclosed by our user study, we proposed a set of requirements that an advanced status message publishing service should satisfy in order to respond to the needs discovered in the user study. A more adequate service should support users in dedicating status messages to people based on:

R 1. Their social graph (their relationships with other users).

R 2. Their affiliation with a certain institution (e.g., school or workplace) as well as with people who are members of a certain online community (e.g., an online forum).

R 3. Their interests and competences (including languages spoken and knowledge about locations visited).

R 4. The intensity of relationship between the status message publisher and the observer.

As well as:

R 5. Support users in dedicating status messages to a certain group of people regardless of the status sharing service they use (i.e., allowing the target audience to be dispersed all over the Social Web).

R 6. Take into account the dynamic and ever changing nature of user properties (for example their current location, interest, etc.).

R 7. Allow users to publish status messages confidentially – in a way that only certain people can get access to the status message.

The dynamic nature of audience that emerged in our study is also present in the works on sociolinguistics (e.g. [5] that includes dynamic factors in the study of speech variation).

In the following sections we investigate the possibilities offered by Semantic Web [6] technologies to help establish a system capable of fulfilling these requirements.

---

[4] http://blogs.zdnet.com/social/?p=53
[5] http://www.mynameise.com/

6 Directing Status Messages: The Linked Data Way

The term Linked Data [7] refers to publishing and interlinking structured data on the Web in RDF[6] with the assumption that the value and usefulness of data increases the more it is interlinked with other data. This effort to publish the data online using open standards and interlink data sources is aimed at transforming the Web of documents towards a more (re)usable, machine readable Web of Data[7].

We argue - and will demonstrate - that additional semantics describing a status message, as well as semantics (partially already published as Linked Data) describing users and their current context can be helpful to direct a status message to its intended audience, and thus reduce information noise and contribute to ensuring privacy. In particular we argue that currently available Linked Data sources, especially from the Linking Open Data initiative[8], can help define the intended audiences of status messages, relying on user properties described in those sources (interests, locations, social graph, etc.)

To enable publishing and exchange of such additional semantics, we decided to enrich an existing vocabulary - the Online Presence Ontology (OPO)[9], that we defined in previous work [8] - with the information about intended audience of a status message. The Online Presence Ontology provides a way to describe a user's current state of presence in the online world, including his/her availability for interaction, current status message, location and other elements of context. As such this vocabulary can be elegantly complemented with a way to direct a status message (but also other presence data) to a certain audience. To enable this, we have extended the OPO with the notion of Sharing Space.

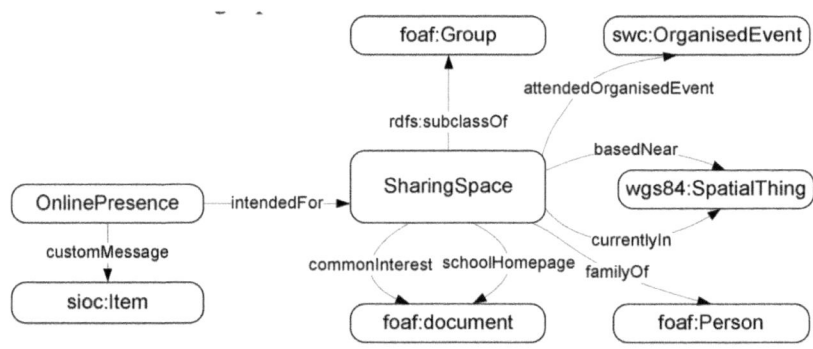

Fig. 2. An excerpt from the Online Presence Ontology

A Sharing Space, in our proposal, is a group of people (or more generally agents) with whom particular information can be shared. As shown on Figure 2, instances of the OnlinePresence class, encompassing (among other properties) the current status

---

[6] Resource Description Framework http://www.w3.org/RDF/
[7] http://www.w3.org/2001/sw/
[8] http://linkeddata.org
[9] http://www.milanstankovic.org/opo/

message of a user, can be connected to its intended audience, represented as an instance of the `SharingSpace` class through a property `intendedFor`. The status message itself is represented using the Item concept from the SIOC[10] ontology [9] in order to enable replies to the status message and make use of this concept's suitable semantics. Sharing Space is also enriched with a list of properties that make it possible to represent some of the common attributes that bind members of the Sharing Space together (e.g., common interest, shared current location). In order to express the semantics of those attributes we relied on concepts from widely used vocabularies (FOAF[11], SWC[12], WGS84[13]). For more details about the ontology design we refer the readers to the project website and the ontology specification[14]. We shall also mention that OPO as well as the extension to enable Sharing Spaces, is designed using existing W3C standards, namely RDF(S)/OWL.

By identifying people who are intended to receive a status message, the notion of Sharing Space can help software systems to deliver status messages to specific people (members of the Sharing Space) and thus deal with information noise and even ensure confidential status message exchange.

In order to properly define Sharing Spaces according to the needs of real life scenarios, we rely on the results of our user study, presented in Section 2. According to our study results, some of the major ways to define the intended audience are: friends of a certain friend; people having a certain interest; friends from a particular online community; people being in a certain location; people having a certain nature of relationship with the user; people who were affiliated in the same institution; and custom assembled groups of contacts.

A lot of information needed to define those groups (users' current and permanent locations, interests, friends' lists, etc.) is already available on the Social Web, and many sources already publish this data using vocabularies such as FOAF and SIOC. Relying on those existing resources, Sharing Spaces could be dynamically defined using simple SPARQL[15] queries that could identify the members of a particular Sharing Space by collecting data across different data sources. We believe that this way of defining Sharing Spaces is flexible enough to cover the needs of real life scenarios identified in our user study, and we will illustrate it on an example in the following subsection.

When proposing to use data from various distributed datasets, we should acknowledge that executing queries over distributed datasets might be a challenging task. However, this challenge has already attracted researchers to develop solutions for this distributed scenario. One of them is a system DARQ [10], an engine for federated SPARQL queries, or the Semantic Web client library[16] that can be used to consider the Semantic Web as a single graph to be quieried from a single entry point.

---

[10] http://sioc-project.org/
[11] Friend-of-a-Friend vocabulary http://xmlns.com/foaf/spec/
[12] Semantic Web Conference Ontology
http://data.semanticweb.org/ns/swc/swc_2009-05-09.html
[13] World Geodetic System ontology http://www.w3.org/2003/01/geo/
[14] Other properties and classes introduced to support the notion of Sharing Space can be found in the specification document http://www.milanstankovic.org/opo/specs/
[15] http://www.w3.org/TR/rdf-sparql-query/
[16] http://www4.wiwiss.fu-berlin.de/bizer/ng4j/semwebclient/

Apart from specifying Sharing Space members using SPARQL, the new version of the OWL language[17], recently adopted as a W3C recommendation [11] will provide a way to define Sharing Spaces through richer restriction axioms such as property chains. Property chains would allow to state that if a user satisfies a certain property then he is automatically a member of a Sharing Space. For example, if the user has interest in the topic that is at the same time associated with a Sharing Space (that is the common interest of all Sharing Space members); an OWL 2 property chain could be created to imply that the user is a member of the Sharing Space. The example definition of this property is given on the Figure 3.

```
SubPropertyOf(
        PropertyChain(
                foaf:interest ObjectInverseOf( opo:commonInterest )
        )
        ex:member
)
```

Fig. 3. OWL 2 Property Chain defining a Sharing Space

However, when we use property chains we should take care not to change the semantics of properties defined elsewhere. This is why in our example we use the property ex:member that is thought of as the subproperty of foaf:member[18] defined in the FOAF ontology. It is introduced since statements made directly about the foaf:member property (that is created and maintained by other people) might redefine its original meaning ant thus be considered as vocabulary hijacking [12]. This subproperty introduced only for the purpose of this example makes the impact of the statement to the semantics of foaf:member property more genuine.

```
Document(
 Prefix(dbpedia <http://dbpedia.org/resource/>)
 Prefix(ex <http://example.org/ns#>)
 Prefix(opo <http://ggg.milanstankovic.org/opo/ns#>)
 Prefix(foaf <http://xmlns.com/foaf/0.1/>)
 Group (
  Forall ?person ?presence (
   ?person[foaf:memberOf -> ex:currentlyInParis] :-
    ?person[
      foaf:topic_interest -> dbpedia:Semantic_Web
      opo:declaresOnlinePresence -> ?presence
    ]
    ?presence[
     opo:currentLocation -> <http://sws.geonames.org/2988507/>
    ]
  )
 )
)
```

Fig. 4. Sharing Space in Object-Oriented Representation in RIF Core presentation syntax

---

[17] http://www.w3.org/2004/OWL/

[18] foaf:member property is used to state that one foaf:Person is a member of a foaf:Group.

We also believe that the emerging Rule Interchange Format [13] – RIF (currently a candidate recommendation) will be a useful way to define and exchange Sharing Space definition rules across different systems that may use different rule languages internally. RIF is meant to serve for the exchange of rules on the Semantic Web, and it could therefore be a good solution for the specific need of sharing Sharing Space definitions.

On Figure 4 we give an example Sharing Space definition represented using RIF Object-oriented syntax. The example defines the Sharing Space called ex:currentlyInParis. All persons having an interest in Semantic Web (the concept is uniquely identified by DBPedia[19] URI) and having declared Paris as their current location in their presence declaration; will according to this rule, be automatically considered as members of this Sharing Space. In our example we rely on the Geonames[20] URI for Paris, to uniquely identify this geographical location.

6.1 Scenario of Use

To better illustrate the flexibility of our approach and the usefulness of Linked Data, we present a scenario of publishing a status message together with a dedication to a particular Sharing Space. Figure 5 will serve as a graphical support to our explanations.

In this scenario, our example user Harry is organizing a reunion for his friends from the Semantic Web community. The reunion will take place in Paris, and Harry wants to announce it in his status message.

Thanks to the open nature of Semantic Web technologies, any status message publishing service (including microblogging platforms, social networks, chat platforms) can publish a status message and describe it using the OPO vocabulary, while translation services can be written for existing services to provide their data as RDF using OPO. Then, Harry's status message publishing service can offer a semantically-rich description of the message and make it available to all status message consuming services. It can further associate it with a particular audience, by using the intended-For property and the concept of a SharingSpace. Along with OPO data about the

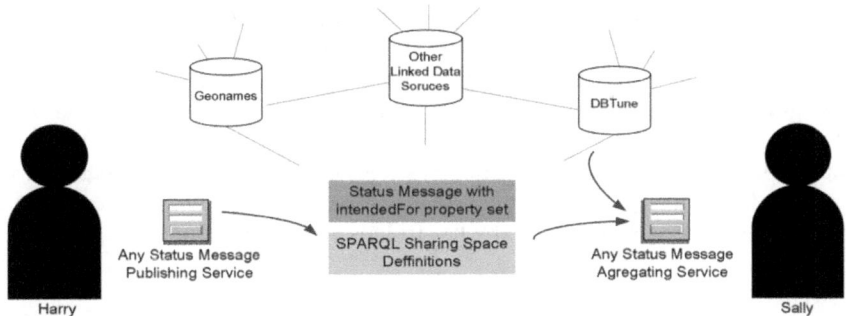

Fig. 5. Publishing a Status Message

---

[19] DBPedia is a semantic Wikipedia – the repository of RDF data extracted from Wikipedia articles; http://dbpedia.org
[20] http://www.geonames.org/

status message itself, Harry's service can publish a SPARQL query to define the members of the Sharing Space. In our case, since Harry's message is intended for people interested in Semantic Web who are currently in Paris, the SPARQL Query would be similar to the one presented in Figure 4.

To make better use of the data available in Linked Data sources, we can reuse existing URIs used by those sources. In this example we rely on DBPedia and Geonames URIs, like in the previous RIF example, to benefit from already existing identifiers to represent respectively an interest and a location.

```
PREFIX opo: <http://http://ggg.milanstankovic.org/opo/ns#>
PREFIX foaf: <http://xmlns.com/foaf/0.1/>
PREFIX rdf: <http://www.w3.org/1999/02/22-rdf-syntax-ns#>

CONSTRUCT
{
    <http://example.org/ns#SWPeopleInParis>
                      rdf:type opo:SharingSpace;
                      foaf:member ?person.
}
WHERE
{
    ?person foaf:topic_interest

<http://dbpedia.org/resource/Semantic_Web>.
    ?person opo:declaresOnlinePresence ?presence .
    ?presence opo:currentLocation
            <http://sws.geonames.org/2988507/>.
}
```

Fig. 6. Example definition of a Sharing Space

Once the message is available together with its semantic description, and a Sharing Space definition, other services can consume it and make it available to their users. Let us take another example user, Sally. She is Harry's friend, interested in Semantic Web and currently visiting Paris (according to her last published status message with associated geographic location information). Although Sally is not using the same status message publishing service as Harry, her Social Network (SN) service, can retrieve semantically described status messages and SPARQL queries defining Sharing Spaces. Since information about Sally's interest is available in one of her FOAF files, and available to her SN, and since her current location is also known to SN, applying the SPARQL query from Figure 6 will put Sally in SWPeopleInParis Sharing Space - the one Harry's status message is intended for.

Sally's interface for browsing status messages can now make sure that status messages intended for her get to her attention and somehow stand out from the abundance of other status messages put online by her friends and other people.

6.2   Benefits of Sharing Spaces

Combining the publishing of status messages using OPO and the extension describe earlier with the definitions of Sharing Spaces can help direct a status message to its audience. As opposed to solutions where particular (sometimes even closed) services are used to dedicate a status message to a certain group of people, our approach offers a way to dedicate a status message to a certain audience regardless of the service being used to publish them and present them (requirement R5). It is the use of widely accepted Semantic Web standards (e.g., RDF(S) and OWL) that make the intended audience specifications universal and thus applicable everywhere.

The approach also allows taking into account the ever-changing nature of user-related data, since membership in a Sharing Space can be defined through a property and not by naming particular members (requirements: R1-R4). Therefore users can belong to a sharing space at one time when they satisfy a certain condition (e.g. currently located in Paris), and not belong to it at all other times, that switch between sharing spaces being done dynamically thanks to the attribute of the users, that change over time and sometime other contexts such as location (requirement R6).

Apart from solving the issue of status message overload and helping relevant messages to reach their audience, Sharing Spaces can serve as a ground for ensuring privacy and confidential status message sharing (requirement R7). Our approach is based on the idea [14] that ensuring trust and privacy on the future Web can be grounded on the interlinked graph of data (i.e. Linked Data) and policies that take advantage of existing data sources. The introduced change in the OPO vocabulary is a first step in this direction, allowing specifying the intended audience of a status message by reusing existing (linked) data on the Web. Further mechanisms to enforce the delivery of a status message to the specified intended audience can be built on top of our presented solution. The advantage of this approach is that dedicating a status message to its audience is quite a general solution, addressing at the same time the challenge of dealing with information noise, and being the ground for ensuring the confidential status message sharing.

Finally we would like to emphasize how the presence diamond helped to summarize the requirements associated with the audience of status messages, and how the Semantic Web solution emerged naturally, as sharing spaces represent in fact facets of the presence diamond.

7 Related Work

Similar to our use of SPARQL to define sharing spaces i.e. intended audience groups, Alessandra Toninelli et al. [15] use RDF and SPARQL triple patterns to build social graph aware policies. Using triple patterns different policies can be created to grant access to user's attention (e.g., ring her phone). However this work is more related to mobile devices as it strongly reflects the specifics of communication using a mobile device, and in this sense it is complementary to our work in effort to make use of social data available in Linked Data sources to enhance user's interaction with devices and make her communications more adapted to her current situation. Another point of difference is that the socially-aware policy model is more concerned at granting/restricting access to a certain resource than dedicating/directing presence information to a certain audience.

Another example of related work is the MyCampus project that was aimed at developing a Semantic Web based platform to support social interactions of students in university campuses [16]. Apart from other aspects of socialization, it deals with presence as well. When it comes to the problem of different audiences of different data, researchers from the MyCampus project proposed a mechanism for providing different granularity and different accuracy of contextual data to different audiences. For example, depending on the presence data consumer, the user's location could be obfuscated or provided in a less precise form (e.g., like saying that the user is on the campus and not disclosing the exact building where she is). Although this approach is quite useful for user's location and more structured data, in case of status messages it is difficult to apply it because of unstructured nature of status messages published as text.

Researchers from Stanford University have noticed the difficulties in keeping track of many e-mail addresses of our contacts, and have designed a system for directing e-mail messages to people who satisfy a certain criteria [17]. Their system allows a user to specify the characteristics of persons that should receive the message, and then uses various Semantic Web data sources (most notably personal data described using FOAF) to select the actual recipients and find their e-mail addresses. Even though the approach is applied on e-mails and not status messages, it is very similar in nature; which leads us to think how the notion of Sharing Spaces could be generalized to serve in scenarios of directing other kind of content (not only status messages and presence data). This generalization will certainly be one of the directions for our future work.

8   Conclusions and Future Work

In this paper we presented the results of our user study, based on qualitative research techniques, which was aimed at identifying the nature of problems surrounding status message publishing. Our study emphasized the need to direct a status message to a particular audience in order to deal with major issues like: Lack of Understanding, Significance, and Privacy.

We have shown how users try to deal with those issues and what solutions did the Social Web sites come up with to help direct a status message to a certain audience. However, we judged all those solutions as incomplete either because they require users to join particular status sharing networks or because they restrain users from publishing certain types of status messages.

Our solution to the problem of dedicating a status message to a particular audience is based on providing semantic descriptions of intended audience and taking advantage of existing data about users published as Linked Data on the Web. Particularly we rely on an extension of the Online Presence Ontology that allows for associating the intended audience information to a status message. Since the solution is based on Semantic Web technologies it allows a high level of interoperability and gives the intended audience information the ability to flow across different status message sharing services. Moreover, our semantic descriptions of intended audiences possess the ability to collect the intended audience members' information from different Linked Data sources across the Web, which makes them universal and based on existing and already available data.

A part of our future work will consist in evaluating the practical aspects of our proposal by extending the distributed microblogging platform SMOB[21], described in [18] to publish and take into account the intended audience information through the use of

---

[21] http://smob.sioc-project.org/

new notion of Sharing Space introduced in the Online Presence Ontology. Among others, the new version of SMOB will make use of data available as Linked Data on the Web to create refined descriptions of audience for its status messages.

While the simple publishing and taking into account of intended audience information would be sufficient to combat the information noise problem, encompassing both issues of Lack of Understanding and Significance; some additional access control mechanisms must be employed to ensure that the intended audience specifications are properly applied across the Web. As a solution to access control we are considering to use the FOAF + SSL protocol [19] – a lightweight solution for authentication and authorization, based on the semantics exposed using the widespread FOAF vocabulary. The OpenID[22] framework for providing a single digital identity across the Internet can also elegantly contribute to achieve simple access control. OAuth[23] authorization protocol could also be helpful in ensuring secure exchange of intended audience information across different services on the Social Web. This protocol might also be of great value to the confidential exchange of other sensitive data (user profiles, locations, etc.) that is relevant for status message directing.

Although our solution for directing a status message to its audience is flexible in specifying the intended recipients of the status message, a lot of work remains to be done to ensure that the unintended recipients do not get access to it. We see the presented extension of OPO and the notion of Sharing Space as a first step in this direction.

References

1. Bell, A.: Language style as audience design. Language in Society 13, 145–204 (1984)
2. Lenhart, A., Fox, S.: Twitter and status updating. Report of Pew Internet and American Life Project (February 12, 2009),
    http://www.pewinternet.org/Reports/2009/
    Twitterand-status-updating.aspx
3. Glaser, B., Strauss, A.: Discovery of Grounded Theory. Aldine, Chicago (1976)
4. Stankovic, M.: Faceted Online Presence – A Semantic Web Approach. Master's Thesis. Université Paris-Sud XI, Orsay, France (2009),
    http://milstan.net/papers/masters.pdf
5. Ladegaard, H.J.: Audience design revisited: persons, roles, and power relations in speech interactions. Language and Communication 15, 89–101 (1995)
6. Berners-Lee, T., Hendler, J., Lassila, O.: The Semantic Web. Scientific American (May 2001),
    http://www.sciam.com/article.cfm?id=
    the-semantic-web&print=true
7. Berners-Lee, T.: Design Issues: Linked Data (2006),
    http://www.w3.org/DesignIssues/LinkedData.html
8. Stankovic, M.: Modeling Online Presence. In: Proceedings of the First Social Data on the Web Workshop, Karlsruhe, Germany (2008),
    http://sunsite.informatik.rwth-aachen.de/Publications/
    CEUR-WS/Vol-405/paper9.pdf

---

[22] http://openid.net/
[23] http://oauth.net/

9. Breslin, J.G., Harth, A., Bojars, U., Decker, S.: Towards Semantically-Interlinked Online Communities. In: Gómez-Pérez, A., Euzenat, J. (eds.) ESWC 2005. LNCS, vol. 3532, pp. 500–514. Springer, Heidelberg (2005)
10. Quilitz, B., Leser, U.: Querying distributed RDF data sources with SPARQL. In: Bechhofer, S., Hauswirth, M., Hoffmann, J., Koubarakis, M. (eds.) ESWC 2008. LNCS, vol. 5021, pp. 524–538. Springer, Heidelberg (2008), http://www.eswc2008.org/final-pdfs-for-web-site/qpII-2.pdf
11. Motik, B., Patel-Schneider, P.F., Parsia, B.: OWL 2 Web Ontology Language: Structural Specification and Functional-Style Syntax (2009), http://www.w3.org/TR/owl2-syntax/
12. Hogan, A., Harth, A., Polleres, A.: Scalable Authoritative OWL Reasoning for the Web. International Journal on Semantic Web and Information Systems 5(2), 49–90 (2009)
13. Boley, H., Hallmark, G., Kifer, M., Pasche, A., Pollares, A., Reynolds, D.R.: RIF Core (2008), http://www.w3.org/TR/rif-core/
14. Passant, A., Kärger, P., Hausenblas, M., Olmedilla, D., Pollares, A., Decker, S.: Enabling Trust and Privacy on the Social Web. In: Proceedings of W3C Workshop on the Future of Social Networks, Barcelona (January 15-16, 2009), http://www.w3.org/2008/09/msnws/papers/trustprivacy.html
15. Toninelli, A., Khushraj, D., Lassila, O., Montanari, R.: Towards Socially Aware Mobile Phones. In: Proceedings of the First Social Data on the Web Workshop, CEUR Workshop Proceedings, Karlsruhe, Germany, October 27 (2008) ISSN 1613-0073, http://ftp1.de.freebsd.org/Publications/CEUR-WS/Vol-405/paper1.pdf
16. Sadeh, N., Gandon, F., Kwon, O.B.: Ambient Intelligence and Pervasive Computing. In: Vasilakos, T., Pedrycz, W. (eds.) Ambient Intelligence: The MyCampus Experience. ArTech House, Norwood (2006), http://www.cs.cmu.edu/~sadeh/Publications/More%20Complete%20List/Ambient%20Intelligence%20Tech%20Report%20final.pdf
17. Kassoff, M., Petrie, C., Zen, L.M., Genesereth, M.: Semantic Email Addressing: Sending Email to People, Not Strings. In: AAAI 2006 Fall Symposium on Integrating Reasoning into Everyday Applications (2006), http://www.aaai.org/Papers/Symposia/Fall/2006/FS-06-04/FS06-04-004.pdf
18. Passant, A., Hastrup, T., Bojars, U., Breslin, J.,, M.: A Semantic Web and Distributed Approach. In: Proceedings of the 4th Workshop on Scripting for the Semantic Web, CEUR Workshop Proceedings, Tenerife, Spain, June 02 (2008) ISSN 1613-0073, http://www.semanticscripting.org/SFSW2008/papers/11.pdf
19. Story, H.: FOAF & SSL: creating a global decentralized authentication protocol. In: W3C Workshop on the Future of Social Networking, Barcelona, Spain, January 15-16 (2009), http://blogs.sun.com/bblfish/entry/foaf_ssl_creating_a_global

Effects of Social Network Topology and Options on Norm Emergence

Onkur Sen[1] and Sandip Sen[2]

[1] Oklahoma School of Science and Mathematics
onkursen@gmail.com
[2] Department of Computer Science
University of Tulsa
sandip@utulsa.edu

Abstract. A social norm is a behavior that emerges as a convention within society without any direction from a central authority. Social norms emerge as repeated interactions between individuals give rise to biases toward actions or behaviors which spread through the society until one behavior is adapted as the default behavior, even when multiple acceptable behaviors exist. Of particular interest to us is how and when norms emerge in social networks, which provide a framework for individuals to interact routinely. We study how quickly norms converge in social networks depending on parameters such as the topology of the network, population size, neighborhood size, and number of behavior alternatives. Our research can be used to model and analyze popular social networks on the Internet such as Facebook, Flickr, and Digg. In addition, it can be used to predict how norms emerge and spread in human societies, ranging from routine decisions like which side of the road to drive on to social trends such as the *green* phenomenon.

1   Introduction

Recent literature in multiagent systems show a significant increase in interest and research on normative systems which are defined as [6]:

A normative multiagent system is a multiagent system organized by means of mechanisms to represent, communicate, distribute, detect, create, modify, and enforce norms, and mechanisms to deliberate about norms and detect norm violation and fulfillment.

Norms or conventions routinely guide the choice of behaviors in human societies and plays a pivotal role in determining social order [19]. Conformity to norms reduces social frictions, relieves cognitive load on humans, and facilitates coordination. "Everyone conforms, everyone expects others to conform, and everyone has good reason to conform because conforming is in each person's best interest when everyone else plans to conform" [21]. Norms or conventions can

J. Padget et al. (Eds.): COIN 2009, LNAI 6069, pp. 211–222, 2010.

therefore be substituted as external correlating signals to promote coordination (all coordination is choosing a solution from a space of possible solutions).

While these aspects of norms or conventions have merited in-depth study of the evolution and economics of norms in social situations [14, 28, 38, 39], we are particularly interested in the following characterization: "... we may define a convention as an equilibrium that everyone expects in interactions that have more than one equilibrium." [39]. This observation has particular significance for the study of norms[1] in the context of computational agents.

As computational agents in a multiagent system often have to coordinate their actions, adoption and adherence to norms can improve the efficiency of agent societies. A large class of interactions between self-interested agents (players) can be formulated as stage games with simultaneous moves made by the players [18]. Such stage games often have multiple equilibria [23], which makes coordination difficult. While *focal points* [31] can be used to disambiguate such choices, they may not be available in all situations. Norms can also be thought of as focal points evolved through learning [39] that reduces disagreement and promote coherent behavior in societies with minimal oversight or centralized control [9]. Norms can therefore have economic value to agents and help improve their efficiency.

To study the important phenomenon of emergence of social norms via private interactions, we use the following interaction framework. We consider a population of agents, where, in each interaction, each agent is paired with another agent randomly selected from the population. Each agent then is learning concurrently over repeated interactions with randomly selected members from the population. We refer to this kind of learning *social learning* [22, 33] to distinguish from learning in iterated games against the same opponent [15].

Our experiments involve symmetric games with multiple pure-strategy equilibria with the same payoff. While some research on norm emergence assumed uniform interaction probabilities between agents [33, 34] others have studied the effect of topologies of agent relationships [11, 20, 22]. This body of research can be further divided into *interaction-based learning* approaches to norm emergence [22] and *observation-based adoption* approaches [11]. In the interaction-based learning mode, agents learn utility estimates of their behavior choices and over time converge on a particular behavior that becomes the norm in the society. In this mode, agents actually do not even need to observe others' behaviors. In the observation-based learning mode, agents' behaviors must be fully observable and typically there is no direct consideration of utilities.

We are interested in studying how different network topologies affect the rate of interaction based norm emergence. In particular, we experiment with (a) scale-free networks, (b) fully-connected networks, and (c) ring networks. Within ring networks we further consider the effect of neighborhood sizes, where a neighborhood size of δ implies that any node in the ring can interact with the δ nearest nodes on the ring. Such ring networks represent realistic situations where the agents are physically situated in space and are more likely to interact with other

---

[1] Henceforth we use the term norm to refer to both social norms and conventions.

agents in their physical proximity[2]. Scale-free networks, on the other hand, represent logical connectivity in social networks [2], and represent situations where the node degrees of the network follow a power law distribution [24]. With the explosion in interest in social networking sites like Facebook, MySpace, Flickr, Digg, etc., understanding and exploiting how information is disseminated and how choices are adopted by individuals in social networks have assumed critical significance both to social scientists who want to study this fascinating social phenomena and to companies who want to benefit from mining these interaction data to produce better marketing and advertising tools.

While our previous work [22,33] has studied the effect of learning algorithms, population biases, physical proximity based interaction likelihood, etc. we have not addressed the issue of scale-up. Whereas studying scaling-up properties of rate of norm convergence for larger agent societies is of obvious interest given rapid growth of user base of social networking sites, we believe that studying norm emergence scale-up properties of different network topologies in face of increasing number of alternate choices or behaviors can also offer key insights to the working of these systems. For example, users face an increasingly diverse set of choices in their everyday interactions, ranging from usage of software and web-based products (email clients, chat facilities, browsers, social networking/blogging sites), availability of TV shows, interaction styles (emoticons, acronyms, etc.). It would be of significant interest and value to better understand how and when the entire society, or any sub-group thereof, adopt a particular choice given a large set of initial choices. Who are the drivers of this adoption, e.g., are the hubs in a social network the drivers or facilitators of the rise of common choices or conventions? While this paper does not purport to answer all of these complex, interrelated issues, we will evaluate how increasing the number of alternative available behaviors affect the rate of norm emergence in the different network topologies described above.

The rest of the paper is organized as follows: in Section 2 we briefly overview relevant literature; in Section 3 we present the network topologies we use in our study; in Section 4 we describe how individuals behave in the network; in Section 5 we analyze our experimental results and their implications; in Section 6, we summarize our results and propose future work.

2   Related Work

Norms may be adhered to in human societies because they facilitate the functioning of individuals, or because of the threat of social disapproval [29] or acceptance by individuals of desired conduct [13]. They are self-enforcing: "A norm exists in a given social setting to the extent that individuals usually act in a certain way

---

[2] In physical environments, e.g., real-life physical interactions between humans in the society, agents are much more likely to interact with those in close physical proximity compared to others located further away. Such physical or spatial interaction constraints or biases have been well-recognized in social sciences [26] and, more recently, in multiagent systems literature [32].

and are often punished when seen not to be acting in this way" [3]. Conventions in human societies range from fashions to tipping, driving etiquette to interaction protocols. Norms are ingrained in our social milieu and play a pivotal role in all kinds of business, political, social, and personal choices and interactions.

Hence, the systematic study and development of robust mechanisms that facilitate emergence of stable, efficient norms via learning in agent societies promises to be a productive research area that can improve coordination in and thereby functioning of agent societies. Establishment of social norms may come about by top-down influences like official edicts and role models, bottom-up processes driven by local customs, and lateral diffusion of established norms between related interaction types [37]. Most research on norms in multiagent systems focus on the *legalistic view* where norms are used to shape the behavior of open systems without using sanctions to enforce desirable behavior. In this approach norms are typically logically specified using a normative language [16] from which rules of behavior can be automatically derived [10]. Our approach to norm emergence from personal interactions is based on the *interactionist view*, which adopts a bottom-up view of individual adoption of norms because of alignment of goals and utilities between agents in a population [7,8].

While researchers have studied the emergence of norms in agent populations, they typically assume access to significant amount of global knowledge [14,28, 38,39]. For example, all of these models assume that individual agents can observe interactions between other agents in the environment. While these results do provide key insights into the emergence of norms in societies where the assumption of observability holds, it is unclear if and how norms will emerge if all interactions were private, i.e., not observable to any other agent not involved in the interaction.

Amaral *et al.* study the topology of various "small-world" networks, which encompass scale-free networks [2]. Noble *et al.* study how the topology of a network affects the rate of spreading of information [25]. The need for effective norms to control agent behaviors is well-recognized in multiagent societies [5,11]. In particular, norms are key to the efficient functioning of electronic institutions [17]. Most of the work in multiagent systems on norms, however, has centered on logic or rule-based specification and enforcement of norms [12]. Similar to these research, the work on normative, game-theoretic approach to norm derivation and enforcement also assumes centralized authority and knowledge, as well as system level goals [4,5]. While norms can be established by centralized diktat, norms in real-life often evolve in a bottom-up manner, via "the gradual accretion of precedent" [39]. In our formulation, norms evolve as agents learn from their interactions with other agents in the society using multiagent reinforcement learning algorithms [27]. Most multiagent reinforcement learning literature involve two agents iteratively playing a stage game and the goal is to learn policies to reach preferred equilibrium [30]. Another line of research considers a large population of agents learning to play a cooperative game where the reward of each individual agent depends on the joint action of all the agents in the population [35]. The goal of the learning agent is to maximize an objective function for the entire population, the world utility. While these learning approaches consider the same set of individuals repeatedly interacting and learning, in our framework an agent learns by interacting with different individuals at each time step.

3   Network Topologies

An important property of the topology of a social network is its *diameter*. A social network's diameter is defined as the largest distance between any two nodes in a network. The diameter represents the largest path within the network and characterizes the compactness and connectivity of the network. A network with a small diameter is very well-connected, and thus the average path length of the network will be small. On the other hand, a network with a large diameter will be very sparsely-connected, and the average path length can be large. In addition, a network with a small diameter is more likely to have many different paths between nodes, but a network with a large diameter will have many longer paths between nodes.

Scale-free networks have the structural property that the connectivity of the network follows a power law distribution. This means that the network has a small number of nodes, designated as *hubs*, which have a very high connectivity. However, the most of the nodes in the network are sparsely-connected. A familiar example is the current airport system: small cities do not have very busy airports, but cities like Atlanta, Chicago, and Los Angeles are analogous to the hubs in the network. The diameter of a scale-free network can be approximated as the largest distance among hubs plus 2 since this is the distance between a neighbor of one hub of the longest path and a neighbor of the other hub of the longest path. We use the algorithm presented by Albert and Barabási [1] to generate scale-free networks (the parameters used were as follows: number of initial nodes = 10, number of links to be added or rewired at each step = 3, probability of adding links = 0.4, probability of rewiring links = 0.4).

We also examine *ring networks*, where nodes are connected in a ring. We actually consider generalized rings where each node is linked to all other nodes within a certain distance δ, the *neighborhood size*. Unlike scale-free networks, in which certain nodes dominate the network, in a ring network, all nodes have the same connectivity and thus are equally important in the network.

A special case of a ring network is a *fully-connected network* (also known in graph theory as a *clique*), in which every node is connected to every other node. Therefore, a fully-connected network is a ring network with diameter 1 or neighborhood size equal to the size of the network.

4   Individual Behavior in Networks

In our framework, an agent interacts with a random neighbor at each time interval. An interaction consists of both agents selecting an action (behavior). The first agent receives a payoff based on the action chosen by both agents: if the actions are identical, the payoff is $+4$; else, the payoff is -1. An agent does not know the identity of its opponent, nor its opponent's payoff, but it can observe the action taken by the opponent (perfect but incomplete information). Note that only one player gains experience from each interaction. This is to ensure that all agents learn at the same rate, as opposed to agents that are randomly chosen more often learning quicker than those who are chosen less often. We present the protocol of interaction for the entire agent society in Algorithm 1.

---

for *a fixed number of time intervals* **do**
    repeat
        remove randomly agents p_a from the population
        randomly choose p_b, one of the neighbors of p_a,
        p_a and p_b choose their respective actions;
        p_a updates its utility estimate for the chosen action based on the
        reward received from the joint action
    until *all agents have been selected during this time interval* ;
end

Algorithm 1. Interaction protocol

Upon receiving the payoff from an interaction, an agent adjusts its estimate of the utility of the action chosen using *Q-Learning* [36]:

$$Q_t(a) = \alpha R + (1 - \alpha)Q_{t-1}(a),$$

where $Q_t(a)$ represents the agent's Q-valuation of the action a at time t, R is the reward received, and α is a learning rate that weights the current reward with the previous valuation of the action to produce a more accurate approximation to the true valuation. Next, the agents semi-deterministically choose the action estimated to be the most profitable, i.e., the agents will choose the action with the highest valuation most of the time, but with a small probability ϵ (we use $\epsilon = 0.2$) they will instead choose a random action. Note that the choice of action does not change their opinion of which action is the most profitable. Algorithm 2 details the behavior followed by an agent at each time interval:

Data: Q-Table $Q[\,]$, action a, Reward R, Learning Rate α
$R = \text{playRandomNeighbor}()$;
$Q[a] \leftarrow \alpha R + (1 - \alpha)Q[a]$;
$probabilityOfRandomAction = \text{generateRandomDouble}()$;
if $probabilityOfRandomAction <= \epsilon$ **then**
    action $= Q[\text{generateRandomInteger(numberOfActions)}]$;
else
    action $= Q.\text{indexOf(max}(Q))$;
end

Algorithm 2. Action selection and Learning algorithm

5   Results

The performance metric for our experiments was the number of time intervals necessary for convergence, i.e., how quickly a norm emerges. As an example, for a population $N = 100$ and the number of actions $A = 5$, we examined how many agents were following each action over time until 100% of the population view the same action to be the most profitable, i.e. that action emerged as the norm in the society. We performed experiments for scale-free and ring networks (in the following, unless otherwise specified, we include the results from the completely connected network as a special case of ring network with diameter 1). The set of experiments that we ran are as follows:

Scale-free networks: We studied how varying the number of actions as well as the population size would affect the rate of norm emergence. We varied A over the set $\{2, 5, 10, 20\}$, and N over the set $\{250, 500, 750, 1000\}$.

Ring networks: Within ring networks, we also studied the variation of the number of actions A over the set $\{2, 5, 20\}$, but instead of varying the population size (fixed at 500), we varied the diameter D of the network over the set $\{1, 2, 3, 4\}$.

Comparing Topologies: We compared the convergence speeds of scale-free and ring networks for $A = 2$ and $A = 20$.

5.1   The Norm Emergence Process

Figure 1 shows graphs for how norms emerge in a society of 100 social learners with 5 action choices. Initially, approximately the same number of agents play each action. Over time, however, through agent-agent interactions, a bias toward one action spreads through the entire network until 100% of the population believes that this action is the most profitable, i.e., its Q-value is the highest. At this point (approximately time 70 for the scale-free network and time 100 for the fully-connected network), we say that a norm has emerged. However, this process may sometime demonstrate surprising complexity. For example, in the graph for fully-connected networks, the blue and orange actions rise at approximately the same rate until about time 35 when the blue action dominates the orange action and later emerges as the norm.

5.2   Scale-Free Networks

Figure 2 show the iterations required to reach different levels of consensus in the network, measured as the largest percentage of agents to prefer the same action, for our experiments on scale-free networks. All scale-free network systems converged to a norm; however, the speed of norm emergence varied. A larger number of available actions resulted in a delayed convergence of the system. This is to be expected as a larger number of actions may produce local norms dispersed

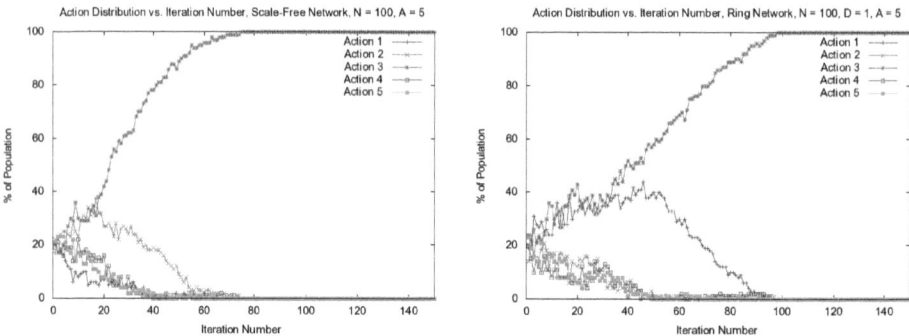

Fig. 1. The process of norm emergence in scale-free (left) and fully-connected (right) networks

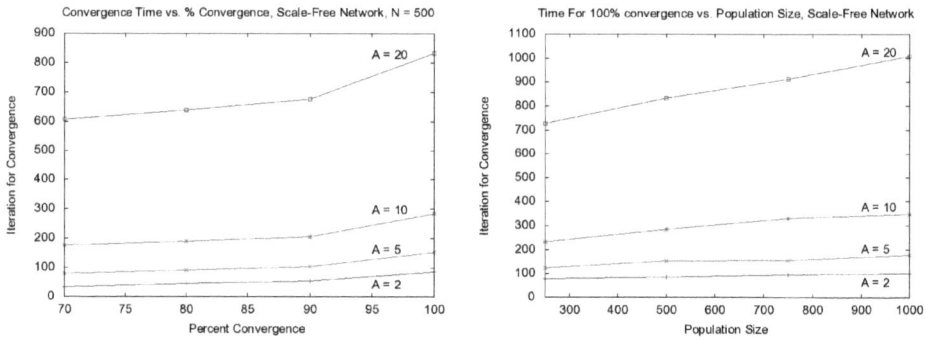

Fig. 2. Iterations required to reach different levels of consensus in scale-free networks with varying number of action options (left) and network size (right)

throughout the network which will lead to many clashes across localities. These conflicting norms must then be resolved and consensus slowly spreads throughout the network until one action emerges as the norm. In addition, a larger population size also delays the emergence of a norm in the network. This is because a larger population size entails that more nodes have to converge to that action based on interaction with other agents.

5.3   Ring Networks

Similar results from ring networks (see Figure 3) shows similar results as scale-free networks in that a larger of number of actions resulted in a slower converge time. In addition, an increase in diameter of the graph causes a near-exponential growth in convergence time. This is because as the diameter of the ring network grows, the spread of bias takes more intermediaries. Hence, biases tend to be

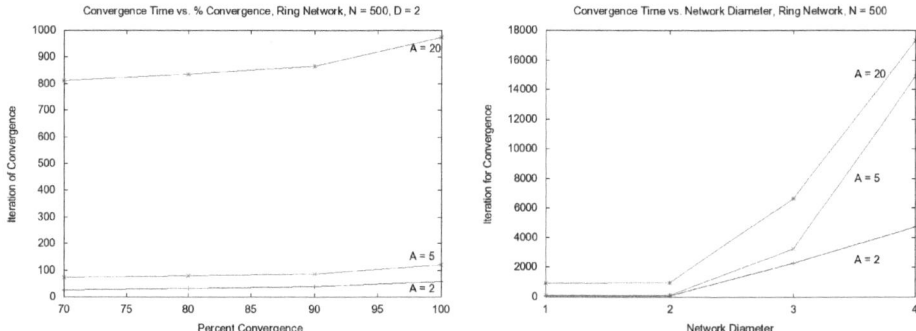

Fig. 3. Iterations required to reach different levels of consensus in ring networks with varying number of action options (left) and network diameter (right)

confined within a locality until the localities converge on an action, at which point the bias toward an action can spread to other areas of the network. However, a notable exception to this is a comparison between $D = 1$, i.e., a fully connected network, and $D = 2$, where the convergence rates are approximately the same. This is because interacting with everybody may, in some cases, lead to more time taken to form a consensus.

5.4   Comparing Scale-Free and Ring Networks

Figure 4 shows the comparison of scale-free, fully-connected, and normal ring networks for both a small and large number of actions. For a small number of actions, the ring network converges the fastest, followed by the fully-connected network, and the scale-free network converges last. However, for a large number of actions, the scale-free network converges much faster than the ring and fully-connected networks. The slight difference between the ring and fully-connected networks can be explained as mentioned above in that interacting with *almost* everybody can strike the right balance between developing and propagating biases in some cases when compared to interacting with everybody. The fact that scale-free is not that effective for small number of actions but is clearly more efficient for a large number of action choices is a very surprising and intriguing result. We conjecture a hypothesis that needs to be further refined and tested to explain this phenomenon. Note that the structure of scale-free networks is based around a small number of hubs which dominate the network. However, in a ring network, every node is equally important since each node has the same degree of connectivity. For a small number of actions, the ring networks converge in a relatively small amount of time as clashes have a smaller probability of occurring. However, as the number of actions available increases, the convergence time for the ring networks will increase rather quickly since clashes are more likely to occur within localities. This delays convergence of a node's locality, and the spread

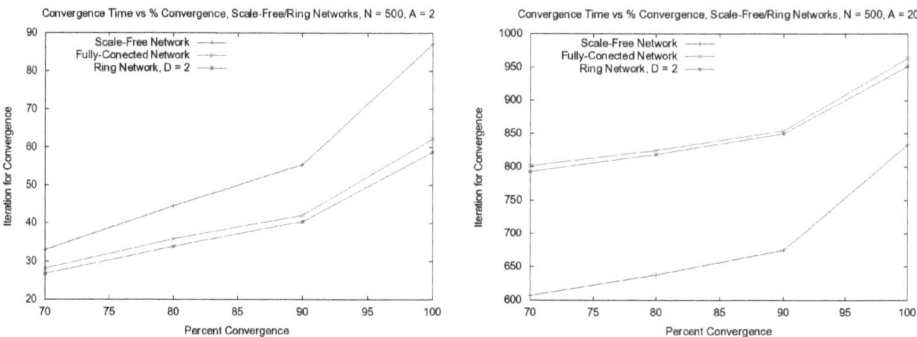

Fig. 4. Comparing convergence speeds of scale-free, normal ring, and fully-connected networks for $A = 2$ (left) and $A = 20$ (right)

of bias throughout the network is slowed, resulting in a longer time for the norm to emergence. However, for scale-free networks, after a certain threshold, the number of actions becomes insignificant since the actions the hubs choose are the ones that will drive the rest of the network. The sparsely-connected nodes will follow the hubs on what action to choose. Therefore, the convergence for a scale-free network is determined by which actions the hubs choose and how quickly the hubs converge and that rate is less affected by an increase in the number of actions available.

6   Conclusions and Future Work

Our research goal was to evaluate how varying topologies of social networks would affect the emergence of norms through interaction-based social learning in these networks. We chose to study scale-free, fully-connected, and ring networks as the topologies. We were particularly interested in understanding the influence of the number of action choices on the rate of norm emergence. An important, counter-intuitive result from our experiments is that although ring networks converge faster for a fewer number of actions, scale-free networks are able to converge faster for a larger number of actions. In addition, we saw the general trend that for both topologies, a larger population size and more actions to choose from delays the emergence of a norm. For future work we first plan to evaluate the hypothesis about the observed phenomena of relative performance of ring and scale-free networks when number of actions is increased. Another interesting set of experiments would be to weigh the experience with each node based on its "status" in the network, e.g., its connectivity. This would mean, e.g., that hub nodes in scale-free networks have more influence than tertiary nodes. We also plan to study the emergence of norms in more topologies, e.g., small-world networks.

References

1. Albert, R., Barabási, A.-L.: Topology of evolving networks: Local events and universality. Phys. Rev. Lett. 85(24), 5234–5237 (2000)
2. Amaral, L., Scala, A., Barthélémy, M., Stanley, H.: Classes of small-world networks. In: Proceedings of the National Academy of Sciences of the United States of America, pp. 11149–11152 (2000)
3. Axelrod, R.: The complexity of cooperation: Agent-based models of conflict and cooperation. Princeton University Press, Princeton (1997)
4. Boella, G., Lesmo, L.: A game theoretic approach to norms. Cognitive Science Quarterly 2(3-4), 492–512 (2002)
5. Boella, G., van der Torre, L.: Norm governed multiagent systems: The delegation of control to autonomous agents. In: Proceedings of IEEE/WIC IAT Conference, pp. 329–335. IEEE Press, Los Alamitos (2003)
6. Boella, G., van der Torre, L., Verhagen, H.: Introduction to the special issue on normative multiagent systems. Autonomous Agents and Multiagent Systems 17(1), 1–10 (2008)
7. Castelfranchi, C.: Modeling social action for AI agents. Artificial Intelligence 103(1-2), 157–182 (1998)
8. Castelfranchi, C.: Formalising the informal? Dynamic social order, bottom-up social control, and spontaneous normative relations. Journal of Applied Logic 1(1-2), 47–92 (2003)
9. Coleman, J.S.: Norms as social capital. In: Radnitzky, G., Bernholz, P. (eds.) Economic Imperialism: The Economic Approach Applied Outside the Field of Economics. Paragon House, New York (1987)
10. da Silva, V.T.: From the specification to the implementation of norms: an automatic approach to generate rules from norms to govern the behavior of agents. Autonomous Agents and Multiagent Systems 17(1), 113–155 (2008)
11. Delgado, J., Pujol, J.M., Sanguesa, R.: Emergence of coordination in scale-free networks. Web Intelligence and Agent Systems 1, 131–138 (2003)
12. Dignum, F., Kinny, D., Sonenberg, L.: From desires, obligations and norms to goals. Cognitive Science Quarterly 2(3-4), 407–430 (2002)
13. Elster, J.: Social norms and economic theory. Journal of Economic Perspectives 3(4), 99–117 (1989)
14. Epstein, J.M.: Learning to be thoughtless: Social norms and individual computation. Computational Economics 18, 9–24 (2001)
15. Fudenberg, D., Levine, K.: The Theory of Learning in Games. MIT Press, Cambridge (1998)
16. Garcia-Camino, A., Rodriguez-Aguilar, J., Sierra, C.: Implementing norms in electronic institutions. In: Proceedings of the Fourth International Conference on Autonomous Agents, pp. 667–673. ACM Press, New York (2005)
17. Garcia-Camino, A., Rodriguez-Aguilar, J., Sierra, C., Vasconcelos, W.: A rule-based approach to norm-oriented programming of electronic institutions. ACM SIGecom Exchanges 5(5), 33–41 (2006)
18. Genesereth, M., Ginsberg, M., Rosenschein, J.: Cooperation without communications. In: Proceedings of the National Conference on Artificial Intelligence, Philadelphia, Pennsylvania, pp. 51–57 (1986)
19. Hume, D.: A Treatise of Human Nature. Oxford University Press, Oxford (1978)
20. Kittock, J.E.: The impact of locality and authority on emergent conventions: Initial observations. In: AAAI, pp. 420–425 (1994)

21. Lewis, D.: Convention: A Philosophical Study. Harvard University Press, Cambridge (1969)
22. Mukherjee, P., Sen, S., Airiau, S.: Norm emergence under constrained interactions in diverse societies. In: Proceedings of the Seventh International Joint Conference on Autonomous Agents and Multiagent Systems, pp. 779–786 (2008)
23. Myerson, R.B.: Game Theory: Analysis of Conflict. Harvard University Press, Cambridge (1991)
24. Newman, M.: The structure and function of complex networks. SIAM Review 45, 167–256 (2003)
25. Noble, J., Davy, S., Franks, D.W.: Effects of the topology of social networks on information transmission. In: From Animals to Animats 8: Proceedings of the Eighth International Conference on Simulation of Adaptive Behavior, pp. 395–404 (2004)
26. Nowak, M., May, R.M.: Evolutionary games and spatial chaos. Nature(London) 359, 826–829 (1992)
27. Panait, L., Luke, S.: Cooperative multi-agent learning: The state of the art. Autonomous Agents and Multi-Agent Systems 11(3), 387–434 (2005)
28. Posch, M.: Evolution of equilibria in the long run: A general theory and applications. Journal of Economic Theory 65, 383–415 (1995)
29. Posner, E.: Law and Social Norms. Harvard University Press, Cambridge (2000)
30. Powers, R., Shoham, Y.: New criteria and a new algorithm for learning in multi-agent systems. In: Proceedings of NIPS (2005)
31. Schelling, T.C.: The Strategy of Conflict. Havard University Press, Cambridge (1960)
32. Schweitzer, F., Zimmermann, J., Muhlenbein, H.: Coordination of decisions in a spatial agent modela. Physica A 303(1-2), 189–216 (2001)
33. Sen, S., Airiau, S.: Emergence of norms through social learning. In: Proceedings of the Twentieth International Joint Conference on Artificial Intelligence (IJCAI'07), January 2007, pp. 1507–1512 (2007)
34. Shoham, Y., Tennenholtz, M.: On the emergence of social conventions: modeling, analysis, and simulations. Artificial Intelligence 94, 139–166 (1997)
35. Tumer, K., Wolpert, D.H.: Collective intelligence and Braess' paradox. In: Proceedings of the Seventeenth National Conference on Artificial Intelligence, pp. 104–109. AAAI Press, Menlo Park (2000)
36. Watkins, C.J.C.H., Dayan, P.D.: Q-learning. Machine Learning 3, 279–292 (1992)
37. Young, H.P.: Social norms. In: Durlauf, S.N., Blume, L.E. (eds.) The New Palgrave Dictionary of Economics, 2nd edn. Macmillan, London (2008)
38. Young, P.H.: The evolution of conventions. Econometrica 61, 57–84 (1993)
39. Young, P.H.: The economics of convention. The Jounal of Economic Perspectives 10(2), 105–122 (Spring 1996)

Part III

Norms and Reasoning

Directed Deadline Obligations in Agent-Based Business Contracts

Henrique Lopes Cardoso and Eugénio Oliveira

LIACC, DEI / Faculdade de Engenharia, Universidade do Porto
R. Dr. Roberto Frias, 4200-465 Porto, Portugal
{hlc,eco}@fe.up.pt

Abstract. There are B2B relationships that presume cooperation in contract enactment. This issue should be taken into account when modeling, for computational handling, contractual commitments through obligations. Deadline obligations have been modeled by considering that reaching the deadline without compliance brings up a violation. When modeling commitments in business contracts, directed obligations have been studied for identifying two agents: the obligation's bearer and the counterparty, who may claim for legal action in case of non-compliance. We argue in favor of a directed deadline obligation approach, taking inspiration on international legislation over trade procedures. Our proposal to model contractual obligations is based on authorizations granted in specific states of an obligation lifecycle model, which we formalize using temporal logic and implement in a rule-based system. The performance of a contractual relationship is supported by a model of flexible deadlines, which allow for further cooperation between autonomous agents. As a result, the decision-making space of agents concerning contractual obligations is enlarged and becomes richer. We discuss the issues that agents should take into account in this extended setting.

1 Introduction

In cooperative B2B Virtual Organizations, agents (representing different enterprises) share their own competences and skills in a regulated way, through commitments expressed as norms in contracts. The importance of successfully proceeding with business demands for flexibility of operations: agents should try to facilitate the compliance of their partners. This common goal of conducting a multiparty business is based on the fact that group success also benefits each agent's private goals. These goals are not limited to the ongoing business relationship, but also concern future opportunities that may arise.

While addressing this problem with norms and multi-agent systems, we find that many approaches to normative multi-agent systems are abstracted away from their potential application domain. As such, deontic operators are often

J. Padget et al. (Eds.): COIN 2009, LNAI 6069, pp. 225–240, 2010.

taken to have a universal semantics. For instance, deadline obligations are violated if the obliged action or state is not obtained until the deadline is reached.

We argue that in some domains – such as in business contracts – such an approach is not desirable. For instance, the United Nations Convention on Contracts for the International Sale of Goods (CISG) [1] establishes what parties may do in case of deadline violations. In some cases they are allowed to fulfill their obligations after the deadline (Article 48), or even to extend the deadlines with the allowance of their counterparties. Furthermore, a party may extend his counterparty's deadlines (Articles 47 and 63), which denotes a flexible and even cooperative facet of trade contracts.

In this paper we propose a different approach (in comparison with [2][3][4][5]) to the use of obligations in MAS in the domain of business contracts. Following a cooperative business performance posture, we argue that obligations should be directed, and that deadlines should be flexible. We start by reviewing, in section 2, the most typical variations regarding the formalization of obligations, after which we propose an approach based on directed obligations with deadlines. The flexibility required when handling temporal restrictions of obligations is addressed in section 3. The proposed approach is based on authorizations, and we present a lifecycle for directed obligations with temporal restrictions. In section 4 we investigate the decision-making process of agents concerning authorizations. Implementation of the proposed model in a rule-based system is discussed in section 5. Section 6 discusses related work and section 7 concludes.

2   Contractual Obligations

The use of norms in MAS makes use of the well-known deontic operators of obligation, permission and prohibition [6]. In theoretical deontic logic approaches, these operators are sometimes used to represent abstract general principles (e.g. it is forbidden to kill). In more applied research, deontic operators are ascribed either to roles or to particular agents in a system; e.g. $O_b(f)$ indicates that agent b is obliged to bring about fact f (a state of affairs or an action) – in this case agent b is said to be the *bearer* of the obligation.

Also, deontic operators are often made conditional and time constrained. Considering obligations, the conditional aspect has taken two different perspectives: conditional obligations of the form $O_b(f/s)$, meaning that agent b is obliged to bring about f when situation s arises; and conditional norms of the form $s \rightarrow O_b(f)$, meaning that if s then b is obliged to bring about f. As for the temporal aspect of deontic operators, deadlines (either time references or more generally defined as states of affairs) are typically employed for stipulating the validity of the operator: $O_b(f, d)$ is a *deadline obligation* indicating that agent b is obliged to bring about f before d.

We will base the following discussion on the *obligation* deontic operator, as it is the most important operator to represent trade relationships in B2B contracts. The meaning of deontic operators has been studied, mainly regarding the use of deadlines (e.g. [2]). Regarding deadline obligations, the usual approach to their semantics is to consider the following entailments[1]:

- $O_b(f, d) \land (f \; B \; d) \models Fulf_b(f, d)$ — If the fact to bring about occurs before the deadline, the agent has fulfilled his obligation.
- $O_b(f, d) \land (d \; B \; f) \models Viol_b(f, d)$ — If the deadline occurs before the fact to bring about, the agent has violated his obligation.

The introduction of *Fulf* and *Viol* enables reasoning about the respective situations. The implementation of this semantics using forward-chaining rules has been studied in [3]. Although intuitive, this semantics is quite rigid in that violations are all defined in a universal way (discounting the fact that different norms can respond to violations in different ways).

The analysis of contracts brings into discussion the notion of *directed obligations* [8]. Obligations are seen as directed from a *bearer* (responsible for fulfilling the obligation) to a *counterparty*. Some authors [4] define the very notion of *contractual obligation* as an obligation with an "obligor" (bearer) and an "obligee" (counterparty). The relationship between these two roles in a directed obligation has been studied, giving rise to two different theories. The *benefit theory* promotes the fact that the counterparty of an obligation is intended to benefit from its fulfillment (see [8] for a benefit theory perspective of directed obligations). A more relevant approach in which contracts are concerned – the *claimant theory* – takes the stance that obligations are interpreted as claims from counterparties to bearers (see [5] for a claimant theory support).

In general, claimant approaches are based on the following definition for directed obligation (adapted from [5]): $O_{b,c}(f) =_{def} O_b(f) \land (\neg f \Rightarrow P_c(la_b))$. A directed obligation from agent b towards agent c to bring about f means that b is obliged to bring about f and if b does not bring about f then c is *permitted* to initiate legal action against b. The concept of legal action is rather vague. A similar approach is taken in [9], where agent c is said to be *authorized* to repair the situation in case b does not fulfill his obligation. Repair actions include demanding further actions from b; e.g., c may demand compensation for damages. It is interesting to note that such definitions are careful enough to base the claims of the counterparty on the *non-fulfillment* of the obligation, not on its violation. In fact, these definitions do not include deadlines, which are the basis for violation detection. Another significant issue is the discretionary nature of the counterparty's reaction (he is permitted or authorized), instead of an automatic response based on the non-fulfillment of the bearer[2].

---

[1] In the following formulae we will follow linear temporal logic (LTL) [7], with a discrete time model. Let $x = (s_0, s_1, s_2, ...)$ be a timeline, defined as a sequence of states s_i. The syntax $x \models p$ reads that p is true in timeline x. We write x^k to denote state s_k of x, and $x^k \models p$ to mean that p is true at state x^k. We use a weak version of the *before* LTL operator B, where q is not mandatory: $x \models (p \; B \; q)$ iff $\exists_j (x^j \models p \land \forall_{k<j}(x^k \models \neg q))$.

[2] As in automatic violation detection approaches based on deadlines, complemented with the definition of violation reaction norms.

We propose the use of *directed deadline obligations* as the basis for defining contractual obligations: $O_{b,c}(f, d)$. In section 3 we describe a model for flexible obligation violation, based on the principle that the deadline is meant to indicate when the counterparty is authorized to react to the non-fulfillment of an obligation directed to him. A possible reaction is to declare the obligation as violated, but there are other means to settle the matter, to the benefit of both involved parties. An extension of directed (contractual) obligations with temporal restrictions is also introduced in [4], but that approach is based on a rigid model of violations, in that they are automatically obtained at the deadline.

2.1   Directed Deadline Obligations

Our proposal combines directed [5][8] and deadline [2] obligations. Although this has been done in the past (e.g. [4]), in our approach deadlines have a distinct role in the definition of obligations. In section 3 we detail such a role.

Directed deadline obligations take the form $O_{b,c}(f, d)$, meaning that agent b is obliged towards agent c to bring about f before d. We do not make obligations conditional (as in [4]), because we assume they are obtained from conditional norms: rules prescribing obligations when certain situations arise.

We consider that if fact f is not yet the case when deadline d arises, the obligation is not yet violated, but is in a state where the counterparty is authorized to take some action. We emphasize the case for a *deadline violation* (as opposed to obligation violation). This comprises a flexible approach to handling non-ideal situations: each deadline violation is different, as each may have a different impact on the ongoing business, and each occurs between a specific pair of agents with a unique trust relationship.

Some evidence from the CISG convention [1] led us to this approach:

> *Article 48: (1) [...] the seller may, even after the date for delivery, remedy at his own expense any failure to perform his obligations, if he can do so without unreasonable delay [...]; (2) If the seller requests the buyer to make known whether he will accept performance and the buyer does not comply with the request within a reasonable time, the seller may perform within the time indicated in his request. [...]*

This means that even though a deadline has been violated, the bearer may still be entitled to fulfill *the same* obligation. This kind of delay is also called a *grace period*: a period beyond a due date during which an obligation may be met without penalty or cancellation.

Figure 1 illustrates the intuitive semantics of a directed deadline obligation. The shaded area represents the period of time within which the achievement of f will certainly bring a fulfillment of the obligation. The region to the right of d indicates that counterparty c is entitled to react if f is not accomplished; however, as long as no reaction is taken, b can still fulfill his obligation.

Therefore, a deadline violation brings a counterparty authorization. Authorizations are taken into account in the normative system by having rules and

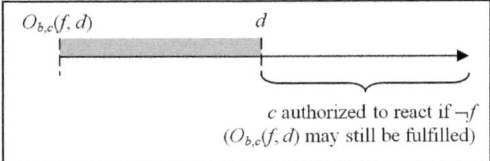

Fig. 1. Directed obligation with deadline

norms that are based on the materialization of such authorizations. The available options are discussed in section 3.

2.2   Livelines and Deadlines

The deadline approach is often taken to be appropriate for specifying temporal restrictions on obligations. However, in certain cases a time window should be provided. In international trade transactions, for instance, storage costs may be relevant. Also, perishable goods should be delivered only when they are needed, not before. This is why in CISG [1] we have:

> *Article 52: (1) If the seller delivers the goods before the date fixed, the buyer may take delivery or refuse to take delivery.*

Therefore, anticipated fulfillments are not always welcome. We find it necessary to include a variation of directed deadline obligations, to which we add a *liveline*: a time reference after which the obligation should be fulfilled. In this case we have $O_{b,c}(f, l, d)$: agent b is obliged towards agent c to bring about f between l (a liveline) and d (a deadline). Figure 2 illustrates the intuitive semantics of this kind of obligation. The shaded area represents the period of time within which the achievement of f will certainly bring a fulfillment of the obligation. If f is accomplished before l, however, it may be the case that c is not willing to accept such a fulfillment, or at least that he may not be happy about it – the region to the left of l entitles c to react if f is accomplished. The region to the right of d is as with (simple) directed deadline obligations.

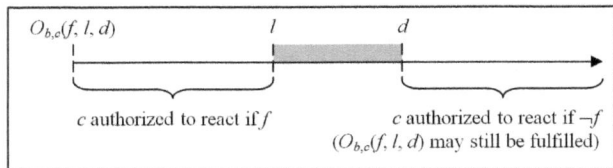

Fig. 2. Directed obligation with liveline and deadline

We escape from an approach with a fixed time reference for obligation fulfillment (an obligation for bringing about f at time t), which would be suggested by the term "date fixed" in CISG's Article 52 transcription above. We find it more convenient to define a fixed date as an interval, say, from the beginning till the end of a specific date[3].

3   Managing Liveline and Deadline Violations

After we have advocated, in the preceding section, a counterparty authorization approach to deadline violations, in this section we address the issue of what kind of actions the counterparty may take in such situations, and what are their effects on the obligation whose deadline has been violated. The same accounts to directed obligations with both livelines and deadlines.

The successful enactment of a contract is dependent on the need to make contractual provisions performable in a flexible way. The importance of having flexible trade procedures is apparent, once again, in the CISG convention [1]:

> *Article 47: (1) The buyer may fix an additional period of time of reasonable length for performance by the seller of his obligations.*

> *Article 63: (1) The seller may fix an additional period of time of reasonable length for performance by the buyer of his obligations.*

These articles emphasize, once more, the need for flexible deadlines. Note that the counterparty's benevolence on conceding an extended deadline to the bearer does not prescribe a new obligation; instead, *the same* obligation may be fulfilled within a larger time window. Furthermore, it is also in the counterparty's best interest that this option is available, given the importance of reaching success in the performance of the contract.

In some other cases, a party may decide that the non-fulfillment of an obligation should be handled in a more strict way. The CISG convention specifies conditions for cancelling a contract in case of breach:

> *Article 49: (1) The buyer may declare the contract avoided: (a) if the failure by the seller to perform any of his obligations [...] amounts to a fundamental breach of contract; [...]; (2) However, in cases where the seller has delivered the goods, the buyer loses the right to declare the contract avoided unless he does so: (a) in respect of late delivery, within a reasonable time after he has become aware that delivery has been made; [...]*

> *Article 64: (1) The seller may declare the contract avoided: (a) if the failure by the buyer to perform any of his obligations [...] amounts to a fundamental breach of contract; [...]; (2) However, in cases where the buyer has paid the price, the seller loses the right to declare the contract avoided unless he does so: (a) in respect of late performance by the buyer, before the seller has become aware that performance has been rendered; [...]*

---

[3] This is actually a matter of time granularity.

These articles allow contract termination in both non-performance and late performance cases. However, the second case is limited to the awareness of the offended party.

From these excerpts we can distinguish two types of reactions to non-fulfill-ments: a smoother one (from articles 47, 48 and 63), in which parties are willing to recover from an initial failure to conform to an obligation; and a stricter one (articles 49 and 64), where the failure is not self-containable anymore. Based on these options, we propose a model for a directed deadline obligation lifecycle.

3.1 Authorizations on Violations

Following the discussion above, we identify the possible states for an obligation, together with the elements we shall use to signal some of those states (when obtained, these elements are supposed to persist over time):

- *inactive*: the obligation is not yet in effect, but will eventually be prescribed by a norm;
- *active*: the obligation was prescribed by a norm – $O_{b,c}(f,d)$ or $O_{b,c}(f,l,d)$
- *pending*: the obligation may be fulfilled from now on;
- *liveline violation*: the fact being obliged has been brought ahead of time – $LViol_{b,c}(f,l,d)$
- *deadline violation*: the fact being obliged should have been brought already – $DViol_{b,c}(f,d)$ or $DViol_{b,c}(f,l,d)$
- *fulfilled*: the obligation was fulfilled – $Fulf_{b,c}(f,d)$ or $Fulf_{b,c}(f,l,d)$
- *violated*: the obligation was violated and cannot be fulfilled anymore – $Viol_{b,c}(f,d)$ or $Viol_{b,c}(f,l,d)$

Starting with the simpler case of directed deadline obligations, we identify the (absolute) fulfillment case:

- $O_{b,c}(f,d) \wedge (f \; B \; d) \models Fulf_{b,c}(f,d)$

Then we state the consequence of reaching a deadline with no achievement of the obligated fact:

- $O_{b,c}(f,d) \wedge (d \; B \; f) \models DViol_{b,c}(f,d)$

Note that, differently from the usual approach, we set the obligation to have a violated deadline – $DViol_{b,c}(f,d)$ – but not to be violated in itself.

The counterparty's reaction to a deadline violation will only change the obliga-tion's state if the option is to deem the obligation as violated, by *denouncing* this situation. For this we introduce the element $Den_{c,b}(f,d)$, which is a denounce from agent c towards agent b regarding the failure of the latter to comply with his obligation to bring about f before d. Since we consider the achievement of facts to be common knowledge, a party may only denounce the non-fulfillment of an obligation while that obligation is not fulfilled yet[4]:

---

[4] This is a simplification of what articles 49 and 64 of CISG suggest.

- $DViol_{b,c}(f,d) \wedge (f\ B\ Den_{c,b}(f,d)) \models Fulf_{b,c}(f,d)$
- $DViol_{b,c}(f,d) \wedge (Den_{c,b}(f,d)\ B\ f) \models Viol_{b,c}(f,d)$

Figure 3 illustrates, by means of a state transition diagram, the lifecycle of directed deadline obligations. We take obligations as being prescribed from conditional norms; the confirmation of the norm's condition will change the prescribed obligation's state from inactive to active. The obligation is also automatically pending, since it may be legitimately fulfilled right away.

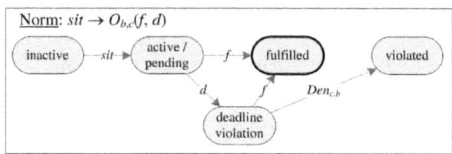

Fig. 3. Lifecycle of a directed deadline obligation

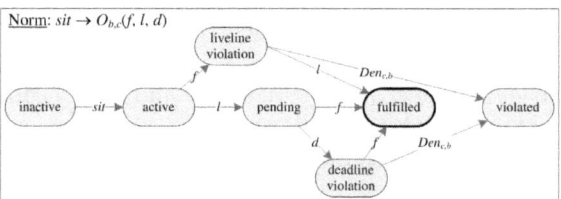

Fig. 4. Lifecycle of a directed obligation with liveline and deadline

Figure 4 contains the state transition diagram for directed obligations with livelines and deadlines. In this case, the obligation will only be pending when l arises, since only then it may be fulfilled in a way that is compliant with the terms of the contract. We define the following relations:

- $O_{b,c}(f,l,d) \wedge (f\ B\ l) \models LViol_{b,c}(f,l,d)$
- $LViol_{b,c}(f,l,d) \wedge (l\ B\ Den_{c,b}(f,l,d)) \models Fulf_{b,c}(f,l,d)$
- $LViol_{b,c}(f,l,d) \wedge (Den_{c,b}(f,l,d)\ B\ l) \models Viol_{b,c}(f,l,d)$
- $O_{b,c}(f,l,d) \wedge (l\ B\ f) \wedge (f\ B\ d) \models Fulf_{b,c}(f,l,d)$
- $O_{b,c}(f,l,d) \wedge (d\ B\ f) \models DViol_{b,c}(f,l,d)$
- $DViol_{b,c}(f,l,d) \wedge (f\ B\ Den_{c,b}(f,l,d)) \models Fulf_{b,c}(f,l,d)$
- $DViol_{b,c}(f,l,d) \wedge (Den_{c,b}(f,l,d)\ B\ f) \models Viol_{b,c}(f,l,d)$

We have now two kinds of temporal violations: liveline violations of the form $LViol_{b,c}(f,l,d)$ and deadline violations of the form $DViol_{b,c}(f,l,d)$. In both cases a denounce may establish the obligation as violated, if issued before l or f, respectively.

3.2   Smoother Authorizations on Violations

The diagrams in figures 3 and 4 only include events that produce a change in an obligation's state. The denouncement of the non-fulfillment of an obligation, making it violated and consequently not fulfillable any longer, denotes a situation in which a bearer's attempt to fulfill the obligation will no longer be significant to the counterparty, and thus a consummated violation should be handled according to applicable norms. These may bring sanctions, further obligations or ultimately a contract cancellation, as in articles 49 and 64 of CISG.

In order to accommodate less strict situations (see articles 47, 48 and 63 of CISG), we consider that in liveline and deadline violation states, while the obligation can still be fulfilled, the counterparty may react to the non-ideal situation. These possibilities are not illustrated in figures 3 and 4, since they do not bring state changes. For instance, in international trade transactions storage costs may be relevant. The counterparty may therefore be authorized to demand for payment of storage costs from an early compliant bearer. Another example for the deadline violation case:

> *Article 78: If a party fails to pay the price or any other sum that is in arrears, the other party is entitled to interest on it [...]*

While obligation state transitions are processed with appropriate rules (including rules that take denounces into account), authorizations expressing the counterparty's right to demand for compensation are handled by the system through appropriate norms, which may be defined in a contract basis.

4   Decision-Making on Directed Deadline Obligations

The authorization approach described above enriches the decision-making space of agents concerning norms. Since commitments can be violated, agents (as human delegates) may decide whether to fulfill them or not. Furthermore, because the violation state is determined by the counterparty's choice to denounce this situation, both parties associated with a directed obligation are in a position to decide over it after the deadline.

In order to model the decision making process, we need to assess each agent's valuations on the obligation states and facts they are able to bring about. We will write $v_a(f)$ and $v_a(S)$ to denote the valuation agent a makes of fact f or state S, respectively (similarly to the valuation model used in [10]). When valuating an obligation's state (namely a fulfillment or a violation), agents should take into account two different sorts of effects. First, since an obligation is taken to be a part of a wider contract that should benefit all participants, the obligation cannot be taken in isolation, as its fulfillment or violation may trigger further commitments. Second, an agent's reputation is affected by whether or not he stands for his commitments. In the following we assume that an agent is capable of anticipating and evaluating the consequences of his actions within a contract.

For an obligation $O_{b,c}(f, d)$ we have the following valuation constraints for b:

$v_b(O_{b,c}(f,d)) < 0$: an obligation is a burden to its bearer

$v_b(f) < v_b(O_{b,c}(f,d))$: there is a heavier cost associated with bringing about f

$v_b(Fulf_{b,c}(f,d)) > 0$: b gains from fulfilling his obligation

$v_b(Viol_{b,c}(f,d)) < 0$: b loses from violating his obligation

The notions of gain and loss for the bearer extend to outside this obligation. For instance, fulfilling an obligation may bring an entitlement (a new obligation where the bearer becomes the counterparty). Violating an obligation will potentially bring penalties to the bearer, hence the negative valuation. In both cases, the reputation of agent b is affected (positively or negatively). Unlike in [10], we do not impose that $v_b(Viol_{b,c}(f,d)) < v_b(f) + v_b(Fulf_{b,c}(f,d))$. An agent may be able to exploit a contract flaw by considering that in a specific situation he is better off violating his obligation than fulfilling it. Of course that even if the above condition holds, agent b may still choose to violate his obligations, because of other conflicting goals: he may lose with respect to the outcome of this contract, but may possibly win across contracts.

As for the counterparty c, we have:

$v_c(O_{b,c}(f,d)) > 0$: an obligation is an asset for the counterparty

$v_c(f) > v_c(O_{b,c}(f,d))$: c benefits from f

$v_c(Fulf_{b,c}(f,d)) \le 0$: c may acquire obligations after fulfillment

$v_c(Viol_{b,c}(f,d)) \ge 0$: c may obtain compensations after violation

Note that both fulfillments and violations may bring no value if they have no further consequences in the contract.

In a rough attempt to model the decision making process of a counterparty of an obligation whose deadline was violated, we could state that he should denounce (and thus obtain the obligation's violation) if[5]

$$v_c(f) + v_c(Fulf_{b,c}(f,d)) < v_c(Viol_{b,c}(f,d)).$$

We consider that valuations may possibly vary with time. Were that not the case, the above condition would only need to be checked right after d, at which point the counterparty would either denounce or decide to wait indefinitely for the bearer to fulfill his obligation. For instance, we believe that it makes sense to think of $v_c(f)$ as possibly decreasing with time (like a resource that should be available but is not yet). Even when the above condition does not hold, the counterparty may still prefer to tolerate the less preferred situation of failure for matters of conflicting goals (just as with the bearer).

Until now we have discussed the possibility of agents (both bearers and counterparties) deciding on breach over compliance (either by assessing intra-contract consequences or by inter-contract conflicts). But in scenarios enriched with social features agents can exploit, it may be the case that agents decide to behave cooperatively even when they have to bear a contained disadvantage. In such settings, more than being altruistic, agents may try to enhance their trust awareness in the community, from which they will benefit in future interactions or contracts.

---

[5] We assume there is no cost associated with the denouncing action.

5   Implementation and Practical Issues

The logical relationships expressed above provide us a formalism to define directed deadline obligations. However, in order to monitor contracts at run-time, we need to ground this semantics into a reasoning engine capable of responding to events in a timely fashion. That is, elements describing obligation states should allow us to reason about those states *as soon as they occur*.

A natural choice we have made before [3] is the use of a rule-based inference engine, with which the following (forward-chaining) rules can be defined to implement the semantics of directed obligations with livelines and deadlines[6]:

- $O_{b,c}(f, l, d) \wedge f \wedge \neg l \rightarrow LViol_{b,c}(f, l, d)$
- $LViol_{b,c}(f, l, d) \wedge l \wedge \neg Den_{c,b}(f, l, d) \rightarrow Fulf_{b,c}(f, l, d)$
- $LViol_{b,c}(f, l, d) \wedge Den_{c,b}(f, l, d) \wedge \neg l \rightarrow Viol_{b,c}(f, l, d)$
- $O_{b,c}(f, l, d) \wedge l \wedge \neg LViol_{b,c}(f, l, d) \wedge f \wedge \neg d \rightarrow Fulf_{b,c}(f, l, d)$
- $O_{b,c}(f, l, d) \wedge d \wedge \neg f \rightarrow DViol_{b,c}(f, l, d)$
- $DViol_{b,c}(f, l, d) \wedge f \wedge \neg Den_{c,b}(f, l, d) \rightarrow Fulf_{b,c}(f, l, d)$
- $DViol_{b,c}(f, l, d) \wedge Den_{c,b}(f, l, d) \wedge \neg f \rightarrow Viol_{b,c}(f, l, d)$

With this approach, we assume an immediate assertion of facts and deadlines when they come into being. Furthermore, rules are expected to be evaluated in every working memory update (e.g. right after a fact is asserted), in order to produce the indicated conclusions, which are added to the normative state in a cumulative fashion. To detect the moment at which the *before* relation holds, we translated terms of the form $(e_1 \ B \ e_2)$ into a conjunction $e_1 \wedge \neg e_2$. The fourth rule demanded for a more careful construction, since we had two consecutive before relations – we needed to ensure that there was no liveline violation when having both l and f.

5.1   Reasoning with Time

In business contracts it is common to have deadlines that are dependent on the fulfillment date of other obligations. Therefore, instead of having fixed (absolute) dates, these may at times be relative, calculated according to other events. CISG [1] expresses this by saying that dates can be *determinable* from the contract:

Article 33: The seller must deliver the goods: (a) if a date is fixed by or determinable from the contract, on that date; (b) if a period of time is fixed by or determinable from the contract, at any time within that period [...]

Article 59: The buyer must pay the price on the date fixed by or determinable from the contract [...]

It is therefore useful to timestamp each event: facts, fulfillments and violations. For that purpose, $Fulf_{b,c}(f, l, d)^t$ will be used to indicate that b has fulfilled at time point t its obligation towards c to obtain f between l and d; similarly for

---

[6] The simpler case of directed deadline obligations is a simplification over these rules.

$Viol_{b,c}(f, l, d)^t$. Since a fact itself has now a timestamp attribute, for ease of reading we will write fact f achieved at time point t as $Fact(f)^t$. A denounce will also be written $Den_{c,b}(f, l, d)^t$.

Norms will be based on these elements and on their time references in order to prescribe other obligations with relative deadlines. For instance,

$$Fulf_{b,c}(Deliver(x, q), \_, \_)^t \rightarrow O_{c,b}(Pay(price), t, t + 10)$$

means that once agent b has fulfilled his obligation to deliver q units of x to agent c, the latter is obliged to pay the former within a period of 10 time units.

5.2   Re-implementing Rules

We also need to update our rules in order to stamp each generated event. In fact, having timestamps also allows us to implement such rules in a way that has a closer reading to the LTL *before* operator:

- $O_{b,c}(f, l, d) \wedge Fact(f)^t \wedge t < l \rightarrow LViol_{b,c}(f, l, d)$
- $LViol_{b,c}(f, l, d) \wedge l \wedge \neg(Den_{c,b}(f, l, d)^u \wedge u < l) \rightarrow Fulf_{b,c}(f, l, d)^l$
- $LViol_{b,c}(f, l, d) \wedge Den_{c,b}(f, l, d)^u \wedge u < l \rightarrow Viol_{b,c}(f, l, d)^u$
- $O_{b,c}(f, l, d) \wedge Fact(f)^t \wedge l < t \wedge t < d \rightarrow Fulf_{b,c}(f, l, d)^t$
- $O_{b,c}(f, l, d) \wedge d \wedge \neg(Fact(f)^t \wedge t < d) \rightarrow DViol_{b,c}(f, l, d)$
- $DViol_{b,c}(f, l, d) \wedge Fact(f)^t \wedge \neg(Den_{c,b}(f, l, d)^u \wedge u < t) \rightarrow Fulf_{b,c}(f, l, d)^t$
- $DViol_{b,c}(f, l, d) \wedge Den_{c,b}(f, l, d)^u \wedge \neg(Fact(f)^t \wedge t < u) \rightarrow Viol_{b,c}(f, l, d)^u$

This kind of approach has the benefit of relaxing the rule evaluation policy: rules do not have to be evaluated after each working memory update, since we are checking the timestamps of each event (see also [3]).

5.3   Example Contract

Considering a two-party business scenario, a contract should be beneficial for both involved parties. Therefore, both are obliged to bring about certain facts (e.g. payments or deliveries) in specific situations, and those facts should benefit the obligations' counterparties. The contract will typically specify remedies for breach situations (such as those pointed out at CISG). For the sake of illustration, we present a possible buyer-supplier contract: agent S commits to supply agent B, whenever he orders, good X for 7.5 per unit. The norms below define this particular contractual relationship. Agent S is supposed to deliver the ordered goods between 3 to 5 days after the order (norm $n1$), and agent B shall pay within 30 days (norm $n2$). Furthermore, if agent B does not pay in due time, he will incur in a penalty consisting of an obligation to pay an extra 10% on the order total (norm $n3$). Finally, if agent S violates his obligation to deliver, the contract will be canceled (norm $n4$).

(n1) $Fact(Order(X, q))^w \rightarrow O_{S,B}(Deliver(X, q), w + 3, w + 5)$
(n2) $Fulf_{S,B}(Deliver(X, q), l, d)^w \rightarrow O_{B,S}(Pay(q * 7.5), w, w + 30)$

(n3) $DViol_{B,S}(Pay(p), l, d) \rightarrow O_{B,S}(Pay(p*0.10), d, d+30)$
(n4) $Viol_{S,B}(Deliver(X, q), l, d)^w \rightarrow Cancel\_contract$

Note that the interest applied on payments is automatic once a deadline violation is detected (norm $n3$). On the other hand, a contract cancellation (norm $n4$) requires that agent B denounces the inability of agent S to fulfill the delivery. It is therefore up to agent B whether to wait further and accept a delayed delivery or not. If the agreed upon contract conditions are important enough, allowing a counterparty deviation (and hence taking a cooperative attitude regarding the compliance of the contract) may be a good decision.

Different kinds of situations may be easily modeled using this kind of norms. Moreover, using flexible deadlines also ensures a degree of freedom for agents to make decisions in the execution phase of contracts, which is important for dealing with business uncertainty.

6 Related Work

Most implementations of norms in multi-agent systems ignore the need for having directed obligations from bearers to counterparties. The most likely reason for this is that in those approaches obligations are seen as (implicitly) directed from an agent to the normative system itself. It is up to the system (e.g. an electronic organization [11] or an electronic institution [12]) to detect violations and to enforce the norms which are designed into the environment (in some cases they are even regimented in such a way that violation is not possible). On the contrary, our flexible approach towards an Electronic Institution allows agents to define the norms that will regulate their mutual commitments.

Other authors have proposed different lifecycles for commitments and deontic operators. Directed social commitments are modeled in [13], in the context of dialogical frameworks. Violated commitments resort to their cancellation, which may bring sanctions. An interesting issue that is explicit in the model is the possibility for the bearer to cancel his commitment, allowing the counterparty to apply sanctions; also, updating is allowed through cancellation of the commitment and creation of a new one. A more compact model is presented in [14], also considering the possibility to update commitments. However, fulfillment and violation are not dealt with explicitly in this model; instead, a commitment is discharged when fulfilled, or else may be canceled.

Taking a cooperative approach to contract fulfillment, in [15] an obligation lifecycle model includes states that are used in a contract fulfillment protocol. Agents communicate about their intentions to comply with obligations, and in this sense an obligation can be refused or accepted. After being accepted, the obligation may be canceled or complied with. These states are obtained according to the performance of a contractual relationship. Our model should also require that agents communicate their intentions regarding an obligation with a violated deadline. In fact, CISG's Article 48 seems to go in this direction, in order to protect the bearer's efforts toward a late fulfillment of the obligation.

The need to identify two opposite roles in deontic operators is not exclusive of obligations. In [5] the concept of directed permission is described on the basis of *interference* and *counter-performance*. If a party is permitted by another to bring about some fact, the latter is not allowed to interfere with the attempt of the former to achieve that fact. The authors also sustain a relation between directed obligations and directed permissions: $O_{b,c}(f) \rightarrow P_{b,c}(f)$, that is, if an agent b has an obligation towards an agent c, then b is permitted (by c) to bring about the obliged fact and c is not permitted to interfere. This is very important in international trade transactions, especially when storage costs can be high. Some evidence from CISG [1] brings us once more the same insight:

> *Article 53: The buyer must pay the price for the goods and take delivery of them [...]*

> *Article 60: The buyer's obligation to take delivery consists: (a) in doing all the acts which could reasonably be expected of him in order to enable the seller to make delivery; and (b) in taking over the goods.*

In this case the permission is described in terms of an obligation of the counterparty (the buyer).

Our model of directed obligations with livelines and deadlines has some connections with research on real-time systems, where a time-value function valuates a task execution outcome depending on the time when it is obtained. *Soft* real-time systems use soft deadlines: obtaining the result after the deadline has a lower utility. In contrast, for *hard* real-time systems the deadline is crisp: after it, the result has no utility at all, and missing the deadline can have serious consequences. Our approach seems to be soft with a hard-deadline discretionally declared by the counterparty of the task to achieve. Deadline goals are also analyzed in [16] in the context of goal-directed and decision-theoretic planning. Goals are given a temporal extent and can be partially satisfied according to this temporal component. The authors propose a *horizon* time point somewhere after the deadline, after which there will be no benefit in achieving the goal. In our case the horizon is not static, but can be defined by the counterparty.

A model for commitment valuations, on which we have based our decision-making prospect, has been proposed in [10]. However, while their work is centered on checking correctness of contracts, we focus on valuations in the course of a contract execution. We do not assume that a contract is correct from a fairness point of view. This difference in concerns has brought divergent considerations when valuating fulfillment and violation states.

Other authors have studied agent decision-making regarding norm compliance. For instance, violation games, put in perspective of a game-theoretic approach to normative multi-agent systems in [17], model the interactions between an agent and the normative system that is responsible to detect violations and sanction them accordingly. That line of research analyses how an agent can violate obligations without being sanctioned. In our case, while we assume that temporal violations are always detected, we explore decision-making from the point of view of both the bearer and the counterparty of a directed obligation.

7 Conclusions

In cooperative B2B Virtual Organizations, contracts specify, through obligations, the interdependencies between different partners, and provide legal options to which parties can resort in case of conflict. However, when this joint activity aims at pursuing a common goal, the successful performance of business benefits all involved parties. Therefore, when developing automated monitoring tools, one should take into account that agents may be cooperative enough to allow counterparties' deviations.

Taking this into account, in this paper we have presented a novel model for contractual obligations – *directed deadline obligations*. Following a claimant theory approach, the directed aspect concerns the need to identify the agent who will be authorized to react in case of non-fulfillment. We started from previous theoretical approaches to model such authorizations, and developed a more concrete formalization by linking authorizations with a flexible model of deadlines. Obligation violations are now dependent on the counterparty motivation to claim them. We have also considered in our model smoother authorizations.

Our approach is based on real-world evidence from business contracts (namely the United Nations Convention on Contracts for the International Sale of Goods), which denotes a flexible and even cooperative facet of trade contracts. This facet extends to the concept of B2B Virtual Organizations, wherein different parties come together to share a business goal that is achievable through the cooperative fulfillment of a common contract.

We addressed the important issue of agent decision-making, which is enriched by our model of authorizations. Both parties involved in a directed deadline obligation may have a say regarding its violation. When considering obligations as interlinked through norms in a contract, agents should evaluate the consequences of fulfillment and violation states as prescribed in the contract. Furthermore, in "socially rich" environments, agents should explore the value of future relationships by enhancing their perceived trustworthiness and predisposition to facilitate compliance, something that is made possible by our directed deadline obligations approach.

Acknowledgments. The first author is supported by FCT (Fundação para a Ciência e a Tecnologia) under grant SFRH/BD/29773/2006.

References

1. UNCITRAL: United nations convention on contracts for the international sale of goods, cisg (1980)
2. Broersen, J., Dignum, F., Dignum, V., Meyer, J.J.C.: Designing a deontic logic of deadlines. In: Lomuscio, A., Nute, D. (eds.) DEON 2004. LNCS (LNAI), vol. 3065, pp. 43–56. Springer, Heidelberg (2004)
3. Lopes Cardoso, H., Oliveira, E.: A context-based institutional normative environment. In: Hübner, J.F., Boissier, O. (eds.) AAMAS'08 Workshop on Coordination, Organization, Institutions and Norms in agent systems (COIN), Estoril, Portugal, pp. 119–133 (2008)

4. Ryu, Y.U.: Relativized deontic modalities for contractual obligations in formal business communication. In: 30th Hawaii International Conference on System Sciences (HICSS), Hawaii, USA, vol. 4, pp. 485–493 (1997)
5. Tan, Y.-H., Thoen, W.: Modeling directed obligations and permissions in trade contracts. In: Proceedings of the Thirty-First Annual Hawaii International Conference on System Sciences, vol. 5. IEEE Computer Society, Los Alamitos (1998)
6. von Wright, G.: Deontic logic. Mind 60, 1–15 (1951)
7. Emerson, E.A.: Temporal and modal logic. In: Leeuwen, J.v. (ed.) Handbook of Theoretical Computer Science. Formal Models and Sematics, vol. B, pp. 995–1072. North-Holland Pub. Co./MIT Press (1990)
8. Herrestad, H., Krogh, C.: Obligations directed from bearers to counterparties. In: Proceedings of the 5th international conference on Artificial intelligence and law, College Park, Maryland, United States, pp. 210–218. ACM, New York (1995)
9. Dignum, F.: Autonomous agents with norms. Artificial Intelligence and Law 7(1), 69–79 (1999)
10. Desai, N., Narendra, N.C., Singh, M.P.: Checking correctness of business contracts via commitments. In: Proc. 7th Intl. Joint Conf. on Autonomous Agents and Multiagent Systems, Estoril, Portugal, IFAAMAS, pp. 787–794 (2008)
11. Vázquez-Salceda, J., Dignum, F.: Modelling electronic organizations. In: Mařík, V., Müller, J.P., Pěchouček, M. (eds.) CEEMAS 2003. LNCS (LNAI), vol. 2691, pp. 584–593. Springer, Heidelberg (2003)
12. Esteva, M., Rodríguez-Aguilar, J.A., Sierra, C., Garcia, P., Arcos, J.L.: On the formal specifications of electronic institutions. In: Sierra, C., Dignum, F.P.M. (eds.) AgentLink 2000. LNCS (LNAI), vol. 1991, pp. 126–147. Springer, Heidelberg (2001)
13. Pasquier, P., Flores, R.A., Chaib-Draa, B.: Modelling flexible social commitments and their enforcement. In: Gleizes, M.-P., Omicini, A., Zambonelli, F. (eds.) ESAW 2004. LNCS (LNAI), vol. 3451, pp. 139–151. Springer, Heidelberg (2005)
14. Wan, F., Singh, M.P.: Formalizing and achieving multiparty agreements via commitments. In: Proceedings of the fourth international joint conference on Autonomous agents and multiagent systems, The Netherlands, pp. 770–777. ACM Press, New York (2005)
15. Sallé, M.: Electronic contract framework for contractual agents. In: Cohen, R., Spencer, B. (eds.) Advances in AI: 15th Conf. of the Canadian Soc. for Computational Studies of Intelligence, pp. 349–353. Springer, Heidelberg (2002)
16. Haddawy, P., Hanks, S.: Utility models for goal-directed, decision-theoretic planners. Computational Intelligence 14(3), 392–429 (1998)
17. Boella, G., van der Torre, L.: A game-theoretic approach to normative multi-agent systems. In: Boella, G., van der Torre, L., Verhagen, H. (eds.) Normative Multiagent Systems (NorMAS07). Dagstuhl Seminar Proceedings, vol. 07122 (2007)

Internal Agent Architecture for Norm Identification

Bastin Tony Roy Savarimuthu, Stephen Cranefield,
Maryam A. Purvis, and Martin K. Purvis

Department of Information Science, University of Otago, Dunedin, P.O. Box 56,
Dunedin, New Zealand
{tonyr,scranefield,tehrany,mpurvis}@infoscience.otago.ac.nz

Abstract. Most works on norms in the multi-agent systems field have concentrated on how norms can be applied to regulate behaviour in agent societies using a top-down approach. In this work, we describe the internal architecture of an agent which identifies what the norm of a society is using a bottom-up approach. The agents infer norms without the norms being given to them explicitly. We demonstrate how the norm associated with using a park can be inferred by an agent using the proposed architecture.

1 Introduction

Software agents that act as proxies to real world entities need to adapt to the changing needs of environments. An example would that be of virtual worlds (e.g. SecondLife [1]). Virtual environments offer a rich and expressive environment for agent interactions. Traditionally, norms have governed the behaviour of agent interactions in a closed system. In open systems such as virtual worlds, agents instead of possessing predetermined notions of what a norm is, should be able to infer and identify norms through observing patterns of interactions and their consequences.

Recognizing the norms of a society is beneficial to an agent. This process enables the agent to know what is permissible within a society and what is not. As the agent joins and leaves different agent societies, these capabilities are essential for the agent to modify its expectations of behaviour depending upon the society it is a part of. As the environment changes, the capability of recognizing the new norm helps an agent to derive new ways of achieving its intended goals.

In this work we describe an internal agent architecture for norm identification. Using a park scenario as an example, we describe the design and implementation of the internal agent architecture which aids the agent to infer what the norms of using the park are.

J. Padget et al. (Eds.): COIN 2009, LNAI 6069, pp. 241–256, 2010.

2   Background and Related Work

2.1   Background on Norms

Norms are expectations of an agent about the behaviour of other agents in the society. Norms are of interest to multi-agent system (MAS) researchers as they help in sustaining social order and increase the predictability of behaviour in the society. However, software agents tend to deviate from these norms due to their autonomy. So, the study of norms has become crucial to MAS researchers as they can build robust multi-agent systems using the concept of norms and also experiment with how norms evolve and adapt in response to environmental changes.

Due to multi-disciplinary interest in norms, several definitions for norms exist. Ullman-Margalit [2] describes a social norm as a prescribed guide for conduct or action which is generally complied with by the members of the society. She states that norms are the resultant of complex patterns of behaviour of a large number of people over a protracted period of time. Coleman [3] describes *"I will say that a norm concerning a specific action exists when the socially defined right to control the action is held not by the actor but by others"*. Elster notes the following about social norms [4]. *"For norms to be social, they must be shared by other people and partly sustained by their approval and disapproval. They are sustained by the feelings of embarrassment, anxiety, guilt and shame that a person suffers at the prospect of violating them. A person obeying a norm may also be propelled by positive emotions like anger and indignation ... social norms have a grip on the mind that is due to the strong emotions they can trigger"*.

Based on the definitions provided by various researchers, we note that the notion of a norm is generally made up of the following two aspects.

- Normative expectation of a behavioural regularity: There is a general agreement within the society that a behaviour is expected on the part of an agent (or actor) by others in a society, in a given circumstance.
- A norm spreading factor: Examples of norm spreading factors include the notion of advice from powerful leaders and the sanctioning mechanism. When an agent does not follow the norm, it could be subjected to a sanction. The sanction could include monetary or physical punishment in the real world which can trigger emotions (embarrassment, guilt etc.) or direct loss of utility resulting in the agent internalising the applicable norm to avoid future sanctions. Other kind of sanctions could include agents not being willing to interact with an agent that violated the norm or the decrease of its reputation score. Other norm spreading factors include imitation and learning on the part of an agent.

It should be noted that researchers are divided on what the differences between a norm and a convention are. Our belief is that convention is a common expectation amongst (most) others that an agent adopts a particular action or behaviour. Conventions may become norms once the non-adherence of the focal action specified by the convention is sanctioned. In this paper our concern is on *norms*.

2.2   Related Work

Several researchers have worked on both prescriptive (top-down) and emergent (bottom-up) approaches to norms. In a top-down approach, an authoritative leader or a normative advisor prescribes what the norm of the society should be [5]. In the bottom-up approach, the agents come up with a norm through learning mechanisms [6, 7]. Researchers have used sanctioning mechanisms [8] and reputation mechanisms [9] for enforcing norms.

The work reported in this paper falls under the bottom-up approach in the study of norms. Many researchers in this approach have experimented with game-theoretical models for norm emergence [6,8]. Agents using these models learn to choose a strategy that maximizes utility . The agents do not possess the notion of a "normative expectation" in these works. Very few have investigated how an agent comes to know the norms of the society. Our objective in this work is to propose an architecture where agents can identify what the norms of the society are. Several researchers have proposed architectures for normative systems. For a comparison of these architectures refer to Neumann's article [10].

We note that our work parallels the work that is being carried out by the researchers involved in the EMIL project [11]. Researchers involved in the EMIL project [11] are working on a cognitive architecture for norm emergence. There have been some attempts to explore how the mental capacities of agents play a role in the emergence of norms.

The EMIL project aims to deliver a simulation-based theory of norm innovation, where norm innovation is defined as the two-way dynamics of an inter-agent process and an intra-agent process. The inter-agent process results in the emergence of norms where the micro interactions produce macro behaviour (norms). The intra-agent process refers to what goes inside an agent's mind so that they can recognize what the norms of the society are. This approach uses cognitive agents that examine interactions between agents and are able to recognize what the norms could be. The agents in this model need not necessarily be utility maximizing like the ones in the learning models. The agents in the model will have the ability to filter external requests that affect normative decisions and will also be able to communicate norms with other agents. Agents just employing learning algorithms lack these capabilities.

Researchers involved with the EMIL project [12, 13] have demonstrated how the norm recognition module of the EMIL-A platform works. In particular they have experimented with an imitation approach versus the norm recognition approach that they have come up with. The norm recognition module consists of two constructs, the normative board and a module for storing different types of modalities for norms (which they refer to as modals). Each modal represents a type of message that is exchanged between agents (e.g. the deontics modal refers to distinguishing situations as either acceptable or unacceptable). The normative board consists of normative beliefs and normative goals. They have shown that norm recognizers perform better than social conformers (imitating agents) due to the fact that the recognizers were able to identify a pool of potential norms while the imitators generated only one type of norm.

The work reported here differs from this work in three ways. Firstly, we have chosen "reaction" (positive and negative) to be a top level construct for identifying potential norms when the norm of a society is being shaped. We note that a sanction not only may imply a monetary punishment, it could also be an action that could invoke emotions (such as an agent yelling at another might invoke shame or embarrassment on another agent), which can help in norm spreading. Agents can recognize such actions based on their previous experience. Secondly, we identify three different sets of norms in agent's mind: suspected norms, candidate norms and identified norms. Thirdly, we demonstrate how our architecture allows for an agent to identify co-existing norms.

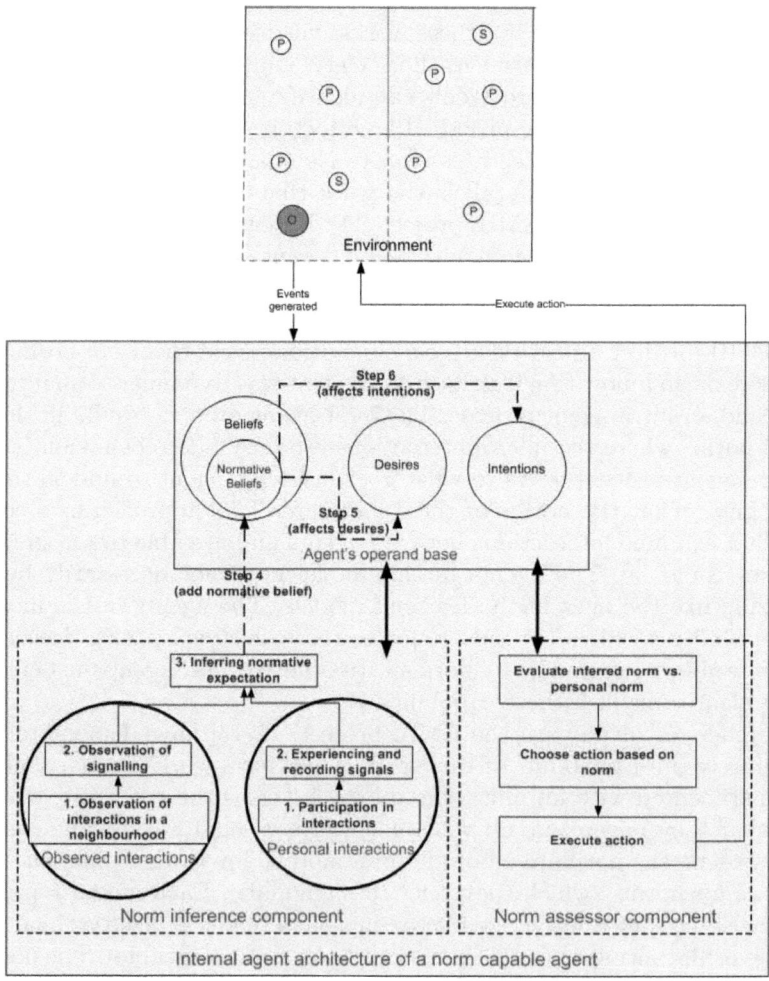

Fig. 1. Higher level architecture of norm identification

3   Architecture for Norm Identification

This section describes the normative inference architecture of an agent. The architecture provides a sequence of six steps that an agent goes through before it comes to know what a norm of the society is, as shown in Figure 1.

To understand the architecture let us assume that an agent society exists. Let us also assume that a norm does not exist to start with or only a few of the agents have a notion of what an appropriate action should be in a particular circumstance (a personal norm). In this architecture a typical agent would first observe the interactions that occur between the agents in the society. The interactions could be of two types. The first type of interaction is the one in which the agent itself is involved and is called a *personnel interaction* (an action that an agent does in an environment). The second type of interaction is an interaction between other agents that is observed by the observer agent, referred to as an *observed interaction*. The agent records these interactions. The top part of Figure 1 shows the types of agents in an agent society. An agent in the society can assume one or more of the three roles: a participant (P) that is involved in a personal interaction, an observer (O) and a signaller (S).The actions observed by an observer are of two types: regular actions and signalling actions. A regular action is an event such as an agent moving to another location in a park or sitting on a bench. Signalling actions can be thought of as special events that agents understand to be either encouraging or discouraging certain behaviour.

For example, let us assume that two agents are in a public park. One agent (A) sees another agent (B) littering the park. Agent B may choose to sanction the agent A (B nods or shakes its head in disapproval and in the worst case yells at the litterer). The observer agent (C) records the signalling that takes place between these agents. The signals can either be positive or negative and it depends on one kind of norm to another. In the case of park littering, agents might issue a negative signal when an agent litters while non-littering might be considered as a normal or routine activity for which there is no positive signalling. In our architecture, signalling is a top level entity because in normative systems it is important for an agent to have an expectation of a particular behaviour. Norms do not appear from nowhere. There might be some norm entrepreneurs or norm innovators who come up with a norm (also known as personal norm (p-norm)). Though few, these agents might sanction or reward others because they violated or followed the norm.

The third step is for the agent to infer normative expectations of a society based on noted observations and signalling. An agent correlates signalling with the observations and infers what its notion of a relevant norm in the society is. A detailed description of how the norm inference works is provided in the next section. The fourth step is to store this newly formed notion of norm in its belief set. We call the beliefs that are based on norms normative beliefs. For every signal that an agent processes, it re-evaluates its notion of the norm. Based on the inference it can modify the notion of what the norm is at any point of time which results in dynamic creation of norms. Once the agent has a norm, its desires and intentions are influenced by the norm which might affect its goals and plans (steps 5 and 6).

Once the agent has inferred what the norm it, it will then have to decide whether to follow the norm. The norm assessor component is responsible for making this decision. The agent weighs its own personal norm against the identified norm in a given circumstance and chooses an appropriate action. The emphasis of this paper is on the norm inference component.

4   Inferring Norms in a Communal Park

This section describes the design and implementation of a norm identification system. The context for norms is the usage of a public park.

In many human societies there exists a norm that one should not litter a communal area such as a park. However, software agents that join open societies do not come to know of the norm of a society *a priori*. Let us assume that software agents stroll through a virtual park in environments such as SecondLife [1]. Let us imagine that the virtual park is a two dimensional grid where agents move around and enjoy the park. Agents sometimes become hungry and eat food. Some agents litter (i.e. drop the rubbish on the ground) and some agents carry the rubbish with them and drop it in a rubbish bin. The actions that can be performed by agent X are *move*, *eat* and *litter*. Some agents consider littering to be an activity that should be discouraged, so they choose to sanction other agents through actions such as yelling and shaking their heads in disapproval. We assume that an agent has a filtering mechanism which categorizes actions such as *yell* and *shake-head* as sanctioning actions. These sanctioning agents can be considered as norm entrepreneurs.

Let us assume that the agents can observe each other within a certain visibility threshold (e.g. agents can only see other agents in a 3 cell neighbourhood). Agents can either be a direct participant in interactions or observers. Some participants can be sanctioning agents . The observer records another agent's actions until it disappears from its vicinity. Whenever it encounters an action of type *sanction*, it recognizes that something has gone wrong (e.g. the action is against the personal norm of the punishing agent). When such an event occurs, the agent may become emotionally charged and perform certain sanctioning action such as yelling at the litterer or shaking its head vigorously in disapproval. Hence, an agent observing this can infer that someone involved in an interaction has violated a norm. We assume that there exists a filtering mechanism in the agent that can recognize sanctioning and rewarding actions when they occur.

Let us assume that an agent perceives other agents' actions. An event that is perceived consists of an event id, an observed action, and the agent(s) participating in that event. For example an agent observing another agent eating will have the representation of *do(1,eat,A)*. This implies that the observer believes that the first event was generated by agent *A* which performs an action *eat*. A sample representation of events observed by an agent is given below.

$$\begin{pmatrix} do(1, eat, A) \\ do(2, litter, A) \\ do(3, move, B) \\ do(4, move, A) \\ do(5, sanction, B, A) \end{pmatrix}$$

Event 5 is a sanctioning event where agent B sanctions agent A. An agent records these events in its belief base. The agent has a filtering mechanism, which identifies signalling events. We can consider the filtering mechanism to be a black box that recognizes an emotionally charged event such as yelling and shaking head in disapproval and categorizes those actions to be sanctions[1]. When a sanctioning event occurs, it triggers the invocation of the norm inference module of the agent. It should be noted that signalling events can both be positive (e.g. rewards) and negative (e.g. sanctions). In this work, we have focused on the latter type of signalling.

Figure 2 shows the architecture of the norm inference component of an agent. The following sub-sections describe the four sub-components of the norm inference component.

4.1   Creating Event-Episodes

Agents record other agents actions in their memory. Let us assume that there are three agents A,B and C. Agent A eats, litters and moves while agent B moves and then sanctions. Agent C observes these events and categorizes them based on which agent was responsible for creating an event. $\{A\}$ followed by right arrow ($\rightarrow$) indicates the categorization of events performed by agent A as observed by agent C. A hyphen separates one event from the next.

$$\begin{pmatrix} \{A\} \rightarrow do(1, eat, A) - do(2, litter, A) - do(4, move, A) \\ \{B\} \rightarrow do(3, move, B) - do(5, sanction, B, A) \end{pmatrix}$$

When a sanction occurs, an observer agent extracts the sequence of actions from the recorded history that were exchanged between the sanctioning agent and the sanctioned agent. In the example shown above, the observer infers that something that agent A did may have caused the sanction. It could also be that something agent A failed to do might have caused a sanction. In this work we concentrate on the former of the two. Agent C then extracts the following sequence of events that take place between A and B based on the information retrieved from its history.

$$\{A, B\} \rightarrow eat(1, A) - litter(2, A) - move(4, A) - sanction(5, B, A)$$

To simplify the notation here afterwards only the first letter of each event will be mentioned (e.g. e for eat). The event episode for interactions between agents A and B shown above will be represented as

---

[1] Recognizing and categorizing a sanctioning event is a difficult problem. In this paper we assume such a mechanism exists (e.g. based on an agent's past experience).

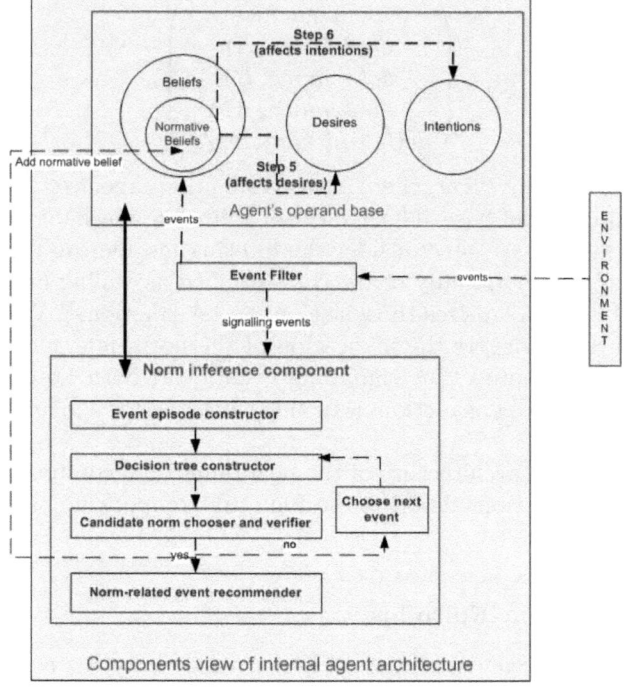

Fig. 2. Architecture of the norm inference component

$$\left(\{A, B\} \to e - l - m - s\right)$$

There might be a few sanctioning events at any given point of time that an agent observes. A sample list containing ten event episodes that are observed by an agent in a certain interval of time is given below.

$$\begin{pmatrix} e - l - m - s, l - e - l - s, m - e - l - s, e - l - e - s, e - l - e - s \\ l - e - l - s, e - e - l - s, m - e - l - s, e - l - m - s, e - l - e - s \end{pmatrix}$$

4.2 Constructing an Event-Tree Based on Conditional Probability

Once the event episodes are constructed, the agent creates a tree of events that occur in all episodes based on the estimation of conditional probabilities for events that might have led to sanctioning. The mechanism for constructing a decision tree is explained below.

For calculating the conditional probabilities for events that precede a sanction, an agent follows the following steps.

1. Categorizes episodes into events belonging to different levels.
2. Constructs a conditional probability tree of sub-episodes
3. Ranks sub-episodes and chooses candidate norms for verification

Categorizing episodes into event levels - Based on a certain fixed number of events that precede a sanction, an agent categorizes events of an episode into certain levels (e.g. single-level events, two-level events and three-level events). Let us assume that an agent is interested in n events in a sequence that precede a sanction. As an example let us consider e-l-m-s, which is the first episode from the sample list of ten episodes. The sequence of events that precede a sanction is e-l-m and hence the value of n is three. A single level event (level 1) is an event that precedes a sanction (i.e. m). Two-level events (level 2) are the events that are a combination of two events that precede a sanction (i.e. e-l and l-m). Three-level events (level 3) are the events that are a combination of three events that precede the sanction (i.e. e-l-m). Let us call each entry in these levels a sub-episode.

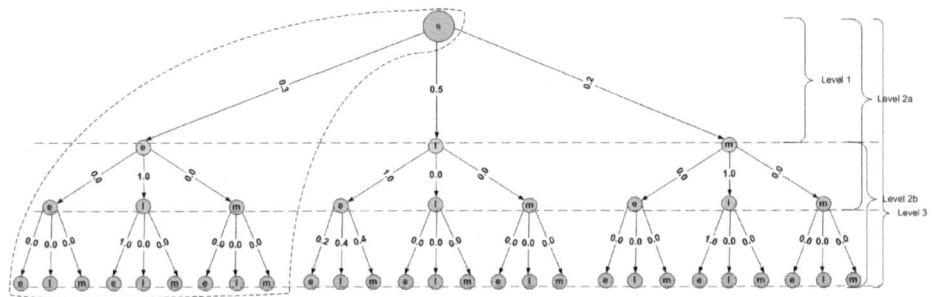

Fig. 3. Events-tree of all episodes based on conditional probability

Constructing a tree based on conditional probability - For each sub-episode in each level, the agent calculates the conditional probability. Sub-episodes for an episode e-l-m are e at level 1, e-l and l-m at level 2 and e-l-m at level three. The conditional probability tree of the sample list of ten events as shown in Section 4.1 is given in Figure 3.

For the sake of simplicity, let us only consider those sub-episodes that end with e in the region encompassed by a dashed line in Figure 3. In the sample list that consists of ten episodes, there are three episodes that end with event e. So, the conditional probability of event e given that a sanction has occurred is p(e|s)=0.3. One of the three events (e or l or m) could have occurred before e. The conditional probability of e occurring given that an e-s has occurred is p(e-e-s|e-s)=0.0 and the other two conditional probabilities are p(l-e-s|e-s)=1.0 and p(m-e-s|e-s)=0.0. Based on these, we know that p(l-e-s|s)=0.3 and the p(e-e-s|s)=0 and p(m-e-s|s)=0. Now again, three events (e or l or m) could have preceded l. The conditional probabilities p(e-l-e-s|l-e-s)=1.0 and p(l-l-e-s|l-e-s)=0 and p(m-l-e-s|l-e-s)=0. From these, we can infer that p(e-l-e-s|s)=0.3, p(l-l-e-s|s)=0 and p(m-l-e-s|s)=0.

At level 2, we are also interested to find out the occurrences of all episodes that are made up of two level events (indicated in figure 3 as levels 2a and

2b). Based on permutations with repetitions we know that for choosing two out of three events, there are 9 possible combinations (ee,el,em,le,ll,lm,me,ml,mm). The respective probabilities of each of these sub-episodes is 0.1,1,0,0.5,0,0.2,0.2 and 0,0.

The list given below shows the conditional probabilities of all sub-episodes that have a non-zero probability for all the three levels. We call these sub-episodes *suspected norms*. Note that for simplicity we assume that the representation of $p(x|s)$ is $p(x)$. Additionally, the hyphens will be omitted from the sub-episodes (e.g. *e-l-m* will be represented as *elm*).

1. p(e)= 0.3, p(l)=0.5, p(m)=0.3
2. p(ee)=0.1, p(el)=1, p(le)=0.5, p(lm)=0.2, p(me)=0.2
3. p(ele) = 0.3, p(eel)=0.1, p(lel)=0.2, p(mel)=0.2, p(elm)=0.2

Ranking sub-episodes and selecting candidate norms - The agent ranks sub-episodes based on these probabilities and creates a ranked list using the norm selection parameter (*ns*). An agent chooses only those sub-episodes that have conditional probabilities greater than *ns*. Elements in this subset of norms are referred to as *candidate norms*. For example, if *ns* is set to 50, the candidate norms chosen from the set of suspected norms will be *el* (100%), *l* (50%) and *le* (50%).Having compiled a set containing candidate norms, the agent passes this information to the norm verification and identification component.

4.3   Norm Verification and Identification

In order to find whether a candidate norm is a norm of the society, the agent asks another agent in its proximity. This happens in certain intervals of time (e.g. once in every 10 iterations). When two agents A and B interact, A chooses its first candidate norm and asks B whether its current norm is A's candidate norm. If true, A stores this norm in its set of *identified norms*. Otherwise, it chooses a sub-episode of the norm and enquires whether that is the norm. It is possible that B might identify the sub-episode as the norm. If not, A moves on to the second candidate norm in its list[2].

In the case of the running example, the sub-episode *el* has the highest probability for selection and it is chosen to be communicated to the other agent. It asks another agent (e.g. an agent who is the closest) whether it thinks that the given candidate norm is a norm of the society. If it responds positively, the agent infers *prohibit(el)* to be a norm. If the response is negative, this norm is stored in the bottom of the candidate norm list. It then asks whether the sub-episodes of *el*, which are *e* or *l* are the reasons for sanction. If yes, the appropriate action is considered to be prohibited. Otherwise, the next event in the candidate norm list is chosen. This process continues until a norm is found or no norm is found in which case, the process is re-iterated once a new signal indicating a sanction

---

[2] Other alternative mechanisms are also possible. For example, an agent could ask for all the candidate norms from another agent and can compare them locally.

is generated. When one of the candidate norms has been identified as a norm of the society, the agent still iterates through the candidate norm list to find any co-existing norms.

It should be noted that an agent will have three sets of norms: suspected norms, candidate norms and identified norms. Figure 4 shows these three sets of norms. Once an agent identifies the norms of the system and finds that the norms identified have been stable for a certain period of time, it can forgo using the norm inference component for a certain amount of time. It invokes the norm inference component in regular intervals of time to check if the norms of the society have changed, in which case it replaces the norms in the identified list with the new ones[3].

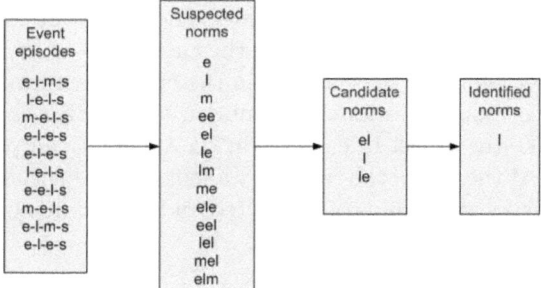

Fig. 4. Three sets of norms

4.4   Related Event Recommender

Even if the event immediately preceding a sanction was responsible for causing the sanction (e.g. event l), the agent would still be watchful of the event sequences that precede the sanctioned action 100% of the time (e.g. event e) for two reasons. One reason is that when it produces events e and then l, it could be sanctioned. Also when other agents produce events e-l, then if the observer were a sanctioning agent, it may have to sanction the litterer. The purpose of the related event recommender is to recommend event episodes that occur 100% of the time preceding a sanctioning action so that the agent can be warned about impending sanctions.

5   Experiments on Norm Identification

In an agent society, one or more norms can co-exist. In this section we demonstrate that the agents using our architecture are able to infer the norms of the society.

---

[3] Alternatively, an agent can wait for certain number of sanctions to occur before it invokes the norm inference component.

5.1   Scenario 1: A Society with One Type of Norm

We have experimented with an agent society comprising 100 agents. There are
agents with three different personality types. They are learning litterers (ll),
non-litterers (nl) and non-littering punishers (nlp). The learning litterers are
litterers who learn to change their behaviour based on normative expectations
inferred through the observation of interactions between agents. Non-litterers do
not litter the park and non-littering punishers are the non-litterers who sanction
littering because that action is against their personal norm.

There are 50 ll and 50 nl agents. Out of these 50 nl agents, 5 are nlp agents.
In each iteration, an agent performs one of m,e,l or s. The agents are initialized
with a uniform probability for choosing actions (p(m)=0.75, p(e)=0.25, p(l) having eaten in the previous interaction =0.5). The nlp agents punish other agents
if they observe a littering action of an agent in the current iteration or the previous iteration with 6% probability (in both the cases). An agent stores the actions
performed by other agents in its vicinity (in the current set up, a fully-connected
network topology is assumed where an agent can see all other agents). We ran this
experiment for 100 iterations. In each iteration an agent can perform one of the
actions (e,l,m,s). At the end of the run every agent looks at the event history it had
recorded and observes what kinds of suspected and candidate norms has emerged.

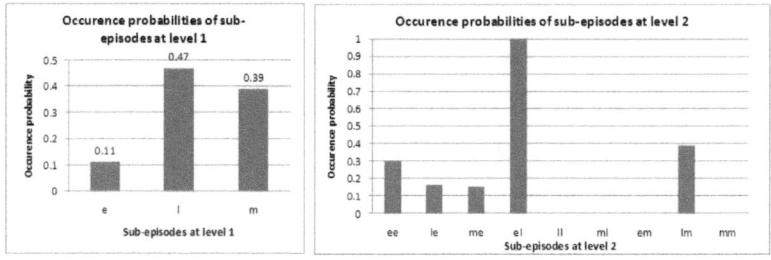

Fig. 5. Sub-episode occurrence probabilities (level 1 and 2)

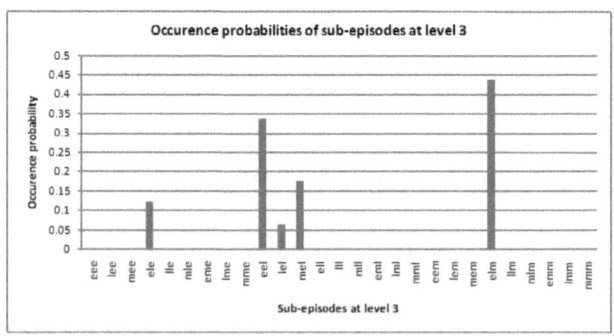

Fig. 6. Sub-episode occurrence probabilities (level 3)

It should be noted that for an episode that is made up of 3 different events, allowing permutation with repetition, 39 sub-episodes can be created (3 in level 1, 9 in level 2 and 27 in level 3). It can be observed from figures 5 and 6 that out of 39 possible sub-episodes, only a subset of sub-episodes (13 of them) happen to appear (i.e. the suspected norms). Assuming that an agent's norm selection threshold is 0.45 to construct the list of candidate norms, there are two such norms, which are norms against *el* and *l*. The agent then moves on to the norm verification stage which identifies the norm against littering.

5.2 Scenario 2: Identification of Co-existing Norms in an Agent Society

Let us assume that there are two types of sanctioning agents, one that sanctions when an agent litters the park and the other sanctions if it sees anyone eating in the park. In these cases, our mechanism will be able to generate different sets of suspected norms. Retaining the experimental set-up used in the previous scenario, we have set the probability of a *nlp* punishing eating action to be 3% and the probability of punishing littering action to be 3%). The norm selection threshold has been set to 0.25. Occurrence probabilities of sub-episodes (i.e suspected norms) at level 2 is given in figure 7. It can be observed that there are more occurrences of events involving *e* that appear in these sub-episodes than event *l*. This is due to the set up of the system since p(e)=0.25 while p(l)=0.125. The important thing to note in this experiment is that our architecture allows for the identification of co-existing norms.

5.3 Scenario 3: Identification of Norms Across Different Societies

Let us assume that there are three sections of a park. At any point of time, an agent might be present in one of these sections. Let us also assume that there are two types of sanctioning agents. One type of agents punish litterers while the other type of agents punish those who eat in the park. Assume that these types of agents are randomly placed in the three sections of a park. Our objective was to see what type of norms might emerge in these three sub-groups.

Figure 8 shows the candidate norms of three different agents that belong to three different sub-groups. The norm selection threshold was set to 0.3. It can be observed that different types of candidate norms are generated in the minds of these agents based on what they had observed in their respective agent society. It can be observed that the agent from sub-group one had identified the norm against littering and the one from the third group had identified the norm against eating while the agent from the second group had identified both these norms.

An extension to this experiment is to allow an agent to move around in these three sections of the park and see how it accommodates the changes to its norms. Another extension will be to allow the sanctioning agents to move around which will enable dynamic change of norms in the society.

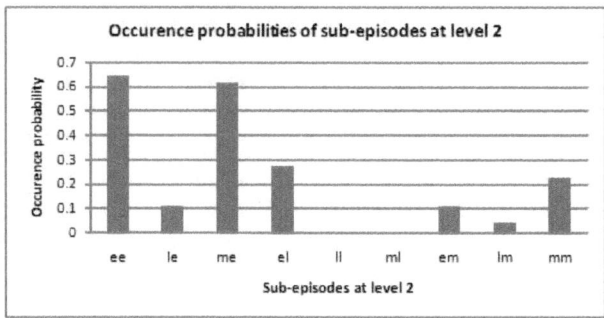

Fig. 7. Sub-episode occurrence probabilities (level 2) when two types of sanctioning agents were present

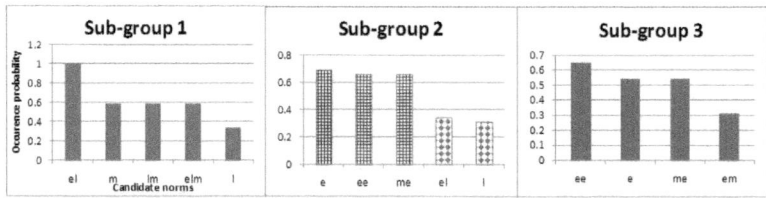

Fig. 8. Candidate norms of three agents that belong to three different sub-groups

6   Discussion

We note that the experimental set up is simple. We have assumed that an agent considers three events ($n=3$) that precede a signal (a sanction or a reward). The value of n can change and an agent being a computation machine should be able to handle a large number of possible events. Most researchers agree that there will be some form of sanction or reward once a norm is established (e.g. [4, 3]). Hence, the notion of a reaction (positive or negative action) has been considered to be a top level entity in our work. We have assumed that even when a norm is being created, the notion of sanction is important for norm identification.

Our experimental set-up can be improved in many ways. Firstly, we do not assume that there is a cost associated with sanctions. The cost for sanctions can be included in the model. Secondly, our model identifies co-existing norms. If the cost of sanctions is considered there could also be competing or conflicting norms. For example, some agents might punish other agents when they litter while some others may punish one when the littering agent is within 20 meters from the rubbish bin. When there are competing norms the society might be divided into groups. This type of dynamics will be interesting to study. Thirdly, the experiments have only made use of observational information ignoring the personal experience. We believe that the inclusion of personal experience will speed up the rate at which norms are identified. Fourthly, we have assumed that when an agent identifies a norm, it will follow the norm. Agents owing to their autonomy do not always follow the norm. An agent might have its own personal agenda and it can be an opportunistic norm follower. Autonomy of an agent needs to be addressed in the future. In our architecture, this has been encapsulated as a part of the norm assessment component which will be elaborated in a future work. Fifthly, it might not always be possible to associate sanctions or rewards with the events that immediately precede them. For example, speeding might result in a fine that is sent to an agent after a couple of days. An observer might not be able to recognize this sanction. In this work, we have only considered those norms where the sanctions can be recognized by an observer and the events that caused the sanction occurred within an immediate window of time before the sanction. Sixthly, the problem of false negatives and positives for norm identification needs to be dealt with in the future. Lastly, our work can take advantage of the work done in the data-mining field on the identification of frequent event sequences [14].

However, we believe that our work reports some advancements. Firstly, the question of "how an agent comes to find out what the norm of society is" is being dealt with by at least one other research group [11]. We have made some progress in that regard by proposing an internal agent architecture and demonstrating how an agent will identify the norms of a society. Secondly, other prominent works identify one norm that exists in the society [15, 8]. In our architecture an agent is able to identify several norms that might exist in the society. Thirdly, most works have not addressed how an agent might be able to identify whether a norm is changing in a society and how it might react to this situation. In our model, the agents will be able to identify the norm change and dynamically add, remove and modify norms. Fourthly, our architecture can be used to study norm emergence. We believe through norm identification at the agent level, we are also in the realm of addressing how norms emerge using a bottom-up approach.

7   Conclusions

In this paper we have explained the internal agent architecture for norm identification. Through simulations we have shown how an agent infers norms in an agent society. We have also discussed the related work and have identified issues that should be addressed in the future.

Acknowledgments

We thank the three anonymous reviewers for their insightful comments.

References

1. Rymaszewski, M., Au, W.J., Wallace, M., Winters, C., Ondrejka, C., Batstone-Cunningham, B., Rosedale, P.: Second Life: The Official Guide. SYBEX Inc., Alameda (2006)

2. Ullmann-Margalit, E.: The Emergence of Norms. Clarendon Press, Oxford (1977)
3. Coleman, J.: Foundations of Social Theory. Belknap Press (August 1990)
4. Elster, J.: Social norms and economic theory. The Journal of Economic Perspectives 3(4), 99–117 (1989)
5. Verhagen, H.: Simulation of the Learning of Norms. Social Science Computer Review 19(3), 296–306 (2001)
6. Shoham, Y., Tennenholtz, M.: Emergent conventions in multi-agent systems: Initial experimental results and observations (preliminary report). In: KR, pp. 225–231 (1992)
7. Sen, S., Airiau, S.: Emergence of norms through social learning. In: Proceedings of Twentieth International Joint Conference on Artificial Intelligence (IJCAI'07), pp. 1507–1512. AAAI Press, Menlo Park (2007)
8. Axelrod, R.: An evolutionary approach to norms. The American Political Science Review 80(4), 1095–1111 (1986)
9. Castelfranchi, C., Conte, R., Paolucci, M.: Normative reputation and the costs of compliance. Journal of Artificial Societies and Social Simulation 1(3) (1998)
10. Neumann, M.: A classification of normative architectures. In: Proceedings of World Congress on Social Simulation (2008)
11. Andrighetto, G., Conte, R., Turrini, P., Paolucci, M.: Emergence in the loop: Simulating the two way dynamics of norm innovation. In: Boella, G., van der Torre, L., Verhagen, H. (eds.) Normative Multi-agent Systems, Dagstuhl Seminar Proceedings, vol. 07122. Internationales Begegnungs- und Forschungszentrum fuer Informatik (IBFI), Schloss Dagstuhl (2007)
12. Andrighetto, G., Campenni, M., Cecconi, F., Conte, R.: How agents find out norms: A simulation based model of norm innovation. In: 3rd International Workshop on Normative Multiagent Systems (NorMAS 2008), Luxembourg, July 15-16 (2008)
13. Campenni, M., Andrighetto, G., Cecconi, F., Conte, R.: Normal = normative? the role of intelligent agents in norm innovation. In: The Fifth Conference of the European Social Simulation Association (ESSA), University of Brescia, September 1-5 (2008)
14. Mannila, H., Toivonen, H., Inkeri Verkamo, A.: Discovery of frequent episodes in event sequences. Data Mining and Knowledge Discovery 1(3), 259–289 (1997)
15. Epstein, J.M.: Learning to be thoughtless: Social norms and individual computation. Comput. Econ. 18(1), 9–24 (2001)

Influence of Communication Graph Structures on Pheromone-Based Approaches in the Context of a Partitioning Task Problem

Thomas Kemmerich

International Graduate School of Dynamic Intelligent Systems
Knowledge Based Systems, University of Paderborn, Germany
`kemmerich@upb.de`

Abstract. This paper introduces and formalizes a multi-objective agent coordination problem, called General Online Partitioning Problem (GOPP). The goal is to find a cost-optimal, distance minimizing, and uniform partitioning of an agent set to a set of targets in a 2-dimensional world. Agents build a communication graph based on local neighborhood relations. We propose a message-based Ant Colony Optimization (ACO) algorithm that disposes target-specific pheromones in this communication graph to solve the GOPP. It is analyzed why different typed and newly arriving pheromone traces are unable to grow into once established pheromone structures. Furthermore, an example is presented in which pheromone-based approaches working on communication graphs are unable to find optimal solutions. We present experimental results and compare the new approach to existing ones. Besides the proved non-optimality of our novel approach, the evaluation shows that the algorithm produces high quality solutions on average.

1 Introduction

Consider a coffee-break scenario at a conference when a large number of Wi-Fi devices at the same time tries to connect to the internet using some provided access points. Usually, the access point with the strongest signal will be selected by each device. However, this could lead to situations where one access point is totally overcharged while others – that are reachable as well – still provide plenty of capacity [1,2]. A possible solution to this problem would be to create equal sized groups of devices. These groups then could assign themselves to the access points. The question of how to create such groups autonomously and in a decentralized manner has to be answered to realize such an approach.

Next, consider a scenario where several agents at the same time cooperatively have to solve different tasks. Every task requires a certain number of agents in order to be completed. Again, the question is how should the agents organize themselves into groups in order to efficiently complete all tasks?

As these two examples show, establishing groups or organizations of agents is a key problem when solving problems that could only be solved using the power of

J. Padget et al. (Eds.): COIN 2009, LNAI 6069, pp. 257–272, 2010.

organizations. The paper on hand handles this question by considering a problem that demands an uniform, distance-minimal and cost-efficient partitioning of an agent set to a set of targets in a 2-dimensional world. In order to solve that problem we will propose an ant-based algorithm and discuss its properties.

Technically, the above mentioned problem is related to decentralized coordination of groups of agents, for which several different techniques have been proposed. Kube and Zhang [3], for instance, implemented an ant-based approach that uses indirect communication for solving a cooperative box-pushing task. The task could only be fulfilled by cooperation since the box is too heavy to be moved by a single robot. Kube and Zhang used the subsumption architecture to arbitrate simple behavioral rules using fixed-priorities. In addition, they experimented with a simple neural network type called Adaptive Logic Networks. Kube and Zhang showed the feasibility of a cooperative task without direct communication using homogeneous robots.

In the early 2000s, further neural network based approaches towards cooperative transport have been developed by Groß and Dorigo [4,5,6] as well as by Groß *et al.* [7]. Their dynamic box-pushing task requires the agents to react on changing target positions and to cope with "blind" robots that are occasionally unable to detect the target. In [4] and [5] a single recurrent neural network and a self-adaptive $(\mu + \lambda)$ evolution strategy are used to accomplish the task. In [6] the authors note that it requires too many generations for a single neural network to produce good results. Accordingly, they divided the task into two subtasks that are performed by two independent neural networks. The results show that the neural network controllers scale better with increasing group sizes than hand-coded controllers.

In contrast to these partially biologically-inspired approaches, market-based coordination methods recently gained the interest of researchers [8]. In [9], Koenig *et al.* describe a sequential single-item auction system to solve an exploration task. In detail, their problem includes a team of robots which has to visit targets located in a 2-dimensional world. Each target has to be visited by at least one robot. The robots know their initial location, the exact positions of all targets, as well as the number of targets in the system. Furthermore, the terrain includes obstacles whose dimensions and locations are unknown to the agents in the beginning. Robots bid on targets whereas the costs to visit the corresponding target on an cost-optimal path determines the bid value. Whenever a robot detects a previously unknown obstacle, it publishes this information. Next, all unvisited targets become subject of new auctions, again. The new bids reflect the updated path costs. Koenig's coordination method allows real time coordination, which is why the robots need to act efficiently in terms of communication and computation. Comparable to the *distance objective* in the GOPP (see Sect. 2), Koenig *et al.* choose the minimization of the sum over all produced path costs as a measure for the team performance. The proposed approach performs well under the given constraints and is proved to gain results bounded by an interval of $[1.5, 2]$ times the optimum [9]. Recently, Koenig *et al.* [10] proposed a method using auctions and regret clearing which further improves the team performance.

Goebels *et al.* [11,12,13] consider a partitioning task, called *Online Partitioning Problem (OPP)*. This problem demands a partitioning of an agent set to a target set in a 2-dimensional world that does not include any obstacles. The partitioning should be calculated according to the following three objectives:

Distribution: Uniform distribution of agents to targets
Distance: Minimize the overall distance between agents and assigned targets
Abilities: Agents should have as limited abilities as possible

To solve the OPP, Goebels [11] proposes several approaches including central instance, non-communicative, and communicative strategies, biologically-inspired techniques, as well as cellular automata, and organization-based methods. He also presents a strategy, to which we will refer as *Two Target Optimal (TTO)* approach, that calculates an optimal solution for two targets and n agents in time $\mathcal{O}(n^2)$. For the general case of m targets the problem is hard to solve and the exact approach proposed by Goebels requires time $\mathcal{O}(m^n)$. The most promising heuristic is called *Exchange Target Strategy (ETS)*. Its basic idea is to optimize the OPP objectives one after the other. Therefore, the strategy begins to optimize the *distribution* objective by assigning all agents to a target using a uniform random number generator. Next, the *distance* objective is improved by repeatedly exchanging target assignments between neighbored agents. Target exchange decisions of an agent are based on information gathered using messages which contain distance and assignment information of neighbored agents. An exchange is performed if it locally improves the distance objective, only. Due to the exchange of target assignments, the *distribution* objective remains unchanged. Later in this work we will use a more efficient ETS which avoids sending not required messages [14].

In contrast to the local exchange strategy, Wehe [15] proposes the *Chainmail Strategy (CMS)* which collects information about all assignments and distances in an extended OPP system. Wehe's OPP version allows a non-transparent wall that can not be penetrated by radio waves. To collect the information, chainmail-like messages are exchanged until, given enough runtime, all information are accumulated into a single message. This message is used locally by some special agents to calculate an optimal solution. For two targets Wehe uses a strategy comparable to the TTO approach, and for the general case of m targets he proposes to use a linear programming technique. This, however, implies agents high computational and storing abilities which in some way contradicts the *ability* objective. CMS is able to produce high quality solutions in the evaluated scenarios.

In Sect. 2 of this paper we propose a formalization of an extended, obstacle containing OPP version whose evaluation function takes the *ability* property into account. Section 3 introduces a novel approach inspired by the foraging behavior of ant societies using pheromones. In addition, we analyze the limitations of pheromone-based approaches working on communication graphs. Section 4 compares the novel approach to existing ones and presents experimental results. Finally, Sect. 5 draws a conclusion and provides an outlook on future work.

2   Problem Definition

The problem considered in this paper is to find a partitioning of an agent set to a target set in a 2-dimensional world containing obstacles and special regions. The novel problem thus can be considered as a refinement of the Online Partitioning Problem (OPP) [11,13] which at the same time overcomes its limitations.

Since the *ability* objective is not formalized within the OPP it is evaluated informally, only. Our idea is to measure the abilities of an agent by considering the costs they produce. In robotics, abilities of single robots emerge by executing different software procedures and/or by using additional hardware. Usually, more complex abilities require more computational effort and probably also additional hardware. In contrast, simple abilities are satisfied with less resources. Support in this idea comes from Šimunić *et al.* [16] who showed varying energy consumption for different software configurations. In addition, Mei *et al.* [17] state

> "As robots become more sophisticated, control, sensing, communication and computation consume higher portions of energy."

and

> "The power consumption of the embedded computer may vary significantly across different programs.".

Consequently, we decided to use energy consumption as indicator for the complexity of agent abilities. Since we deal with an abstract optimization problem, the term energy consumption is abstracted to *general costs*. In order to compare and measure the costs produced during the execution of an algorithm, we developed a cost model and guidelines how to apply that model [14]. Note that different algorithms can only be compared if the same model is used.

Additionally, we allow different types and an arbitrary number of obstacles and special regions. Using areas where agents can move faster or slower, as well as areas where agents can look through but are not allowed to walk across, we are able to model more realistic scenarios, too. However, we currently distinguish between solving the GOPP in a stationary environment and the actual movement of the agents towards the targets in a second step.

In this paper $\mathcal{A} = \{a_i, \ldots, a_n\}$ denotes a non-empty set of agents, $\mathcal{T} = \{T_1, \ldots, T_m\}$ a non-empty target set, $\mathcal{C}$ a cost model, and $\mathcal{R}$ a set of regions. A region r_i is described by a tuple $r_i = (F_i, P_i)$, with F_i denoting the geometrical form and P_i a set of properties, containing at least a region specific weight factor w_i. $\rho : \{\mathcal{A} \uplus \mathcal{T} \uplus \mathcal{R}\} \to \mathbb{R}_0^+ \times \mathbb{R}_0^+$ is a positioning function that maps each object to a position in the Euclidean space. The position of an object is defined as its center point. $\delta(\rho(x), \rho(y))$ denotes the shortest weighted distance between two positions. Furthermore, let $\tau : \mathcal{A} \to \mathcal{T}$ return an agent's currently assigned target. Function $\psi : \mathcal{A} \to \mathcal{T}$ returns the nearest target of an agent (ties are broken by selecting the target T_i with the lowest index i). Based on the given notations, we now define the *General Online Partitioning Problem (GOPP)*:

Definition 1 (GOPP). *The General Online Partitioning Problem (GOPP) is described by* $\mathrm{GOPP} = (\mathcal{A}, \mathcal{T}, \mathcal{C}, \mathcal{R}, \rho)$. *The aim is to find a partition* $\mathcal{S} = \{S_1, S_2, \ldots, S_m\}$ *of* $\mathcal{A}$ *with* $S_i \subseteq \mathcal{A}, i \in \{1, \ldots, m\}$, *such that* $\mathcal{A} = \{S_1 \uplus S_2 \uplus \ldots \uplus S_m\}$. *Any agent* $a \in S_i$ *is assigned to target* T_i. *Such a partition must obey the following three objectives:*

1. *create a **uniform distribution** where* $\forall i, i \in \{1, ..., m\} : \lfloor \frac{n}{m} \rfloor \leq |S_i| \leq \lceil \frac{n}{m} \rceil$, *which is equal to maximizing the product of the subset sizes[1]:*

$$\max \prod_{S_i \in \mathcal{S}} |S_i|$$

2. *minimize the **overall weighted distance sum** over all agents and their assigned targets:*

$$\min \sum_{a \in \mathcal{A}} \delta(a, \tau(a))$$

3. *minimize the **costs** produced to find the partition according to the cost model* $\mathcal{C}$:

$$\min \sum_{a \in \mathcal{A}} f_\mathcal{C}(a) + \lambda_\mathcal{C}(\tau(a)),$$

where $f_\mathcal{C}(a)$ *describes the fixed costs produced by agent* a *and* $\lambda_\mathcal{C}(\tau(a))$ *the costs for finding the assignment of agent* a *to target* $\tau(a)$.

These objectives are normalized against optimal solutions and combined in Equation (1), where o_i *denotes the number of agents that would choose target* T_i *in an optimal distribution according to the first objective. Furthermore, let* $\alpha, \beta, \gamma \geq 0$ *be weight factors with* $\alpha + \beta + \gamma = 1$.

$$f = \alpha \cdot \left(\frac{\prod\limits_{S_i \in \mathcal{S}} |S_i|}{\prod\limits_{i=1}^{m} o_i} \right) + \beta \cdot \left(\frac{\sum\limits_{a \in \mathcal{A}} \delta(a, \psi(a))}{\sum\limits_{a \in \mathcal{A}} \delta(a, \tau(a))} \right) + \gamma \cdot \left(\frac{\sum\limits_{a \in \mathcal{A}} f_\mathcal{C}(a)}{\sum\limits_{a \in \mathcal{A}} f_\mathcal{C}(a) + \lambda_\mathcal{C}(\tau(a))} \right) \quad (1)$$

Since all three objectives are normalized, it holds that the higher the value $f \in [0, 1]$ *the better the solution found with reference to the weighted optimization criteria.*

Using Equation (1) we thus are able to assign a degree of importance to each of the three contrary optimization criteria. By doing so, we obtain a simple measure that allows us to compare different solutions based solely on a single criterion instead of dealing with the Pareto optimality of all three optimization criteria.

---

[1] For this mathematical description we use the fact that a product of m numbers is maximal if the numbers are identical. A proof is available in the appendix of [11].

Referring to the introduction, the *uniform distribution* objective demands the emergence of equal sized agent groups.

In OPP scenarios without obstacles and weighted regions, Euclidean distances are easy to calculate. In the remainder of this paper, however, we consider the GOPP using four different types of rectangular, weighted regions as illustrated in Fig. 1(a). The problem of determining shortest weighted paths in such environments is known as *Weighted Region Problem* (WRP) [18]. Since an $(1 + \epsilon)$-approximation algorithm proposed in [18] requires time $\mathcal{O}(n^8 L)$, where L is a factor based on the precision of the problem instance and n the number of vertices, we implemented and used a heuristic that solves a simplified WRP in time $\mathcal{O}(|R|^3)$ [14]. To further simplify the distance determination, we assume infinite small agents that cannot collide.

3 The ComAnt Approach

The presented communicative approach is inspired by the foraging behavior of ant colonies, hence the name ComAnt. The basic idea is to establish a network of pheromones based on the communication graph structure. Using pheromone evaporation and updates, appropriate pheromone structures should emerge which are used by the agents to find a partitioning according to GOPP's objectives. Algorithm 1 briefly summarizes the four phases of the ComAnt algorithm as they will be described in the remainder of this section.

In the *first phase* each agent initializes its internal variables and determines its (l, k)-neighborhood as defined in Definition 2. Note that the k-neighborhood used in [11] and [15] per definition always contains the k nearest agents, but disregards the maximum communication range of realistic communication devices. We believe that a more realistic neighborhood is required and thus decided to use the (l, k)-neighborhood which better reflects that physical limitation. Neighborhoods are established using an iterative approach which increases the communication range until either the desired number of agents k is reached or the maximum communication range has been exceeded. In order to guarantee proper execution, this and most other (G)OPP algorithms rely on the availability of local information. Therefore, we demand a minimum number of neighbors l. If less than l agents are reachable then the agent is said to be uninformed and it may not properly execute the algorithm. Accordingly, its neighborhood size is set to 0.

Definition 2 $((l, k)$-**neighborhood**)**.** *Let c be the number of agents within the maximum communication range of agent a, a excluded. Then j is defined as follows:*

$$j = \begin{cases} k \text{ for } c \geq k \\ c \text{ for } l \leq c < k \\ 0 \text{ otherwise} \end{cases}$$

The (l,k)-neighborhood $\mathcal{N}_a$ of agent a contains the j nearest agents according to the communication distance δ_c, or more formally $\mathcal{N}_a = \{b_1, \ldots, b_j\} \subseteq \mathcal{A}\backslash\{a\}$

Algorithm 1. ComAnt

1: **procedure** COMANT
2:    */* Phase 1: initialize all agents */*
3:    **for all** $a \in \mathcal{A}$ **do**
4:        initialize variables
5:        determine and store $\mathcal{N}_a$ */* Agents do not move */*
6:    */* Phase 2: Sense targets */*
7:    **for all** $a \in \mathcal{A}$ **do**
8:        sensedTargetList $\leftarrow$ a.senseTargets()
9:        **if** sensedTargetList $\neq \emptyset$ **then**
10:            t $\leftarrow$ nearest target in sensedTargetList
11:            a.assignTo(t)
12:            a.setInitiatorStatus(t, true)
13:    */* Phase 3: Create initial pheromone traces */*
14:    **for all** $a \in \mathcal{A}$ **do**
15:        **if** a.isInitiator() **then**
16:            a.createInitialTrace(maxTraceLength)
17:    */* Phase 4: Find solution */*
18:    **while** the stop condition is false **do**
19:        **for all** $a \in \mathcal{A}$ **do**
20:            t $\leftarrow$ a.getSelectionStrategy().selectTarget()
21:            a.getUpdateStrategy().updatePheromones(t)
22:        **for all** $a \in \mathcal{A}$ **do**
23:            a.evaporatePheromones(evaporationRate)

---

such that $\forall a' \in \mathcal{A} \backslash (\mathcal{N}_a \cup \{a\}), i \in \{1, \ldots, j\} : \delta_c(a', a) \geq \delta_c(b_i, a)$. *By definition,* $\mathcal{N}_a$ *does not contain agent a itself.*

The single neighborhoods form a (l, k)-communication graph such as the one shown in Fig. 1(b).

The *second phase* causes each agent to search for targets located within the maximum view range of its sonar sensor. Agents assign themselves to the nearest sensed target, or, if no target was found, wait for phase three or four to begin.

Target perceiving agents are initiators of the *third phase*. Within this phase an initial network of pheromone traces is established. A pheromone trace belongs to a specified initiator and thus to a unique target. The initial network is created as follows. Each initiator broadcasts a message to all its neighbors which in turn retransmit that message until a specified hop counter value is exceeded. Like in distance vector routing protocols (compare e.g. AODV [19]), these messages are used to create route table entries pointing towards the initiator of a trace. The pheromone concentration of an entry decreases with increasing number of hops to the initiator. If an agent already owns a pheromone entry for the same target with a higher pheromone concentration then the message is discarded. Otherwise, a new trace is created or the existing updated. It is important to point out that initial traces may not reach all agents, since the reachability highly depends on

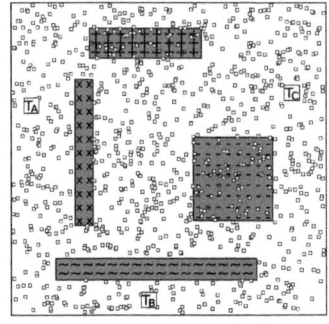
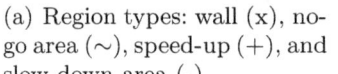
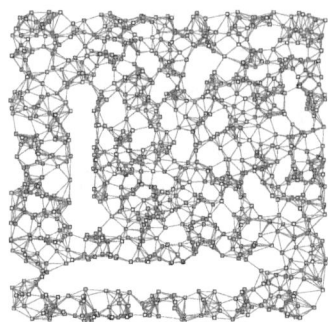

(a) Region types: wall (x), no-   (b) Exemplary communica-
go area ($\sim$), speed-up (+), and   tion graph structure.
slow-down area (-).

Fig. 1. Example scenario

the chosen parameters and the dimensions of the system. Thus, the fourth phase should ensure growing traces.

The *fourth and last phase* of the algorithm is executed repeatedly until a stopping criterion is true. We decided that this stopping condition is true after a certain number of iterations. A single iteration of phase four involves three steps. First, agents select targets based on local (pheromone) information using a *target selection strategy*. Second, the pheromones are updated according to a given *pheromone update strategy*. Third, the artificial pheromones evaporate over time using a constant factor chosen from $[0, 1)$. Due to this evaporation, pheromones on unused traces will diminish, while those on frequently selected trails grow if they are renewed through the update strategy.

It is important that once existing traces are not completely removed from the system since a removal may lead to problems when an update to an entire trace towards a particular initiator has to be performed. Due to this, and since we want to avoid arbitrary large and thus extremely dominating pheromone traces, we enforce each pheromone concentration p to be within a predefined range $(p_{min} \leq p \leq p_{max})$.

Pheromone update strategies are responsible for the emergence of appropriate pheromone traces and thus directly influence the solution quality. In an optimal case, an update procedure should evaluate the current solution and locally update pheromones based on the actual solution quality. This, however, implies a central instance — or at least massive data exchange.

We implemented three different update and selection strategies. The *Pure-Pheromone-Strategy (PPS)* is an approach that bases the target selection only on pheromone information. It locally applies negative feedback to all unselected traces and positive feedback to the entire selected trace down to the initiator. The *Distribution-Pheromone-Dominating-Strategy (DPD)* selects a target based on target recommendations of neighbored agents if there are no pheromone information available. Trace initiators maintain a counter indicating the number of agents that choose the corresponding trace. This value is used by the strategy to determine whether or not the selected target was a good choice regarding the *distribution* objective. Thus, the pheromones are updated according to an assumed distribution. The *Random-Pheromone-Dominating-Strategy (RPD)* strategy also bases its target selection on pheromones or advices but updates the pheromones using a random update factor from [0.9, 1.1]. Details on the strategies and analyses on their message complexity can be found in [14].

3.1   Influence of Communication Graph Structures

In this section we show the influence of communication graph structures to the applicability of pheromone-based approaches. Figure 2(a) shows an optimal solution for an exemplary scenario. The underlying communication graph is based on a (l, k)-neighborhood with $l = k = 2$. We assume that the pheromone traces grow by at least one agent in every iteration.

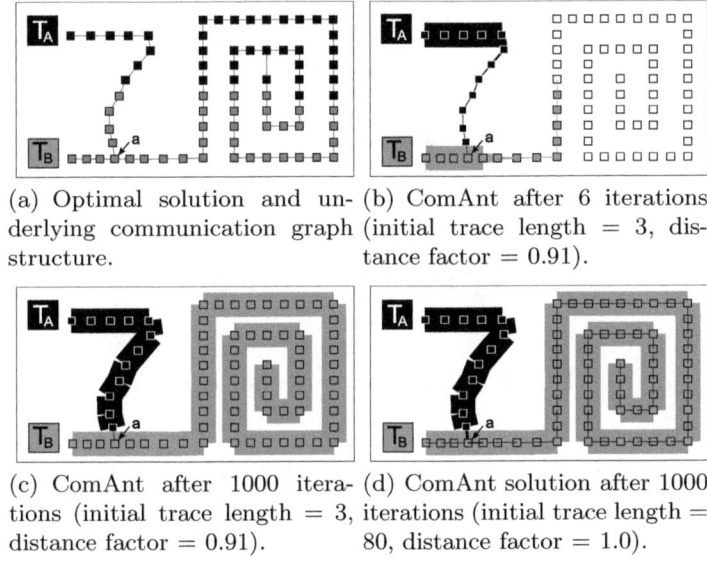

(a) Optimal solution and underlying communication graph structure.

(b) ComAnt after 6 iterations (initial trace length = 3, distance factor = 0.91).

(c) ComAnt after 1000 iterations (initial trace length = 3, distance factor = 0.91).

(d) ComAnt solution after 1000 iterations (initial trace length = 80, distance factor = 1.0).

Fig. 2. Pheromone development on paths restricted by communication structures

Figure 2(b) shows a situation in which the pheromone trace of target T_A reaches agent a several iterations after the trace of T_B. Note that besides agent distribution as in the example, obstacles which are not penetrable like e.g. walls also influence communication graph structures. Consequently, pheromone traces have to surround these obstacles from which follows that it takes more time for them to reach opposed agents. Hence, situations in which a trace reaches a certain agent some time after another trace are very likely to occur in real scenarios with obstacles.

In pheromone-based algorithms, decisions generally are based on the available pheromone concentrations: the higher the concentration, the higher the probability of being selected. As Fig. 2(b) already indicates, the probability for agent a to choose the lately arriving trace thus will be small. Figures 2(c) and 2(d) show that the probability of agent a to select T_A is that low that its pheromones, even after 1000 iterations, are unable to "grow" into T_B's trace. The remainder of this section is used to provide a mathematical analysis of the probability that the lately arriving trace grows into the older one.

Figure 3 shows a schematical representation of this situation. Let us assume an initial trace length $h = 2$ and $h \ll p$, p denoting the number of hops required for trace T_A to reach agent a. Then T_B's trace is available on a directly after the initial pheromone network is established. In contrast, T_A's trace requires $p - h$ iterations until it finally reaches agent a. In each of these $p - h$ iterations T_B's trace, however, can grow by at least one agent. Since a trace is updated by each agent that selects it, pheromone concentrations grow exponentially on agent a for target T_B because all agents a_i right to a select T_B. The reason for this is, that they do not know about A's existence in the beginning. Consequently, the pheromone concentration of T_B at a is reinforced exponentially and continuously, whereas the one of T_A remains unset (i.e. is 0).

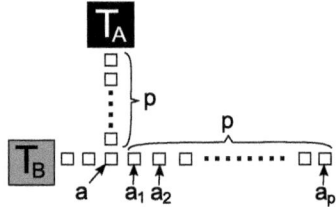

Fig. 3. Schematical problem description

Let $pc_j(a, T)$ denote the pheromone concentration on agent a for target $T \in \{T_A, T_B\}$ at iteration j. c denotes the initial concentration of a trace on an agent that is just connected to the pheromone network, and $f > 1$ is a positive feedback factor used for updating the pheromones. Without loss of generality, we neglect pheromone evaporation and allow unlimited large/small pheromone concentrations to simplify the following explanations.

In the beginning, we start with $pc_0(a, T_A) = 0$ and $pc_0(a, T_B) = c$, since $h = 2$ and $h \ll p$. After the first iteration, it holds that $pc_1(a, T_B) = pc_0(a, T_B) \cdot f$ and $pc_1(a, T_A) = 0$ since a's only choice was T_B. Thus, a updates its pheromone concentration for T_B and expands the pheromone trace to agent a_1. After the second iteration, it holds that $pc_2(a, T_B) = pc_1(a, T_B) \cdot f \cdot f$ since a's and a_1's only choices are to select T_B. Due to the update mechanism down to the initiator, both update the pheromones on a using f. T_B's trace is expanded to a_2. For the third iteration $pc_3(a, T_B) = pc_2(a, T_B) \cdot f \cdot f \cdot f$ follows, since a_1, a_2, as well as a itself select target T_B and so on.

Hence, T_B's pheromone concentration on agent a after the j-th iteration ($0 \le j \le p - h$) follows by Equation (2):

$$
\begin{aligned}
pc_j(a, T_B) &= pc_{j-1}(a, T_B) \cdot f^j \\
&= pc_{j-2}(a, T_B) \cdot f^{j-1} \cdot f^j \\
&= \dots \\
&= pc_0(a, T_B) \cdot f \cdot f^2 \cdot f^3 \cdot \dots \cdot f^{j-1} \cdot f^j \\
&= c \cdot f^{\sum_{\ell=1}^{j} \ell}
\end{aligned}
\tag{2}
$$

After $p - h$ iterations, T_A's trace will reach a. Then, $pc_{p-h}(a, T_A) = c$ holds by definition. According to the explanations above, for T_B's pheromones on a $pc_{p-h}(a, T_B) = c \cdot f^{\sum_{\ell=1}^{p-h} \ell}$ follows. In iteration $p - h + 1$ agent a has to decide between both targets for the first time. Remember that the decision is based on the available pheromone concentrations and that high concentrations are more likely to be chosen. Since proportional selection techniques well reflect this property, we decided to use the *roulette wheel selection* that belongs to this class of techniques [20]. Note that other proportional selection techniques could be used as well.

The following equation calculates the probability that agent a chooses target T_A, whereas α is a parameter that influences the selection procedure:

$$
Pr(\tau(a) = T_A) = \frac{pc_{p-h+1}(a, A)^\alpha}{pc_{p-h+1}(a, A)^\alpha + pc_{p-h+1}(a, B)^\alpha} = \frac{1}{1 + f^{\alpha \cdot \sum_{\ell=1}^{p-h+1} \ell}}
\tag{3}
$$

On the other hand, T_B is selected with a probability of

$$
Pr(\tau(a) = T_B) = \frac{pc_{p-h+1}(a, B)^\alpha}{pc_{p-h+1}(a, A)^\alpha + pc_{p-h+1}(a, B)^\alpha} = \frac{f^{\alpha \cdot \sum_{\ell=1}^{p-h+1} \ell}}{1 + f^{\alpha \cdot \sum_{\ell=1}^{p-h+1} \ell}}
\tag{4}
$$

For fixed h and large p we get $\lim_{p \to \infty} Pr(\tau(a) = T_A) = 0$ and $\lim_{p \to \infty} Pr(\tau(a) = T_B) = 1$. Consequently it follows, that T_A's trace will reach agents $a_i, 1 \le i \le p$, with a *very* small probability, only. Note that if T_A's traces manages to reach agent a_1, say in iteration j, then per definition $pc_j(a_1, T_A) = c$ holds. Consequently, a_1 will be faced to the same probability ratios as just described for agent a. In general, we conclude, that the limit of the probability $Pr(\text{"all agents to the right of } a \text{ have pheromones for } T_A \text{ in iteration } j\text{"})$ as j approaches ∞ is 0.

To put it in other words, agents are unable to switch a once established trace in favor of a new arriving one. This observation is supported by Goss *et al.* [21] who calls this effect the *"irreversible nature of the positive feedback process"*.

3.2   Non-optimality

Again, we use the example shown in Fig. 2 to prove the non-optimality of the ComAnt algorithm. In our understanding, an algorithm is *non-optimal* if there are scenarios in which it is unable to find an optimal solution.

The goal of the ComAnt algorithm is to solve the GOPP using *adequate* pheromone traces. These traces are constrained to follow the underlying communication graph. According to the natural model, adequate traces should emerge during the runtime. For the given example (Fig. 2), we thus expect final pheromones as sketched in Fig. 4(a) and 4(b), since they would result in an optimal solution as calculated by the TTO approach (compare Fig. 2(a)).

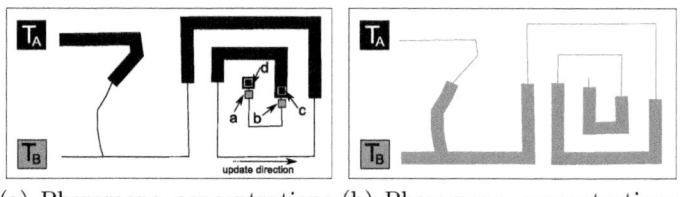

(a) Pheromone concentrations for T_A.   (b) Pheromone concentrations for T_B.

Fig. 4. Expected, optimal pheromone concentrations

Next, we prove that it is impossible for two neighbored agents b and c, as shown in Fig. 4(a), to select different targets with a probability of 1 each. In this proof, c_p denotes the pheromone concentration on an agent when it gets connected to the pheromone network. Furthermore, n is the number of agents (including a and b) that constitute the path between a and b. We consider a single iteration of the ComAnt approach. According to the assumed traces, agents d and c should select target T_A, whereas the n agents which connect a and b should select T_B. These choices are rewarded by a positive update factor $f > 1$. Due to the pheromone update down to an initiator, the pheromone concentrations will develop as follows. On the one hand, the pheromone concentration $pc(c, T_A)$ is updated only twice since solely agents d and c select target T_A's trace. On the other hand, $pc(c, T_B)$ is updated n times using f. Accordingly, we obtain $pc(c, T_A) = c_p \cdot f^2$ and $pc(c, T_B) = c_p \cdot f^n$, as well as $pc(b, T_A) = c_p \cdot f$ and $pc(b, T_B) = c_p \cdot f^n$. Using the roulette wheel selection, b and c will select T_A with a probability of 0 and T_B with a probability of 1 for large n as Equations (5)-(7) show.

$$Pr(\tau(b) = T_A) = \lim_{n \to \infty} \frac{(c_p \cdot f)^\alpha}{(c_p \cdot f)^\alpha + (c_p \cdot f^n)^\alpha} = 0 \tag{5}$$

$$Pr(\tau(c) = T_A) = \lim_{n \to \infty} \frac{(c_p \cdot f^2)^\alpha}{(c_p \cdot f^2)^\alpha + (c_p \cdot f^n)^\alpha} = 0 \tag{6}$$

$$Pr(\tau(b) = T_B) = \lim_{n \to \infty} \frac{(c_p \cdot f^n)^\alpha}{(c_p \cdot f^2)^\alpha + (c_p \cdot f^n)^\alpha} = 1 \tag{7}$$
$$= Pr(\tau(c) = T_B)$$

This, however, is a contradiction to the assumption that b and c are able to choose different targets. Consequently, it follows that c selects the same target

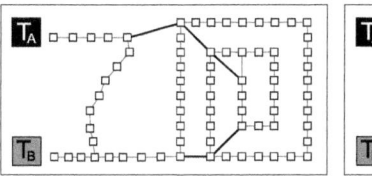 

(a) Different communication graph.

(b) Pheromone distribution required by an optimal solution.

Fig. 5. Different communication graph structure

as b and thus, over time, others than the required pheromones for an optimal solution will emerge. Figures 2(c) and 2(d) show exemplary pheromone results.

Note that the presented properties are independent from the pheromone update strategy, since the latter is only used to determine the update factor which is applied to the entire trace. Accordingly, no pheromone update strategy can guarantee optimal solutions for all possible scenarios. Hence, the non-optimality of the ComAnt algorithm in the proposed and implemented form follows.

Figure 5(a) sketches a communication graph which would enable the ComAnt approach to find an optimal solution for the considered example since proper pheromones may emerge as illustrated in Fig. 5(b).

4   Simulation Results

We simulated the ComAnt algorithm using the three abovementioned strategies DPD, PPS, RPD and compared the results to those of the Chainmail Strategy (CMS), the modified Exchange Target Strategy (ETS_m), as well as to the optimal solution calculated by the Two Target Optimal (TTO) approach. Note that both, CMS and TTO, in the implemented form can only be applied to scenarios with two targets. The simulations have been performed on four scenarios (S1-S4) with 3000 randomly distributed agents. All scenarios contain one speed-up, one slow-down, one no-go area, and one wall which all have random dimensions and are located at random positions. Scenarios S1 and S2 both contain two targets, scenarios S3 and S4 both contain three targets. In S1 and S3 the targets are positioned randomly, while the targets in S2 are located in the top left and bottom right corner of the system and the three targets in S4 constitute a triangle in the middle of the system. We chose these scenarios to demonstrate the importance of non-interfering pheromone traces. The fourth phase of the ComAnt algorithm is executed 12 times and uses a pheromone evaporation rate of 0.95. CMS iterates 13 times and ETS_m 100 times. All algorithms use a (l, k)-neighborhood with $l = 6, k = 8$. Furthermore we chose $\alpha = \beta = \gamma = 0.3333$ for the objective function specified in Equation (1). Since TTO is a central instance approach, no costs are produced. Hence, we set $\alpha = \beta = 0.5, \gamma = 0$ for TTO. Each scenario was simulated 30 times for each algorithm.

Table 1. Simulation results

Scenario	Algorithm	f	var(f)	distance	costs	distribution
1	CMS	0.9581	1e-04	0.9619	0.9125	1.0000
	DPD	0.9492	0.0009	0.9565	0.9871	0.9039
	PPS	0.9507	0.0013	0.9834	0.9872	0.8817
	RPD	0.9482	0.0013	0.9757	0.9872	0.8818
	ETS_m	0.9838	1e-04	0.9522	0.9997	0.9997
	TTO	0.9850	2e-04	0.9766	-	0.9935
2	CMS	0.9703	2e-06	0.9983	0.9126	1.0000
	DPD	0.9918	1e-05	0.9932	0.9871	0.9953
	PPS	0.9792	1e-05	0.9544	0.9872	0.9961
	RPD	0.9920	1e-05	0.9929	0.9872	0.9960
	ETS_m	0.9986	2e-06	0.9965	0.9997	0.9997
	TTO	0.9994	3e-06	0.9990	-	0.9997
3	DPD	0.9042	0.0024	0.8985	0.9871	0.8269
	PPS	0.9070	0.0038	0.9643	0.9872	0.7694
	RPD	0.9027	0.0030	0.9395	0.9872	0.7813
	ETS_m	0.9752	3e-04	0.9270	0.9996	0.9991
4	DPD	0.9343	3e-05	0.8295	0.9872	0.9861
	PPS	0.9799	9e-06	0.9661	0.9872	0.9864
	RPD	0.9605	1e-05	0.9073	0.9872	0.9869
	ETS_m	0.9830	5e-05	0.9504	0.9996	0.9992

Table 1 lists average values of the obtained results and the variance of f for all four scenarios. The results show that all algorithms are able to produce high quality solutions ($f \geq 0.95$) for the two target case, but perform worse for three targets. In S2, DPD and RPD produce almost optimal solutions. Beside of scenario S4, the variances of the ComAnt strategies are higher compared to the other approaches. Furthermore, the results in Table 1 show that the objective function value for the ComAnt strategies is between 3% (PPS, 2 targets) and 8,04% (PPS, 3 targets) better in scenarios with fixed target positions compared to scenarios with random target positions. Moreover, the variance in the scenarios with fixed positions (S2,S4) is lower than in the random scenarios(S1,S3).

The reason for these results can be found in the way how the target positions were selected. In detail, these positions in S2 and S4 were chosen such that the corresponding target pheromones should be able to grow without interfering each other and hence avoiding the effects described in Sect. 3.1. The random alignment, however, may result in situations where the targets are located nearby each other. In such cases, the pheromones interfere and the strongest trace in terms of pheromone concentration will distract the others from adequate growth. According to Sect. 3.2, the two obstacles (wall and no-go area) influence the communication graph structure and thus further influence the growth of pheromones such that the approach is unable to find better solutions in S1 and S3. All ComAnt strategies are more cost-efficient than CMS since the latter repeatedly broadcasts very large messages which results in high communication costs. ETS produces the smallest costs and calculates the best solutions.

5   Conclusion and Future Work

Based on the question how to establish organizations or groups of agents in a decentralized manner, in order to enable the agents to solve problems which involve groups, we introduced and formalized the General Online Partitioning Problem (GOPP). We presented a pheromone-based approach called ComAnt to solve the GOPP. The simulations showed that the algorithm is able to create groups of almost the same size in scenarios with obstacles and special regions. The proposed approach also adequately solves the additional constraints (cost-efficiency and distance minimization) demanded by the GOPP and thus is able to produce high quality solutions on average.

However, we also identified and analyzed situations where the approach does not perform well. We proved that the solution quality of the underlying mechanism using different types of pheromones depends on the communication graph structure of the agents. We showed that pheromones of different types cannot break into already established structures due to the probabilities resulting from proportional selection techniques.

As future work, we plan to evaluate scenarios with more than three targets and update strategies based on internal agent states. Currently, we are developing an hierarchy-based approach inspired by dominance fights in wasp societies to solve the GOPP. Preliminary results are almost optimal for two but worse for three targets.

References

1. Kasbekar, G.S., Kuri, J., Nuggehalli, P.: Online association policies in IEEE 802.11 WLANs. In: 4th International Symposium on Modeling and Optimization in Mobile, Ad Hoc and Wireless Networks, pp. 1–10. IEEE, Los Alamitos (2006)
2. Bejerano, Y., Han, S.J., Li, L.E.: Fairness and load balancing in wireless LANs using association control. In: Proceedings of the 10th Annual International Conference on Mobile Computing and Networking, pp. 315–329. ACM, New York (2004)
3. Kube, C.R., Zhang, H.: Collective robotics: From social insects to robots. Adaptive Behavior 2(2), 189–218 (1993)
4. Groß, R., Dorigo, M.: Cooperative transport of objects of different shapes and sizes. In: Dorigo, M., Birattari, M., Blum, C., Gambardella, L.M., Mondada, F., Stützle, T. (eds.) ANTS 2004. LNCS, vol. 3172, pp. 106–117. Springer, Heidelberg (2004)
5. Groß, R., Dorigo, M.: Evolving a cooperative transport behavior for two simple robots. In: Liardet, P., Collet, P., Fonlupt, C., Lutton, E., Schoenauer, M. (eds.) EA 2003. LNCS, vol. 2936, pp. 305–316. Springer, Heidelberg (2004)
6. Groß, R., Dorigo, M.: Group transport of an object to a target that only some group members may sense. In: Yao, X., Burke, E.K., Lozano, J.A., Smith, J., Merelo-Guervós, J.J., Bullinaria, J.A., Rowe, J.E., Tiňo, P., Kabán, A., Schwefel, H.-P. (eds.) PPSN 2004. LNCS, vol. 3242, pp. 852–861. Springer, Heidelberg (2004)
7. Groß, R., Tuci, E., Dorigo, M., Bonani, M., Mondada, F.: Object transport by modular robots that self-assemble. In: Proceedings of the 2006 IEEE International Conference on Robotics and Automation, pp. 2558–2564. IEEE Computer Society Press, Los Alamitos (2006)

8. Dias, M.B., Zlot, R., Kalra, N., Stentz, A.: Market-based multirobot coordination: A survey and analysis. Proceedings of the IEEE 94(7), 1257–1270 (2006)

9. Koenig, S., Tovey, C.A., Lagoudakis, M.G., Markakis, E., Kempe, D., Keskinocak, P., Kleywegt, A.J., Meyerson, A., Jain, S.: The power of sequential single-item auctions for agent coordination. In: Proceedings of the 21st National Conference on Artificial Intelligence, pp. 1625–1629. AAAI Press, Menlo Park (2006)

10. Koenig, S., Zheng, X., Tovey, C.A., Borie, R., Kilby, P., Markakis, V., Keskinocak, P.: Agent coordination with regret clearing. In: Proceedings of the 23rd National Conference on Artificial Intelligence, pp. 101–107. AAAI Press, Menlo Park (2008)

11. Goebels, A.: Agent Coordination Mechanisms for Solving a Partitioning Task. PhD thesis, University of Paderborn (2006)

12. Goebels, A., Kleine Büning, H., Priesterjahn, S., Weimer, A.: Multi target partitioning of sets based on local information. In: Abraham, A., Dote, Y., Furuhashi, T., Köppen, M., Ohuchi, A., Ohsawa, Y. (eds.) WSTST. Advances in Soft Computing, vol. 29, pp. 1309–1318. Springer, Heidelberg (2005)

13. Goebels, A., Kleine Büning, H., Priesterjahn, S., Weimer, A.: Towards online partitioning of agent sets based on local information. In: Fahringer, T., Hamza, M.H. (eds.) Parallel and Distributed Computing and Networks, pp. 674–679. IASTED/ACTA Press (2005)

14. Kemmerich, T.: Algorithms for the general online partitioning problem. Master's thesis, University of Paderborn (2008)

15. Wehe, B.: Verfahren zur Partitionierung von Multi-Agentensystemen in Szenarien mit Hindernissen. Diploma thesis, University of Paderborn (2008)

16. Šimunić, T., Benini, L., De Micheli, G.: Cycle-accurate simulation of energy consumption in embedded systems. In: Proceedings of the 36th annual ACM/IEEE Design Automation Conference, pp. 867–872. ACM, New York (1999)

17. Mei, Y., Lu, Y.H., Hu, Y.C., Lee, C.G.: A case study of mobile robot's energy consumption and conservation techniques. In: IEEE International Conference on Advanced Robotics, pp. 492–497 (2005)

18. Mitchell, J.S.B., Papadimitriou, C.H.: The weighted region problem: finding shortest paths through a weighted planar subdivision. J. ACM 38(1), 18–73 (1991)

19. Perkins, C.E., Royer, E.M.: Ad-hoc on-demand distance vector routing. In: Proceedings of the 2nd IEEE Workshop on Mobile Computing Systems and Applications, pp. 90–100. IEEE Computer Society Press, Los Alamitos (1999)

20. Engelbrecht, A.P.: Fundamentals of Computational Swarm Intelligence. Wiley, Chichester (2005)

21. Goss, S., Aron, S., Deneubourg, J.L., Pasteels, J.M.: Self-organized shortcuts in the argentine ant. Naturwissenschaften 76, 579–581 (1989)

An Infection-Based Mechanism in Large Convention Spaces

Norman Salazar, Juan A. Rodriguez-Aguilar, and Josep Ll. Arcos

IIIA, Artificial Intelligence Research Institute
CSIC, Spanish National Research Council
{norman,jar,arcos}iiia.csic.es

Abstract. Regulating the behavior of autonomous agents is necessary to solve coordination problems and minimize conflicts in multi-agent systems (MAS). It is well known that in practice centralized approaches are not viable to accomplish this. Thus, distributed regulating mechanisms, such as mechanisms for the emergence of social conventions, are highly needed. Nevertheless, existing studies have not focused on determining how the size of the convention space may influence the emergence of conventions. To that end in this paper we apply a mechanism for the distributed, dynamic emergence of social conventions, to a problem with a large convention space: finding a common vocabulary (lexicon) for the agents of a MAS that allows them to perfectly communicate with neither ambiguity nor inconsistencies. Therefore, we empirically show that the mechanism can cope with large convention spaces.

1 Introduction

Regulating the behavior of autonomous agents in multi-agent systems (MAS) to improve its overall performance and effectiveness is a current subject of interest. In particular, to solve coordination problems and minimize conflicts. It is well known that centralized techniques that depend on global knowledge have become a less than viable approach to accomplish this. Therefore, distributed mechanisms have become highly desirable. In particular, those that coordinate the agents in a MAS through social conventions.

It has been argued that the space of alternative behaviors (or convention space) is an important factor in the outcome of convention problems [8]. In other words, the number of possible conventions the agents can establish may influence the emerging convention(s) (if any). Therefore, mechanisms must be able to cope with convention spaces of different sizes.

In [15,14], Salazar et al. propose, with some success, an evolutionary computing mechanism based on the notion of social contagion to dynamically emerge social conventions, the so-called *infection-based mechanism* (IBM). Nevertheless, their experiments are limited to study cases where the space of conventions agents can reach is somewhat small. With this in mind, this paper focuses on validating the IBM by evaluating it in large convention spaces. To this aim,

J. Padget et al. (Eds.): COIN 2009, LNAI 6069, pp. 273–288, 2010.

we have selected language conventions as our case study domain because: (i) it provides large convention spaces; and (ii) it is a relevant problem for MAS.

In multi-agent systems (MAS), communication is a key factor for agents to successfully interact with each other. In particular, when agents rely on explicit communication, a *shared language or vocabulary* (i.e. communication system) is highly necessary. Nevertheless, in open, heterogeneous MAS, where no central authority exists, such language may not exist. Since no one enforces a common language, agents may have their own, limiting their successful interactions to agents with a similar or the same language (if any exists).

In such MAS, agents may use different terms to refer to the same concept, or may use the same term to refer to different concepts, creating ambiguities in their communications. Therefore, a mechanism that allows agents to distributedly reach language conventions (consensus) that improve their communications is highly desirable. Furthermore, in an open MAS, establishing conventions with an *offline* process may not be reliable. Because, the MAS conditions can change with time (e.g. the number of agents, their objectives, the environment). Hence, the need for a mechanism that allows agents to reach language conventions at the same time they normally operate to achieve their (individual) goals.

From the social sciences perspective, language establishment is a highly studied topic [2,11]. It has been argued that languages are established as a form of a social convention, thus the relationship between a word and a concept is dependent on the interactions between individuals. Several studies have addressed the modeling of such interactions as language games between individuals [12] [4], with various levels of success. These games model language construction at a purely semiotic level, i.e. they neglect the semantic relationships between models and symbols. A common game to study conventionalization is the *naming game* [18]. This game focuses on the interactions of speakers and listeners that try to find names for objects to understand each other. Thus, the aim of the naming game is to study how a common lexicon (vocabulary) is established in a society. Thus, for our purposes we apply this notions from a MAS perspective.

With the purpose of studying different types of large convention spaces, we evaluate two different cases. Firstly, the one created by having the same number of names and concepts (objects). This scenario, is likely to exhibit ambiguity (also called specificity) because there is a high probability that agents assign the same name to different objects. Thus, it represents a behavior space with small number of desired conventions (with respect to the number of possible ones). Secondly, if the number of names is (relatively) much larger than the number of objects, ambiguity may be less likely to occur, but conventions may be harder to reach, since the space of possibilities is larger.

Several studies show that the social structure of a population affects how a language emerges [13,6,10]. This motivates that we further explore how different complex networks, such as small-world [19] and scale-free [1], as underlying topologies of our MAS may influence the adaptation mechanism.

In this paper, as stated above, we propose applying the infection-based mechanism as a distributed adaptation mechanism to engineer the emergence of lexicon conventions in a MAS. Firstly, we model agents' communication interactions as a particular type of naming game. To that end, we base ourselves on the model proposed in [9]. Next, we use the IBM to provide lexicon adoption and adaption. Lastly, we empirically show that thanks to such distributed adaptation mechanism, agents in an open MAS distributedly manage to reach a common lexicon. Furthermore, the emergent lexicon provides the MAS with a so-called, *perfect communication system* [9]. Consequently, this also shows the usefulness of the infection-based mechanism in large convention spaces.

Additionally, we analyze the robustness of the approach in dynamical settings, by allowing new agents to join a MAS at any time and by dynamically changing its interaction topology. Incoming agents are equipped with their own lexicon, which may be different to the one the agents in the MAS have already agreed upon (if any). Thus, we observe that despite changes in the population our adaptation mechanism leads the agents in an open MAS to adapt to the existing lexicon conventions or not.

To summarize, the contributions of this paper are: (1) we show how to successfully apply the IBM to emerge communication in an open MAS; (2) we propose a MAS communication model based on the naming-game; (3) we empirically show that the IBM can cope with large convention spaces; and (4) we empirically show that thanks to IBM a consensus on a single, globally-shared lexicon is feasible despite the interaction topology and dynamic changes.

The paper is organized as follows. Section 2 characterizes an open MAS and defines the communication model agents employ to interact. Section 3 briefly reviews the infection-based mechanism [14] and discusses its application to our problem. Section 4 presents some empirical evaluations. Finally, in section 5 we draw some conclusions and set paths to future research.

2   The Communication Model

In this section we define and characterize the communication model that the agents employ to interact between themselves. We based the model on a well studied one, the *naming game*. Therefore, the first part of the section focuses on describing such game, as well as its shortcomings (from our perspective) if used in MAS. Whereas, the second part proposes a communication model to overcome the identified shortcoming.

The naming game [18] is one of the most used models for studying language evolution. This game consists of two agents, a speaker who utters the name of an object, and a listener who must understand it. Thus, a game is successful if the listener can understand the speaker. Moreover, the game is considered as adaptive if speaker and hearer manage to increase the success of their communications through repeated interactions.

Even though this kind of game is mostly used in linguistics to understand the principles of language evolution [12], it can be highly useful in open MAS for agents to agree upon the lexicon to share. Therefore, in a broad sense it can be regarded as a model for ontology sharing [17]. Nevertheless, currently the most

common formulation of the naming game presents some impractical characteristics to make it useful for open MAS. First of all, it allows agents to create any
word to refer to a particular object, which may be unrealistic in MAS since the
number of concepts to name can most likely be bounded beforehand. Secondly,
it allows the existence of multiple words to refer to the very same object (synonymy), which may cause ambiguities or inconsistencies in the communication
between agents. Moreover, the predominant naming-game formulation makes no
distinction between the communication model and the communication development (language acquisition) algorithm, (i.e. they are inter-wove).

To take into account the above-mentioned issues, we propose a communication model based on the one described by De Jong et al. in [7]. De Jong's model
borrows some of the notions of the naming game and defines them for a MAS.
Moreover, it makes a distinction between the interaction model and the communication development algorithm. Nevertheless, it still considers word creation.
Therefore, we propose to replace word creation with a word selection (from a
finite set), similar to a not commonly used variation of the naming game presented in [16]. Henceforth, we shall refer to this communication model as the
name-matching game, whose mechanics we describe in what follows.

We shall consider an open MAS composed of a set of autonomous agents,
Ag. No central authority exists to rule the agents and agents only work with
local knowledge. Each agent, $ag_i \in Ag$ knows a set of concepts (be them, for
instance, object, topics, actions) O, which it employs to communicate with the
other agents in the MAS. Some or all concepts can be shared between different
agents. We also consider that all agents share a finite set of words, W, which they
employ to refer to the concepts they use. Thus, agents interact with each other by
exchanging messages composed of words from W. To facilitate communication
among agents, each agent has a lexicon, $L_i : O \rightarrow W$, which assigns an external
representation to the concepts it needs to employ. Thus, each agent uses its own
lexicon L_i to find the appropriate word that represents the concept about which
it wants to communicate. Moreover, we restrict the lexicon in such a manner
that only one entry per concept is permitted. Hence, it is not possible to assign
more than one word per concept (synonymy). Finally, the decoding function,
$D_i : W \rightarrow 2^O$, is used to translate a given word to its related concept.

The convention space of this problem, C, stands for the set that contains all
possible agent language conventions. For the sake of simplicity we shall measure
its size as the number of possible lexicons to which all agents may agree to at
one point, namely $|C| = |W|^{|O|}$. Notice that this is a lower bound since it only
considers conventions in which all agents share the same lexicon.

Additionally, we consider that interactions among agents in a MAS are restricted by an interaction topology. We model an interaction topology as a graph
(Ag, E), where $E \subseteq Ag \times Ag$, whose edges correspond to relationships (neighborhoods) between agents. If $(ag_i, ag_j) \in E$, then ag_i and ag_j are neighbors,
and thus they can interact with each other. Since the kind of MAS we consider
is open (agents join or leave at will), interaction topologies may change with
time. Specifically, interactions between agents are pair-wise. Each interaction is a

communication between an agent playing the role of *speaker*, $s \in Ag$, and another one playing the role of *hearer*, $h \in Ag$, relating to a certain concept, $o \in O_s$.

Given some interaction topology, each agent uses the words in its lexicon to build messages that exchanges with its neighboring agents. The recipient of an agent's message may understand a message or not. This directly depends on the degree of agreement on the lexicons of sender and receiver. Overall, the higher the agreement on lexicons, the higher the number of successful interactions (and hence the lower the amount of misunderstandings).

In a MAS context, this interaction framework models various communication situations, in particular petitions. For example, an agent s (speaker) requiring an object available to an agent h (hearer), requesting a service or task, sending instructions, etc. Within this setting, communication is successful if agent s obtains the object or service it requires; or if it perceives that agent h soundly performs the requested task or some instruction. In other words, the game is successful if both agents can match the same word to the same concept.

To summarize, the mechanics of the game that we propose are as follows: (1) Agent s selects a concept, $o_s \in O_s$; (2) Agent s uses its lexicon, L_s, to find the word, w, that refers to o_s; (3) Agent s communicates w to agent h; (4) Agent h uses its decoding function, D_h, to interpret w into a concept $o_h \in O_h$; (5) Agent h responds according to its understanding of o_h; and (6) The game is successful if s is satisfied by h's response (i.e. if $o_s = o_h$).

Our aim will be that agents achieve a so-called perfect communication system [7], where the lexicon mappings between words and concepts are one-to-one. Thus, as with synonymy, a desirable lexicon should not exhibit polysemy (i.e. same word for multiple concepts). The presence of polysemy increases the possibility of *ambiguousness* in the message interpretation of the hearer agent. If a particular agent's lexicon, assigns the same word to two (or more) concepts, at the moment of decoding a message relating to this word, the hearer will have trouble deciding which concept the word refers to. In MAS communications, the specificity of a word quantifies the degree to which it identifies a single concept (the higher the specificity the less ambiguous the word). Thus, from here on we shall measure the specificity of a lexicon as the percentage of words in the lexicon with specificity equal to one. Therefore, a lexicon with 100% of specificity represents a lexicon with one-to-one mappings guaranteeing perfect communication.

Now observe that the ratio between the number of available words ($|W|$) and concepts ($|O|$) to the agents in the MAS depicts scenarios with different degrees of specificity. Hence, if $|W| < |O|$ we obtain games where full understanding (a perfect communication system) is impossible because ambiguity is unavoidable (a 100% lexicon specificity cannot occur). If $|W| = |O|$, ambiguity is likely to happen, but lexicons with a 100% specificity are feasible. Thus, for a large enough number of concepts, the resulting convention space C is large, namely $|C| = |W|^{|O|}$. Nevertheless, only a small number of desirable conventions exist. Finally, when $|W| > |O|$ we obtain games where the likelihood to present ambiguity is low, but where misunderstandings are possible because of different lexicons naming the same object with different words. Moreover, if $|W|$ is considerably large then the resulting convention space is also considerable large.

Notice that the proposed communication model solves to some extent the above-mentioned impracticalities by: i)bounding the number of available words to a particular set; ii) preventing synonymy through lexicon restrictions; and iii) decoupling the communication development algorithm from the communication model. Therefore, the remaining issue to deal with is polysemy. We tackle this issue with the aid of the communication development algorithm, whose aim will be to emerge a common lexicon with high specificity. The next section presents the algorithm we employ to accomplish this aim.

3   IBM for Communication Development

As noticed above, our main goal is to engineer the emergence of desirable lexicon conventions in an open, dynamic MAS. To succeed in this endeavor, we must guarantee that the agents in the MAS converge to a common lexicon. Not only that, because we pursue that convergence occurs despite changes in the agent population caused by the openness of a MAS. Therefore, we aim at endowing a MAS (section 2) with a distributed, adaptive mechanism that ensures a continuous convergence to a common lexicon despite changes in the agent population, hence promoting the development of a common communication system.

In what follows we propose to apply the infection-based mechanism described by Salazar et al. in [15] as a mechanism that promotes communication development. Furthermore, we also discuss how to deploy the infection-based model in an open MAS since it is an issue which is not tackled in [15].

The IBM is a distributed evolutionary algorithm that allows agents in a MAS to self-regulate through the collective emergence of social conventions. It is based on the social phenomenon of social-contagion [5], which relates to the spreading of behaviors/knowledge between individuals akin to an infectious disease.

However, the IBM considers the notion of *positive infection*: agents with *good behaviors / knowledge* that help improve the social welfare become more infectious to spread their behaviors (knowledge). In the context of our problem, an agent whose lexicon is highly unambiguous (close to or no polysemy) and/or highly agrees with its peers' is considered to have a *good lexicon* because it leads to successful communications. Therefore, the agent is more likely to spread his lexicon (infect other agents). An agent whose lexicon shows either a low degree of agreement with its peers' or a considerable number of ambiguous words, is bound to lead the agent to unsuccessful communications. Hence, this agent's lexicon can be regarded as a *bad lexicon*, that should not spread and be positively infected by some agent with a good lexicon instead of being spread. The following subsection details how the infection-based mechanism was implemented.

3.1   Implementation

Here we propose to deploy the infection-based mechanism in an open MAS by embedding an infection-based (adaptation) module within each agent as depicted

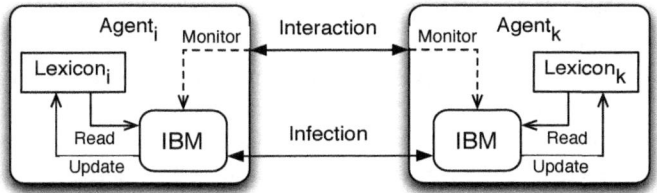

Fig. 1. Infection-based module embedded into agents

by figure 1 (squared boxes within agents labeled as IBM). These adaptation modules collaborate to run a distributed evolutionary algorithm (detailed below) to continuously improve their lexicons. Within this setting, the infection-based mechanism operates as follows. Each adaptation module (IBM) continuously monitors the success of the interactions of the agent where it is embedded, (figure 1). Recall that such interactions occur between agents linked by some interaction topology. Periodically, adaptation modules synchronize to fire a cooperative evolutionary process aimed at improving their agents' lexicons. More precisely, adaptation modules record the results of a fixed number of interactions, namely language games (such as described in section 2). We refer to such number as the *incubation time* ($t_{incubation}$). This parameter bounds the time period for adaptation modules to monitor the success that the lexicons in use bring to their agents.

Once the incubation time expires, each infection-based module starts its adaptation process. It employs two strategies to improve the lexicon of each agent: *spreading* it among the agent's neighbors; and *innovating* it to prevent stagnation. As outlined above, the mechanism gives agents a higher infectious power the higher their success in their interactions. In the context of our problem, agents with a good lexicons (low ambiguity and already adopted by other agents) should have a higher chance of infecting other agents (via their lexicons), thus following the *survival of the fittest* approach.

In order to assess an agent's lexicon success, each adaptation module requires an **evaluation function**. This function allows to value the results of the language games an agent has been engaged in during the incubation time. Moreover, each adaptation module also requires a secondary communication channel. Such channel needs to be specialized for the adaptation module, i.e. independent of the (primary) communication channel used by each agent (see figure 1). Through this secondary channel, adaptation modules realize the spreading (infection attempts) by exchanging information related to their lexicons and their usefulness in preventing misunderstandings.

Henceforth, although the operations described below are run inside agents' adaptation modules, for the sake of simplicity we refer to the agents hosting them. Then, since each agent receives infection attempts from multiple neighbors, a **selection process** is ran by the agent to determine the infecting peer, based on its fitness (namely, on the evaluation of the peer's lexicon). The selection operator is implemented as detailed in [15] by adapting the roulette selection in the classic GA literature [3] to make it decentralized.

Once an agent has chosen a peer, it runs an **infection process** (with probability $p_{infection}$)is ran, to have its lexicon injected with part of the infecting agent's lexicon (both lexicons are represented as genes). The infection process is implemented as a classic crossover recombination. The classic crossover (*single-cut crossover*) randomly selects a cut point in the parents' gene sequences to exchange their genes and produce two new individuals. Consider a contagious agent and an agent to infect as two parents. Instead of creating child individuals, an infection operator combines the genes of both parents. Furthermore, there is no restriction on the number of agents each agent can infect (per iteration), but no agent can be infected twice. Therefore, the fittest agents enjoy more opportunities to spread.

Finally, each agent also runs an **innovation process** that randomly changes (with probability $p_{mutation}$) the word assigned to a concept with one word out the set of words W. The infection-based mechanism is outlined in algorithm 1. Importantly, our algorithm runs distributedly: each agent decides whether to infect or mutate based on its local knowledge. The interactions to which algorithm 1 refers are language games (line 2). As mentioned above, agents in a MAS continuously engage in language games until the incubation time expires. Thereafter, all agents locally start their evolutionary processes. Once this process finishes, agents resume their interactions.

```
1: repeat
2:     Let the agent interact for time t_{incubation};
3:     ag.evaluate();
4:     ag.sendInfectionAttempts();
5:     ag' ← ag.selection();
6:     ag.infection(ag', p_{infection});
7:     ag.innovation(p_{innovation});
8: until MAS stops
```

Algorithm 1. Infection-based Algorithm

Notice that a very important feature of the infection-based mechanism is that it allows to interweave agents' interactions to achieve their goals with their lexicon adaptation. In other words, adaptation occurs at the same time that agents operate.

4   Empirical Evaluation

We hypothesize that the adaptation mechanism detailed in section 3 can be applied to emerge conventions in MAS with large convention spaces. To that end, we use communication development, namely the agreement on lexicon conventions, as our experimental domain. This domain, has the potential of exhibiting an interesting large convention space (depending on the number of words and concepts). Therefore, we shall consider our hypothesis as solved if the IBM allows a MAS to emerge a global (near-) perfect communication system.

Given an open MAS whose agent communication interactions are modeled as a language game, we shall consider the mechanism as successful if it allows: (i) agents in the MAS to reach lexicon convention(s) with a high level of specificity, for different word/concept ratios and under the most common interaction topologies; and (ii) conventions can be maintained despite changes in the agent population and in the underlying interaction topology.

At the aim of validating these hypothesis, we designed various sets of experiments to empirically evaluate the mechanism for communication development (described in section 3) under different conditions of a particular MAS. Next, in subsection 4.1 we describe the interaction topologies that we employed. In subsection 4.2 we detail our empirical settings, and in the rest of subsections we present and discuss our empirical results.

4.1 Interaction Topologies

It has been argued that the social distribution of individuals is an important factor in the evolution of languages [13,6,10]. This distribution is modeled in our MAS by the underlying interaction topology. Thus, in order to empirically analyze the potential of the infection-based mechanism as a tool for lexicon evolution we chose the following interaction topologies:

Small-world. These networks present the small-world phenomenon, in which nodes have small neighborhoods, and yet it is possible to reach any other node in a small number of hops. This type of networks are *highly-clustered* (i.e. have a high clustering coefficient). Formally, we note them as $W_V^{k,p}$, where V is the number of nodes, k the average connectivity, i.e., the average size of the node's neighborhood, and p the re-wiring probability. We used the Watts & Strogatz model [19] to generate these networks.

Scale-free. These networks are characterized by having a few nodes acting as highly-connected hubs, while the rest of them have a low connectivity degree. Scale-free networks are *low-clustered* networks. Formally we note them as $S_V^{k,-\gamma}$, where V is the number of nodes and its degree distribution is given by $P(k) \sim k^{-\gamma}$, i.e. the probability $P(k)$ that a node in the network connects with k other nodes is roughly proportional to $k^{-\gamma}$.

Notice that we discard to consider random networks because they rarely appear in actual-world networked systems.

4.2 Experimental Settings

Each *experiment* consists of 50 discrete event simulations, each one running up to 120000 time-steps (ticks). Each simulation runs with 1000 agents using one of the underlying topologies defined in section 4.1. At the beginning of each simulation, each agent uploads a random lexicon. During each simulation, at

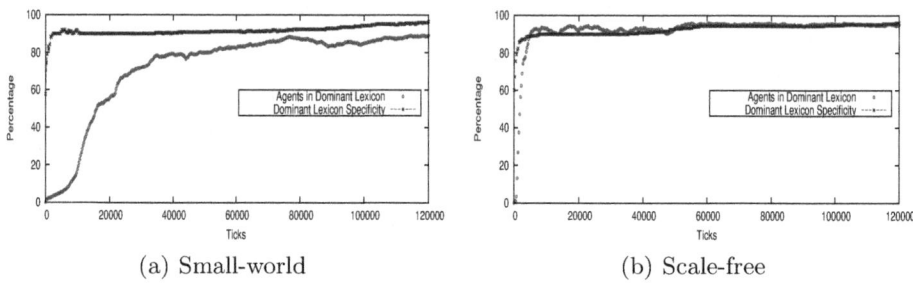

(a) Small-world   (b) Scale-free

Fig. 2. Results of the name-matching game

each time-step agents interact through communication, as defined in sections 2, with a randomly selected neighbor. The interactions occur by agents randomly choosing some concepts to send.

The individual understanding, evaluation function, of each agent is measured as the number of times it has engaged in a successful communication as a speaker. This measure is reset after each incubation period in the infection-based algorithm (algorithm 1), namely once the interaction period is over.

We generate interaction topologies for the simulations as small-world and scale-free networks by setting the following parameters: $W_{1000}^{<10>,0.1}$ and $S_{1000}^{<10>,-3}$. The clustering coefficients of the topologies are 0.492 and 0.056 respectively. Notice that we generate a new interaction topology per simulation.

As to the parameters of the infection-based mechanism, we set them as follows: $p_{infection} = 0.65$, $p_{innovation} = 5 \times 10^{-5}$, and $t_{incubation} = 10$. This setting of the incubation time means that we require a low number of interactions before adapting lexicons. In other words, we can consider a continuous adaptation.

In order to observe the effect of the IBM over a MAS we probe simulations in two ways. On the one hand, to measure whether a lexicon convention is adopted, we observe the number of agents that share each lexicon per tick. We shall refer to the lexicon shared by the largest number of agents as the *dominant* lexicon. On the other hand, we also observe at every tick the *quality* of such lexicon. Given a lexicon its quality is determined by its specificity, namely the percentage of words that represent a single concept. For both dominant lexicons and specificity, we aggregate the measures obtained after 50 simulations using the inter-quartile mean.

We designed different sets of experiments to empirically validate our initial hypothesis regarding the validity of the infection based mechanism. The first set, analyzed in section 4.3, aims at showing that the IBM can guide a MAS to emerge a lexicon with high specificity in a scenario where the likelihood of ambiguity is high ($|W| = |O|$). Next, in section 4.4 we also test the case when the likelihood to present ambiguity is low (but misunderstandings are feasible), namely when $|W| > |O|$. Finally, in section 4.5 we study a dynamic setting where both the agent population and interaction topology change over time to test the robustness of the IBM.

4.3   Matching Game with Same Words and Concepts

The aim of this section is to show that the infection-based mechanism (section 3) can guide a MAS, whose interactions are modeled as a name-matching game, to emerge a lexicon with high specificity. Furthermore, we particularly focus on the case where the existing number of words is equal to the number of objects ($|W| = |O|$). Recall that this scenario is likely to promote the existence of lexicons with low-specificity because given a limited number of words an agent can probably assign the same word to more than one concept.

We set the number of concepts to 10, and the set of words, W, is also composed of 10 different words ($|C| = 10^{10}$). Thus, to prevent ambiguity a lexicon must manage to match each one of the ten concepts to a different word.

Figure 2 shows the evolution of the percentage of agents sharing the dominant lexicon along with the specificity of the lexicon. We observe that, on average, for a small-world topology the dominant lexicon convention exhibits a smooth and slow growth. Nevertheless, at least 80% of the agents reach a consensus regarding their lexicon. The figure also shows that the specificity of the dominant lexicon quickly reaches 90%, which means that one of the words matches two concepts. However, we observe that in the long run there is a trend towards total specificity.

As to scale-free networks, a dominant lexicon shared by a large number of agents emerges in a fast and sharp manner. This dominant lexicon almost immediately encompasses 90% of the agents with a 90% specificity. This state is maintained for some time, but at some point (around 60000 ticks) reaches beyond 95% of the population and the quality or the lexicon improves.

Moreover, observing a particular simulation provides some interesting insights. Figure 3 shows one of the 50 simulations performed for the small-world topology. In this plot, the transition towards a lexicon with 100% specificity is clearer. If we analyze what happens before the lexicon transition, we observe that the agent population sharing the dominant lexicon decreases (around 30000 ticks). This occurs because a lexicon with maximum specificity appears and starts pulling members out of the dominant lexicon at that point. By the 35000 time-step it is able to overtake the previously dominant lexicon and rapidly reaches a global consensus (almost all the agent population shares it).

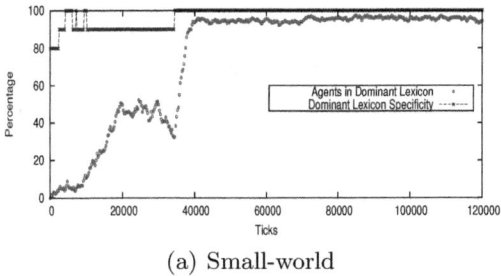

(a) Small-world

Fig. 3. Results of a particular small-world simulation

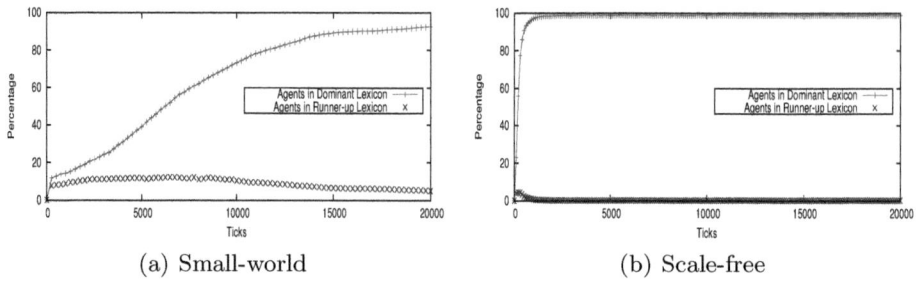

(a) Small-world   (b) Scale-free

Fig. 4. Results of the 2-names-matching game with $|W| = 100$ and $|O| = 10$

Overall, the results of these experiments show that the IBM emerges a perfect communication system for more than 90% of the population. It is called perfect because: i) all the words in the dominant lexicon have a high specificity; ii) once established the lexicon becomes consistent overtime; and iii) the agents' communicative interactions are always successful.

4.4   Matching Game with Many Words

In the previous section we focused on experiments with high potential ambiguity, where there were as many concepts as words. Now we turn our attention to the other extreme of the spectrum, where the number of words is significantly greater than the number of concepts. In this case, the likelihood of ambiguity decreases when the number of words increases. This happens because assigning the same word to more than one concept is less probable. In other words, the number of lexicons with 100% specificity increases.

For this set of experiments we set $|W| \in \{20, 100\}$, whereas we only used 10 concepts ($|C| = 20^{10}$ and $|C| = 100^{10}$). As to the extreme case ($|W| = 100$) for a small-world topology, we observe in figure 4(a) that two (dominant) lexicon conventions with total specificity rapidly appear (< 100 ticks). One of them starts gaining members rapidly ($\sim$89%) while the other one appears to stabilize with a small percentage of the population ($\sim$11%). Since the second (small) agent group has a lexicon with 100% specificity and its communications are most likely occurring between its members, it can withstand infections coming from the dominant group. However, because the topology is a small-world scenario, members of this group may need to communicate with agents sharing the dominant lexicon. Hence, around 1000 ticks, time at which the dominant lexicon is shared by most of the population, the membership of the second group starts swaying towards the biggest group out of necessity. As times goes on (beyond what we show in the plot), the dominant lexicon settles in 98 % of the population. On scale-free topology see figure 4(b), we observe a more straightforward behavior. Almost immediately ($\sim$2000 ticks) a lexicon convention with total specificity is shared by the whole population, swaying over any secondary lexicon intending to rise.

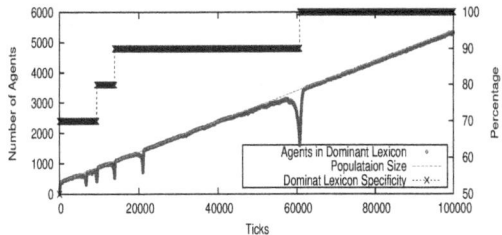

Fig. 5. Evolution of a dominant lexicon for a dynamic agent population over a scale free topology

As to the results with $|W| = 20$, on the small-word topology we observe the same behavior as the one presented in section 4.3 for $|W| = 10$. However, there are significant improvements regarding scale-free networks because there is a larger number of lexicons with high specificity. Furthermore, observe that all the scale-free experiments so far converge to a common lexicon significatively faster than small-world. Such result contrast with results in the literature. This leads us to believe that scale-free is more receptive to large convention spaces.

4.5   Dynamic Population

In previous sections we showed, through multiple scenarios, the usefulness of the infection-based mechanism to engineer the emergence of lexicon conventions. Nevertheless, all scenarios were somewhat static, in the sense that the MAS did not change with time. Hence, the purpose of our last experiments is to show the robustness of the IBM in a MAS that changes with time.

Thus, we model the open dynamics of a MAS by allowing the agent population and their neighborhoods to change over time. In practice, environment changes are achieved by dynamically changing the network topology. Hence, we proceeded as follows: 1) we create a scale-free interaction topology up to certain number of agents; 2) we let agents interact over the topology; and 3) after l simulation ticks, we introduce new agents along with their neighborhoods. Finally, we implemented the open dynamics of a MAS by inter-weaving the Barabasi-Albert (BA) scale-free network generation algorithm [1] with the MAS simulation. In other words, we ran the MAS and the BA algorithm at the same time.

We set the parameters for the experiments as follows. The starting MAS employed a scale-free underlying topology of 400 agents ($S_{400}^{<10>,-3}$). Every 400 iterations, 20 new agents with random lexicons joined the MAS ($l = 400$). The MAS continued growing until reaching the $S_{6000}^{<10>,-3}$ topology (6000 agents).

On average (inter-quartile mean), we can report that IBM helps agents rapidly converge to a lexicon, and incoming agents promptly join the dominant convention. Nevertheless, this initial dominant lexicon presented some ambiguity that diminished with time. Thus, at some point a lexicon with total specificity was found. We illustrate this claim with a particular example.

Figure 5 shows a simulation (a single run instead of the aggregation) where a dominant lexicon is quickly established. Notice that the dominant lexicon grows at almost the same rate as the population (left-hand y-axis). However, the dominant lexicon has an initial lexicon specificity percentage of $\sim 70\%$ (right-hand y-axis). Observe that as time goes on the lexicon specificity starts to improve. Furthermore, notice that improvements in the quality of the global convention lexicon (specificity) seems to be usually preceded by a decrease in the convention size (e.g. ~ 10000, ~ 15000 and ~ 60000 ticks). These downward spikes mark the agent population's transition to better lexicons. Nevertheless, observe that some of the spikes do not improve the unambiguity. This also marks a change in the current dominant lexicon, but one that did not improve the specificity.

5   Conclusions and Future Work

In this paper we proposed the use of a recently studied distributed evolutionary algorithm as a viable tool to emerge conventions in multi-agent systems with large convention spaces. We accomplish this by tackling communication development in MAS, which is a known problem. Through the infection-based mechanism it is possible to engineer the emergence of lexicon conventions in open heterogeneous MAS. The infection-based mechanism allows agents to distributedly converge to a lexicon with high specificity that guarantees the success of their communications, i.e. a perfect communication system. Even more, through this approach lexicon consensus are attainable despite the presence of dynamic changes in the MAS. In particular, changes in the agent population and its underlying topology (e.g. available communication links between the agents).

We apply the infection-based mechanism described in [15] as a communication development mechanism. Moreover, we make use of language games as a model for communication interactions. Hence, the agents' normal interactions are valued as successful or failed. Through these two elements our approach allows agents to find and improve lexicon conventions while they normally interact in the MAS. Nevertheless, notice that different communication models can be employed without changing the IBM.

We ran several experiments to provide empirical evidence of the capabilities of the proposed approach under different (reasonable) circumstances. Furthermore, because it is known that language emergence is influenced by the social structures, our experiments took this into account. Namely, through the use of the most common complex networks as underlying interaction topologies.

On the one hand, the results show that we can direct the emergence of a global lexicon consensus regardless of the topology. Nevertheless, topology affects the time it takes to reach such consensus. Therefore, in contrast with other approaches [6], the IBM reaches a single-vocabulary consensus, in the form of a globally shared lexicon. Moreover, this is accomplished in a largely populated multi-agent systems.

On the other hand, the results also helped to gauge the effect intrinsic to the relation in the number of words and concepts. When the number of words and concepts is equal, some difficulty exists in establishing an unambiguous lexicon, but conventions between agents may be reached faster. However, as the number of words increases, finding a lexicon with 100% specificity becomes somewhat easier, but reaching a common to most agents becomes harder. Nevertheless, despite this it is still possible to agree on a single lexicon global consensus.

Our final experiments showed that our adaptation mechanism can reach an unambiguous lexicon convention even if the agent population in the MAS and its interaction topology are constantly changing. Therefore, our approach shows to be valid even in highly dynamic scenarios.

To summarize, we empirically show that the IBM can reach desirable global conventions even when the convention space is large. Furthermore, this can also be accomplished when the number of desired convention is considerably a small fraction of the convention space.

Finally, as to future work we plan to look to more dynamic settings. For instance, scenarios where agents can introduce new concepts at run-time. Moreover, we also plan to study the effect produced by each agent having a different set of available words.

Acknowledgments

N. Salazar thanks CONACyT. JAR thanks Jose Castillejo (JC2008-00337). Work funded by projects EVE (TIN2009-14702-C02-01), IEA (TIN2006-15662-C02-01), AT (CONSOLIDER CSD2007-0022), and the Generalitat of Catalunya grant 2009-SGR-1434.

References

1. Albert, R., Barabasi, A.-L.: Statistical mechanics of complex networks. Reviews of Modern Physics 74, 47 (2002)
2. Axelrod, R.: The dissemination of culture: A model with local convergence and global polarization. The Journal of Conflict Resolution 41(2), 203–226 (1997)
3. Bäck, T.: Evolutionary Algorithms in Theory and Practice: Evolution Strategies, Evolutionary Programming, Genetic Algorithms. Oxford University Press, Oxford (1996)
4. Baronchelli, A., Felici, M., Loreto, V., Caglioti, E., Steels, L.: Sharp transition towards shared vocabularies in multi-agent systems. Journal of Statistical Mechanics: Theory and Experiment 06, P06014 (2006)
5. Burt, R.: Social contagion and innovation: Cohesion versus structural equivalence. American J. of Sociology 92, 1287–1335 (1987)
6. Dall'Asta, L., Baronchelli, A., Barrat, A., Loreto, V.: Nonequilibrium dynamics of language games on complex networks. Physical Review E (Statistical, Nonlinear, and Soft Matter Physics) 74(3), 36105 (2006)
7. de Jong, E.D., Steels, L.: A distributed learning algorithm for communication development. Complex Systems 14, 315–334 (2003)
8. DeVylder, B.: The Evolution of Conventions in Multi-Agent Systems. PhD thesis, Artificial Intelligence Lab Vrije Universiteit Brussel (2007)

9. Jong, E.D.D., Steels, L.: A distributed learning algorithm for communication development. Complex Systems 14 (2003)
10. Kalampokis, A., Kosmidis, K., Argyrakis, P.: Evolution of vocabulary on scale-free and random networks. Physica A: Statistical Mechanics and its Applications 379(2), 665–671 (2007)
11. Lewis, D.: Convention. Harvard University Press, Cambridge (1969)
12. Loreto, V., Steels, L.: Social dynamics: Emergence of language. Nature Physics 3, 758–760 (2007)
13. Puglisi, A., Baronchelli, A., Loreto, V.: Cultural route to the emergence of linguistic categories. Proceedings of the National Academy of Sciences, 802485105 (2008)
14. Salazar, N., Rodríguez-Aguilar, J.A., Arcos, J.L.: An infection-based mechanism for self-adaptation in multi-agent complex networks. In: Proc. of the Second IEEE International Conference on SASO (2008)
15. Salazar, N., Rodriguez-Aguilar, J.A., Arcos, J.L.: Infection-based self-configuration in agent societies. In: Proc. of the 2008 GECCO conference companion on Genetic and evolutionary computation, pp. 1945–1952. ACM, New York (2008)
16. Steels, L.: Self-organizing vocabularies. In: Langton, C.G., Shimohara, K. (eds.) Artificial Life V, Nara, Japan, pp. 179–184 (1996)
17. Steels, L.: The origins of ontologies and communication conventions in multi-agent systems. Autonomous Agents and Multi-Agent Systems 1, 169–194 (1998)
18. Steels, L.: Grounding symbols through evolutionary language games. In: Simulating the Evolution of Language, ch. 10, pp. 211–226. Springer, Heidelberg (2002)
19. Watts, D.J., Strogatz, S.H.: Collective dynamics of 'small-world' networks. Nature 393(6684), 440–442 (1998)

The Classification Game: Complexity Regularization through Interaction

Samarth Swarup

Network Dynamics and Simulation Science Lab,
Virginia Bioinformatics Institute,
Virginia Polytechnic Institute and State University,
Blacksburg, VA 24061
swarup@vbi.vt.edu

Abstract. We show that if a population of neural network agents is allowed to interact during learning, so as to arrive at a consensus solution to the learning problem, then they can implicitly achieve complexity regularization. We call this learning paradigm, the classification game. We characterize the game-theoretic equilibria of this system, and show how low-complexity equilibria get selected. The benefit of finding a low-complexity solution is better expected generalization. We demonstrate this benefit through experiments.

1   Introduction

In machine learning, simple models are expected to generalize better. More complex models are more likely to overfit the training data, and consequently are less likely to generalize well. Thus, during learning, it is advisable to try to find a low-complexity model that performs well on the training data. How to do this is, in a nutshell, the problem of complexity regularization.

Most attempts to solve this problem proceed by developing an objective function (also called an empirical loss function) which includes a penalty term for the complexity of the model [1,2,3, e.g.]. Here we present a multi-agent solution to this problem, where the objective function used by each individual learner does *not* contain a penalty term for complexity. Instead, low complexity models are found through implicit complexity regularization via interaction during learning. Further, most techniques for complexity regularization try to minimize the complexity of the *weights*, whereas our learning algorithm is best understood as minimizing the complexity of the internal representation, i.e. hidden layer activations, of the neural networks. This is closer in spirit to the idea of learning over the space of input-output functions rather than the weights of the neural network [4]. We call our learning method, the *classification game* [5].

We proceed as follows. First we give a brief introduction to neural networks. Then we demonstrate, through a simple example, that the classification game succeeds in finding simple models. Then we present the learning algorithm in detail. After that we do some analysis to characterize the equilibria of the game, and discuss why certain (low-complexity) equilibria tend to be selected in the game. Then we present another experiment where vanilla neural networks fail to learn altogether, but a population of

J. Padget et al. (Eds.): COIN 2009, LNAI 6069, pp. 289–303, 2010.

neural networks playing the classification game is more successful. We then discuss where our approach fits in the landscape of complexity regularization techniques. In the conclusion, we present a summary of this work as well as some directions for future work.

2   A Brief Introduction to Neural Networks

Artificial neural networks are one of the most commonly used representations in machine learning. They consist of a set of "nodes" with "weights" on the incoming edges to the nodes. Feedforward neural networks generally have the nodes organized into "layers", so that information flows strictly from the inputs to the outputs. The illustration in figure 1 shows an example.

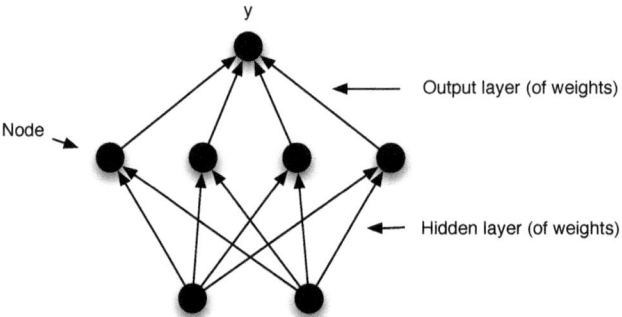

Fig. 1. A schematic of a feed-forward artificial neural network

Each node in a neural network carries out the following computation:

$$u = \sum_i w_i x_i + b, \tag{1}$$

$$y = \frac{1}{1 + e^{-\beta u}}, \tag{2}$$

where y is the output of the node, x_i are the inputs to the node, and w_i are the weights. Additionally, b is known as the *bias weight*, and β is a parameter. The r.h.s. of equation 2 is known as the *logistic* function, which is a *sigmoid* function.

Geometrically, the weights of the node define a line (or a *hyperplane* in higher dimensions), and the computation above can be seen to be the dot product between a point (given by the inputs, x_i) and the line. u will be positive for points on one side of the line, and negative for points on the other side of the line. Passing u through the sigmoid function (equation 2) "squashes" the output to be between 0 and 1. Points on the positive side of the line will evaluate to $y > 0.5$ and points on the negative side will evaluate to $y < 0.5$. More importantly, though, the sigmoid function introduces a non-linearity, so that the neural network as a whole computes a non-linear function. It can be shown that a feed-forward neural network with two layers of weights is capable of approximating any continuous function arbitrarily closely, given enough hidden layer nodes.

Given a set of samples from an unknown function (as input-output pairs), known as the *training set*, the weights of a feedforward neural network can be estimated, to fit the function, using a learning procedure known as error backpropagation. We define an error function,

$$e = (t - y)^2, \tag{3}$$

where t is the target output for an input x, and y is the actual output generated by the neural network. Then we calculate the gradient of the error function with respect to all the parameters w_i (using the chain rule when necessary), and update the weights to descend the gradient. Thus, after several iterations, the neural networks ends up in a *local* minimum of the error functions. Details about various kinds of neural networks and their training can be found in several textbooks on the topic [6, e.g.].

3   Complexity Regularization in Neural Networks

If the training set is too small, or noisy, then the learning procedure can lead to *over-fitting*, where the weights start to adapt to the noise in the data, rather than finding true regularities. When this happens, the neural network becomes too complex. Thus, there have been several modifications suggested for the basic error function defined above, to avoid overfitting by keeping the complexity of the weights low. This is known as complexity regularization, as discussed earlier.

Most approaches work by augmenting the objective function with a penalty term for the complexity of the solution, so that by minimizing the objective function, both error and complexity are minimized. These penalty terms are often derived from information-theoretic (minimum description length) considerations. For example, Hinton [7] showed early on that minimizing the squared error function above corresponds to minimizing the description length of the "data misfits", and adding a penalty term for the magnitude of the weights ($\sum_{ij} w_{ij}^2$) corresponds to minimizing the description length of the weights as well (with the assumption that the data misfits and the weights of the trained network are each drawn from Gaussian distributions). Hinton and van Camp [2] presented a more sophisticated method utilizing noisy weights and a coding scheme based on a mixture of Gaussians. The main limitation of their approach was that it relied on a "good" initialization of the weights, since the description complexity is shown to be equivalent to the Kullback-Leibler divergence between the prior and the posterior distribution over the weights.

Hochreiter and Schmidhuber [3] showed how a minimum description length argument could be interpreted as a search for large *flat* minima in the weight space, which results in a considerably more complex penalty term in the objective function, but also shows very robust performance.

More recently, researchers have turned to ensemble methods for complexity regularization, where the complexity of the ensemble can be adjusted by making the weight of each trained learner depend on its complexity [8]. The difference between the classification game and this approach (and also other ensemble methods like boosting [9] and bagging [10]) is that in the classification game all the learners converge towards a single model of low complexity, i.e., the complexity of each learner is reduced. Further, we do not rely on a combination (by voting etc.) of the learned models at the end.

Before discussing the classification game in detail, we present a small demonstration that shows that the classification game manages to perform complexity regularization implicitly through interaction during learning, without modifying the error function.

4   A Demonstration of the Classification Game

We have a population of four artificial neural networks, with a fixed number (4, in this example) of hidden layer nodes, and 1 output node. We train them on the *xor* problem. Thus each neural network has 2 inputs, and the set of possible inputs is $\{(0, 0), (0, 1), (1, 0), (1, 1)\}$. The expected output is the logical xor of the inputs, i.e. the output is 1 when the inputs are different, and 0 when the inputs are the same.

We interpret each hidden layer node as a hyperplane, where the weights to the node are the coefficients of the hyperplane. Since the input space is two-dimensional, we can draw these hyperplanes (straight lines), to visualize how they dissect the input points.

Figure 2 shows the result of training a single neural network on the xor problem. The hyperplanes in the figure are labeled and also indicate orientation. Hyperplane A, e.g., labels the point $(0, 0)$ as 1, and all other points as 0. The output neuron of the neural network converts the encoding generated by all four hidden layer hyperplanes into a label. The neural network obtains zero error, i.e. perfect classification accuracy, very easily, but we can see that the found solution uses all four hidden layer nodes whereas we know that only two are really necessary. This means that the neural network has found an overly complex model, though it is not a problem here because all possible inputs are presented during training. This tendency to use all the hidden layer nodes available is general behavior for a neural network, however, and if we used a more complex problem where only some of the possible inputs are presented during training,

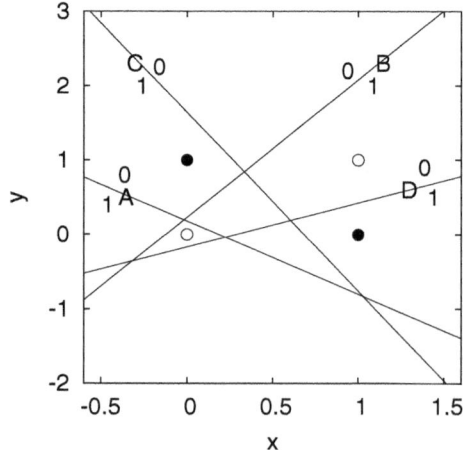

Fig. 2. A neural network typically finds overly complex solutions to the xor problem

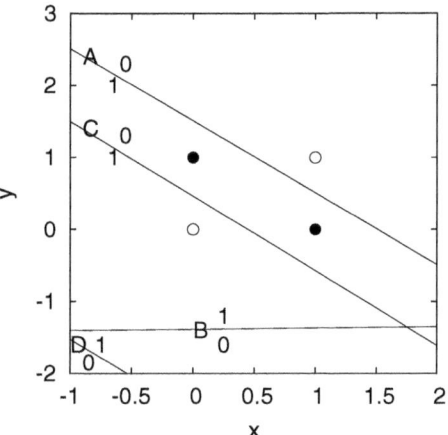

Fig. 3. A population of neural networks playing the classification game typically finds the optimal solution to the xor problem

then generalization is the key measure, and we would not expect the found model to generalize well.

In contrast, if we have a population of such neural networks playing the classification game, then they almost always converge on a solution such as the one illustrated in figure 3. The details of the classification game are described in section 5. At present we want to point out that the model that is found by the learners in this case is the optimal model. Even though the neural networks are again provided with four hidden layer nodes, we see that they are only "using" two of them. Two others have been "pushed away".

We now describe the learning algorithm that implicitly obtains this complexity regularization phenomenon. It should be noted that we are not claiming that the classification game always finds the optimal solution. It only does so for toy problems like xor; in general, though, it does reduce the complexity of the model substantially.

5   The Classification Game

Assume that we have a population of neural networks that are initialized with random weights. The learning algorithm then proceeds as follows. At each step, we select two of the learners randomly and designate them *speaker* and *hearer*. They are both presented with the same training example to classify.

The speaker *encodes* this example into a set of hidden-layer activations, by passing it through its hidden layer of weights and sigmoid activation functions in the usual way. It also generates a label by passing the hidden layer activations through the output layer. The hidden layer activations are also converted into a boolean vector by thresholding the neuron activations at 0.5. The speaker then passes this boolean vector to the hearer.

The hearer ignores the example itself, and uses the encoding provided by the speaker to try to predict the label, using its own output layer. In other words, the hearer sets the

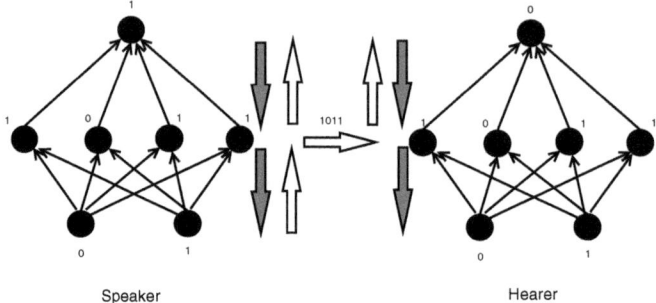

Fig. 4. A single interaction in the classification game. The white arrows show signal flow, and the grey arrows show error flow.

activations of its own hidden layer using the boolean values provided by the speaker, and passes this vector through its output layer in the usual way to generate a label.

The speaker and hearer are then both given the expected label and update their weights through error backpropagation. The entire process is illustrated in figure 4. Notice that the speaker does not get any feedback about the error made by the hearer[1]. Thus the speaker is simply trying to minimize its own error, whereas the hearer is trying to minimize error on an encoding provided by the speaker. The error function (also known as the objective function or loss function) being minimized by the learners is simply the squared difference between the expected label and the actual output of the neural network. The error function does not contain a term for the complexity of the internal representation (weights or hidden layer activations). This means that the agents are not explicitly trying to find a low-complexity solution.

Note that hidden layer weight updates for the hearer are slightly tricky because the hidden layer activations for the hearer came from the speaker, and not the hearer's own hidden layer weights. Therefore, to update these weights, we proceed as follows. The hearer backpropagates the error from the output layer to generate a set of hidden layer activations. These are, in essence, what the hidden layer activations *should have been*, to generate the right output. It then treats these as the expected outputs for its own hidden layer. It generates the actual outputs of its hidden layer from the input vector, compares them with these expected hidden layer outputs, and performs weight updates in the usual manner.

We then return these learners to the population, choose two learners again and repeat the process until we are satisfied (i.e., until the error drops low enough, or we reach an arbitrary number of iterations).

6   Analysis

We now write down the above description formally, in an attempt to give a theoretical description of what is going on in the classification game.

---

[1] Agents take on the role of both speaker and hearer over the course of learning. Thus information is shared between all agents, and information flow is not uni-directional.

Following the formalism of Haussler [11], we assume that the learners are provided with a *training set* $z = \{z_1, z_2, ..., z_n\}$ where each *example* $z_i = (x_i, y_i)$ consists of an *input* $x_i \in X$ and an *expected output* $y_i \in Y$. The learners are also provided with a *loss function* $l : Y \times Y \rightarrow \Re$, and a *hypothesis space* $\mathcal{H}$ containing functions $h : X \rightarrow Y$. We assume that the training set is generated by sampling n times independently from a probability distribution P, and that the *true loss* of a hypothesis h with respect to P is defined as,

$$E(h, P) = \int_{X \times Y} l(y, h(x)) dP(x, y).$$

The goal of the learners is to find a hypothesis h that minimizes the true loss. The learners proceed, as usual, by trying to minimize the *empirical* loss,

$$E(h, z) = \sum_{i=1}^{n} l(y_i, h(x_i)),$$

where the loss function, as mentioned earlier, is simply,

$$l(y, h(x)) = (y - h(x))^2.$$

It has been shown that the difference between the empirical loss and the true loss is related to the *complexity* of h, and that low-complexity hypotheses that minimize the error on the training set are also expected to have low true loss. This is known as Occam's razor for machine learning [12,13,14].

To quantify the complexity of our hypothesis space, we introduce the notion of an internal representation space, V, by splitting the hypothesis space into two parts, $\mathcal{H} = \mathcal{F} \circ \mathcal{G}$, where $\mathcal{G} : X \rightarrow V$, and $\mathcal{F} : V \rightarrow Y$. We assume that points in V are binary vectors, and functions $g \in \mathcal{G}$ are of the form of n_h-hyperplanes. Finally, functions $f \in \mathcal{F}$ are simply hyperplanes. Note that this matches the architecture of an artificial neural network with n_h hidden-layer nodes and a single output node. Points in V are, thus, the vector of labels assigned to points in X by the n_h hyperplanes corresponding to the n_h hidden-layer nodes. We call g an *encoding function* or simply *encoder*, and f a *decoding function* or simply *decoder*.

Now, a low-complexity function g is one which "uses" a small number of the n_h hyperplanes available. This is intuitively obvious from figures 2 and 3. We will make this more precise a little later.

Let $x = \{x_1, x_2, ..., x_n\}$ be the set of training set inputs. We define $x^+ = \{x_i \in x \mid y_i \text{ is positive}\}$, and $x^- = \{x_i \in x \mid y_i \text{ is negative}\}$, to be the positive and negative subsets of x. Note that here, and henceforth, we will always use the term "positive point" to refer to an input for which the expected output is positive, i.e. an input which belong to the class of postively-labeled points (and the same for "negative point"). An encoder, g, transforms x^+ and x^- into internal representations v^+ and v^- respectively. Since we have a population of (say, m) learners, we obtain m internal representations, denoted by v_j, where, $\forall j \in \{1, ..., m\}$, $v_j = v_j^+ \cup v_j^-$, through the action of m encoders, $g_1...g_m$, corresponding to the m learners. The encoding of a particular point, say x_i^+, by agent j is denoted by $v_{j,i}^+$.

6.1 Characterizing Nash Equilibria

From a game-theoretic perspective, the classification game proceeds as follows. Given an example, the speaker chooses the encoding of it both for the speaker itself and for the hearer. The payoff to the speaker and the hearer can be thought of as the negative of their error on the given example. Thus, maximizing the payoff is equivalent to minimizing the error. Note that, in an interaction, the speaker is essentially unaware of the hearer, since it gets no feedback about the hearer's error on the example. The speaker, thus, chooses its encoding of the given example purely to minimize its own classification error.

We are now ready to characterize the Nash equilibria of the classification game. Note that while each encoder, g_j, only produces its own internal representation, v_j, each decoder, f_j, has to decode not just v_j, but $\cup_j v_j$, i.e. each decoder has to decode the internal representations generated by *all* the encoders.

It is possible that the encoding, $v_{j,p}$, generated by learner j for a positively-labeled input, x_p^+, is the same as encoding $v_{k,q}$ generated by learner k for a negatively-labeled input, x_q^-. We denote this event as a *conflict*. A conflict implies that decoders f_j and f_k are guaranteed to make at least one classification mistake because they cannot distinguish positive input x_p^+ from negative input x_q^-, when learners j and k interact with each other. In this case, either one of the learners can change its internal representation by choosing a different encoding function, and can thus reduce its error. This leads straightforwardly to the first condition for an equilibrium:

$$\cup_j v_j^+ \cap \cup_j v_j^- = \emptyset, \tag{4}$$

where $\emptyset$ is the null set. In plain English, this condition is satisfied when there are no conflicts. Note that this condition can always be achieved simply by making all the learners have the same internal representations.

Each learner must choose its internal representation to satisfy two other conditions:

$$v_j^+ \cap v_j^- = \emptyset, \text{ and} \tag{5}$$

$$v_j \text{ must represent an attainable dichotomy for } f_j. \tag{6}$$

Condition 5 simply states that a learner's internal representation must be self-consistent, i.e. it shouldn't assign the same encoding to both a positive and a negative input. Condition 6 states that the encoder should transform the inputs in such a way that the decoder can actually decode them into the right labels. For example, for the xor problem, if the encoder is the identity function, the decoder will not be able to solve the problem, since at least two hyperplanes are needed to separate the positive from the negative points.

Together, these three conditions specify the equilibria for the system, assuming that $\mathcal{G}$ contains functions that are complex enough (i.e., the neural network has enough hidden layer nodes). Note that condition 4 implies condition 5. However, we state them separately because that will facilitate the discussion of equilibrium selection ahead.

There are two different "incentives" for modifying an encoding. In the role of speaker, an agent modifies its encoding to solve the classification problem. In the role of hearer, an agent modifies its encoding to be compatible with the encodings of the other agents. Further, note that the equilibria are not *strict* Nash equilibria, because it is possible for a learner at equilibrium to change its internal representation without increasing the number of conflicts, and without increasing its error.

The complexity of an encoding. The complexity of an encoding, v_j, corresponds essentially to the number of points in v_j, which we denote as $|v_j|$. If more than one point in x is mapped onto the same point in v_j, then $|v_j| < |x|$, and the complexity of v_j is lower than that of x. The complexity of v_j can be quantified by, e.g., the entropy[2] of v_j,

$$H(v_j) = \sum_{i=1}^{|v_j|} p(v_{j,i}) \, log \, p(v_{j,i}).$$

For maximally complex encodings, $|v_j| = |x| = n$, i.e., a different point in V is assigned to each input x_i. When this happens, we say the learner has *memorized* the data. The number of such encodings is $^{2^k}C_n$. Such encodings will generalize poorly. On the other hand, for minimally complex encodings, $|v_j| = 2$, i.e., all the positive inputs are labeled with one point in V, and all the negative inputs are labeled with another point in V, making the decoder's task trivial. The number of such encodings is $^{2^k}C_2$. Such encodings are expected to generalize well, but may not be attainable, depending on the structure of the problem.

When two points have the same encoding, it means that there is no hyperplane separating them (or that hyperplane would assign different labels to the two points, giving them different encodings). As the number of points that share their encoding increases, we are in effect "using" fewer and fewer hyperplanes to separate the points. This corresponds to encodings of low complexity, as mentioned in section 6. In the limit, when all positive points have the same encoding and all negative points have the same encoding, it means that there is essentially only one hyperplane separating them (though in practice we might end up with multiple hyperplanes, nearly aligned with each other, separating the positive from the negatively labeled points). This happens when we have a *linearly-separable* problem.

6.2   Equilibrium Selection

The number of states of the population satisfying the three equilibrium conditions above is large, yet we generally observe the emergence of low-complexity equilibria. To understand why this happens, we turn to the dynamics of the classification game.

To analyze this equilibrium selection problem, we assume that the learners all learn individually for a while before they start interacting and playing the classification game. It turns out that this makes no difference to the complexity regularization phenomenon in practice, but it allows us to ignore the learning transient in the analysis.

Thus, we assume that the learners have all found internal representations that minimize the error on the training set. In other words, they have found internal representations that satisfy conditions 5 and 6 above. They are unlikely to be at an equilibrium point of the classification game, however, because condition 4 might still not be satisfied.

---

[2] Note that there are some learning approaches that explicitly try to maximize information gain, such as ID3 [15]. Here, on the other hand, we are just using entropy to quantify the complexity of the model, not to derive the learning algorithm.

The system dynamics are determined by the backpropagation algorithm. In particular, we are interested in the dynamics of the points in V space, which is the space of hidden layer activations. Ideally, we should set up a full dynamical model of the internal representation of an agent's neural network and show that the stationary state of this dynamical model corresponds to a low-complexity equilibrium. This is not possible, unfortunately, because the learning dynamics of even a single neural network are not yet fully understood [16,17, e.g.], not to mention that we have a population of *interacting* neural networks. Nevertheless, we can gain a qualitative understanding of the dynamics of the classification game by considering the following situations.

1. Input point x_p^+ is mapped onto $v_{j,p}$ by learner j and input point x_q^- is mapped onto $v_{k,q}$ by learner k, where $v_{j,p} = v_{k,q}$ (we keep the j and k subscripts to differentiate which learner is producing the point). This is a conflict and causes the hearer to update its internal representation.
2. Input point x_p^+ is mapped onto $v_{j,p}$ by learner j and input point x_p^+ (note that this is also a positive point) is mapped onto $v_{k,q}$ by learner k, where $v_{j,p} = v_{k,q}$. This is *not* a conflict, even if k does not map x_p^+ to $v_{k,q}$, since both j and k will produce the correct label, but this event plays an important role in equilibrium selection, as will be discussed presently.

First case. In the first case above, if j is the speaker and k is the hearer and they are presented with x_p^+, then j will produce the correct label, but k will generate a mis-classification because it cannot distinguish positive point x_p^+ from negative point x_q^- in this case. If the roles were reversed and they were given input x_q^- to classify, learner j would produce a mis-classification and k would not.

Without loss of generality, if we assume the former situation, then k will alter its encoding of x_p^+ to bring it closer to the encoding provided by j. This will create a violation of condition 5, because k will now have the same encoding for positive point x_p^+ and negative point x_q^-. This violation will eventually be resolved by k when it takes the role of speaker and has to classify these two points.

In general, violations of condition 4 are detected and corrected by agents when they are in the role of hearer, and violations of conditions 5 and 6 are detected and corrected by agents when they are in the role of speaker. The combined effect of learning in both roles is to arrive eventually at a state in which none of the conditions are violated.

Now consider the case where j's internal representation, v_j, is less complex than k's internal representation, v_k, which means $|v_j| < |v_k|$. Further, suppose that v_j and v_k are inconsistent with each other. This means that for some pair of points x_p^+ and x_q^-, $v_{j,p} = v_{k,q}$ (or vice-versa). Also, since v_j is less complex than v_k, there is a higher probability that $v_{j,p}$ is the encoding assigned to more than one input point by j, than the probability that $v_{k,q}$ is assigned to more than one input point by k. In this case, if j is the speaker and k is the hearer, there is a higher probability of a conflict being detected by the hearer than if the roles are reversed. This implies that higher complexity encodings will change more rapidly during learning than lower-complexity encodings. In other words, lower-complexity encodings are more stable.

In this sense, lower-complexity encodings are preferred in the classification game. This is not the only pressure towards selecting low-complexity equilibria however. A second one corresponds to the second situation above, and is described below.

Second case. Now consider the case where v_j and v_k *are* consistent with each other, but are not identical. In particular, suppose that the two learners assign the same encoding to two different points in the same class, i.e. $v_{j,p} = v_{k,q}$, where x_p and x_q are both positive (say), but $v_{k,p} \neq v_{k,q}$, i.e. k assigns different encodings to x_p and x_q.

If they are presented with x_p, the speaker, j, will not make a classification error, and thus will not update its internal representation. The hearer, k, will not make a classification error either. However, since $v_{k,p} \neq v_{k,q}$, k will change its internal representation of x_p to bring it closer to its internal representation of x_q. This means that the complexity of v_k will get reduced, since it will end up assigning the same encoding to both x_p and x_q.

Thus, even if the population is at a state that satisfies the three conditions for equilibrium, the learners will still change their internal representations in a manner that simplifies them. It is possible that this process will introduce violations of conditions 5 or 6, which will then have to be corrected by the agents when they have the role of speaker.

Note that the two cases described do not proceed one after the other in an orderly manner. Rather, they are happening simultaneously as the agents play the classification game. The net result is that the agents converge upon a state of low-complexity. Indeed, since we are always updating the hidden layer for the hearer in each interaction, any equilibrium in which the internal representations of the population are not aligned is unstable, since the hearer will update its internal representation even if it does not make a classification error.

We now present another experiment to show that the classification game can result in significant learning even in a case where vanilla neural networks fail to learn altogether.

7 Experiments

To show the dynamics of the complexity of the solution during learning, we present the following experiment. We extend the xor task to 3 bits (i.e. 3 bit odd-parity), and extend the inputs with 9 irrelevant bits. Thus each input example has 12 bits, and the output is determined by the xor of the first three bits. We refer to this as the 12-input-first-3-xor task. The total number of possible input examples is $2^{12} = 4096$. Of these, we construct a training set by randomly selecting 50 examples. The testing set consists of all 4096 possible examples.

We train a population of ten neural networks on this task. They are each given 10 hidden layer nodes, though only 3 are needed to solve the task. Additionally, to follow the paradigm of the analysis section, we let the networks train individually for the first 2 million time steps, after which we "turn on" the interaction. The resulting error curves and entropy curve are shown in figure 5.

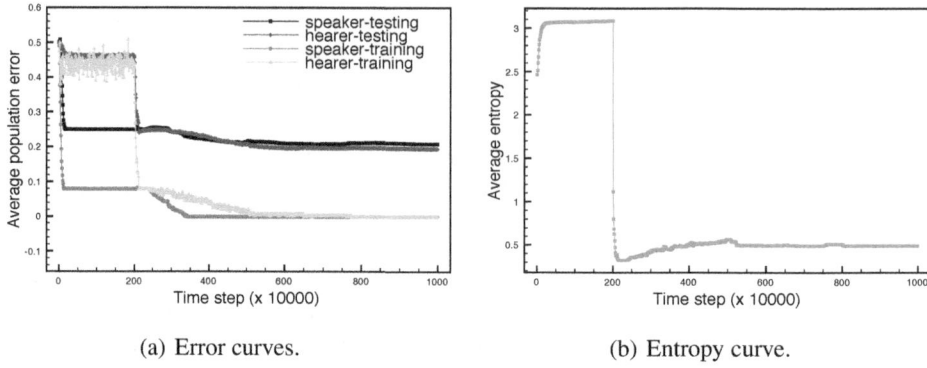

(a) Error curves.   (b) Entropy curve.

Fig. 5. Learning and entropy curves on the 12-input-first-3-xor task

We see that in the initial phase of individual learning, the training error and testing error[3] both drop immediately (figure 5(a)). This corresponds to an *increase* in the complexity of the solution as shown by the initial rise in the entropy curve in figure 5(b). The training error drops to about 0.08 and stabilizes there, and the corresponding testing error stabilizes at 0.25. There hearer errors remain around 0.5 during this time, which shows that the learners are discovering different solutions at this stage. When we turn on interaction at time step 2 million, there is an immediate drop in the complexity of the solutions, matched by a similarly sharp drop in the hearer errors. The training error then goes to zero, and the testing error drops to 0.2. This result shows how a lower complexity solution is discovered through interaction, and that this lower complexity solution leads to better generalization.

For a more "real-world" test, we trained a population of 10 neural networks, using the classification game, on a gender discrimination task. The dataset we used is the Stanford Medical Students database [18].

The database contains four hundred images of faces, of which two hundred are male and two hundred female. Twenty images from each class were randomly chosen to make up the training set, and the remaining three hundred and sixty were put into the testing set. Figure 6 shows some of these images. We reduced the images to size 32 × 32. The neural networks thus had 1024 inputs. We set each neural network to have 50 hidden layer nodes, and, to force them to extract "good" features, we made them reconstruct the image at the output of the neural network, in addition to classifying it. Thus they had 1025 outputs, of which the first one was treated as the classification. Note that we are giving raw pixel data to the neural networks, without any preprocessing. This representation is much more difficult to learn from than, e.g., using the principal components or eigenfaces [19,20], because the raw values don't correct for differences in background lighting, position of the face, etc. Even though the images are taken to minimize differences in orientation, size, etc., it is still significantly difficult to use the pixel data directly. In fact, when we try to use a standard neural network (i.e. the

---

[3] Note that the testing error is just plotted for comparison. This information is not available to the learners themselves.

Fig. 6. Samples from the Stanford medical students database. The learning task is to classify each face correctly by gender.

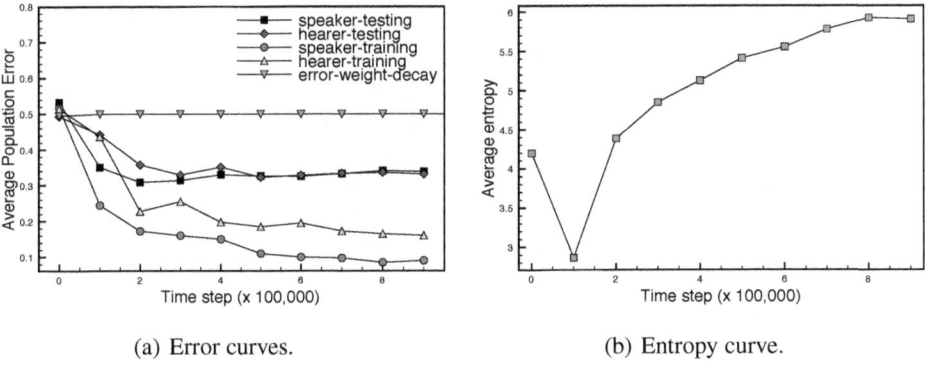

(a) Error curves.   (b) Entropy curve.

Fig. 7. Learning and entropy curves on the gender classification task

no communication case), it is completely unable to improve classification performance through learning: the error always remains around 50%.

To compare with a standard complexity regularization approach, we also implemented weight decay [21], where at each update a weight is also decremented by a fraction d, so that weights tend to go to zero unless reinforced by backpropagation. In this case also, the neural network was not able to learn, and the error remained around 50%.

When the agents were trained using the classification game we got significant improvement, as shown by the learning curves in figure 7. The figure shows five learning curves: two are for the training set and two are for the testing set. The speaker error is simply the average number of misclassifications by the population on the training (or testing) set. To calculate the hearer error, we put each agent in the role of the hearer and choose a speaker randomly from the population. The hearer then has to classify all the points using encodings provided by this random speaker. Averaging all the hearer errors gives the hearer learning curve (over time). The fifth learning curve is for neural network training (without interaction) with weight decay. As mentioned above, this fifth learning curve shows no improvement; the error remains at 0.5 even if we extend training for several more time steps than shown in the figure. Figure 7(b) shows the complexity of the solutions found.

As figure 7(a) shows, the agents were unable to converge on a shared representation (the hearer error remains high), at least in the time for which we ran the experiment. Further, there is some evidence of overfitting, as the speaker error on the testing set increases slightly after dropping initially. Despite these issues, we believe that it is impressive that the classification game enables the neural networks to significantly improve performance in a situation where individual neural networks fail to learn.

8   Conclusion

We have shown that a population of learners can *implicitly* perform complexity regularization by interacting with each other during learning. We have characterized the equilibria of this game, and discussed why low-complexity equilibria tend to be selected by the dynamic induced by the classification game learning algorithm. We have also shown that the classification game results in better performance than plain neural networks trained with error backpropagation, with or without weight decay.

The rate of convergence of the classification game, though we have not discussed it here, tends to be quite slow. This is not unexpected, since it is hard to compute Nash equilibria. However, we have some evidence that learning can be speeded up by altering the topology of interaction of the learners [22], by making it scale-free, for example, or dynamic, where the topology updates according to noisy preferential attachment [23]. Detailed exploration of the role of the interaction topology from a game-theoretic viewpoint remains to be done, and the tradeoff with respect to how well the Nash equilibrium is approximated in each case is also an important question that needs to be worked out.

In general, we believe that there may be many other cases of important computations that can be performed implicitly through interaction by a population of agents. Designing multi-agent learning algorithms that can achieve these results represents, in our view, an interesting and potentially very useful twist on mechanism design in game theory.

Acknowledgments

I thank my external collaborators and members of the Network Dynamics and Simulation Science Laboratory (NDSSL) for their suggestions and comments. This work has been partially supported NSF Nets Grant CNS-0626964, NSF HSD Grant SES-0729441, CDC Center of Excellence in Public Health Informatics Grant 2506055-01, NIH-NIGMS MIDAS project 5 U01 GM070694-05, DTRA CNIMS Grant HDTRA1-07-C-0113 and NSF NETS CNS-0831633.

References

1. Barron, A.R.: Complexity regularization with application to artificial neural networks. In: Roussas, G. (ed.) Nonparametric Functional Estimation and Related Topics, pp. 561–576. Kluwer Academic Publishers, Boston (1991)

2. Hinton, G., van Camp, D.: Keeping neural networks simple by minimizing the description length of the weights. In: Pitt, L. (ed.) Proceedings of the Sixth ACM Conference on Computational Learning Theory, Santa Cruz, CA, USA, pp. 5–13. ACM, New York (1993)

3. Hochreiter, S., Schmidhuber, J.: Flat minima. Neural Computation 9(1), 1–42 (1997)

4. Wolpert, D.: Backpropagation over i-o functions rather than weights. In: Cowan, J.D., Tesauro, G., Alspector, J. (eds.) Advances in Neural Information Processing Systems, vol. 6, pp. 200–207. Morgan Kaufmann, San Mateo (1994)

5. Swarup, S., Gasser, L.: The classification game: Combining supervised learning and language evolution. Connection Science (to appear, 2010)

6. Haykin, S.: Neural Networks: A Comprehensive Foundation, 2nd edn. Prentice-Hall, Englewood Cliffs (1998)

7. Hinton, G.E.: Learning translation invariant recognition in a massively parallel network. In: Goos, G., Hartmanis, J. (eds.) PARLE 1987. LNCS, vol. 258, pp. 1–13. Springer, Heidelberg (1987)

8. Jin, Y., Okabe, T., Sendhoff, B.: Neural network regularization and ensembling using multiobjective evolutionary algorithms. In: Proceedings of the Congress on Evolutionary Computation (CEC), pp. 1–8. IEEE Press, Los Alamitos (2004)

9. Mason, L., Baxter, J., Bartlett, P., Frean, M.: Boosting algorithms as gradient descent. In: Solla, S.A., Leen, T.K., Muller, K.R. (eds.) Advances in Neural Information Processing Systems, vol. 12, pp. 512–518. MIT Press, Cambridge (2000)

10. Breiman, L.: Bagging predictors. Machine Learning 24(2), 123–140 (1996)

11. Haussler, D.: Decision-theoretic generalizations of the PAC model for neural net and other learning applications. Information and Computation 100(1), 78–150 (1992)

12. Blumer, A., Ehrenfeucht, A., Haussler, D., Warmuth, M.K.: Occam's razor. Information Processing Letters 24(6), 377–380 (1987)

13. Board, R., Pitt, L.: On the necessity of Occam algorithms. In: Proceedings of the Twenty Second Annual ACM Symposium on the Theory of Computing (STOC), pp. 54–63 (1990)

14. Li, M., Tromp, J., Vitányi, P.: Sharpening Occam's razor. Information Processing Letters 85(5), 267–274 (2003)

15. Quinlan, J.R.: Induction of decision trees. Machine Learning 1, 81–106 (1986)

16. Luo, P., Wong, K.Y.M.: Dynamical and stationary properties of on-line learning from finite training sets. Physical Review E 67(1) (2003)

17. Ampazis, N., Perantonis, S.J., Taylor, J.G.: Dynamics of multilayer networks in the vicinity of temporary minima. Neural Networks 12, 43–58 (1999)

18. Diaco, A., DiCarlo, J., Santos, J.: Stanford medical students database (2000), http://scien.stanford.edu/class/ee368/projects2001/dropbox/project16/med_students.tar.gz.

19. Sirovich, L., Kirby, M.: Low-dimensional procedure for the characterization of human faces. Journal of the Optical Society of America A 4, 519–524 (1987)

20. Turk, M.A., Pentland, A.P.: Face recognition using eigenfaces. In: Proceedings of the IEEE Conference on Computer Vision and Pattern Recognition, CVPR (1991)

21. Werbos, P.: Backpropagation: Past and future. In: Proceedings of the IEEE International Conference on Neural Networks, pp. 343–353. IEEE Press, Los Alamitos (1988)

22. Swarup, S., Gasser, L.: Language evolution on a dynamic social network. In: The MORS Conference on Analyzing the Impact of Emerging Societies on National Security, Argonne, IL, April 14-18 (2008)

23. Swarup, S., Gasser, L.: Unifying evolutionary and network dynamics. Phys. Rev. E 75, 66114 (2007)

Dealing with Incomplete Normative States

Juan Manuel Serrano and Sergio Saugar

Computing Department
University Rey Juan Carlos
Madrid, Spain
juanmanuel.serrano@urjc.es, sergio.saugar@urjc.es

Abstract. This paper puts forward a normative framework which enables the specification of incomplete theories and their management through incomplete normative states. In particular, attempts to perform a social action are evaluated either as permitted, prohibited (i.e. not permitted) or *pending* for execution (i.e. neither permitted nor prohibited). The framework lets designated agents resolve this latter category of attempts through the speech acts *allow* and *forbid*. We build upon action language K and its support for incompleteness in the formalisation of the framework. The proposal is illustrated with some scenarios drawn from the management of university courses.

1 Introduction

Empowerments and permissions are two common normative devices in the design of computational societies [1,2,3,4,5]. The former notion allows us to model the institutional capabilities ascribed to agents of the society; the latter one serves to represent those desirable institutional states or courses of action which do not lend themselves to violation. Concerning permissions, a difference is made between regimentation and enforcement mechanisms in the implementation of normative systems [6]: regimented infrastructures (e.g. AMELI [7]) effectively prevent agents from executing some action if the corresponding permission does not hold; on the contrary, systems based upon enforcement rely on a subsidiary normative corpus of checking and sanctioning rules to bias the behaviour of agents towards the desired courses of actions. Which approach is better (either regimentation or enforcement) essentially depends on the application domain. For instance, regimentation may simply not be an option in a purely decentralised, large-scale, open system, whereas enforcement alone may not be sufficient in some business process management settings.

This paper addresses the issue of normative incompleteness, mainly from a regimented perspective. A normative theory is *incomplete* when it is unable, in certain situations, to draw a definite conclusion on the truth or falsity of some normative relation. For instance, the theory does not allow us to infer whether some action is either permitted or not permitted (i.e. prohibited). There are two major approaches for dealing with incomplete theories. First, the theory could be extended with default assumptions that automatically complete the inferences of

J. Padget et al. (Eds.): COIN 2009, LNAI 6069, pp. 304–319, 2010.

the theory when necessary. For instance, the general default "everything which is not permitted, is prohibited" may be added to a normative theory in order to account for a closed-world assumption concerning permissions. Notice that even if the normative theory is incomplete, this approach leads to complete normative states, i.e. every normative relation is either true or false at runtime. The second approach consists of allowing a third truth value, *undefined* or *unknown*, which holds for those normative relations which are affected by incompleteness. This paper revolves around this second approach.

Another dimension of analysis which is also relevant for our proposal concerns the *sources* of incompleteness. Roughly speaking, a normative theory may be incomplete due to two different reasons. First, the theory may be *underspecified*, i.e. there are general rules which would allow us to resolve the incompleteness, but they are not implemented in the normative system as yet. Second, the normative deficiency of the theory may be a symptom of *inherent* incompleteness. In the former case, the normative program may be enhanced with rules of the application domain which can handle those situations of incompleteness. In the latter case, which is the one mainly addressed by this paper, those situations can not be tackled through general rules but only on a case by case basis by proper agents at runtime[1].

For instance, let us consider a computational society designed to support the management of *university courses*. As part of the resulting specification, empowerment and permission rules are defined which partially regulate the social processes of the application domain, namely *assignments, examinations, tutoring, lecturing*, and so forth. In particular, the following norms concerning the membership of assignment working groups are considered. Firstly, some *student* is granted empowerment to *join* a working group *if and only if* she has not passed the corresponding assignment, and is not currently participating in any other working group for that assignment. Secondly, permission to join some group is granted *only if* the specified submission deadline has not yet passed. Note that the empowerment rule is complete, whereas the permission rule only states a necessary condition. Thus, if some empowered student attempts to join some working group and the corresponding submission deadline passed, then the attempt will be prohibited. On the contrary, if the deadline has not yet passed, then there will be grounds neither for prohibiting nor permitting the attempt. To handle this situation, we may add the general default "everything which is not prohibited, is permitted", but this does not seem adequate since the ultimate decision on the permission or prohibition of the attempt should lie with the initiator of the working group (i.e. the student who *set up* the group). Hence, sufficient conditions for permitting the joining action can not be specified in advance by the designer of the society.

This paper attempts to provide a normative framework which enables the specification of inherent incomplete theories of empowerment and permission

---

[1] These agents may indeed follow general decision rules in order to allow or forbid someone to do something. However, these are not institutional but private rules which govern the internal dynamics of the agent components.

rules, such as the one described above for the course management application. The normative framework shall deal with incomplete theories through normative incomplete states, and will provide agents with adequate mechanisms to resolve the incompleteness at runtime. In order to formalise this framework, we first build upon the support for incompleteness of action language K [8], which, in turn, builds upon the two characteristic negation operators (weak and strong) of Answer Set Programming (ASP) [9]. In fact, action language K is implemented as a frontend to the answer set solver DLV [11], called DLV^K [10]. Second, the normative framework shall rely upon the notions of empowerment, permission and social actions reported in [5], where action language C+ is used as formal device [12]. That paper introduces the operational semantics of a language for programming computational societies called SPEECH [13,14,5,15], where social actions (e.g. speech acts) are not treated as events but as *social entities* which have an execution state, viz. *prohibited* or *performed*. This paper extends the operational specification reported in [5] in such a way that social actions can also be in a *pending* state, which holds when the normative program does not allow to infer whether the social action being attempted is either permitted or prohibited. Lastly, this paper will provide a mechanism for resolving pending attempts through a formalization of artificial counterparts of the English speech acts verbs *allow* and *forbid* [18].

The rest of the paper is structured as follows. Firstly, the most salient features of action language K for the purpose of this paper will be reviewed. Then, the general framework for social action processing in SPEECH will be introduced, describing the major features of the action description in language K. Next, the speech acts *allow* and *forbid* will be formalised and some experiments using DLV^K will be described. Lastly, the major differences with previous work will be discussed and future work briefly described.

2 Review of Action Language K

Action languages are formal techniques for representing and reasoning about the performance of actions in dynamic domains. The semantics of action languages is given in terms of transition systems, namely graphs whose states and arcs represent, respectively, the possible configurations of the domain and its evolution due to the concurrent execution of a set of actions. Commonly, action languages such as C+ describe transitions between states of the *physical* world, i.e. states which represent complete configurations of the domain, where each fluent is necessarily either true or false. In contrast, action language K [8,10] allows us to describe transitions between states of *knowledge*, where the truth values of some fluents may be neither true nor false, but *unknown*. The motivation behind action language K was thus to support agents with an incomplete view of the world in their planning processes.

An specification in language K is divided into three major parts (figure 1): the *action description*, the *background knowledge* and the *planning query*. The action description declares the set of fluents and actions which define the state

```
% Action description

fluents:
    f₁(X₁,...) requires t₁(X₁), ..
    ...
actions:
    a₁(X₁,...) requires t₁(X₁), ..
    ...
initially:
    caused f if B
    ...
always:
    caused f if B after A
    ...
```

```
% Background knowledge

% Instances of types
t₁(a₁₁).
t₁(a₁₂).
...

% Subsumption rules
tₙ(X) :- t₁(X).
...
```

```
% Planning goal
goal:
    f₁, ..., fₙ? (n)
```

Fig. 1. Structure of K-specifications

parameters and characteristic events of the system being modeled, respectively; moreover, it includes the set of causation rules and executability conditions which define the dynamics of the system. The background knowledge represents static knowledge which does not depend on particular configurations of the system. Lastly, the planning goal specifies a desirable class of system's configurations. More precisely:

– A fluent or action p is declared using an expression of the form:

$$p(X_1,...,X_n) \text{ requires } t_1(X_1),...,t_n(X_n)$$

where X_i are variables and t_i are type predicates which specify the sorts of the corresponding variables[2]. Type predicates are part of the background knowledge, where their corresponding instances are defined (figure 1). The background knowledge may also include different subsumption relationships amongst types. Thus, the rule $t_n(X)$:- $t_1(X)$ establishes that any instance of type t_1 is also an instance of type t_n. This has as an immediate consequence that any fluent or action declaration, as well as any causation rule and executability condition, declared within the scope of type t_n also pertain to instances of type t_1.
– Causation rules are expressions of the form:

caused f if B after A

If the subexpression **f** is a fluent literal (i.e. an atom **a**, or one prefixed by the strong negation operator, **-a**), the causation rule expresses that **f** holds in the current state if **B** holds in the current state and **A** also holds in the preceding state. The subexpressions **B** and **A** are actually sequences of literals, possibly

---

[2] This is actually a slightly simplified version of this construction. See [8] for the full version.

prefixed with the default (or weak) negation operator **not**. The expression **not a**, where **a** is an atom, holds if **a** is not known to be true, whereas the expression **not -a** holds if **a** is not known to be false. If both expressions hold then the truth value of **a** is *unknown*.

- The subexpression **B** can only refer to type or fluent predicates, whereas **A** can also refer to action predicates. If sequences **B** and **A** are empty, the corresponding **if** and **after** parts can be dropped from the expression. If the **after** part is empty the rule is called *static*, otherwise the causation rule is *dynamic*. Moreover, if **f** is the reserved atom **false**, the causation rule represents an static (resp. dynamic) integrity constraint which allows us to filter out from the transition system ill-formed states (resp. transitions). Dynamic rules can be used to represent the non-executability conditions and effects of actions. In particular, the following macro rule is a shorthand of a dynamic constraint to represent that condition **B** blocks the execution of action **a** [8, sec. 2]:

$$\textbf{nonexecutable a if B} \Leftrightarrow \texttt{caused false after a, B}$$

- Executability statements are primitive (i.e. not macro) expressions of the form

$$\textbf{executable a if B}$$

This kind of declaration expresses that action **a** is *eligible* for execution in any state of knowledge in which **B** holds. If we want the execution of action **a** to be not only possible but also mandatory, then a dynamic constraint can be declared. Since this a common requirement in this paper, we introduce the following macro rule which allows us to declare **B** as a sufficient condition for executing **a**:

$$\textbf{executed a if B} \Leftrightarrow \begin{array}{l} \textbf{executable a if B} \\ \texttt{caused false after not a, B} \end{array}$$

This macro is specially useful for representing reactive rules defined over *endogeneous* actions, i.e. actions whose causes for execution are to be found within the system being modeled. These actions contrast with so-called *exogeneous* actions, viz. actions whose causes for execution are not modeled by the action description. For this latter type of actions, executability statements suffice.

- Causation rules of an action description may be declared within the scope of the **initially** or **always** keywords. In the former case, only static rules are allowed which characterise the class of initial states of the system that will be considered in the planning problem. In the latter, the rules apply to any state of the system.

- The goal of the planning problem to be solved by the DLV^K interpreter is an expression of the form:

$$\texttt{f}_1, \ \ldots, \ \texttt{f}_n? \ (n)$$

where each f_i is a fluent literal and n is a natural number. The output of the DLV^K interpreter consists of a sequence of n sets of actions, whose execution leads the system from one of the initial states to a state in which the goal literals are true.

3   Social Action Processing

Departing from its original motivation, action language K is used in this paper for describing transitions between states of *institutional* worlds, rather than states of *knowledge* of some planning agent. In particular, the technical apparatus of language K is exploited to represent institutional states where some normative fluents (e.g., permissions) may have an objective, non-epistemic indeterminacy. In software engineering terms, the dynamic system to be modeled is thus the social middleware infrastructure in charge of the management of the institutional state of the computational society, rather than the software components participating as agents in the society.

The action description of the social middleware is partitioned in several sub-specifications corresponding to the different types of social entities which make up a computational society according to the SPEECH language, namely *social interactions*, *agents* and *social actions*. A complete account of the whole specification is beyond the scope of this paper. Instead, the focus here is on the major features concerning the normative framework, and the specifications of the *allow* and *forbid* speech act types, which are part of the standard library of the language.

3.1   Social Interactions

The institutional state of computational societies is hierarchically structured in terms of a tree of *social interactions*. The root of this tree, or top-level interaction, represents the social context within which the whole agent activity takes place; the other sub-interactions represent the social contexts for particular joint activities (i.e. social processes). For instance, assignment working groups are represented by social interactions which are sub-interactions of courses, another type of social interaction. Social interactions may be *initiated* within the context of some other interaction, and eventually *finished* by the social middleware. The conditions which cause the execution of these actions are, in general, dependent on the type of interaction. Thus, university courses are automatically initiated when the new academic year begins, and assignment groups are initiated when some student successfully declares its initiation through the performance of the *set up* social action – in accordance with the empowerment and permission rules of the society. In this latter case, the *initiator* of the social interaction can be defined as the performer of the *set up* action.

3.2 Agents

Agents are roles[3] played by software components interacting through the social middleware which purport to achieve some goal as members of some interaction context. In order to do so, agents are empowered to perform social actions such as *setting up* new interactions, *joining* existing interactions, and so forth. For instance, the purpose of students is to pass the course to which they belong as members. In order to achieve this (purported) goal, students are empowered to set up working groups or to join existing ones in order to carry out some mandatory assignment. When the purpose of some agent is too complex, its whole activity may be structured into a role-playing hierarchy of further agents. Thus, the activity of a course student within the context of a working group is represented by *working group students*, a new kind of agent. Agent roles are *played* and *abandoned* by the social middleware according to certain conditions. For instance, a course student role is automatically abandoned as soon as the agent passes the course's subject; a working group student is automatically created for the initiator of the working group, and for any student who successfully manages to *join* a pre-existing working group.

Listing 1 partially shows the K-specification of the `agent` type, which includes the declarations of general fluents and actions which characterise and, respectively, affect the institutional state of any kind of agent. Particularly, it shows the declaration of the fluents `state_a`, `context_a` and `player`, which represent the runtime state of agents (`playing` or `abandoned`), the social interaction context to which the agent belongs and its player agent, respectively. Also, it shows the declaration of the actions `play` and `play_for`. According to the rules declared in the **always** section, the former action causes some agent to be created within some social interaction context. The specification only includes its non-executability condition and effect (lines 14–16). The action `play_for` causes some agent to be created (line 18) for a particular player agent (line 19).

3.3 Social Actions

The activity of agent components within a multiagent society manifests itself through the performance of *attempts*. This external action allows an agent component to perform a given *social action*, namely to *say* something, *manipulate* the environment or *observe* the current state of some social entity. Due to lack of space, this paper refers only to speech acts and, particularly, to declarations such as *set up, join, allow* and *forbid*. The processing of attempts by the social

---

[3] The word "agent" is used to denote agent *roles*, whereas the expression "agent *component*" is used to denote those software components (outside the social middleware) playing some agent role within the computational society. For instance, in the course management application, the human users are the actual students, teachers, and so forth, which employ common user interfaces (e.g. a web browser) to interact as *student agents, teacher agents*, etc., through the social middleware. Thus, agent components for this application domain are not BDI intelligent agents but plain user interfaces.

```
fluents:                                                              1
    state_a(A,S)    requires agent(A), agent_state(S).               2
    context_a(A,I) requires agent(A), interaction (I).              3
    player(A1,A2)   requires agent(A1), agent(A2)                    4
    ...                                                               5
actions:                                                              6
    play(A,I) requires                                                7
        interaction(I), agent(A).                                     8
    play_for(A1,A2,I) requires                                        9
        agent(A1), agent(A2), interaction(I).                        10
    ...                                                              11
always:                                                              12
    % play/2                                                         13
    nonexecutable play(A,I) if state_a(A,playing).                   14
    caused state_a(A,playing) after play(A,I).                       15
    caused context_a(A,I) after play(A,I).                           16
    % play_for/3                                                     17
    executed play(A1,I) if play_for(A1,A2,I).                        18
    caused player(A1,A2) after play_for(A1,A2,I).                    19
    ...                                                              20
```

Listing 1. K-specification of *agents*

middleware takes into account the *empowerment* and *permission* rules of the society. In particular, empowerments shall represent the institutional capabilities of agents, i.e. which social actions a given agent is capable of performing in virtue of the role it represents; permissions shall denote the circumstances under which these institutional capabilities can be exercised. Attempts by agent components are processed according to the following procedure:

- If the agent is empowered to perform the specified social action, then the attempt will be taken into account; otherwise, i.e. either if it is known for certain that the agent is not empowered, or it can not be concluded that it is empowered, the external action will be dismissed. In this latter case, the institutional state of the multiagent society will not be altered at all.
- If the agent is empowered to perform the action, but it is known that the specified performer is not permitted to perform it (i.e. it is prohibited), then the process is finished with a *prohibited* attempt status.
- On the contrary, if the agent is both empowered and permitted, then the social action is performed by the middleware. The effects caused through this execution depend on the kind of social action being performed.
- If the agent is empowered to perform that action, but it is neither known that the action is permitted nor prohibited, then the social action is kept in a *pending* state. This state persists by inertia until it is eventually resolved into a *performed* or *prohibited* state as soon as it is known whether the action is permitted or prohibited.

This procedure is formalised as part of the `social_action` type specification, whose major features are shown in listing 2. The fluents which characterise the institutional state of a social action, declared in lines 2–8, represent its runtime state (fluent `state_sa`, which may hold one of the values `pending`, `prohibited` or `performed`); its context of execution (`context_sa`); its performer agent (`performer`); and the empowerment and permission evaluations of the social action (`empowered` and `permitted`).

```
fluents:                                                          1
    state_sa(Act,S)     requires  social_action(Act),             2
                                   social_action_state(S).        3
    context_sa(Act,I)   requires  social_action(Act),             4
                                   interaction (I).               5
    performer(Act,A)    requires  social_action(Act), agent(A).   6
    empowered(Act)      requires  social_action(Act).             7
    permitted(Act)      requires  social_action(Act).             8
    ...                                                           9
actions:                                                          10
    attempt(Act) requires  social_action(Act).                   11
    perform(Act) requires  social_action(Act).                   12
always:                                                           13
    % attempt/1                                                   14
    executable attempt(Act,A) if not ill_formed(Act) ...          15
    caused state_sa(Act,prohibited) after                         16
        attempt(Act), empowered(Act), -permitted(Act).            17
    executed perform(Act) if                                      18
        attempt(Act), empowered(Act), permitted(Act).             19
    caused state_sa(Act,pending) after                            20
        attempt(Act), empowered(Act), not permitted(Act),         21
        not -permitted(Act).                                      22
    ...                                                           23
    % pending attempts                                            24
    caused state_sa(Act,prohibited) if                            25
        empowered(Act), -permitted(Act)                           26
        after state_sa(Act,pending).                              27
    executed perform(Act) if                                      28
        state_sa(Act,pending), empowered(Act),                    29
        permitted(Act).                                           30
    caused -state_sa(Act,pending) after   .                       31
        state_sa(Act,pending), not empowered(Act).                32
    ...                                                           33
    % perform/1                                                   34
    caused state_sa(Act,performed) after perform(Act).            35
```

Listing 2. K-specification of *social actions*

Attempts by agent components to execute some social action `Act` are represented through the action `attempt(Act)`. This action is exogenous, so that it is just declared as **executable** (line 15) subject to the action not being *ill-formed* (e.g. the interaction context being closed) and other preconditions not shown in listing 2. The different scenarios described above concerning the processing of attempts are modeled through different groups of dynamic rules:

- Lines 16–22 describe the effects of executing the `attempt` action. Note that all these rules require the performer agent to be empowered; otherwise, the attempt is dismissed. The first rule (line 16) declares a resulting `prohibited` state for the social action if it is known that its execution is not permitted (i.e. `-permitted(Act)`). The second rule declares the performance of the action when it is known that its execution is permitted (line 18). Execution of social actions is represented by the action `perform`, whose only effect at this level of abstraction is the change in the runtime execution state (line 35). Lastly, if the execution of the social action is neither known to be permitted nor prohibited, then the social action is kept in a pending execution state in the resulting system state (line 20).
- Pending attempts are eventually resolved according to causation rules in lines 25–31. The first two rules refer to those circumstances in which the system evolves in such a way that the social action becomes permitted or prohibited. In those cases, its runtime state will be resolved to the `performed` (line 28) or the `prohibition` values (line 25) by the corresponding rules. Otherwise, the social action will persist by inertia until the performer agent becomes unempowered (line 31) or the social action becomes ill-formed.

3.4   Forbidding and Allowing Social Actions

Those social actions pending for execution will be resolved as prohibited or permitted attempts as soon as the rules of the society enable the social middleware to draw a definite conclusion on its permission status. As a complementary mechanism, particularly useful in the absence of general rules, designated agents may also change the permission status through the speech acts *allow* and *forbid*. The specification of a new type of social action t_1 proceeds, firstly, by declaring the rule `social_action(X) :- t₁(X)` as part of the background knowledge. This rule establishes that any entity of type t_1 shall be regarded as a social action, so that rules which define the general structure and dynamics of social actions (listing 2) are applicable for entities of that type. Secondly, new fluents representing the additional arguments of the new social action type must be declared. Lastly, new rules for representing the post-conditions of the performance of the new type of action, as well as their additional non-executability conditions, etc., have to be declared as well.

For instance, listing 3 shows the formalisation of the `join` speech act type. By performing a speech act of this type, the speaker declares that she plays a new role within the social action's execution context. The interaction context and the player agent are represented by the inherited social actions fluents `context_sa` and `performer` (listing 2). The new role to be played is declared as a new fluent, `new_role`. The rest of the specification includes the particular effects associated to the execution of this kind of declaration, which are indirectly achieved through the internal action `play_for` (listing 2).

```
fluents:                                                                 1
   new_role(Join,A) requires join(Join), agent(A).                       2
   ...                                                                   3
always:                                                                  4
   executed play_for(A1,A2,I) if                                         5
      join(Join), perform(Join), context_sa(Join,I),                     6
      performer(Join,A2), new_role(Join,A1).                             7
   ...                                                                   8
```

Listing 3. K-specification of the *join* social action

Figure 4 shows the partial specification of the `allow` speech act. In this case, the generic social action specification is extended with the new fluent `action_a`, which represents the social action targeted by the *allow* speech act. The effect of performing the *allow* action is to explicitly cause that the social action is permitted (line 6). The specification of the *forbid* speech act is similar to the one shown in listing 4. The only major difference pertains to its post-condition, which in this case resorts to the strong negation operator, i.e.

```
caused -permitted(Act) after
   forbid(Forbid), perform(Forbid), action_f(Forbid,Act)
```

```
fluents:                                                                 1
   action_a(Allow,Act) requires allow(Allow),                            2
                                 social_action(Act).                     3
   ...                                                                   4
always:                                                                  5
   caused permitted(Act) after                                           6
      allow(Allow), perform(Allow), action_a(Allow,Act).                 7
   ...                                                                   8
```

Listing 4. K-specification of the *allow* social action

4   Planning Problems

This section illustrates the normative framework described above through some planning problems defined over a simplified implementation of the course management application. The bulk of this implementation consists of a collection of action descriptions which specifies the domain-dependent types of the application domain, namely *courses, working groups, students,* and so forth. These subspecifications are added to the action description of the normative framework and standard library to obtain a working prototype. Thus, students of courses are represented by the type `courseStudent` which is modeled as a particular subtype of agent (i.e. the rule `agent(X) :- courseStudent(X)` is part of the background knowledge). The additional fluents, actions, causation rules, etc., which pertain to agents of this particular type (besides the standard ones, described in listing 1) are declared by the corresponding action description. The full implementation of the course management example, the normative framework and the standard speech act library, can be downloaded from the address http://www.speechlang.org/k. Due to lack of space, this section just describes the implemented planning scenarios.

1st *scenario: Allowing to join.* The implementation of the first scenario is partially shown in listings 5 and 6. Listing 5 represents the background knowledge of the planning problem, which basically consists of the declarations of the different objects which populate the computational society. Thus, s1 and s2 are course students and the top object is a course interaction (lines 2–4). Concerning listing 6, it declares the initial state of the system as well as the goal state to be achieved. Thus, lines 3–6 state that, initially, the two course students are being played within the context of the top course; that there is an open working group within the course, which has been initiated by student s1; and, that this student participates in that working group by playing role s11. The goal posed to the DLV^K planner asks for the possible ways in which student s2 may play a role within the working group wg1, in exactly three planning steps (line 13).

```
% Top-level interaction                                1
course(top).                                           2
courseStudent(s1).                                     3
courseStudent(s2).                                     4
...                                                    5
% Assignment working Group                             6
assignmentGroup(wg1).                                  7
assignmentGroupStudent(s11).                           8
assignmentGroupStudent(s21).                           9
join(join1).                                          10
allow(allow1).                                        11
```

Listing 5. Background knowledge of the planning problem

```
initially:                                                         1
   % objects ''instantiated'' in the initial state                2
   state_a(s1,playing). context_a(s1,top).                         3
   state_a(s2,playing). context_a(s2,top).                         4
   state_i(wg1,open). context_i(wg1,top). initiator(wg1,s1)        5
   state_a(s11,playing). context_a(s11,wg1). player(s11,s1)        6
   % objects to be instantiated in future states                  7
   -has_state_sa(join1). new_role(join1,s21).                      8
   -has_state_a(s21).                                              9
   -has_state_sa(allow1). action_a(allow1,join1).                 10
   ...                                                            11
goal:                                                             12
   state_a(A,playing), context_a(A,wg1), player(A,s2)? (3)        13
```

Listing 6. Initial and final states of the planning problem

The output of the DLV^K planner is shown in figure 2. As expected, the first action to be performed is an attempt by agent s2 to join the working group. Two additional objects have to be declared in the background knowledge in order for this action to be performed: a *join* speech act, join1 and the student agent to be played within the working group, s21. These objects initially belong to the pool of objects which are made available for the planning process (lines 8–10 of listing 6), and might be instantiated in future states. Since the student is empowered to perform the join action but no permission rules are declared (according to the specification of the *working group student* type, not shown in the paper), the attempt to perform it results in a pending status. The next state features an attempt by agent s11 to allow the performance of the join action. Since this agent is both empowered and permitted to perform social action allow1, the permissions to execute the join1 action are in effect in the next state. This, in turn, causes the performance of the join action and the consequent playing of the student agent within the working group, which, in turn, causes the goal to be satisfied.

```
STATE 0:  state_a(s2,playing) state_i(wg1,open)
          context_sa(join1,wg1) performer(join1,s2)
          new_role(join1,s21) empowered(join1) ...
ACTIONS:  attempt(join1)
STATE 1:  state_sa(join1,pending) state_a(s11,playing)
          context_sa(allow1,wg1) performer(allow1,s11)
          action_a(allow1,join1) empowered(allow1)
          permitted(allow1) ...
ACTIONS:  attempt(allow1) perform(allow1)
STATE 2:  state_sa(allow1,performed)
          state_sa(join1,pending) performer(join1,a1)
          permitted(join1) ...
ACTIONS:  perform(join1) play_for(s21,s2,wg1) play(s21,wg1)
STATE 3:  state_a(s21,playing) player(s21,s2)
          context_a(s21,wg1) ...
```

Fig. 2. DLV^K answer to a planning problem

2nd scenario: Prohibiting attempts to join. The planning query for the second scenario asks for the different ways in which some attempt to join the working group may be prohibited. The answer of the DLV^K planner outputs two solutions: in the first one, the group's initiator ignores the pending attempt, whereas in the second one the initiator explicitly forbids the attempt. In the former case, the attempt is prohibited when the deadline for submitting the assignment passes, in accordance to the prohibition rule shown in listing 7. This rule, which states a necessary condition for joining assignment working groups, is part of the specification of the *working group student* type.

```
caused -permitted(Join) if Deadline < Now,
   % where
   join(Join), performer(Join,S),
      context_sa(Join,G), new_role(Join,GS),
   courseStudent(S),
   assignmentGroup(G), assignment_g(G,A),
   assignment(A), deadline(A,Deadline),
   assignmentGroupStudent(GS),
   now(Now).
```

Listing 7. Prohibition rule for joining working groups

3rd *scenario: Authorization hierarchies.* The third planning scenario features the emergence of authorization hierarchies to resolve some pending attempt. This phenomenon is due to the fact that *allow* and *forbid* are social actions, and hence their performance is also governed by permission rules. Thus, if some agent attempting to allow other agent to do something lacks permission to perform this authorization, the *allow* action will be frozen in a pending state. This pending attempt may be resolved through the performance of a (meta-)allow speech act; and so forth. For instance, let us assume that teachers want to have a finer grained control over the membership of working groups. In order to support this requirement, the normative program establishes that each group's initiator needs the teacher's authorization in order to allow or forbid some colleague to join their working groups.

5   Discussion

This paper has introduced a normative framework for computational societies which makes possible the specification of incomplete sets of permission rules. Rather than automatically completing the resulting normative state with defeasible assumptions (using negation as failure, abductive reasoning, etc.), the framework is able to handle incomplete normative states where some permission fluents are neither true, nor false, but have an *undefined* truth value. Attempts to perform speech acts which are neither permitted nor prohibited lead to the creation of *pending* speech acts, which may be eventually resolved as prohibited or permitted (and hence executed). Therefore, speech acts are not treated as events but as social entities, which contrasts with other approaches based on Answer Set Programming (ASP) [3], the event calculus [4] or the C+ action language [2], which revolve around complete normative states.

The proposed normative framework depends upon the features of action language K for reasoning with incomplete information, which in turn build upon the two kinds of negation operators (weak and strong) provided by ASP. Using weak negation, the designer may resort to a general default like "everything which is not permitted, is prohibited" whenever it is adequate for some particular type of attempt. Using strong negation, the programmer may represent necessary conditions of permissions, thereby endorsing an open-world assumption over designated types of attempts. These features make our work closely aligned with the proposal of [16], where ASP is also used as the underlying technical framework. Basically, [16] puts forward a language for representing authorization policies in terms of defeasible and strict permission/prohibition rules. Although the language allows in principle for the representation of *incomplete* policies, that paper focuses in ASP-based methods for checking compliance of events. Using the terminology of [16], this paper primarily focuses instead on *weakly compliant* events (i.e. attempts to perform some action which are not prohibited), which at the same time are not *strongly compliant* (i.e. are not permitted).

Moreover, our framework lets designated agents "manually" resolve the incompleteness resulting from these kinds of events by using the tailor-made speech acts *allow* and *forbid*. This possibility makes the approach specially suited to normative domains featuring an inherent incompleteness problem, although the framework could also be fruitfully exploited in cases of underspecification. In this latter class of systems, however, incompleteness may also be resolved dynamically by upgrading the normative program at runtime through additional permission rules, something undertaken in [17]. Future work will address this issue through the formalization of rule-oriented speech acts such as *permit* and *prohibit*, which complement the ad-hoc character of the speech acts *allow* and *forbid* [18].

The normative framework reported in this paper is part of a larger research project aimed at the specification of SPEECH, a language for programming software systems designed to support human interaction in arbitrary social contexts, viz. social applications. This general goal partly explains some of the features of the proposed normative framework, such as its bias towards regimentation. Nevertheless, the approach may not be plainly qualified as "regimented", since some attempts which are not permitted may eventually be executed. It should be noted that the eventual execution of pending speech acts may involve the participation of a hierarchy of authorities. In future work we plan to compare these ad-hoc hierarchies with other kinds of permission hierarchies found in the literature [19].

Acknowledgments. The authors wish to thank the anonymous reviewers for their detailed comments and suggestions. Research sponsored by the Spanish Ministry of Science and Innovation, project TIN2006-15455-C03-03.

References

1. Jones, A.J.I., Sergot, M.J.: A formal characterisation of institutionalised power. Logic Journal of the IGPL 4(3), 427–443 (1996)
2. Artikis, A., Sergot, M., Pitt, J.: Specifying norm-governed computational societies. ACM Transactions on Computational Logic 10(1), 1–1 (2009)
3. Cliffe, O., Vos, M.D., Padget, J.: Answer set programming for representing and reasoning about virtual institutions. In: Inoue, K., Satoh, K., Toni, F. (eds.) CLIMA 2006. LNCS (LNAI), vol. 4371, pp. 60–79. Springer, Heidelberg (2007)

4. Fornara, N., Colombetti, M.: Specifying artificial institutions in the event calculus. In: Dignum, V. (ed.) Handbook of Research on Multi-Agent Systems: Semantics and Dynamics of Organizational Models, pp. 335–366. IGI Global (2009)
5. Serrano, J.M., Saugar, S.: Run-time semantics of a language for programming social processes. In: Fisher, M., Sadri, F., Thielscher, M. (eds.) CLIMA IX. LNCS, vol. 5405, pp. 37–56. Springer, Heidelberg (2009)
6. Grossi, D.: Designing Invisible Handcuffs. SIKS Dissertation Series No. 2007-16 (2007)
7. Esteva, M., Rosell, B., Rodríguez-Aguilar, J.A., Arcos, J.L.: AMELI: An agent-based middleware for electronic institutions. In: Proceedings of the Third International Joint Conference on Autonomous Agents and Multiagent Systems, vol. 1, pp. 236–243 (2004)
8. Eiter, T., Faber, W., Leone, N., Pfeifer, G., Polleres, A.: A logic programming approach to knowledge-state planning: Semantics and complexity. Technical Report 1843-01-11, INFSYS Research Report (2002)
9. Eiter, T., Ianni, G., Krennwallner, T.: Answer set programming: A primer. In: Tessaris, S., Franconi, E., Eiter, T., Gutierrez, C., Handschuh, S., Rousset, M.-C., Schmidt, R.A. (eds.) Reasoning Web. Semantic Technologies for Information Systems. LNCS, vol. 5689, pp. 40–110. Springer, Heidelberg (2009)
10. Eiter, T., Faber, W., Leone, N., Pfeifer, G., Polleres, A.: A logic programming approach to knowledge-state planning, II: The DLV^K system. Artif. Intell. 144(1-2), 157–211 (2003)
11. Leone, N., Pfeifer, G., Faber, W., Eiter, T., Gottlob, G., Perri, S., Scarcello, F.: The dlv system for knowledge representation and reasoning. ACM Trans. Comput. Log. 7, 499–562 (2006)
12. Giunchiglia, E., Lee, J., Lifschitz, V., McCain, N., Turner, H.: Nonmonotonic causal theories. Artif. Intell. 153(1-2), 49–104 (2004)
13. Serrano, J.M., Saugar, S.: Operational semantics of multiagent interactions. In: Durfee, E.H., Yokoo, M., Huhns, M.N., Shehory, O. (eds.) AAMAS'07, pp. 889–896. IFAAMAS (2007)
14. Saugar, S., Serrano, J.M.: A web-based virtual machine for developing computational societies. In: Klusch, M., Pěchouček, M., Polleres, A. (eds.) CIA 2008. LNCS (LNAI), vol. 5180, pp. 162–176. Springer, Heidelberg (2008)
15. Serrano, J.M., Saugar, S.: Programming social middlewares through social interaction types. In: Dastani, M., Seghrouchni, A.E.F., Leite, J., Torroni, P. (eds.) Proceedings of the workshop on Languages, methodologies and Development tools for multi-agent systems (2009)
16. Gelfond, M., Lobo, J.: Authorization and obligation policies in dynamic systems. In: Garcia de la Banda, M., Pontelli, E. (eds.) ICLP 2008. LNCS, vol. 5366, pp. 22–36. Springer, Heidelberg (2008)
17. Artikis, A.: Dynamic protocols for open agent systems. In: Sierra, C., Castelfranchi, C., Decker, K.S., Sichman, J.S. (eds.) AAMAS (1), IFAAMAS, pp. 97–104 (2009)
18. Wierzbicka, A.: English speech act verbs. A semantic dictionary. Academic Press, Australia (1987)
19. Boella, G., van der Torre, L.W.N.: Permissions and obligations in hierarchical normative systems. In: ICAIL, pp. 109–118 (2003)

Towards an Architecture for Self-regulating Agents: A Case Study in International Trade

Brigitte Burgemeestre[1], Joris Hulstijn[1], and Yao-Hua Tan[1,2]

[1] PGS IT Audit, Faculty of Economics and Business Administration, Vrije Universiteit
[2] Department of Technology, Policy and Management, Delft University of Technology
{jhulstijn,cburgemeestre}@feweb.vu.nl, Y.Tan@tudelft.nl

Abstract. Norm-enforcement models applied in human societies may serve as an inspiration for the design of multi-agent systems. Models for norm-enforcement in multi-agent systems often focus either on the intra- or inter-agent level. We propose a combined approach to identify objectives for an architecture for self-regulating agents. In this paper we assess how changes on the inter-agent level affect the intra-agent level and how a generic BDI architecture IRMA can be adapted for self-regulation. The approach is validated with a case study of AEO certification, a European wide customs initiative to secure the supply chain while facilitating international trade.

Keywords: Self-regulation, agent architectures, compliance.

1 Introduction

To make autonomous agents comply with norms, various enforcement mechanisms have been proposed. Norms here are defined as standards of behavior that are acceptable in a society, indicating desirable behaviors that should be carried out, as well as undesirable behaviors that should be avoided [14]. Enforcement mechanisms often require special 'observers' or 'regulator agents' that actively monitor the behavior of the other agents, and sanction them in case of norm violations. When developing norm enforcement mechanisms for multi-agent systems, the modeling is often focused on the inter-agent level (between agents). Models aim to construct norm enforcement mechanisms by agent interaction. The intra-level (inside the agent) is mainly treated as a black box. We argue that the intra- and inter-agent aspects cannot be viewed separately, especially in norm enforcement where external stimuli should motivate an agent to adapt its behavior and thereby its internal mechanisms.

Norm-enforcement models applied in human societies may serve as an inspiration for the design of electronic institutions and open agent systems. An enforcement mechanism that is based on an agent's internal architecture to achieve compliant behavior, and does not require additional 'observers' is self-regulation. Self-regulation is a control approach in which rule making and enforcement are carried out by the agent itself, instead of by the regulator. Self-regulation is an alternative for direct control, when external supervision and enforcement is not possible, ineffective or when there is a lack of controlling resources. For example, in an e-institution it might be impossible to check all agent actions for compliance in real time. A solution might

J. Padget et al. (Eds.): COIN 2009, LNAI 6069, pp. 320–333, 2010.

be to do a code review and determine whether an agent is compliant by design [17]. In human societies, programs of self–regulation have been found to contribute to expanded control coverage and greater inspectorial depth [3]. Self-regulation can be implemented in various ways, ranging from voluntary self-regulation, where a group of agents chooses to regulate themselves, to mandated or enforced self-regulation, where a government agency delegates some of its regulative and enforcing tasks to the agents subjected to the norm, but retains the supervision [16]. Each model of self-regulation causes different dependencies among agents and different information needs, which imposes different requirements on the agent architecture.

A specific case of self-regulation is the Authorized Economic Operator (AEO) program [12]. The AEO program is a European wide customs initiative that aims to secure international trade while at the same time reducing the administrative burden for companies through the use of self-control. Companies that are trustworthy in the context of customs related operations and have a good internal control system may apply for the AEO certificate and receive operational benefits from simplified customs procedures, preferential treatment, and less physical inspections. Companies that do not have an AEO certificate remain subject to the current level of customs controls. Participation in the AEO program is voluntary, but demonstrating effective self-control mechanisms is a necessary requirement.

Implementing self-regulation as a control mechanism thus results in a redistribution or delegation of control tasks among the actors. Agents have to adapt their internal mechanisms to cope with these tasks. We see that changes at the inter-agent level affect the intra-level. We therefore propose to use a combined approach to develop an architecture which can use self-regulation as a control mechanism for multi-agent systems. The research questions we would like to answer are:

1. What objectives need to be met by an architecture for self-regulating agents?
2. How should the existing BDI-agent architecture be adapted for self-regulation?

We use a combination of frameworks to cover the inter- as well as intra-agent aspects. For intra-agent analysis the Intelligent Resource-Bounded Machine Architecture (IRMA) [4] is a good starting point, because it is a general BDI architecture [15], which is well accepted and forms the basis for more recent agent architectures, such as AgentSpeak or 3APL. Software engineering methodology TROPOS [5] provides suitable concepts to analyze agents' dependencies at the inter-agent level.

The remainder of the paper is structured as follows. In Section 2 we analyze the difference between direct control and self-regulation using TROPOS. Using this analysis we generate objectives for the internal architecture of a self-regulating agent. We apply these objectives to IRMA and propose some adaptations (Section 3). Using the extended architecture and the TROPOS model, we analyze a case study of AEO (Section 4). We examine if our adapted version of the architecture covers the findings of the case study. We identify its suitability and shortcomings.

2 Inter-agent Analysis

We first analyze the types of agents involved in regulation, and the dependencies between them. To do so we use concepts from the early requirements phase of the TROPOS methodology [5], which is derived from the *i** framework [18]. The key concepts we use are: actor, goal, plan, resource and dependency. An actor can be an autonomous agent that has a goal or strategic interest, based on its organizational role. A goal can be satisfied through the execution of a plan, which is an abstract representation of a way of doing something. A resource can be a physical or informational entity. Actors can depend on each other to reach a certain goal, to execute a plan or to obtain resources. The agent that depends on another agent is called the depender, the agent he depends on is called the dependee. The object which is the subject of the dependency relation is called the dependum.

We first model direct control, where actions of autonomous agents are regulated by special regulator agents. After that we analyze self-regulation and assess what should change when an autonomous agent internalizes control tasks of the regulator agent.

2.1 Agents' Dependencies in Direct Control

In direct control we have two types of agents: an Actor agent (A) that is carrying out an activity and a Regulator agent (R) that is responsible for regulating A's actions such that agent A complies with the norms that are applicable to A. An agent can violate the norms through pursuing an illegal goal or by performing an illegitimate action. We assume that R has a norm framework from which it derives the set of norms tailored to an agent's specific situation. To regulate A, agent R must have plans for executing the following activities: R1 'Specify norms for actor', R2 'Determine control indicators of actor', R3 'Monitor actor's actions' and R4 'Sanction actor'. R1 generates a set of norms for A. R uses information about A and A's actions to select the appropriate norms from the norm framework that apply to A's specific situation. R2 determines appropriate 'control indicators'. A control indicator is the kind of evidence required to demonstrate compliance of a norm, as well as infrastructural requirements to collect that evidence. For example: when a company sends an invoice, they make a copy of the invoice and store the copy to be able to check later whether all collected payments are correct and complete. R3 concerns the monitoring performed by R on A's actions, based on information provided by A about the control indicators. R4 describes the plan of R to sanction A in case of a norm violation. Agent A's model is quite simple, as A is a 'blind' agent that has no knowledge about the norms or control indicators and can only act. Therefore it is possible that A unknowingly engages in an activity that violates a norm that is imposed upon A by R. However, we do assume that A remembers action-sanction relations and that it can decide to cancel an action that will lead to a sanction.

Figure 1 shows the results of the dependency analysis for direct control.

A consequence of this division of tasks, where the regulator is responsible for the majority of control tasks, is that it is very labor intensive for the regulator. The regulator needs to specify norm sets and control indicators for all agents and needs to do all the verification and auditing. Furthermore the suitability of the rules can be disputable. Overregulation can occur when all the characteristics of the individual agents and possible exceptions need to be taken into account in the rules. Or rules can become ill fitting when they are supposed to be suitable for the majority of the agents but turn out to be compromises, which are not suitable for any individual agent. In direct control relations, Actor agents often have little influence on the rules that are assigned to them and simply have to adapt to the rules that are given.

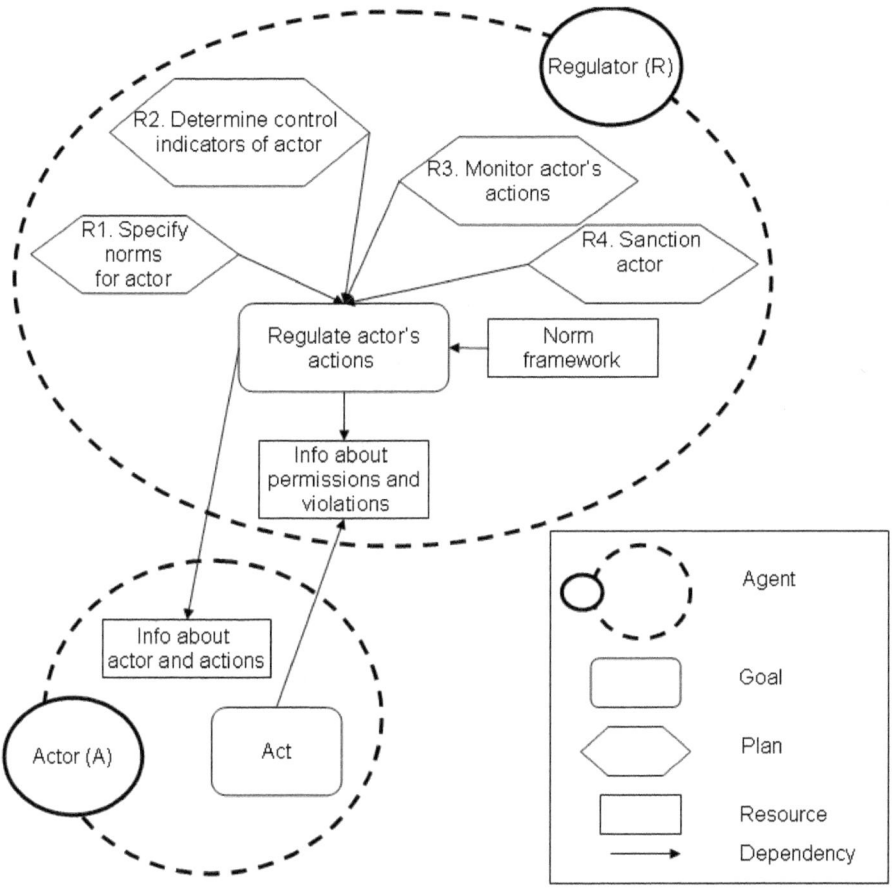

Fig. 1. TROPOS model of direct control. The actions of an actor (A) are regulated by a regula-tor (R). Note that arrows depict dependency, not information flow. So to regulate A's actions, R depends on A for information about actor and actions.

2.2 Agents' Dependencies in Self-regulation

For self-regulation we start again with two types of agents: the actor agent (A) and the regulator agent (R). In self-regulation several control tasks are delegated from R to A. Since A is autonomous, R can never be absolutely certain that A complies. R thus has to implement a mechanism to make A regulate itself appropriately. Furthermore, to maintain the power of the regulator to handle non-compliant agents, the sanctioning task (R4) remains the regulator's responsibility.

We first consider the consequences of the internalization of control tasks by A. Plans R1, R2 and R3 may be internalized by agent A as plans: A1 'Specify norms', A2 'Determine control indicators' and A3 'Monitor actions'. A1 specifies norms based on a norm framework which originates from R. This entails a new dependency between A and R: A now depends on R for communicating the norm framework.

When the norm specification is done by A, A is also supposed to be able to differentiate between norm violations and norm compliance. A therefore no longer depends for
information about violations and permissions on R, but has to do it himself. A2 defines control indicators about A's actions, based on the norms defined in A1. A3 describes the monitoring actions of A which it performs in the context of the control
indicators from plan A2. The plans A1, A2, and A3 together, should support A to act
in compliance with the norms. The acts of A in turn affect the nature of the control
actions. If A starts doing different activities the control indicators may become less
effective and A therefore has to determine new control indicators that cover the
norms. For example, if A replaces the process of sending paper invoices to its cus-
tomers by sending electronic invoices, new control indicators are required: e.g. log
files and encryption proof instead of paper copies of the invoice.

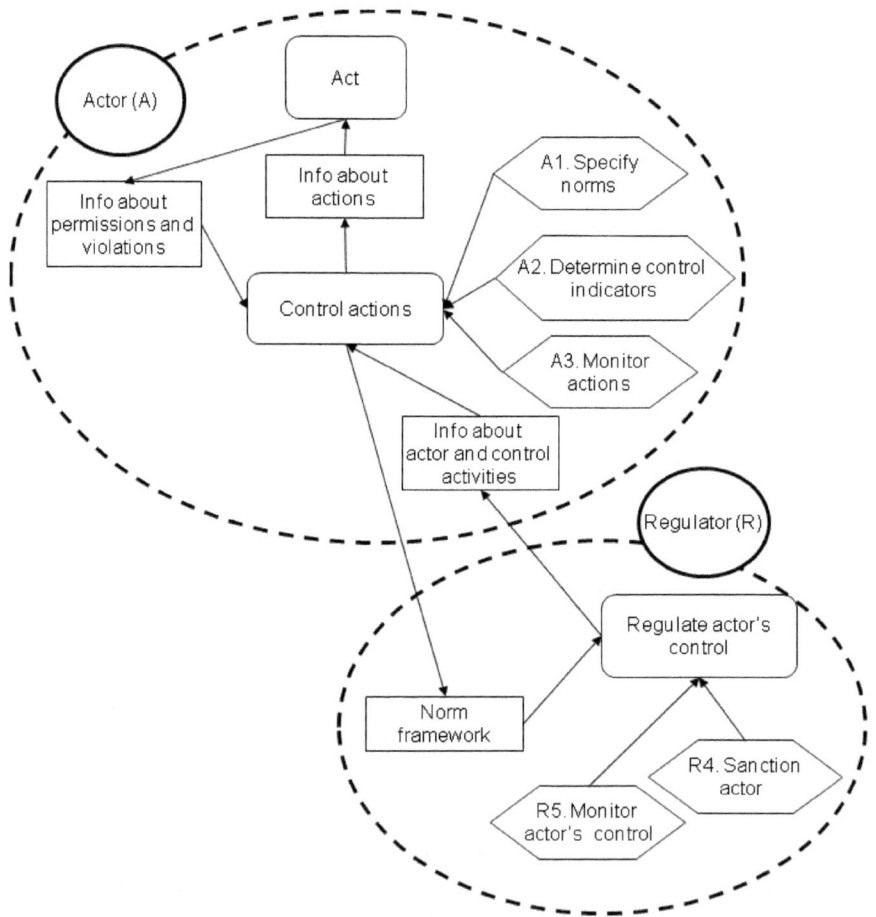

Fig. 2. TROPOS model of self-regulation, control tasks of the regulator are internalized by the
actor agent

Now we describe the consequences of A's internalization of the control tasks of R's goals and plans. Since A now has to control its own actions, the goal of R to regulate A's actions is supposed to be met by the control activities of A. To determine if this delegation of control is effective, R has adopted a new goal which is to regulate the control activities of A. To reach this goal, R also has defined a new plan (R5), which describes the activities of R to monitor and evaluate A's control actions. Note that R now depends on A for information about its control activities instead of its activities, so R5 is a kind of meta-control plan. In auditing practice, R5 refers to a system-based audit, were the focus is the internal control system instead of on business transactions. Before an agent can enter a self-regulative relation, it has to provide an authenticated control architecture or control script to the regulator.

A similar solution would work for a code review, mentioned in the introduction. An electronic marketplace, for example, may want to provide assurance that its members generally comply with the norms. In addition to monitoring and sanctioning violations when they occur, the institution can require the owner of an agent to provide documentation and programming code before an agent is allowed into the environment. In this documentation the owner must make explicit how the agents internal control architecture assures compliance to the norms defined by the marketplace. Using this evidence, the institution can verify (up to a point) whether the agent is compliant by design, compare [17]. Such a verification can be automated, but that is not necessary, as the review takes place off-line.

Figure 2 shows dependencies between agents A and R engaged in self-regulation.

When we compare direct control with self-regulation we see that A internalizes some of R's control activities on A. New information resources are gathered to be used within the control activities. Also new goals evolve and lead to the adoption of new plans. Corresponding new dependencies between R and A develop for the acquisition of these new information resources.

These inter-agent changes are reflected in a number of objectives for intra-agent architectures. Summarizing the objectives, self-regulating agent must have at least the capabilities to:

1. Detect, internalize and store the norms which are applicable in the environment,
2. Translate norms into measurable control indicators, and
3. Monitor, detect and mitigate possible norm violations.

In the next section we show the internal architecture of the actor in self-regulation.

3   Inter-agent Analysis

We now analyze how the new tasks and dependencies revealed by the TROPOS models will affect an agent's internal architecture. We acknowledge that these tasks are complex normative tasks. We use the Intelligent Resource-Bounded Machine Architecture (IRMA) [4]. The architecture is a BDI architecture where the intentions are structured into plans. A plan can be a plan that an agent has actually adopted, or a plan-as-recipe that is stored into the plan library. Plan options are proposed as a result of means-end reasoning or by the opportunity analyzer. The opportunity analyzer detects changes in the environment and determines new opportunities, based on the agent's desires. The options are filtered through a compatibility filter, that checks the options to determine compatibility with the agent's existing plans, and a filter override mechanism, in which the conditions are defined under which (portions) of plans need to be suspended and replaced by another option. The deliberation process determines the best option on the basis of current beliefs and desires.

Consider an autonomous agent that likes to achieve a certain goal. The agent has already several plans of action available (in its plan-library) to reach this goal. Before deliberating on a plan, the agent engages in a filtering process. This process constrains the agent's possible plans to plans that can be completed given its available (sub) plans in the plan library, its beliefs and desires. The agent chooses from this selection the best plan, given its beliefs and desires, and executes the plan. Figure 3 shows our extension of the IRMA architecture, adapted for self-regulation. Norm related adaptations are shown in grey and dotted lines. The ovals in the figure are information stores (repositories) and the rectangles are process modules.

Within IRMA we like to implement the processes and information stores that are needed for self-regulation. A self-regulating agent needs to internalize certain control activities to control its actions. The activities are: 'specify norms' (A1), 'determine control indicators' (A2), and 'monitor actions' (A3). These control activities require input from the agent's actions, and the actions in turn are influenced by the norms. We first analyze which IRMA modules are possibly affected by normative reasoning.

Norms can impact the information stores or processes of the architecture. A norm can be implemented in plans and function as a threshold to restrict the outcome. For example, a thermostat function that tries to keep the room heated at a certain temperature. Norms can also restrict the possible set of plans. Plans that violate a norm are no longer stored in the plan library. Or in means-end reasoning: there are illegal plans in the plan library but they are not considered as appropriate options to reach a goal; such plans are temporarily 'suppressed', as in [14]. Norms can also prevent the actual execution of a plan. For example, a person can plan to rob a bank, but decide not to do so at the last moment.

Besides that, norms affect the beliefs. After all, agents are expected to know the general norms. Beliefs also affect the norms, in the sense that beliefs about the context help to identify applicable norms. An agent may also realize, based on its beliefs, that it is acting in violation with the norms. Or, an agent realizes that due to a change in activities certain norms are no longer applicable and new norms must be incorporated. Whenever an agent adopts a new norm, this must be known (believed).

Norms are also related to the desires of an agent. An agent's desires may violate the norms. For example, an agent may desire a handbag that is made of the skin of a protected snake. A norm is that killing a protected animal is illegal. If norms are included in the compatibility filter, an agent can check if an option is compatible with its norms. If norms are part of the filter override mechanism, non-compliance can be a condition under which an agent must reconsider its plans. Both implementations make it possible for an agent to decide not to consider a plan option of buying a snake skin handbag. The opportunity analyzer may use the norms and beliefs to search for an alternative, such as a fake snake skin handbag.

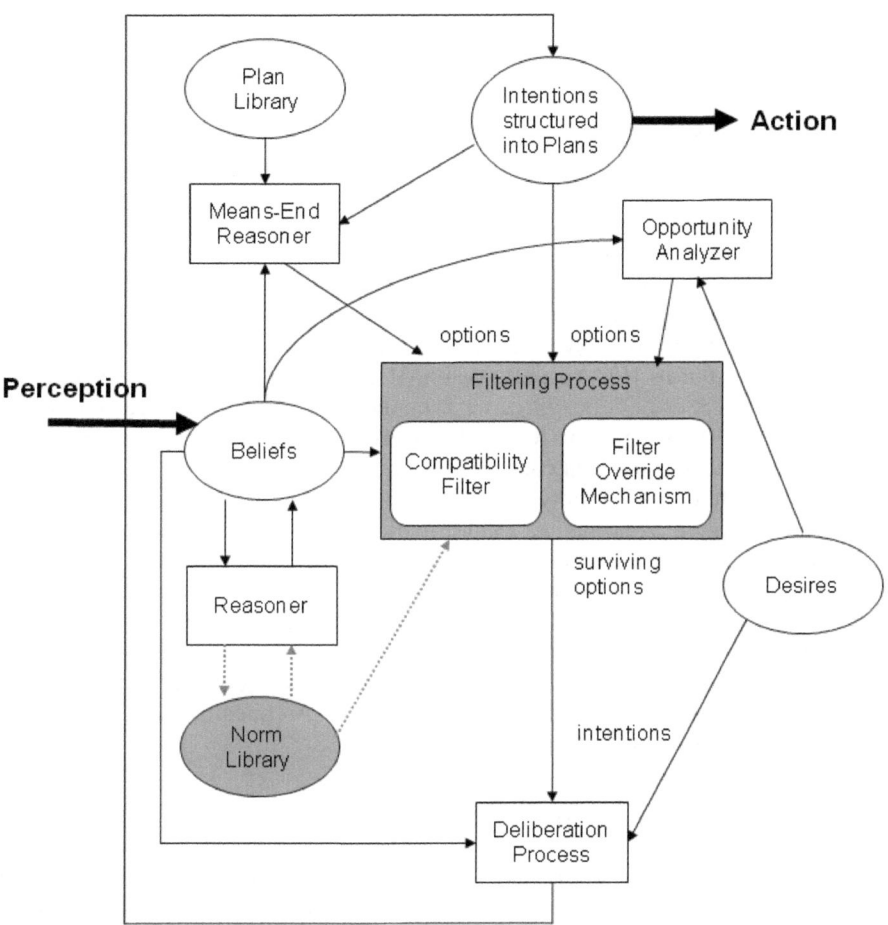

Fig. 3. A reasoning component for self-regulating agents adapted from [4]. Norm related adaptations are shown in grey and with dotted lines.

We find that norms can impact all components of the architecture. To assure consistent norm application we propose a central storage for norms similar to what the plan library is for plans. Activity A1 updates the norm library according to the beliefs of the agent. Only norms that are considered to be applicable to the agent's specific situation are included. To make an agent aware of a norm (violation) we connect the norm library with the reasoner module that is attached to the beliefs. If an agent then reasons about its beliefs, it will take the relevant norms into account. Beliefs about a norm (violation) can be used as input for the means-end reasoner, opportunity analyzer and the deliberation process. Besides that, the agent may use its knowledge about norms to determine the control indicators of A2. We consider the filtering process the best location to implement the control indicators. Beliefs about norms are already included in the other reasoning processes. The filtering process and reasoning thus together consider (non-) compliant behavior. We think that the majority of the control indicators should be embedded in the compatibility filter and only severe violations should be handled by the filter override mechanism. Otherwise it could happen that the filtering is too strict. The monitoring in A3 is handled through a comparison of the beliefs about the data on the indicators with the norms. Based on results from this analysis, controls in the filtering process may be adapted. Figure 3 shows a version of the IRMA architecture specifically adapted for self-regulation.

Our approach of embedding norms into the filter override mechanism is comparable with the framework that is proposed by [14]. Norms can also be implemented into the goal generation mechanism as was done in the BOID architecture [6]. In BOID one can distinguish two kinds of goals: internal motivations (desires), representing individual wants or needs, and external motivations (obligations) to model social commitments and norms [6]. All these potential goals may conflict. To resolve conflicts among the sets of beliefs, obligations, intentions and desires, a priority order is needed. In the BOID, such a (partial) order is provided by the agent type. In [8] we discuss the use of values for goal conflict resolution.

Note that we have so far only considered adaptations to the agent architecture based on a conception of norms as a kind of filtering: actions, plans or goals which might lead to violation are filtered out or suppressed. Instead of filtering, we can also consider norm adoption [9,11]. Here, a norm is simply adopted as a goal. The rest of the architecture will then ensure compliance. Note that adopted norms will often correspond to so called maintenance goals: goals to make sure that some desirable state of affairs subsists or that an undesirable state is avoided, by contrast to achievement goals, which are about reaching a new state of affairs. Architectures for dealing with maintenance goals are discussed in [13].

4   Case Study: AEO Certification

We illustrate and validate our models by analyzing a specific case of self-regulation: AEO certification. The case study results are based on document analysis and a series of semi-structured interviews with experts from Dutch Tax and Customs Administration, held in the period of May till November 2009. Meeting notes were made by the authors and verified by interview partners. Intermediate results of the case study were validated in a one-day workshop with domain experts.

An Authorized Economic Operator (AEO) can be defined as a company that is in-control of its own business processes, and hence is considered trustworthy throughout the EU in the context of its customs related operations [12]. Typically, modern enterprise information systems (ERP, CRM etc.) play an essential role for companies to be in-control. AEO's will receive several benefits in customs handling, such as a "Green Lane" treatment with a reduced number of inspections. This can lead to considerable cost-reductions for businesses. For non-certified enterprises customs will continue to carry out the traditional supervision. Customs can direct their efforts towards non-certified companies to increase the security of international supply chains, while at the same time reducing the administrative burden for AEOs.

To qualify as AEO, a company must meet a number of criteria, which are described in the community customs code and the AEO guidelines [12], developed by the European Commission. Part of the application procedure is a self-assessment on the quality of the company's internal control system for aspects that are relevant to the type of AEO certificate ('Customs simplifications', 'Security and safety' or 'Combined') [12]. The company's approach and the results of the self-assessment are inspected by customs. Customs officers determine whether the self-assessment is performed well and whether the results indicate that a company is able to control its business processes such that they contribute to a secure supply chain. If this is the case and other criteria are met (e.g. solvency, no known tax evasions etc.) an AEO certificate is issued by the customs office. Next we focus on the self-assessment task.

4.1 The Self-assessment Task

The company's first task is to collect information related to the specific nature of the company to focus the self-assessment. This step is called 'Understanding the business'. The next step is to identify (potential) risks to which the business is exposed using the AEO guidelines, which provide an overview of general risk and attention points. The company determines which sections are important according to the nature of the business activities. A company then has to identify, what risks affect the supply chain's safety, and are therefore of interest of the customs authorities. So the company takes over the customs' task of risk identification. For example, computer components are valuable goods, which are subject to theft. Trading valuable goods requires more security measures, than, say, trading in a mass product like fertilizer. However, some ingredients of fertilizer may be used to assemble explosives, leading to a different set of risks.

A company must then assess if appropriate internal control measures are taken to mitigate these risks. The vulnerability of a company to threats depends on its current control measures. Control measures either reduce the likelihood, by dealing with vulnerabilities (preventative controls), or reduce the impact (detective and corrective controls). A robust system of controls is thus able to prevent, detect and correct threats. A robust system of controls should also monitor its own functioning. For risks that are not controlled, additional measures may be implemented or the risk is "accepted". Risks can be accepted, if the likelihood of a threat is limited and the risk is partially covered, or if the costs for complete coverage are very high.

The company must show how its risk management contributes to its being trustworthy. In addition, the company must evaluate whether the proposed measures are implemented effectively. To provide some guidance on what is considered 'effective implementation' customs refer to the COSO internal control guidelines. COSO is a general framework for risk management and internal control [10]. The scores range from 0 "no control measures in place", 1 "internal control is ad hoc and unorganized", 2 "internal control has a structured approach", 3 "internal control is documented and known", 4 "internal control is subject to internal audits and evaluation" until 5 "internal control measures are integrated into the business processes and continuously evaluated". This scoring provides the customs with an indication of the maturity level of the company's self-controlling abilities.

4.2 Case Analysis

In the AEO case study we see the implementation of tasks A1, A2, and A3 at the company's side. A company has to define a control system appropriate to handle its specific risks. The company therefore translates the general AEO guidelines into norms that are applicable in its own practice and circumstances (compatible with A1). Thereby a company determines parameters to monitor and control its business processes (A2). A company with a control system of a high maturity level monitors its actions (A3) through internal audits and controls that are integrated in the processes. The customs replace their traditional controls of the company's processes (R1,R2,R3) with an assessment of the company's self-regulating capabilities and control actions (R5). To check the reliability of the company's controls, customs may still take samples of business transactions, but these will now be much more focused, for instance on areas with an increased risk. To make R5 and the delegation of tasks A1, A2, A3 more manageable, we see that additional guidelines and principles must be formulated. An example of such additional guidelines is the set of AEO guidelines specified by the EU, indicating examples of risk areas for different domains. Another example is given by local customs directives. For instance, the Dutch customs refer to the COSO maturity levels as a way of objectively measuring 'effective implementation' of control measures. Such additional guidelines are needed for both implementing and auditing control systems. They help to specify under what circumstances a company can be said to be 'in control' of safety and security.

We also observe dependencies regarding information resources. The company depends on abstract norms (e.g. the AEO Guidelines) provided by the customs, which they try to apply to themselves as they believe the customs would do. The customs on the other hand depend on the company for information about their control system. For instance, why have they chosen for a certain implementation of the norms? Why have they decided to accept a certain risk, and not take additional control measures?

The AEO case provides us with a new approach to control that could also be applied to a multi-agent system. It shows that norm enforcement is a task that can be distributed among various types of agents. Furthermore we learned that self-regulation only works under certain conditions and that delegating control tasks is not simple. In general companies find it difficult to do a self-assessment as they do not know what customs expect from them (open norms). The translation of the abstract AEO guidelines into company specific norms turns out to be hard. For companies it is unclear when they have taken sufficient measures. Companies sometimes expect customs to indicate what is sufficient: "A fence for a chemical company should be X meters high". Even for customs such knowledge is often only implicitly available as expert knowledge that is difficult to externalize and make accessible for companies. In the AEO case, implemented measures are based on the risks in the environment. This corresponds to our observation in the architecture that norms depend on the beliefs. In the AEO case, we find both the adoption of new policies and procedures (norm adoption), as well as a redesign of existing business processes (norm filtering). Mature companies have their controls integrated in the business processes, and have regular audits to check the functioning of controls (reflective capabilities).

Summarizing, we can say that the internal control system of a company can be seen as the implementation of an architecture for self-regulation. In the AEO case, customs must provide a kind of quality assessment of this control architecture (system based audit), rather than verifying business transactions. This fundamental change in the role of customs, shows a transformation from operational control to meta-control. Therefore issues like trust and integrity now play a role at two levels. First there is the trustworthiness of the company's management, or in the case of an electronic institution, of the agent owner. In the AEO case, we find that historical indicators of fraud always lead to a rejection of the certificate. In electronic institutions a rule could be that agents from proven untrustworthy owners are denied access to the community. Second, there is the reliability of the control system or agent architecture itself. If the control system is not reliable, it cannot be used to take over the delegated control tasks. Therefore the company can't function as a trusted partner of customs. Electronic institutions may also require that agent behavior is controlled to assure the correctness of the transactions. In that case, the owner of must prove that the agent is compliant by design. Such a proof depends on the internal architecture of the agent.

5 Discussion

We use a combination of TROPOS and IRMA as a means to identify requirements for self-regulating agents at the intra- and inter-agent level. We do not claim that these are the best approaches currently available, there are some limitations.

The most important limitation of IRMA as the internal architecture is that it is not reflective. By this we mean that agents cannot learn from their mistakes. When the agent finds that a plan leads to a norm violation it is only able to cancel this plan as a possible option. It lacks mechanisms to delete or change such plans in a plan library. Desires that violate norms cannot be changed either. The agent therefore keeps proposing violating plans and desires. Since norms are context dependent it is quite complex to differentiate violating plans from non-violating plans. Plans that are allowed in one situation may be a violation under different circumstances. An adaption of the planning mechanism is needed.

Second, there seems to be a fundamental problem in the delegation of control: often it is not clear how to communicate the delegated norms from the regulator to the actor. For companies it is difficult to interpret and implement the EU guidelines. Should customs and companies implement a communication protocol, a shared vocabulary or procedures such that they can more effectively communicate information? How should a company make its internal control system available to customs, such that they can determine the quality of a control system in a specific context with limited expert knowledge? These questions have to be answered by a detailed study of norm communication, both in practice, and for multi-agent systems.

Third, our case study reveals issues which may inspire the development of norm enforcement mechanisms for multi-agent systems. Open norms and forms of self–regulation enable heterogeneous agents to enter environments as the entrance requirements (open norms) leave room for specific implementations (control architectures). In particular, it suggests how agents can be verified to be 'compliant by design' before entering into an agent environment. Agents have to map their control architecture to the norm framework of the environment. The communication problem in the case emphasizes the need for well defined norm frameworks. Norm frameworks should be abstract enough to allow agents to enter an environment and specific enough to support compliance and enforcement of the norms. However, exactly how to translate such ideas depends on the particular set-up of the multi-agent system. In most cases, there will be a large role for the human owner of the agent, similar to the role of management. They must provide the evidence to demonstrate that they are 'in control' regarding compliance.

6 Conclusions and Further Research

In this paper we have argued that, with regard to norms, the macro-level definition of tasks and dependencies in a multi-agent system and the internal architecture of agents are crucially interconnected. A combined approach, that analyses the inter- (between agents) and intra-agent level (inside agents), was suitable to identify objectives for an architecture for self-regulation. We identified key processes and their influence on the dependencies between agents and the internal agent architecture. The models provide an insight in the differences in requirements for direct controlled agents and self-regulating agents. The analysis also points out the limitations of some well-known existing approaches. IRMA lacks reflective capabilities and is therefore not sufficient to model a truly self-regulating agent: an agent that is able to learn from its mistakes. In [8] we look in more detail at various cognitive architectures and how they account for compliance and norm adoption. Also unaddressed were aspects of norm communication. For two agents to engage in self-regulation relation, they must be able to communicate the norms effectively. Since the agents are autonomous we cannot simply assume that both agents use similar vocabularies or protocols [7]. So a solution for norm communication should take the agent's autonomy into account. One of our current research projects examines the use of argumentation theory [1] for norm implementation and communication. Future research thus concerns the role of reflection for normative behavior and norm communication. We hope to specify our ideas more formally in a declarative agent architecture (e.g. based on [13]). This will allow agent-based simulation of the regulatory process. We are also interested in the evolution process from direct control to self-regulation.

Acknowledgments. We would like to thank the Dutch Tax and Customs Administration for their cooperation and insights.

References

1. Atkinson, K., Bench-Capon, T., McBurney, P.: Computational representation of practical argument. Synthese 152(2), 157–206 (2006)
2. Boella, G., van der Torre, L., Verhagen, H.: Introduction to normative multiagent systems. Computational and Mathematical Organization Theory 12, 71–79 (2006)
3. Braithwaite, J.: Enforced self-regulation: a new strategy for corporate crime control. Michigan law review 80, 1466–1506 (1982)
4. Bratman, M.E., Israel, D., Pollack, M.: Plans and resource-bounded practical reasoning. In: Cummins, R., Pollock, J.L. (eds.) Philosophy and AI: Essays at the Interface, pp. 1–22. MIT Press, Cambridge (1991)
5. Bresciani, P., Perini, A., Giorgini, P., Giunchiglia, F., Mylopoulos, J.: Tropos: An agent-oriented software development methodology. Journal of Autonomous Agents and Multi-Agent Systems 8, 203–236 (2004)
6. Broersen, J., Dastani, M., Hulstijn, J., van der Torre, L.: Goal generation in the BOID architecture. Cognitive Science Quarterly 2(3-4), 431–450 (2002)
7. Burgemeestre, C.B., Liu, J., Hulstijn, J., Tan, Y.: Early Requirements Engineering for e-Customs Decision Support: Assessing Overlap in Mental Models. In: Proceedings of the CAiSE Forum, pp. 31–36 (2009)

8. Burgemeestre, C.B., Hulstijn, J., Tan, Y.: Agent Architectures for Compliance. In: Aldewereld, H. (ed.) ESAW 2009. LNCS, vol. 5881, pp. 68–83. Springer, Heidelberg (2009)
9. Conte, R., Castelfranchi, C.: Cognitive and Social Action. UCL Press (1995)
10. COSO enterprise risk management framework, http://www.coso.org
11. Dignum, F.: Autonomous agents with norms. Artificial Intelligence and Law 7, 69–79
    (1999)
12. European Commission: AEO Guidelines, TAXUD/2006/1450 (2007),
    http://ec.europa.eu/taxation_customs/customs/policy_issues/
13. Hindriks, K., van Riemsdijk, M.B.: Satisfying maintenance goals. In: Baldoni, M., Son,
    T.C., van Riemsdijk, M.B., Winikoff, M. (eds.) DALT 2007. LNCS (LNAI), vol. 4897, pp.
    86–103. Springer, Heidelberg (2008)
14. Meneguzzi, F., Luck, M.: Norm-based behaviour modification in BDI agents. In: Proceed-
    ings of the 8th International Conference on Autonomous Agents and Multiagent Systems
    (AAMAS'09), Budapest, Hungary, pp. 177–184 (2009)
15. Rao, A.S., Georgeff, M.P.: Modelling rational agents within a BDI-architecture. In: Princi-
    ples of Knowledge Representation and Reasoning (KR'91), San Mateo CA (1991)
16. Rees, J.: Self-regulation: An Effective Alternative to Direct Regulation by OSHA? Policy
    Studies Journal 16(3), 602–614 (1988)
17. Sadiq, S.W., Governatori, G., Namiri, K.: Modeling control objectives for business process
    compliance. In: Alonso, G., Dadam, P., Rosemann, M. (eds.) BPM 2007. LNCS,
    vol. 4714, pp. 149–164. Springer, Heidelberg (2007)
18. Yu, E.K.S.: Towards Modelling and Reasoning Support for Early-Phase Requirements
    Engineering. In: Proceedings of the 3rd IEEE International Symposium on Requirements
    engineering, pp. 226–235 (1997)

Author Index